FATHERS AND SONS IN THE BOOK OF MORMON

· ·

E. DOUGLAS CLARK
AND
ROBERT S. CLARK

Deseret Book Company
Salt Lake City, Utah

Library of Congress Cataloging-in-Publication Data

Clark, E. Douglas, 1953–
    Fathers and sons in the Book of Mormon / E. Douglas Clark and
  Robert S. Clark.
        p. cm.
    Includes bibliographical references and index.
    ISBN 0-87579-567-6
    1. Book of Mormon—Criticism, interpretation, etc.   2. Fathers and
sons. I. Clark, Robert S., 1954–   . II. Title.
BX8627.C53 1991
289.3'22—dc20   91-35112
                                                                          CIP

Printed in the United States of America

10   9   8   7   6   5   4   3   2

"The Book of Mormon was meant for us. It was written for our day. Its scriptures are to be likened unto ourselves.

"With that understanding, let us consider from the Book of Mormon the responsibility fathers have to teach their sons, and the responsibility sons have to take direction from their fathers. This counsel also applies to all parents and their children."

—President Ezra Taft Benson,
A Witness and a Warning

CONTENTS

ACKNOWLEDGMENTS
. . . .

We, the authors, express our appreciation to John A. Tvedtnes, Roy W. Doxey, and Terrance D. Olson for their review of the manuscript and their helpful suggestions and insights. For any errors that this book may contain, however, we remain solely responsible.

We also wish to thank Loretta Woodmansee, whose patience and perseverence in typing the manuscript were indispensable in the realization of this project.

Writing this book on Book of Mormon parents has given us a profoundly new appreciation of our own parents, who not only taught us to love the Book of Mormon, but also taught us according to the pattern of the great Book of Mormon parents. To our parents, we owe an eternal debt of loving gratitude, and it is our hope to prove to be as worthy sons as they are parents.

The completion of this project would not have been possible without the patience and support of our wonderful wives, Mila and Wendy. They are also wonderful mothers, and with their continued patience and support, we hope to become the kind of fathers portrayed in the Book of Mormon.

Doug and Rob Clark

ABBREVIATIONS

. . . .

AB   The Anchor Bible.

Abraham   "The Book of Abraham," in The Pearl of Great
          Price.

AI   Roland de Vaux, *Ancient Israel*.

CWHN   Hugh Nibley, *The Collected Works of Hugh Nibley*
          (titled separately).

D&C   The Doctrine and Covenants of The Church of Je-
          sus Christ of Latter-day Saints.

EJ   *Encyclopedia Judaica*.

JD   *Journal of Discourses*.

JS–H   "Joseph Smith–History," in The Pearl of Great
          Price.

JST   Joseph Smith's "New Translation" of the Bible.

LF   *Lectures on Faith,* in Larry E. Dahl and Charles D.
          Tate, Jr., *The Lectures on Faith in Historical Perspec-
          tive*.

LJ   Louis Ginzberg, *The Legends of the Jews*.

Moses   "Selections from the Book of Moses," in The Pearl
          of Great Price.

NASB   New American Standard Bible, in Master Study
          Bible.

NIDNTT   Collin Brown, ed., *The New International Dictionary
          of New Testament Theology*.

NIV   New International Version, in The NIV Study
          Bible.

NJB   The New Jerusalem Bible.

NJoBC   Raymond E. Brown, Joseph A. Fitzmeyer, and Ro-
          land E. Murphy, eds., *The New Jerome Biblical Com-
          mentary*.

NJPS   New Jewish Publication Society translation of the
          Hebrew Bible, in Tanakh: A New Translation of
          THE HOLY SCRIPTURES According to the Tradi-
          tional Hebrew Text.

NRSV   Holy Bible: New Revised Standard Version.

OTP   James H. Charlesworth, ed., *The Old Testament
          Pseudepigrapha*.

REB   The Revised English Bible.

TDNT   Gerhard Kittel and Gerhard Friedrich, eds., *Theo-
          logical Dictionary of the New Testament*.

TDOT   G. Johannes Botterweck and Helmer Ringgren,
          eds., *Theological Dictionary of the Old Testament*.

TETB   Ezra Taft Benson, *The Teachings of Ezra Taft Benson*.

TPJS   Joseph Fielding Smith, ed., *Teachings of the Prophet
          Joseph Smith*.

W&W   Ezra Taft Benson, *A Witness and A Warning: A
          Modern-day Prophet Testifies of the Book of Mormon*.

WTNID   *Webster's Third New International Dictionary of the
          English Language, Unabridged*.

INTRODUCTION

· ·

Superlatives can be valuable in providing perspective, establishing limits, and pointing the way. So it is with two superlatives announced by latter-day prophets. The first concerns the Book of Mormon, about which the Prophet Joseph Smith recorded: "I told the brethren [the Twelve Apostles] that the Book of Mormon was the most correct of any book on earth, and the keystone of our religion, and a man would get nearer to God by abiding by its precepts, than by any other book."[1]

The second superlative concerns the paramount duty of parents to teach their children; it has been expressed in various ways. President Ezra Taft Benson has stated that "the family is a divine institution established by our Heavenly Father"[2] and is "the rock foundation, the cornerstone of civilization,"[3] so that "proper training of children is a duty of the highest order"[4] and "a most sacred responsibility"[5]

---

1. TPJS 194.
2. TETB: 496.
3. Ibid. 522.
4. Ibid. 496.
5. Ibid. 502.

for which "God holds parents responsible."[1] Accordingly, "for a man, there is no calling as high as that of a righteous patriarch," and "for a woman there is no calling as high as that of a righteous mother."[2]

President Benson is hardly the first latter-day prophet to speak of parental duty in such emphatic terms. For example, President Harold B. Lee told husbands that "the most important of the Lord's work that you will ever do will be the work you do within the walls of your own home."[3] Earlier President David O. McKay similarly taught that "nothing can take the place of home in rearing and teaching children, and no other success can compensate for failure in the home."[4] Earlier still, the First Presidency under President Heber J. Grant stated:

> By bringing . . . spirits to earth, each father and each mother assume towards the tabernacled spirit and towards the Lord Himself . . . an obligation of the most sacred kind, because the fate of that spirit in the eternities to come, the blessings or punishments which shall await it in the hereafter, depend, in great part, upon the care, the teachings, the training which the parents shall give to that spirit.
>
> No parent can escape that obligation and that responsibility, and for the proper meeting thereof, the Lord will hold us to a strict accountability. No loftier duty than this can be assumed by mortals.[5]

These two superlatives regarding the Book of Mormon and parental duty have been accepted and valued independently, but the connection between the two is often missed. Could we not expect that the book that is most correct in leading us to God would have something important to say about the highest duty God has entrusted to mortals, that of parenthood? Such a connection has not escaped the attention of President Benson, much of whose inspired burden has been to persuade the Church to mine the rich treasures contained in the Book of Mormon. Thus after emphasizing the preeminent value

---

1. Ibid.
2. Ibid. 496.
3. Lee 1973:7.
4. Quoted in TETB:526.
5. Clark, *Messages of the First Presidency* VI:178.

of the Book of Mormon in leading us to God,[1] President Benson has counseled the Church to "consider from the Book of Mormon the responsibility fathers have to teach their sons, and the responsibility sons have to take direction from their fathers."[2] He added that "this counsel also applies to all parents and their children," which follows from the fact that "the Book of Mormon was meant for us," was "written for our day," and is "to be likened unto ourselves."[3] In other words, the father-son portraits in the Book of Mormon — which almost totally predominate the presentation of parent-child relationships — are intended to provide guidance for all parent-child relationships, whether of a mother with her daughter or son, or of a father with his son or daughter.

That the parent-child relationships depicted in the Book of Mormon are almost all father-son relationships has usually been explained by the fact that the record keepers were apparently all men. But another and more important factor may also have been operative: the relationships depicted in the Book of Mormon all deal with principal characters occupying key roles in a story set in a society structured patriarchally (not only the record keepers, but also the ecclesiatical leaders, the monarchs, the chief judges, and the military leaders were apparently all men). Nowhere does the Book of Mormon stop and devote space exclusively to a model parent-child relationship *per se;* instead, constraints of space on the plates dictated that the depiction of such relationships and, in fact, the presentation of all timeless truths, be skillfully interwoven with the historical narrative. And because the principal characters appearing on that very limited stage happened mostly to be men, talk of mothers is rare.

But it is there, offering in fact one of the most poignant parent-child portraits in the Book of Mormon — and, notably, by far the largest portrait in terms of sheer numbers. Two thousand Lamanite young men, whose parents had been converted to the truth and had joined with the Nephites, entered the Nephite army in a war of self-defense

---

1. See W&W vii.
2. Ibid. 67.
3. Ibid.

against Lamanite aggression. Unlike their parents, these young men were under no covenant not to take up arms; in fact, they considered it their solemn duty to assist in defending their families, whose protection theretofore had been so magnanimously furnished by the Nephites. Accordingly, these young Lamanite men "entered into a covenant to fight for the liberty of the Nephites, yea, to protect the land unto the laying down of their lives," covenanting "that they never would give up their liberty, but they would fight in all cases to protect the Nephites and themselves from bondage,"[1] and so "defend their country."[2]

In abridging the account, Mormon describes these two thousand volunteers:

> They were all young men, and they were exceedingly valiant for courage, and also for strength and activity; but behold, this was not all—they were men who were true at all times in whatsoever thing they were entrusted.
>
> Yea, they were men of truth and soberness, for they had been taught to keep the commandments of God and to walk uprightly before him.[3]

Such soldiers would be the pride and joy of any commander, as they were to the Nephite commander assigned to lead them. His name was Helaman, and his regard for his young soldiers was such that he referred to them as "my sons"—a term of endearment reflective of its range of use in ancient Israel,[4] and indicative apparently of his deep regard not only for his young soldiers ("for they are worthy to be called [my] sons"[5]) but also for their actual parents, mothers in particular. In Helaman's own words, his "sons"

> never [before] had fought, yet they did not fear death; and they did think more upon the liberty of their fathers than they

---

1. Alma 53:17.
2. Alma 53:18.
3. Alma 53:20–21.
4. TDOT II:149, 152.
5. Alma 56:10.

did upon their lives; yea, they had been taught by their mothers, that if they did not doubt, God would deliver them.

And they rehearsed unto me the words of their mothers,
saying: We do not doubt our mothers knew it.[1]

Fortified by the faith instilled by their mothers, when the young
soldiers confronted a circumstance in which they thought—but were
not sure—that their help might prove critical, they opted to respond
without hesitation[2] and thereby faced the most powerful army of the
Lamanites,[3] causing Helaman later to write: "Never had I seen so
great courage, nay, not amongst all the Nephites."[4] Their courage
persisted as they engaged in battle—their first ever. As Helaman
describes,

They . . . fought as if with the strength of God; yea, never
were men known to have fought with such miraculous
strength; and with such mighty power did they fall upon the
Lamanites, that they did frighten them.[5]

Their intervention and valor proved decisive in the terrible battle. And
not a single one of Helaman's sons fell.[6]

Subsequent conflict proved them equally valiant, as when, in
Helaman's words, "they were firm before the Lamanites,"[7] and

did obey and observe to perform every word of command with
exactness; yea, and even according to their faith it was done
unto them; and I did remember the words which they said
unto me that their mothers had taught them.[8]

The fighting grew fierce, with heavy casualties on both sides.
When it was over, Helaman gave the order—as must be done after

---

1. Alma 56:47–48.
2. See Alma 56:43–46.
3. See Alma 56:34.
4. Alma 56:45.
5. Alma 56:56.
6. See Alma 56:49–54, 56.
7. Alma 57:19.
8. Alma 57:21.

every battle—to separate the wounded from the dead. Two hundred
of his beloved young Lamanite soldiers had fainted from loss of blood.
However, as Helaman later reported,

> according to the goodness of God, and to our great astonish-
> ment, and also the joy of our whole army, there was not one
> soul of them who did perish; yea, and neither was there one
> soul among them who had not received many wounds.
>
> And now, their preservation was astonishing to our whole
> army, yea, that they should be spared while there was a thou-
> sand of our brethren who were slain. And we do justly ascribe
> it to the miraculous power of God, because of their exceeding
> faith in that which they had been taught to believe—that there
> was a just God, and whosoever did not doubt, that they should
> be preserved by his marvelous power.
>
> Now this was the faith of these of whom I have spoken;
> they are young, and their minds are firm, and they do put
> their trust in God continually.[1]

So ends the remarkable account of the two thousand young Lamanite soldiers, whose words ring in our ears as they did in
Helaman's, that "their mothers had taught them."[2] We end up longing to know more about those wonderful mothers, that host of righteous women whose maternal influence determined the course of
battles and, more importantly, the course of their children's lives. But
their names, the circumstances of their lives, how they taught their
children so effectively—all such details elude us in the Book of Mormon, a history that has been compacted, as we are repeatedly told,
to less than one percent of the full account.[3] We begin to suspect that
the intriguing account of those righteous Lamanite mothers is but the
tip of the iceberg in Book of Mormon history, and that it was no
different there than it has been throughout the rest of history—that,
as one modern has expressed it, "The hand that rocks the cradle is
the hand that rules the world."[4] For as President Brigham Young

---

1. Alma 57:25–27.
2. Alma 57:21.
3. See Jacob 3:13; Words of Mormon 1:5; Helaman 3:14; 3 Nephi 5:8; 26:6; Ether
15:33.
4. William Ross Wallace, in Bartlett 1968:699.

observed, "It is the experience of people generally, that what they [learn] from their mothers in infancy, is the most lasting upon the mind through life,"[1] so that

> it is the mothers, after all, that rule the nations of the earth. They form, dictate, and direct the minds of statesmen, and the feelings, course, life, notions, and sentiments of the great and the small, of kings, rulers, governors, and of the people in general.[2]

Wilford Woodruff similarly stated, "I have often said it is the mother who forms the mind of the child."[3] And President Benson has observed, "It is mother's influence during the crucial formative years that forms a child's basic character."[4] That all these prophets were speaking partially from their own experience is evident from a recent study demonstrating the paramount role of maternal influence in shaping the lives of the latter-day prophets.[5]

But full documentation of the role of maternal influence in history will have to await greater disclosure of what really has transpired on this planet, as Elder Neal A. Maxwell has suggested:

> When the real history of mankind is fully disclosed, will it feature the echoes of gunfire or the shaping sound of lullabies? The great armistices made by military men or the peacemaking of women in homes and in neighborhoods? Will what happened in cradles and kitchens prove to be more controlling than what happened in congresses?[6]

As we have noted, the Book of Mormon makes no claim to being a complete history; quite to the contrary, it repeatedly purports to be but a brief abridgment. What it does claim, however, is to be a writing

---

1. JD 1:67.
2. JD 9:38; and see JD 19:69.
3. JD 15:12.
4. TETB 523.
5. See Arrington and Madsen 1987.
6. *Ensign* 8:5 (May 1978), pp. 10–11.

inspired of God[1] and intended particularly for our generation.[2] The Book of Mormon, says President Benson, was written by men who "saw our day, and chose those things which would be of greatest worth to us."[3] As we read the book, then, "we should constantly ask ourselves, 'Why did the Lord inspire Mormon (or Moroni or Alma) to include that in his record?' "[4]

When we ask that question about the Book of Mormon's predominant focus on father-son pairs in its depiction of parent-child relationships, while considering the ever paramount role of maternal influence, one answer that suggests itself is that such focus may have been intentionally designed to speak that much more emphatically to the fathers of our generation. Such an idea conforms to Brigham Young's repeated insistence that men's natural inclination to righteousness does not generally measure up to that of women: "Women are more ready to do and love the right than men,"[5] for women are "altogether of a finer nature" with "stronger moral inclinations."[6] It may be, then, that fathers tend to need more encouragement in fulfilling their divinely ordained parental role, and the Book of Mormon has prophetically provided that encouragement.

So until more is revealed about the great Book of Mormon mothers, we can at least rejoice in the "plain and precious"[7] truths that the Book of Mormon *does* disclose, not the least of which is the powerful pattern of parenting presented in a number of father-son portraits applicable to all parent-child relationships. In fact, the presentation of that pattern as a guide for this most significant of all duties may well be an important reason as to why the Book of Mormon is the most correct of any book.

---

1. See 2 Nephi 33:10–11; Moroni 10:27–29.
2. See Mormon 8:14–41; 9:1–37.
3. W&W 20.
4. Ibid.
5. JD 12:194, reading "than" for "that."
6. JD 18:233.
7. 1 Nephi 13:34.

Chapter 1

FOUNDING FATHERS
· ·
LEHI AND NEPHI

THE INFLUENCE OF THE FATHERS IN NEPHI'S RECORD

The Book of Mormon owes its existence to the power of parental influence, as the first writer expressly acknowledges from the outset in a tribute to his parents: "I, Nephi, having been born of goodly parents, therefore I was taught somewhat in all the learning of my father."[1] The context is important. This was an Israelite family who had lived near Jerusalem prior to the Babylonion destruction in the sixth century B.C.; so that in teaching his son Nephi, Lehi was discharging the important parental responsibility incumbent upon every father in ancient Israel. As one eminent scholar has explained, "One of [the father's] most sacred duties was to teach his son the truths of religion and to give him a general education."[2] But Lehi could hardly have guessed that the education of his son Nephi would exert such profound influence upon generations to come; indeed, of all the young men then receiving an education in ancient Israel, few would have such critical need of it or would put it to such important use as would

---

1. 1 Nephi 1:1.
2. AI I:49.

Nephi, of whom we must suppose—even as he would write of John the Revelator—that "the Lord God [had] ordained [him] . . . that he should write"[1] mighty revelations from God. Nephi's record would guide generations of his descendants and would eventually—like John's record—go forth to all nations. Furthermore, Nephi's record would serve as the most influential writing in the latter-day gathering of Israel and establishment of Zion. Such a significant calling easily qualifies as one of those spoken of by Joseph Smith: "Every man who has a calling to minister to the inhabitants of the world was ordained to that very purpose in the Grand Council of heaven before this world was."[2]

How well Nephi was taught is reflected in his ability, even at an "exceedingly young" age,[3] not only to recount important scriptural events but also to apply them to his own experience in order to encourage himself and others, seen early in his account. After Lehi had led his family out of Jerusalem in response to a divine command, he was further commanded to send his sons back to obtain a certain set of brass plates in the possession of one Laban that contained the Hebrew scriptures. The difficulties that Lehi's sons faced caused the two oldest, Laman and Lemuel, to want to abandon the enterprise. But Nephi had an altogether different view of what was possible, based on the experience of their ancestral fathers as recorded in the very record they were seeking to obtain. He encouraged his older brothers:

> Therefore let us go up; let us be strong like unto Moses; for he truly spake unto the waters of the Red Sea and they divided hither and thither, and our fathers came through, out of captivity, on dry ground, and the armies of Pharaoh did follow and were drowned in the waters of the Red Sea.
>
> Now behold ye know that this is true. . . . Let us go up; the Lord is able to deliver us, even as our fathers, and to destroy Laban, even as the Egyptians.[4]

---

1. 1 Nephi 14:25.
2. TPJS 365.
3. 1 Nephi 2:16.
4. 1 Nephi 4:2–3.

Nephi's reference to his "fathers" clearly means his "forefathers"; our English word *father*, like its Hebrew counterpart *av*, can mean not only a male parent but also a more remote male ancestor.[1] Such usage of the term "father" is, as we shall see, found throughout the Book of Mormon and is an authenticating mark that its authors originated in ancient Israel, where the concept of "the fathers" figured prominently.[2]

Also authentic is *how* Nephi remembers his fathers: "Let us be strong like unto Moses; . . . the Lord is able to deliver us, even as our fathers." In ancient Israel, as an eminent scholar has explained, "the saving deeds of Yahweh [Jehovah, or the Lord] to the fathers are treasured by the godly, and they receive courage and confidence from them" that God "will deal with the present generation as he dealt with the fathers. . . . Thus the history of the fathers is a living heritage."[3] And the pivotal event of that history in terms of God's direct intervention and deliverance to form the Israelite nation[4] was the Exodus, an event that ancient Israel was repeatedly adjured to remember.[5] For example, Moses himself had warned the children of Israel, "Take heed that you do not forget the LORD who freed you from the land of Egypt, the house of bondage,"[6] for if "you forget" then "I warn you this day that you shall certainly perish."[7]

The threatened penalty of destruction was finally in Nephi's day about to violently fall on Jerusalem, out of which the Lord had led Nephi and his family. In the Book of Mormon the contrast between Nephi and those at Jerusalem is sharp and significant. They had forgotten their forefathers' divine deliverance from Egypt, but Nephi had not—and was therefore being preserved from the penalty. And ironically, Nephi now had to rely on that same kind of divine deliverance to preserve him and his family as they fled from a corrupt

1. See WTNID 828; TDOT I:7; TDNT V:961.
2. See TDOT I:7–6; TDNT V:976–977.
3. TDOT I:12.
4. See EJ 6:1064–66.
5. See Wigoder 1989:249–250; Yerushalmi 1982:11.
6. NJPS Deuteronomy 6:12.
7. NJPS Deuteronomy 8:14, 19.

Jerusalem. To extend the irony, they were forced to flee from the land promised to Abraham in order to help fulfil his covenant in a new promised land.

Such a scenario constitutes a striking introduction to the central significance of the theme of fathers and sons in the Book of Mormon, which thus commences with a group of Israelites owing their very lives to their obedience to the divine imperative to remember their fathers. It will be no coincidence that when Nephite history finally and tragically ends a millennium later, the cause will be the Nephites' collective failure to remember their righteous fathers.

Nephi's own experience, then, turned out to be a reenactment of the experience of his forefathers, a kind of new Exodus as they were divinely led out of a corrupt society and through the wilderness toward a promised land—all of which resounds with yet another authentic echo of ancient Israelite society during Nephi's day when, as modern scholars have shown, much of the literature reflects "the relatively common seventh-sixth century [B.C.] themes of the new exodus, the new trek through the wilderness, and the restoration and resettlement in the land."[1] It is no wonder, then, that as one Latter-day Saint scholar has shown, Nephi's own account of his family's journeyings contains numerous and striking parallels to the Exodus account of the children of Israel, indicating that Nephi consciously patterned his own record after the Exodus account.[2]

In a more immediate sense, though, Lehi is the one whose fatherly influence looms the largest in Nephi's record, not merely because of the education that Lehi provided (Nephi expressly says that "I make a record in the language of my father"[3]), but also because of Lehi's example in making his own record—"my father hath written . . . many things"[4] in his own "record."[5] But here again we should not miss the connection with the forefathers, for Lehi in turn was apparently following an ancestral pattern. In searching the brass plates

---

1. Michael L. Barré and John S. Kselman, in Meyers and O'Connor 1983:98.
2. See Terrence L. Szink, in Sorenson and Thorne 1991:38–51.
3. 1 Nephi 1:2.
4. 1 Nephi 1:16.
5. 1 Nephi 1:17.

he discovered that he and their previous owner (Laban) were both descended from the patriarch Joseph, whose descendants had kept the records. The record that Lehi wrote thus appears to be a continuation of his ancient ancestral record going back to Joseph and beyond—a record that, since the beginning of time, was handed down from father to son.[1] Furthermore, Joseph receives special emphasis in Nephi's narrative about Lehi's discovery of his genealogy; not content simply to specify Lehi's ancestor as Joseph, Nephi tells us that it was "even that Joseph who was the son of Jacob, who was sold into Egypt, and who was preserved by the hand of the Lord, that he might preserve his father, Jacob, and all his household from perishing with famine."[2] Why the elaboration? Perhaps because Joseph served as a pattern for his descendant Lehi, whom the Lord is likewise removing from his Israelite brethren (like "a branch . . . broken off"[3]) to another land in order to eventually bring salvation to the house of Israel—in fulfillment, in fact, of Joseph's own prophecy recorded on the brass plates![4] And the means of that salvation would be the record kept by Lehi's descendants, beginning with Nephi, who was following Lehi's lead. In fact, Lehi's record served as the beginning point of the record of Nephi, who made "an account of my proceedings in my days" beginning with "an abridgment of the record of my father."[5] As one latter-day saint scholar has emphasized, Lehi's record was "very important to Nephi" and constituted "a rich source of the knowledge [that Nephi has] given us."[6]

AN EXEMPLARY FATHER TEACHES AN EXEMPLARY SON

When Nephi begins his account, then, the reference point is naturally Lehi: "It came to pass that my father, Lehi, as he went forth prayed unto the Lord . . . "[7] This same reference point continues

1. See CWHN 2:145–148.
2. 1 Nephi 5:14.
3. 1 Nephi 19:24.
4. See 2 Nephi 3:12.
5. 1 Nephi 1:17.
6. S. Kent Brown, in Sorenson and Thorne 1991:4, 14.
7. 1 Nephi 1:5.

throughout Nephi's repeated mention of "the tent of my father," as when Nephi "returned from speaking with the Lord, to the tent of my father,"[1] or when Nephi and his brothers journeyed back to "the tent of our father" (first with the brass plates and later with Ishmael's family).[2] According to Hugh Nibley, "Nephi seems to think of his father's tent as the hub of everything"[3] and "refers constantly to his father's tent as the center of the universe."[4] Nibley has rightly pointed out the authentic Bedouin frame of mind reflected by Nephi's perspective.[5]

But that perspective also accurately reflects the ideal role of the father in his family in ancient Israel; according to one scholar, in the Israelite family the father was "the centre from which strength and will emanate through the whole of the sphere which belongs to him and to which he belongs."[6] So it was with Lehi's family; Nephi constantly identifies with his father, who at every turn serves as Nephi's teacher and exemplar. For example, when Nephi records that "the Lord spake unto my father,"[7] Nephi can soon likewise record that "the Lord spake unto me."[8] When Nephi records that "the Lord commanded my father,"[9] Nephi can soon say the same about himself.[10] Similarly when Nephi records that Lehi "was obedient unto the word of the Lord,"[11] Nephi himself will soon demonstrate unquestioning obedience to the word of the Lord.[12] When Nephi records that Lehi "took the records which were engraven upon the plates of brass, and . . . did search them,"[13] Nephi also will search them,[14] will be able

---

1. 1 Nephi 3:1.
2. 1 Nephi 4:38, 34; 7:5, 21–22; see also 1 Nephi 9:1; 10:16; 15:1; 16:6.
3. CWHN 5:52.
4. Ibid. 51.
5. See Ibid. 51–52.
6. TDOT I:8.
7. 1 Nephi 2:1.
8. 1 Nephi 2:19.
9. 1 Nephi 2:2.
10. 1 Nephi 3:1–7; 5:20.
11. 1 Nephi 2:3.
12. See 1 Nephi 3:7.
13. 1 Nephi 5:10.
14. See 1 Nephi 5:21.

to say "my soul delighteth in the scriptures, and my heart pondereth them,"[1] and will even devote lengthy portions of his own limited record to quote and expound the prophecies of Isaiah taken from those same brass plates that Lehi had been inspired to acquire and had then searched. When Nephi records that "my father . . . was filled with the Spirit, and began to prophesy concerning his seed,"[2] and "prophesied many things concerning his seed,"[3] Nephi also will be "filled with the spirit of prophecy" and will "prophesy"[4] through "the spirit which is in me"[5] concerning "my seed, from generation to generation."[6]

The context of Lehi's prophesying is noteworthy: it was immediately after he had searched the brass plates "from the beginning" and "discover[ed] the genealogy of his fathers" along with their sacred history all the way back to "Adam and Eve, who were our first parents."[7] When Lehi "saw all these things, he was filled with the Spirit, and began to prophesy concerning his seed."[8] The connection seems more than coincidental: a knowledge of his fathers prompted inspiration regarding his posterity. Furthermore, if the account that Lehi read contained (as seems likely) the record of Adam that Joseph Smith restored, then Lehi would have read how Adam himself had prophesied of his own seed, even "all the families of the earth."[9] Lehi would thus have been following an earlier ancestral model about which he had just read. And as Adam's example had influenced his son and posterity—"Seth . . . prophesied in all his days, and taught his son Enos in the ways of God; wherefore Enos prophesied also"[10]— so it was that Lehi prophesied and taught Nephi; therefore Nephi prophesied also.

---

1. 2 Nephi 4:15.
2. 1 Nephi 5:17.
3. 1 Nephi 5:19.
4. 2 Nephi 25:4.
5. 2 Nephi 25:11.
6. 2 Nephi 25:21.
7. 1 Nephi 5:10, 16.
8. 1 Nephi 5:17.
9. Moses 5:10.
10. Moses 6:13.

In obeying and honoring his father, Nephi was conforming to the commandment given to his forefathers to, as the Decalogue commands, "Honour thy father and thy mother."[1] As one Old Testament scholar explains, "It was the duty of the children to obey their parents" and "to hearken to their father." Hence the Old Testament emphasizes "the mutual responsibilities of parents and children."[2] These same responsibilities are found in modern-day Israel. According to President Benson, "Good fathers teach their sons, and good sons listen and obey."[3]

Nephi's tenacious following of his father's example also reflects the principle that a modern expert on childhood education tells parents, "What tiny children want *is to be you.*"[4] And could this natural inclination of children to become like their parents be what we are most meant to recapture when the Savior emphatically and repeatedly commands us to "become as a little child"[5] in order to be saved? Perhaps only those who become as little children will have the necessary desire to become fully like their Father in Heaven.

The pattern of Nephi following Lehi's example seems aptly symbolized in the vision that Lehi had of the tree of life. After Lehi had traveled the "strait and narrow path" and had arrived at the tree and tasted its sweet fruit, he looked around for his family, and seeing them a short distance away, in his own words, "I beckoned unto them; and I also did say unto them with a loud voice that they should come unto me, and partake of the fruit, which was desirable above all other fruit." Nephi followed his father's example; Laman and Lemuel did not.[6]

Significantly, Lehi was teaching by both example and word, an effective combination that President Ezra Taft Benson has called "a divine pattern."[7] Lehi had first shown the way by treading the path

1. Exodus 20:12.
2. TDOT I:9–10.
3. W&W 67.
4. Doman 1984:129.
5. 3 Nephi 11:37–38.
6. 1 Nephi 8:10–18.
7. W&W 68.

and eating the fruit. He could thus say with the Master Teacher, Christ, "Follow me" – as Nephi would later write about.[1] "A good model," explains President Benson, "is the best teacher. Therefore, a father's first responsibility is to set the proper example."[2] The same responsibility rested upon the fathers in ancient Israel, where "the first requirement of a father," explains one scholar, "was to fear God; then he will be a refuge to his children."[3]

Lehi's example was then made all the more emphatic by his express instructions: he "beckoned" to his family and called to them "with a loud voice" to come join him in eating this most desirable of all fruits. Lehi's fatherly leadership had what President Harold B. Lee insisted was necessary for effective leaders – "a certain, sure trumpet sound to their instructions."[4] Lehi's plainness not only convinced Nephi but also became a pattern for him; Nephi would later write that "my soul delighteth in plainness unto my people, that they may learn,"[5] and he would write his sacred record "according to the plainness of the truth."[6]

The symbolic depiction of Lehi's exemplary teaching in the vision of the tree is consistent with Lehi's actual leadership, as when he obeyed the word of the Lord by moving his family out of Jerusalem and out of the way of the impending Babylonian destruction.[7] Their first camp was "a valley by the side of a river of water,"[8] a topography from which Lehi derived lessons for his sons as he spoke to them "with power, being filled with the Spirit"[9]:

> He spake unto Laman, saying: O that thou mightest be like unto this river, continually running into the fountain of all righteousness!

---

1. See 2 Nephi 31:13.
2. W&W 67.
3. TDOT I:10, citing Proverbs 14:26.
4. Lee 1974a:105.
5. 2 Nephi 25:4.
6. 2 Nephi 33:5.
7. See 1 Nephi 2:2–4.
8. 1 Nephi 2:6.
9. 1 Nephi 2:14.

> And he also spake unto Lemuel: O that thou mightest be
> like unto this valley, firm and steadfast, and immovable in
> keeping the commandments of the Lord![1]

And to emphasize the point, Lehi even named the river "Laman"
and the valley "Lemuel."[2] Lehi's masterful use of metaphor in instructing his sons is noteworthy, for as Elder Boyd K. Packer has
pointed out, this teaching principle was the one used more than any
other by Jesus himself.[3] Lehi's use of metaphor will, as we shall see,
provide a pattern for some of the greatest teachers among his posterity.

Lehi also led his family in worship and prayer, as when they
repeatedly "did offer sacrifice and burnt offerings unto the Lord; and
they gave thanks unto the God of Israel."[4] Lehi likewise led his family
in the study of scripture, as he "took the records which were engraven
upon the plates of brass, and he did search them from the beginning,"[5]
and also discussed them with his family.[6] Lehi's family heard him
prophesy,[7] preach the gospel,[8] testify of the Savior,[9] share profound
spiritual experiences,[10] and counsel them to keep the commandments.[11]
Lehi further directed his children to perform specific tasks that the
Lord had revealed to him.[12] Also, he gave his children individual
counsel and inspired blessings about the future.[13] And with all of this,
Nephi repeatedly reminds us that he is recording merely a fraction
of Lehi's teachings and labors.[14]

In providing this excellent example, Lehi was, once again, fol-

---

1. 1 Nephi 2:9–10.
2. 1 Nephi 2:8, 14.
3. See Packer 1979:20.
4. 1 Nephi 5:9; 7:22.
5. 1 Nephi 5:10.
6. See 1 Nephi 5:11–19.
7. See 1 Nephi 5:17–19; 10:15.
8. See 1 Nephi 8:2–35.
9. See 1 Nephi 2:9–10; 8:38.
10. See 1 Nephi 8:37; 2 Nephi 2.
11. See 1 Nephi 10:4–6; 2 Nephi 2.
12. See 1 Nephi 3:2–4.
13. See 2 Nephi 1 through 4:11.
14. See 1 Nephi 5:19; 8:29–30; 9:1; 10:15.

lowing the example first set by father Adam, who (as was probably recorded on the brass plates that Lehi had searched) was taught the gospel and was then commanded to teach it freely to his children — which he did.[1] Adam's example was followed by his righteous descendants, as when Abraham received divine approval because the Lord knew he would "instruct his children and his posterity to keep the way of the Lord"[2] — an event certainly known to Lehi through the brass plates.

NEPHI SEES WHAT HIS FATHER SAW

As Lehi told his family about his vision of the tree and other prophecies,[3] he found in Nephi not only an attentive and perceptive pupil, but also a son anxious to experience firsthand the divine instruction that had been granted to his father. President Benson has observed that

> Nephi had listened to his father, had believed his father, but he wanted to know through the same source his father knew — revelation. Worthy sons are entitled to receive from their Heavenly Father confirmation concerning the direction their mortal fathers give them. . . . So Nephi diligently sought the Lord.[4]

As Nephi records,

> After I, Nephi, having heard all the words of my father, concerning the things which he saw in a vision, and also the things which he spake by the power of the Holy Ghost, . . . I, Nephi, was desirous also that I might see, and hear, and know of these things, by the power of the Holy Ghost.[5]

The same vision was indeed granted to Nephi, but only, as Nephi again recorded, "after I had desired to know the things that my father had seen."[6] When the Spirit in the form of a man first appeared to

---

1. See Moses 6:51–68; 7:1.
2. NJPS Genesis 18:19.
3. See 1 Nephi 8; 10:1–16.
4. W&W 68.
5. 1 Nephi 10:17.
6. 1 Nephi 11:1.

Nephi and asked him what he desired, Nephi unhesitatingly responded, "I desire to behold the things which my father saw."[1] Whereupon the Spirit queried, "Believest thou that thy father saw the tree of which he hath spoken?" To which Nephi answered, "Yea, thou knowest that I believe all the words of my father."[2] The Spirit's response demonstrates the greatness of Lehi's teachings: the Spirit exclaimed "with a loud voice" to Nephi,

> Hosanna to the Lord, the most high God; for he is God over all the earth, yea, even above all. And blessed art thou, Nephi, because thou believest in the Son of the most high God; wherefore, thou shalt behold the things which thou hast desired.[3]

There could be no greater tribute to Lehi's fatherly teaching than this — that to believe Lehi's words was to believe "in the Son of the most high God." It demonstrates unequivocally that Lehi had taught his family and testified to them of Christ — who should still, observed President Spencer W. Kimball, be the focus of "all our teaching in the home."[4] And from Nephi's perspective, his willingness to learn from his righteous mortal father opened the door to knowledge of a higher Father-Son relationship. This will become a pronounced pattern throughout Book of Mormon history as many sons likewise learn of the Son of God through their righteous fathers. Such sons in turn become righteous fathers and teach their sons, continuing the tradition. Nephi recorded, "We talk of Christ, we rejoice in Christ, we preach of Christ, we prophesy of Christ . . . that our children may know to what source they may look for a remission of their sins."[5]

As we read Nephi's account of his vision as he relates the introduction and explanation of heavenly messengers, we are constantly reminded of Lehi's earlier experience: "the fruit which thy father tasted,"[6] "the tree which my father had seen,"[7] "the rod of iron,

---

1. 1 Nephi 11:3.
2. 1 Nephi 11:4–5.
3. 1 Nephi 11:6.
4. Kimball 1982:333.
5. 2 Nephi 25:26.
6. 1 Nephi 11:7.
7. 1 Nephi 11:8, 21.

which my father had seen,"[1] "the building which my father saw,"[2] and "the Redeemer of the world, of whom my father had spoken."[3] Similarly when Nephi saw in vision John the Baptist and the twelve apostles,[4] he was seeing what his father had spoken of earlier.[5] Likewise when Nephi was told that "thou also hast heard that whoso repenteth not must perish,"[6] he had heard it from his father.[7] And when Nephi was asked, "Rememberest thou the covenants of the Father unto the House of Israel?" he could answer in the affirmative[8] because he had learned of those things from his father.[9] Finally as Nephi closed the record of his vision, he stated in summary, "I bear record that I saw the things which my father saw, and the angel of the Lord did make them known unto me."[10] In all of scripture there is no more emphatic illustration of the power of parental example than this vision of Nephi, who over and over again explains that he experienced what his father had experienced. It is the ultimate tribute to both Lehi and Nephi, and a powerful lesson to all parents and children. It also echoes the relationship between the Father and his Son, Jesus Christ, who in his mortal ministry would explain that "I do nothing of myself; but as my Father hath taught me, I speak these things."[11] Or, as Joseph Smith explained, "The Son doeth what he hath seen the Father do."[12]

LAMAN AND LEMUEL: INVIOLABLE AGENCY

Significantly, it is to "the tent of my father"[13] that Nephi once again returns after his vision, where a scene of arresting contrast

---

1. 1 Nephi 11:25.
2. 1 Nephi 11:35, 12:18.
3. 1 Nephi 11:27.
4. See 1 Nephi 11:27–29.
5. See 1 Nephi 1:10; 10:7–10.
6. 1 Nephi 14:5.
7. See 1 Nephi 1:4.
8. See 1 Nephi 14:8, 5.
9. See 1 Nephi 10:12–14; 15:8.
10. 1 Nephi 14:29.
11. John 8:28.
12. TPJS 312.
13. 1 Nephi 15:1.

unfolds. Having so soon been taught from on high concerning the things his father had taught, Nephi encounters Laman and Lemuel

> disputing one with another concerning the things which my father had spoken unto them.
> For he truly spake many great things unto them, which were hard to be understood, save a man should inquire of the Lord; and they being hard in their hearts, therefore they did not look unto the Lord as they ought.[1]

If Lehi's teachings were, as discussed previously, so plain, why did even Nephi have to "look unto the Lord" to understand them? Because, in words that Nephi's brother Jacob would later write, "No man knoweth of [God's] ways save it be revealed unto him."[2] Or, as the Apostle Paul explained, a mortal must have the Spirit of God to understand the things of God.[3] Ultimately the best that any father or other teacher can hope to do, then, is to plainly invite and persuade another mortal to look to God, without whose Spirit neither understanding of salvation nor salvation itself can come. Hence even Nephi, who gloried in plainness and wrote in plainness, could warn his readers that "if ye cannot understand" his plain words "it will be because ye ask not, neither do ye knock."[4] That Lehi, for all his plain and powerful example and teaching, could not persuade Laman and Lemuel to come and eat of the fruit attests to the reality of individual agency, which even God himself will not violate. Joseph Smith is reported to have said that "God would not exert any compulsory means, and the devil could not," so that "all was voluntary."[5] Hence when Lehi later tells Laman's children, "I know that if ye are brought up in the way ye should go ye will not depart from it,"[6] we must suppose this to be either a general statement with possible exceptions because of agency, or a remark intended to apply specifically to the individuals he was addressing.

---

1. 1 Nephi 15:2–3.
2. Jacob 4:8.
3. See 1 Corinthians 2:11 (and see JST).
4. 2 Nephi 32:4.
5. TPJS 187.
6. 2 Nephi 4:5.

But asking and knocking were the very things Laman and Lemuel refused to do, even as they had refused to eat of the fruit in Lehi's dream. That refusal had caused Lehi great distress, as he had "exceedingly feared" for them[1] and,

> exhort[ed] them then with all the feeling of a tender parent, that they would hearken to his words, that perhaps the Lord would be merciful to them, and not cast them off; yea, my father did preach unto them.[2]

Nephi's sensitivity and empathy in reporting[3] Lehi's anguish over the prospect of losing Laman and Lemuel was undoubtedly heightened by what Nephi learned in his own vision about the future destruction of his own posterity—that "because of the pride of my seed, and the temptations of the devil," the posterity of Laman and Lemuel would "overpower the people of my seed" and entirely "overcome my seed."[4] The vision of that future destruction created the kind of distress in Nephi that only a righteous parent can feel for wayward children. As Nephi reports,

> I was overcome because of my afflictions, for I considered that mine afflictions were great above all, because of the destruction of my people, for I had beheld their fall.[5]

One cannot fully appreciate Nephi's grief over the eventual destruction of his posterity without considering the larger context of Nephi's preoccupation—seen throughout his writings—with his forefather Abraham and the Abrahamic covenant.[6] As one eminent modern scholar has observed about that covenant, "Its core is the blessing and promise of posterity; this is linked with a promise of victory, and the effect of the blessing on the nations."[7] Specifically, because Abra-

---

1. 1 Nephi 8:36, 4.
2. 1 Nephi 8:37.
3. Obviously Nephi reported this after his own vision. See 1 Nephi 9.
4. 1 Nephi 12:19–20.
5. 1 Nephi 15:5.
6. See, e.g., 1 Nephi 6:4; 15:18; 17:40; 19:10; 22:9; 2 Nephi 8:2; 27:33; 29:14.
7. Westermann 1985:364 (internal verse citations omitted).

ham had not withheld his son Isaac, the Lord had sworn to him, "In blessing I will bless thee."[1] (This slavishly literal translation in the King James tends to obscure the meaning; in Hebrew the juxtaposition of the different forms of the same verb acts as an intensifier,[2] so that the meaning is, as more modern translations express it, "I will indeed bless you"[3] or "surely bless you"[4] or "greatly bless you"[5] or "bless you abundantly"[6] or "shower blessings on you."[7]) Furthermore, the Lord promised, "In multiplying I will multiply thy seed" (again the verbal intensifier) "as the stars of the heaven, and as the sand which is upon the sea shore; and thy seed shall possess the gate of his enemies"[8] (a promise of victory[9]), "and in thy seed shall all the nations of the earth be blessed"[10] (but as one eminent scholar says, the form of the verb translated here "can be reflexive or reciprocal, but not passive,"[11] so that the meaning is more accurately conveyed in the translation, "bless themselves"[12] — a meaning which, as Martin Luther noted, "should be carefully noted and pondered"[13] as pointing to the voluntary nature of receiving such a blessing through Abraham's descendant — Christ).

Against such a background Nephi's grief becomes as profound as was his "delight" in the Lord's covenant to Abraham.[14] For Nephi's feeling was not merely the natural pain of a righteous parent for his wayward posterity, but also the anguish of a faithful Abrahamic descendant who could not have missed the contrast between the destiny

---

1. Genesis 22:17.
2. See Cowley 1910:214, 342.
3. NRSV Genesis 22:17; Fox 1983:84.
4. NIV Genesis 22:17.
5. NASB Genesis 22:17.
6. REB Genesis 22:17; Vanter 1977:258.
7. NJB Genesis 22:17.
8. Genesis 22:17.
9. See Sarna 1989:154.
10. Genesis 22:18.
11. Speiser 1979 (ABI):86.
12. Genesis 22:18: NJPS, NJB, NRSV ("gain blessing for themselves"), Speiser 1979 (ABI):162.
13. Pelikan 1964:158.
14. See 2 Nephi 11:5.

of his own posterity and that of Abraham: if Abraham's seed would be multiplied exceedingly to become as the stars and sand, Nephi's seed would mostly be tragically cut off; if Abraham's seed would win victory over their enemies, Nephi's seed would be mostly destroyed by their enemies; and if through Abraham's seed all nations would bless themselves, there would remain none of Nephi's righteous seed to provide such blessing.[1]

All of this makes Nephi's own arduous labors in engraving his record all the more remarkable, for from the very start he knew that he was writing not only to his own posterity, but ultimately to us in the latter days, which should elicit our increased attention to the powerful lessons on fathers and sons that Nephi recorded.

No sooner had Nephi "received strength" from being "overcome" with anguish[2] than he patiently explained to his short-sighted older brothers—they whose descendants would destroy Nephi's descendants—about the things Lehi had taught,[3] finally concluding by

> exhort[ing] my brethren, with all diligence, to keep the commandments of the Lord.
> And it came to pass that they did humble themselves before the Lord; insomuch that I had joy and great hopes of them, that they would walk in the paths of righteousness.[4]

Nephi had, of course, been inclined all along to help his unbelieving older brothers, even when they "would not hearken unto my words; and being grieved because of the hardness of their hearts I cried unto the Lord for them."[5] His charitable behavior towards those who from the beginning gave him nothing but trouble is a sure mark of Nephi's spiritual progress, as judged by the standard explained by Joseph Smith: "The nearer we get to our heavenly Father, the more we are disposed to look with compassion on perishing souls; we feel

---

1. See 1 Nephi 13:30.
2. 1 Nephi 15:5–6.
3. See 1 Nephi 15:6–36; 16:1–3.
4. 1 Nephi 16:4–5.
5. 1 Nephi 2:18.

that we want to take them upon our shoulders, and cast their sins behind our backs."[1]

LOYALTY AND UNITY

Nephi's behavior toward his brothers also manifested his intense loyalty for his father, whom he always supported and with whom he constantly identified. When Laman and Lemuel "did murmur against their father," Nephi was insightful enough to comprehend — and a loyal enough son to record — that "they did murmur because they knew not the dealings of that God who had created them."[2] Furthermore, Nephi took it upon himself, voluntarily and spontaneously, to persuade his younger brother Sam to believe in Lehi's divine inspiration.[3] Nephi was more than an obedient son; he was Lehi's staunch ally, an active force in furthering the cause that Lehi was called upon to direct. Nephi's solidarity with his father is reflected, for example, in his observation after he had brought the brass plates to Lehi and after Lehi had searched them: Nephi observes that "thus far I and my father had kept the commandments wherewith the Lord had commanded us."[4] Then, when Nephi becomes more specific about what had been accomplished to date, he couches the report in terms of joint effort and achievement:

> And we had obtained the records which the Lord had commanded us, and searched them and found that they were desirable; yea, even of great worth unto us, insomuch that we could preserve the commandments of the Lord unto our children.[5]

It was a joint effort also to attempt to bring Laman and Lemuel to understanding and faithfulness. When they rebelled and threatened to return to Jerusalem, Nephi attempted to dissuade them by speaking of (among other things) the example of Lehi who, with the other

---

1. TPJS 241.
2. 1 Nephi 2:12.
3. See 1 Nephi 2:17.
4. 1 Nephi 5:20.
5. 1 Nephi 5:21.

prophets, had been rejected by Jerusalem.[1] Nephi also followed Lehi's lead[2] in encouraging Laman and Lemuel to "keep the commandments of the Lord"[3] and in explaining Lehi's teaching.[4] Such unity seems to have been one of the principal objectives for the Lord giving Lehi the round brass ball "of curious workmanship,"[5] later referred to as the "Liahona," or compass.[6] Significantly, it was not given to Lehi until the very morning he was preparing to leave the valley of Lemuel and journey into the wilderness pursuant to the Lord's command the previous night. According to Nephi, within that amazing instrument "were two spindles; and the one pointed the way whither [they] should go into the wilderness";[7] but the spindles worked only "according to the faith and diligence and heed which [they] did give unto them."[8] The point is worth emphasizing because it is easily overlooked: the instrument did not work according to the faith of the group's most faithful member but rather according to the group's collective faith (as poignantly demonstrated later in the story[9]). Clearly the Lord wished to cultivate and extend the principle of unity that existed between Nephi and Lehi, the same principle that has ever been one of the foundational principles of Zion, whose inhabitants in Enoch's day "were of one heart and one mind."[10] It was the same object for which Christ himself prayed for his followers, that they "all may be one; as thou, Father, art in me, and I in thee."[11] And it is the same condition that Christ has commanded for latter-day Zion: "Be one; and if ye are not one ye are not mine."[12]

Nephi's loyalty to his father assured from the start that Laman

---

1. See 1 Nephi 7:14.
2. See 1 Nephi 8:38.
3. 1 Nephi 15:10, 25.
4. See 1 Nephi 15:7–36; especially vv. 13, 17–18, 21–30.
5. 1 Nephi 16:10.
6. Alma 37:38.
7. 1 Nephi 16:10.
8. 1 Nephi 16:28.
9. See 1 Nephi 18:12.
10. Moses 7:18.
11. John 17:21; 3 Nephi 19:21.
12. D&C 38:27.

and Lemuel's murmuring and persecution against Lehi would also include Nephi. Beginning with the return to Jerusalem to obtain the brass plates, Laman and Lemuel were, says Nephi, "angry with me, and also with my father."[1] During the second trip to Jerusalem, Laman and Lemuel were again, says Nephi, "angry with me" and this time even "sought to take away my life."[2] The pattern continues throughout the account of the long journey." Laman and Lemuel "did murmur against my father, and also against me,"[3] saying, "Thou art like unto our father,"[4] and "let us slay our father, and also our brother Nephi."[5]

The recurrent murmurings of Laman and Lemuel may be taken as some indication of how difficult the journey was. Nephi probably had to endure the same hardships, plus the added burden of his brothers' constant murmuring. The amazing thing, then, is not that Laman and Lemuel continue to murmur but that Nephi never does — even when other stalwarts finally capitulate and join in the murmuring. For example, Sarai, Lehi's wife, once bitterly complained against Lehi, calling him a "visionary man" who had led them into the wilderness to perish.[6] And even Lehi himself, facing the most dire circumstances with no food for his family, once faltered and "began to murmur against the Lord his God."[7] The incident occurred after Nephi's bow broke and the other bows "lost their springs,"[8] so that, in Nephi's words, "it began to be exceedingly difficult, yea, insomuch that we could obtain no food."[9] Reading Nephi's account of what followed, one can sense his high regard for his father, whose failure Nephi is obviously reluctant to mention. In fact, only at the point where the narrative would become unintelligible without that piece of information does Nephi include it, apprising us that Lehi had in

---

1. 1 Nephi 3:28.
2. 1 Nephi 7:16, 19.
3. 1 Nephi 16:36.
4. 1 Nephi 17:20.
5. 1 Nephi 16:37.
6. 1 Nephi 5:2.
7. 1 Nephi 16:20.
8. 1 Nephi 16:18, 21.
9. 1 Nephi 16:21.

fact murmured and temporarily estranged himself from God. What Nephi cannot bring himself to expressly say, however, is that he found it necessary to chasten his father; Nephi reports merely that he spoke to "them" and to "my brethren." As Nephi tells it,

> I, Nephi, did speak much unto *my brethren*, because *they* had hardened their hearts again, even unto complaining against the Lord their God.
>
> And it came to pass that I, Nephi, did make out of wood a bow, and out of a straight stick, an arrow; wherefore, I did arm myself with a bow and an arrow, with a sling and with stones. And I said unto my father: Whither shall I go to obtain food?
>
> And it came to pass that he did inquire of the Lord, for *they* had humbled themselves because of my words; for I did say many things unto *them* in the energy of my soul.[1]

And as impressive as Nephi's recording of the incident was the part he played in it, regarding which Elder Marion D. Hanks commented:

> Nephi went to his father and said, "Dad, the Lord has blessed you. You are his servant. I need to know where to go to get food. Dad, you ask him, will you?" [Nephi] could have gone to his own knees. He could have taken over.
>
> I count this as one of the really significant lessons of life in the book. . . . A son who had strength enough, and humility enough, and manliness enough, to go to his superior and say, "You ask God, will you?" . . . Lehi asked God, and God told him, and Lehi's leadership was restored.[2]

Significant also is how God answered Lehi's prayer—by directing him to look at the brass ball, which contained the directions as to where Nephi could go to obtain food.[3] Why were the directions committed first to the brass ball rather than directly to Lehi? Could it have been that he was not yet sufficiently contrite and receptive to the required

---

1. 1 Nephi 16:22–24; emphasis added.
2. Hanks 1960:7.
3. See 1 Nephi 16:30.

revelation? (Joseph Smith prefaced the record of one of his greatest revelations, received in dire circumstances in Liberty Jail, with the words, "and when the heart is sufficiently contrite, then the voice of inspiration steals along and whispers."[1]) And if Lehi was not quite ready, why not give the answer to Nephi, who was? Because God was endeavoring the same thing Nephi was—to restore Lehi to his patriarchal leadership role.

Having been so restored, Lehi would have resumed leadership of the journey. But this did not prevent the Lord from occasionally giving Nephi inspiration directly for the good of the group. So it was when the time came to construct a ship for the oceanic crossing. Once the ship was built, the divine order to embark was given through Lehi;[2] but the divine order to build it in the first place came directly to Nephi.[3] His youth and strength[4] were marshalled to direct the physically demanding construction, in which Lehi himself apparently did not participate,[5] he being "stricken in years."[6]

Accordingly, Nephi solicited the help of his two older brothers; predictably, they resisted, accusing Nephi of being "like unto our father, led away by the foolish imaginations of his heart. . . . Yea, and our brother [Nephi] is like unto him. And after this manner of language," Nephi observes, "did my brethren murmur and complain against us."[7] In his lengthy response, Nephi tells them that because they, like the Jews at Jerusalem, had sought to kill Lehi, "wherefore, ye are murderers in your hearts and ye are like unto them."[8] In fact, Laman and Lemuel had also threatened and tried to kill Nephi at least twice,[9] but Nephi does not mention this. Nephi also tells Laman and Lemuel "that they should murmur no more against their father; nei-

1. TPJS 134.
2. See 1 Nephi 18:5.
3. See 1 Nephi 17:7–8.
4. See 1 Nephi 2:16.
5. See 1 Nephi 17:55; 18:1–4.
6. 1 Nephi 18:17.
7. 1 Nephi 17:20, 22.
8. 1 Nephi 17:44.
9. See 1 Nephi 7:16; 16:37.

ther should they withhold their labor from me . . . [to] build a ship."[1]
Once again, Nephi also had been the object of their murmuring,[2] but
this he does not mention. It would seem that due respect for Lehi is
what concerns him most. More telling still is what happens after Nephi
physically shocks his two brothers by the power of God: according
to Nephi's account, they did an about-face and

> they said: We know of a surety that the Lord is with thee, for
> we know that it is the power of the Lord that has shaken us.
> And they fell down before me, and were about to worship me,
> but I would not suffer them, saying: I am thy brother, yea,
> even thy younger brother; wherefore, worship the Lord thy
> God, and honor thy father and thy mother, that thy days may
> be long in the land which the Lord thy God shall give thee.[3]

Besides saying that his brothers should worship God instead of
Nephi and should honor their father, Nephi may also be saying that
they should worship God *by* honoring their father. At every turn
Nephi upholds Lehi's patriarchal position and the honor that should
be accorded him; Nephi is ever the devoted and loyal son. He also
succeeded in engaging the help of Laman and Lemuel to build the
ship, the craftsmanship of which was so fine as to cause the two older
brothers to "humble themselves again before the Lord."[4]

Regrettably, their humility did not last even through the ocean
journey, during which they became boisterous and rude, "forget[ting]
by what power they had been brought thither."[5] Once again it was
Nephi, rather than the aged Lehi, who had to confront them. Nephi's
account of the incident is revealing as he rather tersely tells that his
brothers "did take me and bind me with cords, and they did treat me
with much harshness."[6] Four days later when he is finally unbound,
Nephi expends a few more words to describe his affliction, telling
how Laman and Lemuel

---

1. 1 Nephi 17:49.
2. See 1 Nephi 3:28–31; 16:36; 17:17–23.
3. 1 Nephi 17:55.
4. 1 Nephi 18:4.
5. 1 Nephi 18:9.
6. 1 Nephi 18:11.

loosed the bands which were upon my wrists, and behold they
had swollen exceedingly; and also mine ankles were much
swollen, and great was the soreness thereof.[1]

Nephi had borne terrible abuse for leading out in trying to preserve
their safety by subduing his boisterous brothers, "lest the Lord should
be angry with us, and smite us because of our iniquity."[2] While Nephi
was bound, Lehi had spoken up in his behalf, which evoked "much
threatenings" against him. But although the abuse that Lehi endured
was strictly verbal, Nephi devotes significant space to describing his
father's pain:

> My parents being stricken in years, and having suffered much
> grief because of their children, they were brought down, yea,
> even upon their sickbeds.
>   Because of their grief and much sorrow, and the iniquity of
> my brethren, they were brought near even to be carried out
> of this time to meet their God; yea, their grey hairs were about
> to be brought down to lie low in the dust; yea, even they were
> near to be cast with sorrow into a watery grave.[3]

Such are the words of a sensitive and compassionate son who
was as concerned about his parents' well being as that of his own.
And such was the behavior of a son whose commitment to Lehi and
to God was absolute and unwavering even in the face of the most
intense persecution and adversity. Nephi's loyalty is a moving demonstration of obedience to the law of sacrifice, and of the kind of
loyalty exhibited for another prophet, Joseph Smith, by Brigham
Young and Heber C. Kimball, who despite persecution and adversity
never "lifted their heel against" the Prophet Joseph.[4]

LEHI AND NEPHI AS PATTERNS

Nephi's faithfulness brought the joy to Lehi that every good parent
feels for a righteous child. Even as early as when Nephi responded

1. 1 Nephi 18:15.
2. 1 Nephi 18:10.
3. 1 Nephi 18:17–18.
4. TPJS 307.

with such enthusiasm to Lehi's request to go and obtain the brass plates, Lehi "was exceedingly glad, for he knew that I had been blessed of the Lord."[1] Similarly, after Lehi had seen in vision that Nephi partook of the fruit of salvation, Lehi had "reason to rejoice in the Lord because of Nephi."[2] Finally, the depth of Lehi's feeling for this son who had been his unswerving ally and friend is also partially manifest in what the aged Lehi tells the other members of the group in the new world. To Laman and Lemuel he says:

> Rebel no more against your brother, whose views have been glorious, and who hath kept the commandments from the time that we left Jerusalem; and who hath been an instrument in the hands of God, in bringing us forth into the land of promise; for were it not for him, we must have perished with hunger in the wilderness.[3]

Lehi's statement about Nephi saving their lives is true, but it should be read in conjunction with Nephi's earlier statements about how Lehi had saved them from perishing in Jerusalem.[4] Each played an essential role in achieving the purposes of God for each other and for their posterity.

It is not just for past accomplishments that Lehi commends Nephi, but also for future guidance, as Lehi counsels Laman, Lemuel, Sam, and the sons of Ishmael: "If ye will hearken unto the voice of Nephi ye shall not perish."[5] Then to Laman and Lemuel,[6] Lehi says:

> If ye will hearken unto him I leave unto you a blessing, yea, even my first blessing.
> But if ye will not hearken unto him I take away my first blessing, . . . and it shall rest upon him.[7]

What was rightfully theirs would be given to another if they would

---

1. 1 Nephi 3:8.
2. 1 Nephi 8:3.
3. 2 Nephi 1:24.
4. See 1 Nephi 3:18; 7:15; 17:43–44.
5. 2 Nephi 1:28.
6. See 1 Nephi 2:22; 3:29.
7. 2 Nephi 1:28–29.

not obey. They did not,[1] and—fittingly—Lehi's spiritual successor became his most loyal and faithful son and comrade, Nephi.

Lehi's emphasis on Nephi in counseling Laman and Lemuel was just the first of repeated times when the aged father left his last counsel by referring to Nephi. Thus to Zoram (Laban's erstwhile servant) Lehi stated: "I know that thou art a true friend unto my son, Nephi, forever. Wherefore, because thou hast been faithful thy seed shall be blessed with his seed."[2] To his son Jacob, Lehi promised, "Thy soul shall be blessed, and thou shalt dwell safely with thy brother, Nephi."[3] To his son Joseph, Lehi counseled, "Behold, thou art little; wherefore hearken unto the words of thy brother, Nephi, and it shall be done unto thee even according to the words which I have spoken."[4] And to his son Sam, Lehi said:

> Blessed art thou, and thy seed; for thou shalt inherit the land like unto thy brother Nephi. And thy seed shall be numbered with his seed; and thou shalt be even like unto thy brother, and thy seed like unto his seed; and thou shalt be blessed in all thy days.[5]

The story comes full circle as Nephi becomes as much of a reference point for Lehi in directing his posterity as Lehi had earlier been a reference point for Nephi in directing his own life.

But that should not divert our attention from Lehi's own exemplary action in calling his posterity together to leave them his final counsel, prophecies, and blessings—which in turn leave us with some of the most valuable passages in all of scripture regarding the fall of Adam, the atonement of Christ,[6] and the prophecies of the patriarch Joseph in Egypt.[7] The occasion of Joseph's prophecies was (according to the Joseph Smith Translation of Genesis) to his brethren just before

---

1. See 2 Nephi 5:1–8.
2. 2 Nephi 1:30.
3. 2 Nephi 2:3.
4. 2 Nephi 3:25.
5. 2 Nephi 4:11.
6. See 2 Nephi 2.
7. See 2 Nephi 3.

he died[1]—the same context in which the dying Lehi repeated those very prophecies to his son. But the pattern was far older than Joseph; Adam himself, according to both latter-day revelation[2] and pseudepigraphical sources,[3] called together his righteous posterity shortly before his death to leave his final testimony, counsel, prophecies, and blessings. As reported in the pseudepigrapha, the pattern was followed in turn by all the antediluvian patriarchs,[4] and later by Abraham,[5] Jacob[6] (also reported in Genesis[7]), and each of Jacob's twelve sons.[8] The brass plates would have contained at least the accounts of Joseph and Jacob, and probably of others as well.

With the mention of Lehi's death, he is all too often forgotten in favor of Nephi, who—unlike Lehi—never murmured. But no sooner does Nephi recount Lehi's death than he discloses for the first time his own heartfelt struggles with weaknesses and sins, which caused him no small distress:

> Nevertheless, notwithstanding the great goodness of the Lord, in showing me his great and marvelous works, my heart exclaimeth: O wretched man that I am! Yea, my heart sorroweth because of my flesh; my soul grieveth because of mine iniquities.
>
> I am encompassed about, because of the temptations and the sins which do so easily beset me.
>
> And when I desire to rejoice, my heart groaneth because of my sins.[9]

Is it mere coincidence that Nephi's lament follows immediately after Lehi's death? Or is this an indication of how acutely Nephi felt the loss of his father, whose towering strength had been the formative

---

1. See JST Genesis 50:24.
2. See D&C 107:53–56.
3. See Combat of Adam II:VIII, in Malan 1882:114–16; Cave of Treasures, in Budge 1927:72–73.
4. See Combat of Adam II:XII-XXII; III:I-V, in Malan 1882:119–50.
5. See Jubilees 20–22, in OTP 2:93–99.
6. See Testament of Jacob 4–5, in OTP 1:915–16.
7. See Genesis 48–49.
8. See Testaments of the Twelve Patriarchs, in OTP 1:775–828.
9. 2 Nephi 4:17–19.

and predominant force throughout Nephi's life? One Latter-day Saint scholar has observed that in Lehi's death "Nephi lost a friend as well as a father and prophet; he lost his confidant, advisor, and shield against the hatred of his brothers. Thus Nephi had ample reason to reflect on his distress."[1]

Nephi's lament also demonstrates that he shared the same inherent vulnerability that plagues all humanity, who (in Lehi's words) "were in a lost and in a fallen state, and ever would be save they should rely on [the] Redeemer."[2] Nephi's reliance is clear:

> Nevertheless, I know in whom I have trusted. My God hath been my support. . . . Awake, my soul! No longer droop in sin. . . . O Lord, wilt thou redeem my soul? . . . O Lord, I have trusted in thee, and I will trust in thee forever.[3]

Nephi's reliance on his Redeemer is in fact what Lehi had expressly urged for his sons, telling them that

> No flesh . . . can dwell in the presence of God, save it be through the merits, and mercy, and grace of the Holy Messiah. . . . And now, my sons, I would that ye should look to the great Mediator, and hearken unto his commandments; and be faithful unto his words, and choose eternal life.[4]

As with Lehi, Nephi could attain salvation only by, in Nephi's own words, "relying wholly upon the merits of him who is mighty to save."[5] The news about Lehi and Nephi is not that they were imperfect—as all mortals save One have been—but rather that they chose to keep repenting and pressing forward in faith by relying wholly upon the merits of Christ. In fact, Lehi and Nephi were both mighty prophets who unitedly accomplished an amazing mission in which each apparently was indispensable to the other. That Nephi became strong enough not to murmur when his father momentarily

---

1. John S. Tanner, in Sorenson and Thorne 1991:55.
2. 1 Nephi 10:6.
3. 2 Nephi 4:19–20, 28, 31, 34.
4. 2 Nephi 2:8, 28.
5. 2 Nephi 31:19.

did must be seen, at least in part, as a tribute to Lehi, whose powerful teaching and example had nourished Nephi from the beginning. By the strength of his righteous leadership, Lehi had been the dominant force in cultivating that strength of character needed for Nephi to strengthen Lehi when he momentarily faltered. And what parents have not wished to see their child one day excel and exceed them? Even so, Lehi and Nephi, despite their individual imperfections, functioned as a powerful team in achieving God's purposes. As a reward for their mortal efforts, according to the vision that they both saw, both would partake of the precious fruit of eternal life.[1]

Additionally, both were establishing a pattern for their posterity, who would ever hold them in highest esteem. Lehi's righteous posterity would always call themselves Nephites, whether or not directly descended from Nephi himself.[2] Even so, the honor of being directly descended from Nephi is indicated by the final two Book of Mormon writers, Mormon and his son Moroni, each of whom is careful to record that he is a descendant of Nephi.[3] Lehi was no less venerated; Mormon also recorded that he was "a pure descendant of Lehi."[4] Elsewhere when Mormon and other Book of Mormon writers refer to Lehi, it is nearly always "our father Lehi"[5]—the same honored designation traditionally given to Abraham—*avinu Avraham*, "our father Abraham"—by Jews[6] and, as would be expected, by their Nephite kinsmen.[7] As father Abraham was once divinely commended because he would "instruct his children and his posterity to keep the way of the Lord by doing what is just and right,"[8] so father Lehi instructed his children to keep the way of the Lord. And as father Abraham once obtained a divine covenant and promised land for his posterity,[9]

---

1. See 1 Nephi 8:10–16.
2. See, e.g., Jacob 1:13–14; Mosiah 25:12; Alma 53:16; 3 Nephi 2:14–16; 4 Nephi 1:37.
3. See Mormon 1:5; 8:13.
4. 3 Nephi 5:20.
5. Jacob 2:34; Enos 1:25; Mosiah 1:4; 2:34; Alma 9:9; 36:22; 56:3; Helaman 8:22; 3 Nephi 10:17.
6. See Arieti 1981:171.; John 8:53; TDNT V:976.
7. See Alma 13:15.
8. NJPS Genesis 18:19.
9. See Genesis 12:1–3, 7; 15:1–21; 22:15–18.

so father Lehi obtained a divine covenant and promised land for his posterity,[1] in further fulfillment of the earlier covenant to Lehi's ancestor Abraham.[2]

But perhaps the greatest tribute to Lehi and Nephi together was that given in the first century B.C. by one of their descendants,[3] Helaman, a righteous chief judge who "had two sons" and named the older Nephi and the younger Lehi[4] so that, as he explained to them, "when you remember your names ye may remember them; and when ye remember them ye may remember their works; and when ye remember their works ye may know how that it is said, and also written, that they were good."[5]

The pattern that Lehi and Nephi established for their posterity was also intended for us, the latter-day readers of the Book of Mormon. After Mormon had partially completed the monumental task of abridging nearly a millennium of Nephite history, as he searched among the voluminous[6] records he happened upon a set of small plates that covered part of what he had already abridged. The plates were a separate record that Nephi had been commanded to keep, and upon which he had been commanded to write only the sacred things of the ministry.[7] Nephi's obedience in making the sacred and smaller record was, in his words, "for a wise purpose in [the Lord], which purpose I know not."[8] When Mormon discovered this small set of plates, he found that they were "choice"[9] and that there were "great things written upon them."[10] And even though he had already covered the same historical period in his abridgment from other records, he chose to include these small plates in his account:

---

1. See 2 Nephi 1:5. The portion of that land originally settled by Lehi and Nephi would for generations fear their names. See 2 Nephi 5:8; Omni 1:12, 27–30; Words of Mormon 1:13; Mosiah 7:1–4; Alma 58:38; Helaman 4:12.
2. See 1 Nephi 15:18; 3 Nephi 20:25.
3. See Heading to 3 Nephi.
4. Helaman 3:21.
5. Helaman 5:6–7.
6. See Words of Mormon 1:5.
7. See 1 Nephi 9:2–6.
8. 1 Nephi 9:5.
9. Words of Mormon 1:6.
10. Words of Mormon 1:11.

I do this for a wise purpose; for thus it whispereth me, according to the workings of the Spirit of the Lord which is in me. And now, I do not know all things; but the Lord knoweth all things which are to come; wherefore, he worketh in me to do according to his will.[1]

That divine purpose kept hidden from both Nephi and Mormon dealt with the future destiny of the first 116 pages of the Book of Mormon manuscript, which Joseph Smith had translated from Mormon's abridgment and then lent out and lost. Rather than retranslating, Joseph was instructed to translate the set of small plates;[2] that translation constitutes the first portion of the current edition of the Book of Mormon.[3] It includes Nephi's first-person record of his life and comprises, by the way, a highly disproportionate portion of the Book of Mormon based on the time period it covers (over 20 percent of the book but not even 6 percent of the time[4]). It also contains the most detailed account of any father-son relationship in the entire Book of Mormon. This relationship between Lehi and Nephi was surely one of "the great things" that Mormon discovered, and its presentation to us in the record that Nephi was commanded to make was surely part of the "wise purpose" that the Lord had in mind for our benefit.

---

1. Words of Mormon 1:7.
2. See D&C 10:38–45.
3. Through Omni.
4. 117 pages (current English edition) v 531 pages = 22%; 600 (B.C.) + 421 (A.D.) = 1021 years; 1021 years v 56 years = 5.48%.

Chapter 2

KEEPERS OF A RIGHTEOUS TRADITION

• •

JACOB AND ENOS

JACOB AND HIS NAMESAKE FOREFATHER

We are never expressly told why the first son born to Lehi in the wilderness was named Jacob. What we know generally from the Old Testament and related sources is that Israelites anciently had a "custom of calling a child after the circumstances of its birth."[1] But a name could also serve as "the expression of a hope"[2] in that it could be used "to express a special Godward wish for the child thus named" as well as for the child's future posterity; hence "the name [could have] meaning for more than its bearer."[3] Or, expressed another way, "a man's name" was thought to "live on in his descendants,"[4] an idea that found its most obvious expression in "the custom of giving a patronymic name" derived from a paternal ancestor.[5] Furthermore, the very act of naming "establishes a relation of dominion and possession," as when the Lord calls his people "Israel by name and

---

1. AI 1:44.
2. AI I:43.
3. TDNT V:254.
4. TDNT V:253.
5. AI 1:45.

thereby establishes His claim to it."[1] That claim went back, of course, to the patriarch Jacob whom an angel renamed Israel[2] — a name that connotes God's reign and supremacy[3] and that "has by nature a special religious aura."[4] Hence the appropriateness of the name *Israel* for the patriarch Jacob, who in rabbinic tradition is "regarded as a model of virtue and righteousness,"[5] "a great and holy man,"[6] and also a symbol of his posterity[7] — God's covenant people. Forever after they would be called "Israel," even though the Patriarch himself would be remembered and referred to still as "Jacob," following the general practice of the book of Genesis and subsequent biblical books to refer to him by his first name.[8]

Against such a backdrop the naming of Lehi's son *Jacob* makes immediate sense. The righteous Lehi, descendant of the patriarch Jacob, had just departed by divine mandate from the main body of his fellow Israelites whose iniquity would soon bring destruction upon themselves. And even as Lehi began to lead his family into the wilderness, he understood perfectly, and explained to his family, that they were like a branch broken off from the tree of Israel in order to be transplanted elsewhere,[9] in fulfillment of the ancient covenant made to the house of Israel.[10] Furthermore, Lehi's party had been preserved because of their greater faith and righteousness,[11] a tradition Lehi zealously attempted to instill in his sons. Under such circumstances he would naturally memorialize their endeavor by naming his first son born in the wilderness after the ancient patriarch whose

1. TDNT V:253.
2. See Genesis 32:28.
3. See TDOT VI:401.
4. TDOT VI:412.
5. EJ 9:1198.
6. EJ 9:1201.
7. See EJ 9:1199.
8. See Genesis 32:29 and forward; and see Exodus 2:24; 32:13; Leviticus 26:42; Deuteronomy 29:12; Joshua 24:4; 2 Kings 13:23; Psalms 105:23; Ezekiel 28:25; 37:25; Isaiah 41:8; 44:1; Malachi 1:2–3. In contrast, Jews are forbidden to call Abraham by his first name, Abram. (See Wiesel 1976:146.)
9. See 1 Nephi 10:12–14.
10. See 1 Nephi 15:12–18.
11. See 1 Nephi 3:16–18; 5:4; 7:13–14.

covenant they were bringing to fruition—Jacob. Hence the name of Lehi's son Jacob expressed at once not only the circumstances of his birth but also Lehi's wish for the righteousness of his son and his son's posterity in order to continue the example of Lehi, who as a descendant of the patriarch Jacob was helping fulfil the covenant to that same patriarch—a covenant concerning which Lehi "spake much."[1]

In addition, the name *Jacob* for Lehi's son also turned out to be prophetic in terms of his general life circumstances, which were unusually difficult both emotionally (because of the hatred of his brothers) and physically (because he was born in the wilderness and arrived as a first-generation settler in an untamed new world). These themes appear in his own synopsis of his life written shortly before his death:

> Our lives passed away like as it were unto us a dream, we being a lonesome and a solemn people, wanderers, cast out from Jerusalem, born in tribulation, in a wilderness, and hated of our brethren, which caused wars and contentions; wherefore, we did mourn out our days.[2]

All of this presents striking parallels with the hardships faced by his ancient namesake, the patriarch Jacob, who near the end of his mortal sojourn said that the years of his life had been "few and hard"[3] (or "few and difficult"[4] or "few and unhappy"[5]). The patriarch Jacob had likewise incurred the hatred of a brother, Esau, over the issue of birthright, in consequence of which he also had been forced to leave his homeland and become a wanderer.[6] He also had known solemnity, loneliness, and mourning as he lost first his beloved wife Rachel in childbirth[7] and later his beloved son Joseph, sold by his brothers, who made it appear that he had been devoured by a wild animal. Even

---

1. 1 Nephi 10:12; and 15:18.
2. Jacob 7:26.
3. Genesis 47:9 in NJPS, NRSV, REB, and Speiser 1979 (AB 1):348.
4. NIV.
5. NJB.
6. See Genesis 27–28.
7. See Genesis 35:16–20.

the dream motif ("our lives passed away like as it were unto us a dream") figures into the patriarch Jacob's life through his dream of the ladder[1] and through the dreams of his son Joseph.[2] Fortunately, other and happier parallels will later become apparent in the similar blessings received by these two Jacobs.

REMEMBERING THE FATHERS AND LOOKING TO THE SON

As remarkable as are such resemblances, more significant still is Lehi's son Jacob's own keen awareness of and emphasis on the heritage inherent in his name, as seen first in his early preaching. Nephi devotes significant space—no less than five chapters[3]—to a verbatim account of some of his younger brother Jacob's preaching. Some of that material is direct quotation from Isaiah 49:22 through 52:2 (a passage about which Nephi had expressly asked Jacob to speak[4]), but the rest is Jacob's own exposition of what Isaiah meant. As John Tvedtnes has pointed out, the themes and language of Jacob's sermon mirror many of the same themes and much of the same language recorded in Lehi's prior counsel to Jacob as recorded in 2 Nephi 2[5]— showing how well Jacob was remembering his own father, Lehi. But perhaps the most conspicuous aspect of Jacob's preaching in comparison with the rest of the Book of Mormon is his constantly repeated designation of God as "the Holy One of Israel."

That this title would surface somewhere in Jacob's preaching about Isaiah is no surprise, of course, since the title occurs in the Old Testament primarily in Isaiah but only infrequently elsewhere (usually in dependent passages).[6] Furthermore, the title as used in the later chapters of Isaiah (from which Jacob quotes) emphasizes the Lord's "saving power and protection"[7] in his role as Redeemer[8] pursuant to

---

1. See Genesis 28:11–16.
2. See Genesis 37.
3. 2 Nephi 6–10.
4. See 2 Nephi 6:4.
5. In John A. Tvedtnes, "The Influence of Lehi's Admonitions on the Teachings of His Son Jacob" (forthcoming article).
6. See TDNT 1:93; North 1964:100.
7. North 1964:100.
8. See TDNT 1:94.

his covenant[1] – the very themes Jacob was expounding. Moreover, his brother Nephi[2] and their father, Lehi,[3] had already used the title in speaking of God. Even so, Jacob's usage of the title stands out for two reasons: first, the particular Isaiah passage he quotes never expressly uses the title; and second, and most notably, Jacob uses the title far more frequently (some seventeen times[4]) in just two chapters than any other primary Book of Mormon writer does elsewhere in the rest of the book.[5]

Why, then, does Jacob draw so frequently on the title "the Holy One of Israel"? The answer at least in part could be because of his own heightened awareness of and identification with his ancient namesake, the patriarch Jacob (Israel), and the covenants he had received. This could also explain Jacob's continued obsession (once Nephi turned the sacred record over to him) with the destiny of the house of Israel: nearly one-third of Jacob's own writing (in the book of Jacob) is devoted to reproducing the lengthy and elaborate allegory by the prophet Zenos comparing the house of Israel to an olive-tree.[6]

A variation of this theme that is also continued by Jacob from his early preaching to his later writing is that of Abraham (the earlier Jacob's grandfather and initial recipient of the covenant later renewed with the patriarch Jacob), who receives such emphasis in the Isaiah passage that Jacob had quoted:

> Hearken unto me, ye that follow after righteousness. Look unto the rock from whence ye are hewn, and to the hole of the pit from whence ye are digged.
> Look unto Abraham, your father, and unto Sarah, she that bare you; for I called him alone, and blessed him.[7]

---

1. See Westermann 1969:81.
2. See 1 Nephi 19:14–15; 22:5, 18, 21, 24, 26, 28.
3. See 2 Nephi 1:10; 3:2.
4. In 2 Nephi 6 and 9.
5. Nephi uses it in his own writing some twelve times (1 Nephi 19:14–15; 22: 5, 18, 21, 24, 26, 28; 2 Nephi 25:29; 28:5; 30:2; 31:13); and Amaleki uses it twice (Omni 1:25–26). The title also appears some seven times in Isaiah passages quoted in the Book of Mormon.
6. See Jacob 5.
7. 2 Nephi 8:1–2 (Isaiah 51:1–2).

That Jacob himself followed Isaiah's counsel to look to father Abraham is evident when Jacob in his own writing selects from "all the holy prophets which were before us"[1]—they who "believed in Christ and worshiped the Father in his name"[2]—the one event that particularly foreshadowed God's giving up his Son for mankind:

> Abraham in the wilderness [was] obedient unto the commands of God in offering up his son Isaac, which is a similitude of God and his Only Begotten Son.[3]

Jacob's selection of this event from Abraham's life as particularly symbolic is noteworthy in light of the symbolic value that Judaism has always attached to Abraham's life in general and his offering of Isaac in particular. "What Abraham did prefigured the future history of Israel,"[4] observes an eminent Judaic scholar, and "If we have to choose the single paradigmatic event in Abraham's life, it is his binding of Isaac as a sacrifice to God."[5] Indeed, the binding—Hebrew *akedah*—of Isaac, as another eminent Jewish writer observes, "is a story that contains Jewish destiny in its totality, just as the flame is contained in the single spark by which it comes to life. Every major theme [in] Judaism . . . can be traced back to it."[6]

Jacob's recognition of atonement symbolism in the *akedah* is also notable because the *akedah* would, some six centuries later after Christ's mortal ministry, become a favorite among the Church fathers in their finding types of Christ in the Old Testament.[7] Jacob is unique, however, in being the first and only prophet on record *before* the time of Christ to recognize the atonement symbolism inherent in the *akedah*.

But Jacob is by no means unique in being led to the Father and Son by remembering his own fathers. We have already seen how Nephi believed and remembered the words of his father and thereby

---

1. Jacob 4:4.
2. Jacob 4:5.
3. Ibid.
4. Neusner 1985:136.
5. Ibid. 97.
6. Wiesel 1976:84.
7. See Danielou 1960:115–30.

acquired revelation about the Son of God. Similarly, we will yet see how other Book of Mormon prophets repeatedly urge their listeners to learn of the Son of God by remembering their righteous forefathers.

JACOB—MAN OF RIGHTEOUSNESS AND POWER

Perhaps the most personally significant aspect of Jacob's remembering his forefathers Abraham and Jacob was his emulation of their righteousness despite extreme hardship. The dying Lehi told his son Jacob:

> And now, Jacob, I speak unto you: Thou art my first-born in the days of my tribulation in the wilderness. And behold, in thy childhood thou hast suffered afflictions and much sorrow, because of the rudeness of thy brethren.
>
> Nevertheless, Jacob, my first-born in the wilderness, thou knowest the greatness of God; and he shall consecrate thine affliction for thy gain.
>
> Wherefore, thy soul shall be blessed, and thou shalt dwell safely with thy brother, Nephi; and thy days shall be spent in the service of thy God. Wherefore, I know that thou art redeemed, because of the righteousness of thy Redeemer; for thou hast beheld that in the fulness of time he cometh to bring salvation unto men.
>
> And thou hast beheld in thy youth his glory; wherefore, thou art blessed even as they unto whom he shall minister in the flesh.[1]

Jacob's vision of Christ also elicited comment from Nephi, who observed that "my brother, Jacob, also has seen him [Christ] as I have seen him."[2]

Such sharing of vision qualified Jacob to share in the ministry. He was consecrated by Nephi to be a priest and teacher[3] and was finally given charge of Nephi's small plates containing the sacred record[4] as he became Nephi's spiritual successor among the Nephite

---

1. 2 Nephi 2:1–4.
2. 2 Nephi 11:3.
3. See 2 Nephi 5:26.
4. See Jacob 1:1–4.

people. Jacob's writing reveals a man of consummate faith and righteousness: he had "many revelations, and the spirit of much prophecy";[1] he had seen angels who had ministered to him, and had even "heard the voice of the Lord speaking unto [him] in very word, from time to time."[2] All of this recalls parallel events in the life of the ancient patriarch Jacob, who likewise had seen and been ministered to by angels[3] and had heard the voice of God[4] — these being but typical examples of the many revelations he received, since (according to the pseudepigraphical Testament of Jacob) it was "his custom every day to speak . . . with the angels."[5]

The effect of such revelations in the life of the Book of Mormon prophet Jacob was profound: "Having all these witnesses [he] obtain[ed] a hope, and [his] faith [became] unshaken, insomuch that [he] truly [could] command in the name of Jesus and the very trees obey . . . , or the mountains, or the waves of the sea."[6] Furthermore, he, along with others, "labored diligently" among his people to "persuade them to come unto Christ, and partake of the goodness of God,"[7] and thereby "did magnify [his] office unto the Lord, taking upon [himself] the responsibility, answering the sins of the people upon [his] own [head] if [he] did not teach them the word of God with all diligence."[8] Part of what he had to teach was against the rising tide of materialism sweeping Nephite society, as well as — ironically — against the breach of family obligations occasioned by the gross sins of infidelity and adultery.[9] The irony was that Jacob, who was faithfully keeping the righteous family heritage of his namesake forefather, had to preach to a people whose sins were ripping apart their own immediate families.

---

1. Jacob 1:6. These are Jacob's words referring to himself and others.
2. Jacob 7:5.
3. See Genesis 28:12; 32:25–30 (that the divine personage described in these verses was an angel, see Hosea 12:4 and Sarna 1989:227).
4. See Genesis 28:13–15.
5. Testament of Jacob 1:7, in OTP 1:914.
6. Jacob 4:6. These are Jacob's words referring to himself and others.
7. Jacob 1:7.
8. Jacob 1:19.
9. See Jacob 2:22 through 3:11.

JACOB AS A FATHER

As to Jacob's own family, his effort to continue the heritage of righteousness seems to be evidenced in the name he gave his son— Enos—the name of Adam's grandson, the venerable antediluvian patriarch who, although he lived in an idolatrous generation, was—says ancient tradition—a "type of the pious,"[1] a "model of undaunted faith,"[2] and a critical "link in the chain of ancient righteous ancestors."[3] And "he, like the other links in the chain, provide[d] a model of piety and a proof of God's regard for those who despite temptation and adversity maintain complete faith in Him."[4] The antediluvian Enos also "exemplifie[d] the . . . messianic expectation of the faithful" and was even viewed by the early Christians as "typologically . . . fore-shadowing Jesus and the Christian faithful."[5] The name Enos for Jacob's son thus fits the circumstances of his birth and his father's wish for him—to serve as a link in continuing the chain of righteous prophets testifying of Christ, despite the trends in Nephite society toward materialism and immorality. Jacob thus conferred the same benefit upon his son as Lehi had done upon Jacob—a patronymic name that recalled a righteous forefather and called for emulation of that righteousness.

The book of Moses attributes the righteousness of Enos to the teaching he had received from his father, Seth, by way of example and instruction: "Seth . . . prophesied in all his days, and taught his son Enos in the ways of God; wherefore Enos prophesied also."[6] Jacob supplied the same for his son Enos, as we learn from Enos' own account—a record that begins, as did Nephi's, with a filial tribute to a father's example and teaching:

> Behold, it came to pass that I, Enos, knowing my father
> that he was a just man—for he taught me in his language, and

---

1. LJ V:151.
2. Fraade 1984:230.
3. Ibid. 229.
4. Ibid. 104.
5. Ibid. 230.
6. Moses 6:13.

also in the nurture and admonition of the Lord — and blessed
be the name of my God for it. . . . I had often heard my father
speak concerning eternal life, and the joy of the saints.[1]

Significantly, what Jacob taught Enos — "concerning eternal life,
and the joy of the saints" — was what Lehi had earlier taught Jacob —
that "men are, that they might have joy" by choosing "eternal life."[2]
And as Lehi had taught these things after first being an example, so
now did Jacob, whom Enos acknowledges was "a just man." And
Jacob's instruction to his son was "often" — providing a pattern still
relevant for parents. "Repetition is a key to learning," notes President
Benson. "Our children need to hear the truth repeated, especially
because there is so much falsehood abroad. Devoted Book of Mormon
fathers constantly reminded their sons of saving truths"[3] — as Jacob
did Enos, who, like children today, was confronted by great falsehood
in his society.

But such repetition need not be overbearing, as is clear from how
Enos says he was taught by his father — "in the nurture and admonition of the Lord." The English word *nurture* is derived from the
same Latin verb as is the word *nourish* and carries much the same
meaning, including not only "to train by or as if by instruction," but
also "to supply with food, nourishment, and protection" and "to
further the development of" or "promote the growth of."[4] One thinks
of the principles of priesthood leadership enumerated in modern-day
revelation: persuasion, long-suffering, gentleness, meekness, love,
and kindness.[5] And balancing Jacob's parental nurturing was "admonition," defined as a "gentle or friendly reproof, warning, or re-
minder" or "counsel against a fault, error, or oversight."[6]

The phrase "nurture and admonition of the Lord" occurs in one
other passage of our English scriptures, in the King James translation
of the Apostle Paul's counsel to fathers at Ephesus to "provoke not

1. Enos 1:1, 3.
2. 2 Nephi 2:25–28.
3. W&W 69.
4. WTNID 1552.
5. D&C 121:41–42.
6. WTNID 28.

your children to wrath: but bring them up in the nurture and admonition of the Lord"[1] – or, as more modern translations express, "in
the discipline and instruction of the Lord."[2] The Greek original for
"discipline [nurture] of the Lord" is the identical phrase used in the
(Greek) Septuagint translation of Deuteronomy 11:2, which calls on
Israel to "consider the discipline of the Lord";[3] so that Paul's counsel
to fathers directly echoed the ancient Mosaic instruction to remember
the discipline (nurture) of the Lord. It is possible, then, that Jacob
also, in teaching Enos in the nurture (discipline) of the Lord, may
have been fulfilling the ancient Mosaic instruction given to his Israelite
forefathers.

Even older, according to the Testaments of the Twelve Patriarchs,
is the idea expressed by the patriarch Jacob's son Reuben that "obeying
the admonitions of [one's] fathers" leads to "understanding the law
of God"[4] – which suggests that when the Book of Mormon prophet
Jacob gave his son admonition concerning the Lord, he was following
an ancient precedent followed by his namesake forefather, the patriarch Jacob.

With so much of Jacob's parental instruction so applicable to parents today, we might well ask whether the language instruction Enos
received from Jacob ("he taught me in his language") is of passing
historical interest only. After all, the reference appears to be not to
the vernacular of the day but rather to the written language (involving
Egyptian[5]) of the plates – which Jacob in fact passed down to Enos
for further addition by him.[6] The situation is obviously not generally
applicable to parents, but there may be a larger principle that is urgently applicable. According to the book of Moses, writing was originally a gift of God given to humanity in order to keep sacred records,[7]

---

1. Ephesians 6:4.
2. NRSV, REB.
3. NIDNTT 3:777; NRSV, REB, and NIV also translate here "discipline of the Lord."
4. Testament of Reuben 3:8, in Hollander and de Jonge 1985:92; and see commentary on that verse on p. 96.
5. See 1 Nephi 1:2; Mormon 9:32–33.
6. See Jacob 7:27.
7. See Moses 6:5–6, 46.

the keeping and study of which are the highest exercise of mankind's capacity to read and write. Teaching this truth to children, and teaching them to feast from the sacred scriptural records, is as pertinent today as it was in Enos' day.

THE STORY OF ENOS

One would expect that such a model father as Jacob would have a model son. Apparently it was not so with Enos—at least, not at first. While there is no evidence that he was ever openly rebellious, his own account seems to imply at least an early lack of commitment to the principles his father taught. Perhaps peer pressure from a Nephite society engulfed in pride, materialism, and immorality[1] took its toll on the young Enos.

But if the seeds of powerful parental instruction delayed in sprouting, they did at last sprout, as Enos himself tells in one of the most moving of all Book of Mormon accounts of a father's influence on a son:

> I will tell you of the wrestle which I had before God, before I received a remission of my sins.
>
> Behold, I went to hunt beasts in the forests; and the words which I had often heard my father speak concerning eternal life, and the joy of the saints, sunk deep into my heart.
>
> And my soul hungered; and I kneeled down before my Maker, and I cried unto him in mighty prayer and supplication for mine own soul; and all the day long did I cry unto him; yea, and when the night came I did still raise my voice high that it reached the heavens.
>
> And there came a voice unto me, saying: Enos, thy sins are forgiven thee, and thou shalt be blessed.
>
> And I, Enos, knew that God could not lie; wherefore, my guilt was swept away.
>
> And I said: Lord, how is it done?
>
> And he said unto me: Because of thy faith in Christ, whom thou hast never before heard nor seen. And many years pass away before he shall manifest himself in the flesh; wherefore, go to, thy faith hath made thee whole.[2]

---

1. See Jacob 2–3.
2. Enos 1:2–8.

Enos's experience in hearing God's voice recalls Jacob's experience in likewise hearing God's voice.[1] Furthermore, Enos's "wrestle with God" and the blessings that Enos thereby obtained recall the ancient patriarch Jacob's wrestle with an angel, which also resulted in blessings[2]—yet another echo of the life of the ancient Jacob in this Book of Mormon story of Jacob and Enos. The new tranquility of soul that Enos experienced by being made "whole" allowed him to feel concern for the plight of others, for whom he now pled—first for his own people, the Nephites. Again the Lord answered Enos, who still was not satisfied; he now pled for his brethren, the Lamanites. A third time the Lord answered, and this time made a covenant with Enos to preserve the Nephite records for the future benefit of the Lamanites.[3] And then the Lord observed, "Thy fathers have also required of me this thing; . . . for their faith was like unto thine."[4] Like his ancient forefather for whom he was named, Enos now became a link in a chain of righteous prophets. As the righteous life of the ancient Enos had stood out from his wicked contemporaries, so now did the righteous life of the Nephite Enos, who lamented that his people were "stiffnecked" and "hard to understand" and would respond to only the harshest and plainest preaching.[5] And as the ancient Enos had prophesied and typified Christ, so now the Nephite Enos "went about among the people . . . prophesying . . . and testifying,"[6] being "wrought upon by the power of God" to "declare the word according to the truth which is in Christ."[7] It could thus be written of Enos and his father what had been written earlier of his namesake ancestor, Enos, and his father, Seth: "Seth . . . prophesied in all his days, and taught his son Enos in the ways of God; wherefore Enos prophesied also."[8]

1. See Jacob 7:5.
2. See Genesis 32:24–32.
3. See Enos 1:9–17.
4. Enos 1:18.
5. Enos 1:22–23.
6. Enos 1:19.
7. Enos 1:26.
8. Moses 6:13.

JOY AND REJOICING

Enos closes his record by looking both back and forward:

> I have declared [the word] in all my days, and have rejoiced
> in it above that of the world.
>   And I soon go to the place of my rest, which is with my
> Redeemer; for I know that in him I shall rest. And I rejoice in
> the day when my mortal shall put on immortality, and shall
> stand before him; then shall I see his face with pleasure, and
> he will say unto me: Come unto me, ye blessed, there is a
> place prepared for you in the mansions of my Father.[1]

Noticeably different in tone from the way Jacob had closed his
record ("we did mourn out our days"[2]) is Enos' focus on joy, which
he mentions twice. To what did he owe his joy? Ultimately, of course,
to his Redeemer, but also to his father — for whom Enos had at the
opening of his record "blessed . . . the name of [his] God."[3] Despite
the extreme hardships of Jacob's life that had caused him to mourn
out his days to the very last, he had longed for joy, having spoken
of it not only to Enos but also to the people he served, reminding
them of "that happiness which is prepared for the saints."[4] But if
sorrow seemed to be mostly his mortal lot in the face of much hardship,
he nevertheless labored diligently that his posterity might have joy
and somehow avoid the sorrow that he had known — a labor that gave
him joy! As he explained,

> I cannot write but a little of my words, because of the difficulty
> of engraving our words upon plates . . . ; but we can write a
> few words upon plates, which will give our children . . . a
> small degree of knowledge concerning us, or concerning their
> fathers —
>   Now in this thing we do rejoice; and we labor diligently to
> engraven these words upon plates, hoping that . . . our chil-
> dren will receive them with thankful hearts, and look upon

---

1. Enos 1:26–27.
2. Jacob 7:26.
3. Enos 1:1.
4. 2 Nephi 9:43.

them that they may learn with joy and not with sorrow . . . concerning their first parents.[1]

Here again we see Lehi's influence in Jacob's life, for Lehi had
taught Jacob "that men are, that they might have joy."[2] And in light
of Jacob's unyielding faithfulness despite affliction and his unselfish
labor to procure joy for his posterity despite his own mortal sorrow,
we need to read his son's last words as applying also to Jacob, who
would also "rejoice in the day" of resurrection when he and his son
would be invited into the Father's mansions prepared by the Son. Joy
would be Jacob's final lot, as it was for his ancient namesake, the
patriarch Jacob—who on his deathbed, according to the Testament of
Jacob, was told by an angel that "the time has drawn near for you to
go to your fathers to rejoice with them forever."[3] And so will it be
for all who follow the examples of the patriarch Jacob and his namesake
descendant in the Book of Mormon. To use the Prophet Joseph Smith's
words, "in the end they shall have joy."[4]

---

1. Jacob 4:1–3.
2. 2 Nephi 2:25.
3. Testament of Jacob 1:6, in OTP 1:914.
4. TPJS 257.

Chapter 3

MONARCHS AND MISSIONARIES

. . . .

MOSIAH, BENJAMIN, MOSIAH, AND THE SONS OF MOSIAH

THE EARLY NEPHITE MONARCHY

History bears sad record that good kings are the exception rather than the rule. Rare is the person, it would seem, whom absolute power will not quickly corrupt, as keenly perceived by the framers of the United States Constitution with its various divisions of power and ingenious system of checks and balances. The vulnerability of most people to the corrupting influence of power is also attested in latter-day revelation: "It is the nature and disposition of almost all men, as soon as they get a little authority, as they suppose, they will immediately begin to exercise unrighteous dominion."[1] No wonder that hereditary monarchies throughout history have tended, in the words of Will and Ariel Durant, to be characterized by "stupidity, nepotism, irresponsibility, and extravagance."[2] One of the rare exceptions to this dismal record is the remarkable history of the Nephite

---

1. D&C 121:39.
2. Durant 1968:70.

monarchs, particularly the final three, plus the last monarch's four sons who refused the throne to become missionaries.

The Nephite monarchy had originated with Nephi himself, although he had wished it otherwise. When his people became established in the New World, they—like their Israelite ancestors in the Old World[1]—wanted to be ruled by a king. They naturally selected Nephi, but he resisted. "They would that I should be their king," he tersely records, "but I, Nephi, was desirous that they should have no king; nevertheless, I did for them according to that which was in my power."[2] His comment is modest in light of what was written of him after his death:

> The people ha[d] loved Nephi exceedingly, he having been a great protector for them, having wielded the sword of Laban in their defence, and having labored in all his days for their welfare.[3]

We also learn that shortly before his death Nephi "anointed a man to be a king and a ruler over his people"[4] when he was gone. Out of regard for their beloved Nephi, who had magnanimously protected and served his people with no desire for royal power or wealth, "the people were desirous to retain in remembrance his name." Accordingly his successors were given the throne-name of Nephi (second Nephi, third Nephi, and so on) regardless of their actual names.[5] (When this practice ceased, we are not told; it had fallen out of use by the time of the first King Mosiah.)

That the Book of Mormon gives none of those actual names of the Nephite kings for the first three to four centuries may at first appear remarkable. Most works of history, after all, take precisely the opposite approach, demarcating and structuring the story around heads of state. But the first portion of the Book of Mormon is not an ordinary work of history and is not even part of Mormon's abridgment

---

1. See 1 Samuel 8.
2. 2 Nephi 5:18.
3. Jacob 1:10.
4. Jacob 1:9.
5. See Jacob 1:11.

of the large plates kept by the Nephite kings. Rather, it is an account taken from the small plates of Nephi, a record devoted mostly to things of the ministry and kept by a different line of writers.[1] Hence, of kings there is but little mention during this era, save for the encouraging word by one writer that in his day "our kings and our leaders were mighty men in the faith of the Lord; and they taught the people the ways of the Lord; wherefore, we withstood the Lamanites."[2] Unfortunately, withstanding and standing against the warring Lamanites was a constant task during this period so characterized by "wars and contentions."[3]

THE FIRST KING MOSIAH

Only when the threat of war became so great as to require removal of the Nephites from their original land are we introduced for the first time to a specific Nephite king, Mosiah (father of Benjamin). That he was a righteous man is implied by the fact that he was

> warned of the Lord that he should flee out of the land of Nephi, and as many as would hearken unto the voice of the Lord should also depart out of the land with him, into the wilderness —
>
> And it came to pass that he did according as the Lord had commanded him. And they departed out of the land into the wilderness.[4]

Mosiah's life thus echoes that of his forefather, Nephi, who likewise had fled into the wilderness after being warned by the Lord concerning Lamanite aggression.[5]

The divine direction dispensed to Mosiah's people in the wilderness purposefully led them to a site he had selected.

They were led by many preachings and prophesyings. And

---

1. See 1 Nephi 9:1–6; Jacob 3:13–14; Jarom 1:14; Omni 1:11, 23–25; see also chapter 1.
2. Jarom 1:7.
3. Jacob 7:26; Enos 1:13–14, 20, 24; Jarom 1:6–10, 13; Omni 1:2–3, 10.
4. Omni 1:12–13.
5. See 2 Nephi 5:5–7.

they were admonished continually by the word of God; and
they were led by the power of his arm, through the wilderness
until they came down into the land which is called the land
of Zarahemla.[1]

There they discovered a people who had fled Jerusalem at the Babylonian destruction—just a decade after Lehi had left—and had been
divinely led across the ocean to settle in this new land. Unlike Lehi's
party, however, these people had brought no records, so that through
the centuries "their language had become corrupted," and they even
came to "den[y] the being of their Creator."[2] Now, however, once
the language barrier was broken between Mosiah's people and those
of Zarahemla, the latter "did rejoice exceedingly, because the Lord
had sent the people of Mosiah with the plates of brass which contained
the record of the Jews."[3]

The two peoples, actually long-lost kinsmen, united under the
leadership of Mosiah. The last thing we hear of him is that when a
large stone with ancient writings was brought to him, he was able to
interpret it "by the gift and power of God," thereby revealing a brief
account of a still more ancient people who had come from the great
tower to this land but who had been destroyed by the judgments of
God.[4]

KING BENJAMIN EMULATES HIS FATHERS AND
TEACHES HIS SONS

Mosiah's successor was Benjamin, who merits mention in the
small plates not only for his successful military defense against the
aggression of their old enemy, the Lamanites,[5] but also because in
his day the keeper of the small plates, having "no seed"[6] decided to
deliver these plates to Benjamin, known to be "a just man before the

---

1. Omni 1:13.
2. Omni 1:17.
3. Omni 1:14.
4. Omni 1:20; see vv. 20–22.
5. See Omni 1:24.
6. Could mean no sons.

Lord."[1] So ends the account written on the small plates; and so the record as we have it shifts back to Mormon's abridgment of the large plates kept by the kings. Fortuitously, the shift occurs just in time to give us a good look at the righteous and remarkable King Benjamin.

It is King Benjamin the warrior upon whom Mormon first focuses. When the Lamanite armies descended upon Benjamin's people, he "gathered together his armies, and he did stand against them; and he did fight with the strength of his own arm, with the sword of Laban. And in the strength of the Lord they did contend against their enemies."[2] One thinks immediately of the first Nephite king, Benjamin's ancestor[3] Nephi, who similarly "wielded the sword of Laban in . . . defence"[4] of his people, and yet did "not put [his] trust in the arm of flesh" but rather in the Lord.[5] The similarity increases when we read that Benjamin "labor[ed] with all the might of his body and the faculty of his whole soul" for the benefit of his people[6] – again reminiscent of Nephi, who also "labored in all his days for [his people's] welfare,"[7] doing "for them according to that which was in [his] power."[8] And as Benjamin did not labor alone but "with the help" of "many holy men in the land, [who] did speak the word of God with power and with authority,"[9] so Nephi had consecrated priests and teachers[10] who also "labored diligently among [the] people"[11] in teaching the word of God.[12]

But as the story of King Benjamin unfolds, there emerges a pattern even more ancient than that of Nephi. King Benjamin's people, we are told, were at first a stiffnecked and contentious people with diverse

---

1. Omni 1:25.
2. Words of Mormon 1:13–14.
3. See Mosiah 25:13.
4. Jacob 1:10.
5. 2 Nephi 4:34.
6. Words of Mormon 1:18.
7. Jacob 1:10.
8. 2 Nephi 5:18.
9. Words of Mormon 1:17–18.
10. See 2 Nephi 5:26.
11. Jacob 1:7.
12. 2 Nephi 6–10.

deceptions, including false teachers, false prophets, and even false Christs.[1] But the king himself was "a just man"[2] and "a holy man, and he did reign over his people in righteousness."[3] And by exercising "all the might of his body and the faculty of his whole soul" in "speak[ing] the word of God with power and with authority"[4] and teaching his people "to keep the commandments of God,"[5] King Benjamin "establish[ed] peace in the land"[6] and "had continual peace all the remainder of his days."[7]

All of this presents a striking parallel to an ancient king of Abraham's day, Melchizedek, who receives but passing mention in our traditional Genesis account[8] but whose life and activities were much discussed anciently[9] and were obviously written in greater detail on the brass plates — which King Benjamin possessed and had searched diligently.[10] At least part of what the brass plates said about Melchizedek is evident from a later Book of Mormon passage:

> Now this Melchizedek was a king over the land of Salem; and his people had waxed strong in iniquity and abomination; yea, they had all gone astray; they were full of all manner of wickedness;
>
> But Melchizedek having exercised mighty faith, and received the office of the high priesthood according to the holy order of God, did preach repentance unto his people. And behold, they did repent; and Melchizedek did establish peace in the land in his days; therefore he was called the prince of peace, for he was the king of Salem.[11]

Furthermore, the order of priesthood that Melchizedek obtained

---

1. See Words of Mormon 1:12, 15–17.
2. Mosiah 2:4; Omni 1:25.
3. Words of Mormon 1:17.
4. Words of Mormon 1:17–18.
5. Mosiah 2:4.
6. Words of Mormon 1:18.
7. Mosiah 1:1.
8. See Genesis 14:18–20.
9. See generally Horton 1976; Kobelski 1981.
10. See Mosiah 1:3–8.
11. Alma 13:17–18; see also JST Genesis 14:25–40.

was the order of the son of God; it was a "type" with ordinances that "look[ed] forward" to the Son of God.[1] Additional information that may well have also appeared on the brass plates comes from Joseph Smith's inspired translation of Genesis, which tells, among other things, that Melchizedek's people "wrought righteousness, and obtained heaven"[2] and thus called Melchizedek "the king of heaven . . . , or, in other words, the King of peace."[3] The parallels with King Benjamin are compelling: both kings reigned over a wicked people; both exercised mighty faith and preached the word of God; as a result, both established peace in the land. Additional parallels will later be evident when Benjamin will speak about the "heavenly King"[4] who shall soon descend from heaven and "be called Jesus Christ, the Son of God."[5] And after King Benjamin reports this to his people, they fervently petition God for forgiveness and then receive "a remission of their sins,"[6] whereupon Benjamin urges his people to steadfastness so they "may be brought to heaven."[7]

In his righteous conduct, King Benjamin is also, of course, following the more immediate pattern of previous Nephite kings (presumably his ancestors) who were also "mighty men in the faith of the Lord" and who "taught the people the ways of the Lord."[8] including Benjamin's own father, Mosiah, who had done "according as the Lord had commanded him."[9] In turn, King Benjamin passed this heritage on to his own three sons, whom he taught

> in all the language of his fathers, that thereby they might become men of understanding; and that they might know concerning the prophecies which had been spoken by the mouths of their fathers. . . .

---

1. Alma 13:16, 1–2.
2. JST Genesis 14:34.
3. JST Genesis 14:36.
4. Mosiah 2:19.
5. Mosiah 3:8; see also v. 5.
6. Mosiah 4:1–3.
7. Mosiah 5:15.
8. Jarom 1:7.
9. Omni 1:13.

And he also taught them concerning the records which were
engraven on the plates of brass.[1]

At this point, Mormon reproduces verbatim an impressive discourse by King Benjamin as he emphatically teaches his sons about
the sacred cultural heritage being transmitted to them from previous
generations:

> My sons, I would that ye should remember that were it not
> for these plates, which contain these records [on the brass
> plates] and these commandments, we must have suffered in
> ignorance, even at this present time, not knowing the mysteries
> of God.[2]

In the not-too-distant background, of course, was the experience
of the people of Zarahemla—now part of Benjamin's own people—
who had come from Jerusalem at nearly the same time as the Nephites
and to nearly the same place, but who had suffered cultural and
spiritual deterioration through the centuries for lack of written records
like the brass plates. Thus when Benjamin's father, Mosiah, discovered the people of Zarahemla, these "did rejoice exceedingly, because
the Lord had sent the people of Mosiah with the plates of brass."[3]
That Benjamin would now draw on the experience in instructing his
sons about the value of those brass plates is mark of his expertise as
a teacher.

But if the ignorance of the people of Zarahemla was now being
rectified, the ignorance of the Lamanites was not, as Benjamin also
explained to his sons:

> For it were not possible that our father, Lehi, could have
> remembered all these things, to have taught them to his chil-
> dren, except it were for the help of these plates; for he having
> been taught in the language of the Egyptians therefore he could
> read these engravings, and teach them to his children, that

---

1. Mosiah 1:2–3.
2. Mosiah 1:3.
3. Omni 1:14.

thereby they could teach them to their children, and so fulfilling
the commandments of God, even down to this present time.

I say unto you, my sons, were it not for these things, which
have been kept and preserved by the hand of God, that we
might read and understand of his mysteries, and have his
commandments always before our eyes, that even our fathers
would have dwindled in unbelief, and we should have been
like unto our brethren, the Lamanites, who know nothing
concerning these things, or even do not believe them when
they are taught them, because of the traditions of their fathers,
which are not correct.[1]

Having so recently wielded the sword of Laban to defend his
people from aggression by the seemingly incorrigible Lamanites, King
Benjamin could have hardly suspected that in describing the state of
Lamanite ignorance he was planting a seed that would germinate
when his grandsons helped rectify that ignorance by their missionary
labors in taking the gospel and the scriptures to the Lamanites. But
the point King Benjamin was consciously making was the value of
the records and their contents:

O my sons, I would that ye should remember that these
sayings are true, and also that these records are true. And
behold, also the plates of Nephi, which contain the records
and the sayings of our fathers from the time they left Jerusalem
until now, and they are true; and we can know of their surety
because we have them before our eyes.[2]

The written wisdom and heritage of the fathers — this was the treasure
that Benjamin was urging his sons to value and follow.

But all this was prelude to the counsel that the king now gave:

And now, my sons, I would that ye should remember to
search them diligently, that ye may profit thereby; and I would
that ye should keep the commandments of God, that ye may
prosper in the land according to the promises which the Lord
made unto our fathers.[3]

---

1. Mosiah 1:4–5.
2. Mosiah 1:6.
3. Mosiah 1:7.

This is the end of the quotation from Benjamin but not the end of what he taught his sons, for "many more things did [he] teach his sons, which are not written in this book."[1]

To one of those sons King Benjamin had given the name Mosiah, after Benjamin's father; this was the son that Benjamin finally appointed as his successor to the throne. To effect the transfer, a proclamation was sent throughout the kingdom instructing the people to gather at a central location, the temple, where the king would address them. So numerous were they that a tower was built from which he would speak; and when many were still out of earshot, his words were written and relayed.[2]

KING BENJAMIN'S POWERFUL DISCOURSE

This occasion of gathering may also have had ritualistic significance as being one of the three Israelite festivals for which the law of Moses required the people to gather at the temple.[3] If so, the powerful blessings that would accrue on this occasion of King Benjamin's speech would be a direct result of the people following the righteous traditions of their forefathers.

That the historian Mormon, carefully and drastically abridging the voluminous Nephite records, would include a full account of King Benjamin's lengthy discourse reveals Mormon's high esteem for it. Even from our larger perspective of world history, King Benjamin's discourse remains unsurpassed among recorded royal orations. His overall intent is clear from the beginning, as he urges his people, "Hearken unto me, and open your ears that ye may hear, and your hearts that ye may understand, and your minds that the mysteries of God may be unfolded to your view."[4] He will speak to his people of those things which God "hath commanded me concerning [them]."[5] King Benjamin can teach about these things not only because he has received revelation, but also because of his possession and study of

---

1. Mosiah 1:8.
2. See Mosiah 1:9–18; 2:1–8.
3. See Welch 1990:29.
4. Mosiah 2:9.
5. Mosiah 2:27.

the brass plates containing God's revelations and laws to ancient Israel; and in all this Benjamin accurately mirrors the picture of any ancient Israelite king, who was "possessor of the Tablets of Law" and "proclaimer of God's revealed will."[1] Indeed, one of the Deuteronomic laws expressly commands the Israelite king to keep near to him a copy of the Torah and to study it daily "that he may learn to fear the Lord his God" and "that his heart be not lifted up above his brethren."[2]

How well King Benjamin followed this instruction is evidenced by what he says of himself in his discourse—that as a mere "mortal man" he, like his people, is "subject to all manner of infirmities in body and mind."[3] Nevertheless, having been consecrated as king by the will of God, he has spent his days serving his people with "all [his] might, mind and strength."[4] Even so, he has not sought riches from his people, nor has he been a harsh ruler, but he has taught his people to keep God's commandments.[5] Furthermore, so as not to burden his people with taxes, he has "labored with [his] own hands" to serve them[6]—an arresting contrast to so many ambitious monarchs throughout history. And how did Mosiah achieve this? By following the Deuteronomic law given to his ancient Israelite forefathers.

King Benjamin is saying this not to boast, however, but to teach— that he has a clear conscience, and that service to one's fellow beings is in fact service to God. And if he merits any thanks from his people, how much more should they thank their heavenly King, who has created them and blessed them, requiring only that they keep his commandments.[7] This is, as we shall later see, reflective of what Abraham told the many grateful recipients of his hospitality; so that once again, King Benjamin is following an ancient ancestral pattern.

Next Benjamin announces that his son Mosiah will replace him as king, and he urges his people to follow Mosiah and to avoid con-

---

1. Widengren 1958:168.
2. Deuteronomy 17:18–20.
3. Mosiah 2:10–11.
4. Mosiah 2:11.
5. See Mosiah 2:12–13.
6. Mosiah 2:14.
7. See Mosiah 2:15–27.

tending among themselves and hearkening to the evil spirit, especially since they have been taught the commandments from the brass plates as well as from the Nephite records. Happy are the people who keep the commandments, and unhappy the people who don't—both here and hereafter. Accordingly, any transgression must be rectified by repentance.[1] And "I have spoken plainly unto you that ye might understand," he says, thus following Nephi's pattern of plain and unambiguous language.[2]

But King Benjamin has saved the most powerful part of his message for last, as he suddenly announces that he has recently been visited by an angel, whose message the king now proceeds to quote:

> I am come to declare unto you the glad tidings of great joy.
>
> For the Lord hath heard thy prayers, and hath judged of thy righteousness, and hath sent me to declare unto thee that thou mayest rejoice; and that thou mayest declare unto thy people, that they may also be filled with joy.
>
> For behold, the time cometh, and is not far distant, that with power, the Lord Omnipotent who reigneth, who was, and is from all eternity to all eternity, shall come down from heaven among the children of men, and shall dwell in a tabernacle of clay, and shall go forth amongst men, working mighty miracles. . . .
>
> And lo, he shall suffer temptations, and pain of body, hunger, thirst, and fatigue, even more than man can suffer, except it be unto death; for behold, blood cometh from every pore, so great shall be his anguish for the wickedness and the abominations of his people.
>
> And he shall be called Jesus Christ, the Son of God. . . .
>
> And lo, he cometh unto his own, that salvation might come unto the children of men even through faith on his name; and even after all this they shall consider him a man, and say that he hath a devil, and shall scourge him, and shall crucify him.
>
> And he shall rise the third day from the dead; and behold, he standeth to judge the world. . . .
>
> For behold, and also his blood atoneth for the sins of those who have fallen by the transgression of Adam, who have died

1. See Mosiah 2:29–41.
2. 2 Nephi 31:3; 32:7.

not knowing the will of God concerning them, or who have ignorantly sinned.

But wo, wo unto him who knoweth that he rebelleth against God! For salvation cometh to none such except it be through repentance and faith on the Lord Jesus Christ.

And the Lord God hath sent his holy prophets among all the children of men, to declare these things to every kindred, nation, and tongue, that thereby whosoever should believe that Christ should come, the same might receive remission of their sins. . . .

Yet the Lord God saw that his people were a stiffnecked people, and he appointed unto them a law, even the law of Moses.

And many signs, and wonders, and types, and shadows showed he unto them, concerning his coming. . . .

And moreover, I say unto you, that there shall be no other name given nor any other way nor means whereby salvation can come unto the children of men, only in and through the name of Christ, the Lord Omnipotent. . . .

And moreover, I say unto you, that the time shall come when the knowledge of a Savior shall spread throughout every nation, kindred, tongue and people. . . .

And now I have spoken the words which the Lord hath commanded me.

And thus saith the Lord: They shall stand as a bright testimony against this people, at the judgment day.[1]

So powerful was the effect of this message upon the audience that "they had fallen to earth, for the fear of the Lord had come upon them. And they had viewed themselves in their own carnal state," and "cried aloud with one voice, saying: O have mercy, and apply the atoning blood of Christ that we may receive forgiveness of our sins, and our hearts may be purified; for we believe in Jesus Christ, the Son of God." Then "the Spirit of the Lord came upon them, and they were filled with joy, having received a remission of their sins, and having peace of conscience, because of the exceeding faith which they had in Jesus Christ who should come, according to the words which king Benjamin had spoken unto them."[2]

---

1. Mosiah 3:3–5, 7–15, 17, 20, 23–24.
2. Mosiah 4:1–3.

Additional instructions followed, as Benjamin taught the people how to "retain a remission of [their] sins" and "grow in the knowledge of the glory of him that created [them]," or, as he would presently say, how to continue to be what they had now become: children of Christ. He told them not "to injure one another, but to live peaceably"[1] and to succor the needy.[2] He also instructed them to teach their children not to quarrel with each other, but rather "to love one another, and to serve one another," thus "walk[ing] in the ways of truth and soberness"[3] (a charge that he himself had followed with his own sons). In other words, parents cannot qualify as children of Christ without properly teaching their own children.

King Benjamin then asked if they believed what he had spoken; they responded:

> Yea, we believe all the words which thou hast spoken unto us; and also, we know of their surety and truth, because of the Spirit of the Lord Omnipotent, which has wrought a mighty change in us, or in our hearts, that we have no more disposition to do evil, but to do good continually. . . .
>
> And it is the faith which we have had on the things which our king has spoken unto us that has brought us to this great knowledge, whereby we do rejoice with such exceedingly great joy.[4]

The people entered into a covenant and took upon themselves the name of Christ, as King Benjamin explained to them that thenceforth they would "be called the children of Christ . . . ; for behold, this day he hath spiritually begotten you."[5] King Benjamin encouraged them to be ever "steadfast and immovable"[6] and then recorded the names of all who had entered into the covenant. It turned out that every adult had entered the covenant. King Benjamin then consecrated his son Mosiah to be the new king, and he also "appointed

---

1. Mosiah 4:12–13.
2. See Mosiah 4:17–26.
3. Mosiah 4:14–15.
4. Mosiah 5:2, 4.
5. Mosiah 5:7.
6. Mosiah 5:5–15.

priests to teach the people, that thereby they might hear and know the commandments of God, and to stir them up in remembrance of the oath which they had made."[1]

King Benjamin's instrumental role in the dramatic cleansing of his people is expressly noted throughout the account: his prayers had been heard and his righteousness accepted by God, who had sent his angel with the message of joy for King Benjamin to declare to his people.[2] Upon hearing that message and praying for mercy, they were filled with joy because of their faith in "Christ who should come, according to the words which king Benjamin had spoken unto them"[3] — even as they gratefully acknowledged: "It is the faith which we have had on the things which our king has spoken unto us that has brought us to this great knowledge, whereby we do rejoice with such exceedingly great joy."[4] As a divine instrument in blessing his people, King Benjamin is following the pattern of his father, King Mosiah: he was an instrument of blessing not only by heeding God's warning to have his people flee into the wilderness but also in bringing the brass plates to the people of Zarahemla, who in turn joined with Mosiah's people under his rule.[5]

THE SECOND KING MOSIAH AND HIS SURPRISING SONS

But King Benjamin is also furthering, and in a sense completing, the work begun by his father. The coming of Mosiah to Zarahemla with the brass plates had caused "great rejoicing" among the people of Zarahemla, because without written records of their own they had lapsed into such a state of affairs that they even "denied the being of their Creator."[6] Mosiah's bringing the records thus began to reverse the process, which was furthered by his son Benjamin when he with other holy men under him "did speak the word of God with power and with authority" to the people,[7] which included, of course, all

---

1. Mosiah 6:1–3.
2. See Mosiah 3:4.
3. Mosiah 4:3.
4. Mosiah 5:4.
5. See Omni 1:12–19.
6. Omni 1:17.
7. Words of Mormon 1:17.

those formerly designated as the people of Zarahemla. These were gradually brought again to a knowledge of their God—a process that came to full fruition with King Benjamin's discourse, whose power had induced every adult in the multitude of listeners to enter into the covenant and take upon them the name of Christ.[1]

No sooner do we begin to read about the activities of the new King Mosiah, Benjamin's son, than we learn that he, in turn, is following the pattern of *his* father. As King Benjamin had been "a holy man, . . . reign[ing] over his people in righteousness"[2] and had exhorted Mosiah and his other sons to "keep the commandments of God,"[3] so now Mosiah did indeed "walk in the ways of the Lord, and did observe his judgments and his statutes, and did keep his commandments in all things whatsoever he commanded him."[4] And lest there be any doubt as to the pattern, Mosiah himself "did till the earth, that thereby he might not become burdensome to his people, that he might do according to that which his father had done in all things."[5]

And also according as his grandfather had done, as seen further along in the story. When one of Mosiah's subjects learns of the twenty-four gold plates (the Jaredite record) containing strange and ancient engravings, he immediately offers the services of King Mosiah, who "can translate the records" because he possesses "a gift from God" called "interpreters," thus making him a "seer." Furthermore, "a seer is a revelator and a prophet also; and a gift which is greater can no man have," for by this gift "a seer can know of things which are past, and also of things which are to come" and can make "hidden things . . . come to light . . . which otherwise could not be known." And "thus God has provided a means that man, through faith, might work mighty miracles; therefore he becometh a great benefit to his fellow beings."[6]

---

1. See Mosiah 6:2.
2. Words of Mormon 1:17.
3. Mosiah 1:7.
4. Mosiah 6:6.
5. Mosiah 6:7.
6. Mosiah 8:13, 16–18; see also 21:28.

One is reminded, of course, of Mosiah's father, Benjamin, who also through faith became a great benefit to his fellow beings. But the particular way in which Mosiah is now said to be of benefit directly echoes the experience of his grandfather for whom he was named, for that first Mosiah also had "interpret[ed] . . . engravings by the gift and power of God."[1] When the twenty-four gold plates were eventually delivered to the second Mosiah, he "translated them by the means of those two stones which were fastened into the two rims of a bow,"[2] or the "interpreters," and thereby brought to light an account of the people who had come to that same land from the great tower but were eventually destroyed.[3] Coincidentally, it was the very people mentioned in the engravings that had been translated earlier by the first Mosiah.[4]

Another echo of the first Mosiah's reign occurs when the second Mosiah was joined by other peoples, first Limhi's people and then Alma's people. All these were only too glad to join with King Mosiah, who "received them with joy."[5] So had his grandfather, the first King Mosiah, likewise taken under his rule the rejoicing people of Zarahemla.[6]

With the people of Limhi and Alma newly arrived in his realm, King Mosiah immediately called together all his people. If this seems to fit the pattern set by his father,[7] the parallels increase as we read of what transpired at this new assembly. After he reads the accounts of both Limhi's group and Alma's group, the people are "struck with wonder and amazement" as they feel pain for their deceased brethren and for the sinful state of the Lamanites, but also joy for the deliverance of some of their brethren. Thus "they did raise their voices and give thanks to God."[8] Their reactions are not unlike those of the prior

---

1. Omni 1:20.
2. Mosiah 28:13.
3. See Mosiah 28:17.
4. See Omni 1:20–22.
5. Mosiah 22:14; see also 24:25.
6. See Omni 1:19.
7. See Mosiah 1:10.
8. Mosiah 25:5–11.

assembly when Mosiah was consecrated king and his father delivered the powerful discourse that caused the people to fall to earth with fear and cry aloud for mercy, whereupon they were filled with joy.[1]

King Mosiah then has Alma preach faith and repentance to the people. He also has him organize churches and ordain priests and teachers, whose labors cause the Lord to "pour out his Spirit" upon the people.[2] And the Lord commends the people for being "willing to bear my name."[3] Once again the situation roughly reflects King Benjamin's prior assembly, when "the Spirit of the Lord came upon them"[4] and they took upon themselves the name of Christ,[5] and when King Benjamin "appointed priests to teach the people."[6]

The reverberations of righteousness extending through these three generations of righteous monarchs leave us totally unprepared to discover that, among those of the "rising generation" who were unbelieving and rebellious were Mosiah's own four sons—Ammon, Aaron, Omner, and Himni.[7] Their unbelief was more than passive; they joined with one of the sons of Alma, also called Alma, in actively leading people to wickedness and idolatry, causing dissension, and "seeking to destroy the church, and to lead astray the people of the Lord, contrary to the commandments of God, or even the king."[8] How could there be such a radical departure from the otherwise repeating pattern of righteousness in this royal family? Noticing that the record never expressly says, as it does of Benjamin, that Mosiah taught his sons, one might be tempted to conclude that this silence indicates that in fact he never—or perhaps hardly ever, or only poorly did—teach his sons; this then, could explain their otherwise surprising rebellion. To draw such a conclusion, however, seems contrary to what the record implies. Not only did Mosiah "do according to that

---

1. See Mosiah 4:1–3.
2. Mosiah 25:24.
3. Mosiah 26:18.
4. Mosiah 4:3.
5. See Mosiah 5:7–12.
6. Mosiah 6:3.
7. Mosiah 26:1–6; 27:8, 34.
8. Mosiah 27:10.

which his father had done in all things,"[1] which would presumably include teaching his own children, but he also walked "in the ways of the Lord, . . . and did keep his commandments in all things,"[2] which would presumably include the commandment given by Benjamin that his people should "teach [their children] to walk in the ways of truth and soberness."[3]

How, then, can we explain the unexpected departure of King Mosiah's sons from the path that their fathers had so assiduously followed? In the ultimate sense we are faced with the reality and inviolability of individual agency (even Lehi, it will be remembered, could not save Laman and Lemuel). But Mosiah's sons may have been influenced by peer pressure from what Mormon characterizes as "the rising generation" who "did not believe the tradition of their fathers."[4] And preeminent among those peers was Alma the younger, who besides being the son of the Nephite High Priest happened to be one of the glibbest characters in Nephite history, being "a man of many words" who "did speak much flattery to the people," "stealing away the hearts of the people" and leading "many . . . to do after the manner of his iniquities."[5] That this Alma should have associated closely with Mosiah's sons seems only natural, since their fathers were the two highest-ranking Nephite authorities and were close associates.[6] Such was the context in which Mosiah's sons surprisingly and drastically departed from the righteous path of their fathers.

Equally surprising, however, is what ensued. According to Mormon's account, as Alma the younger and the sons of Mosiah

> were going about rebelling against God, behold, the angel of the Lord appeared unto them; and he descended as it were in a cloud; and he spake as it were with a voice of thunder, which caused the earth to shake upon which they stood;
> And so great was their astonishment that they fell to the

1. Mosiah 6:7.
2. Mosiah 6:6.
3. Mosiah 4:15.
4. Mosiah 26:1.
5. Mosiah 27:8–9.
6. See Mosiah 24:25; 25:6, 14, 19; 26:8–12.

earth, and understood not the words which he spake unto them.

Nevertheless he cried again, saying: Alma, arise and stand forth, for why persecutest thou the church of God? . . .

And again, the angel said: Behold, the Lord hath heard the prayers of his people, and also the prayers of his servant, Alma, who is thy father; for he has prayed with much faith concerning thee that thou mightest be brought to the knowledge of the truth; therefore, for this purpose have I come to convince thee of the power and authority of God, that the prayers of his servants might be answered according to their faith.

And now behold, can ye dispute the power of God? For behold, doth not my voice shake the earth? And can ye not also behold me before you? And I am sent from God.[1]

The angel further instructed Alma to remember his heritage and to cease trying to destroy the church, even if he himself would be cast off.[2]

At this point, according to Mormon's abridgment, "Alma and those that were with him fell again to the earth," but when they subsequently arose, Alma did not, having lost his strength and become helpless and speechless. In this state he was carried to his father, who rejoiced because "he knew that it was the power of God." Alma the father immediately called others to "witness what the Lord had done for his son, and also for those that were with him." He further had the priests fast and pray with him, asking God to restore Alma the younger to strength. The prayer was answered two days later when Alma stood up and announced that he had repented and had been redeemed, thanks to divine mercy. From then on he and those with him when the angel appeared made an irrevocable about-face as they traveled around "publishing to all the people the things which they had heard and seen, and preaching the word of God in much tribulation."[3]

As with the similar experience of Saul (Paul) in the New Testa-

---

1. Mosiah 27:11–15.
2. See Mosiah 27:16.
3. Mosiah 27:18–32.

ment,[1] the purpose of this dramatic divine intervention seems to have been twofold: the stopping of the persecution and the conversion of the persecutors. But here is an additional element: the instrumental role of a father, Alma the elder, in obtaining divine intervention on behalf of his wayward son. Others of the Lord's servants had also prayed for this, as the angel told Alma the younger,[2] and that these may have included Mosiah on behalf of his own sons seems plausible since they also saw the angel and fell to the ground in astonishment when they heard him speak and felt the earth shake at his voice.[3] That the angel singled out Alma and addressed him directly is understandable because of his leadership role among the wrongdoers. But the parallel account given in Alma's own words later in the Book of Mormon reveals that after Alma had fallen to the ground and could no longer hear what was spoken, the angel continued and spoke more things "which were heard by my brethren, but I did not hear them."[4] Thus the experience was intended to impress them all, as Alma emphasizes: "God sent his holy angel to stop *us*," and "he spake unto *us*, . . . and the . . . earth did tremble beneath *our* feet; and *we all* fell to the earth, for the fear of the Lord came upon *us*."[5] All of this is, admittedly, only circumstantial evidence that what befell the sons of Mosiah was pursuant to the faith of their father. But such a conclusion would certainly be in harmony with the divine protection later accorded these same sons, concerning whom the Lord promised Mosiah that they would be delivered "according to thy faith."[6] And if it was Mosiah's faith that had obtained the conversion of his sons who "fell to the earth" when "the fear of the Lord came upon" them,[7] Mosiah's life again echoes that of his own father, King Benjamin, who after his powerful discourse saw that his people had similarly "fallen to the earth, for the fear of the Lord had come upon them."[8]

---

1. See Acts 8–9.
2. See Mosiah 27:14.
3. See Mosiah 27:18.
4. Alma 36:11.
5. Alma 36:6–7, emphasis added.
6. Alma 19:23; 17:35; Mosiah 28:7.
7. Alma 36:7.
8. Mosiah 4:1.

The reality of what Mosiah's sons had experienced was confirmed by their good works that followed, as

> they traveled throughout all the land of Zarahemla, and among all the people who were under the reign of king Mosiah, zealously striving to repair all the injuries which they had done to the church, confessing all their sins, and publishing all the things which they had seen, and explaining the prophecies and the scriptures to all who desired to hear them.
>
> And thus they were instruments in the hands of God in bringing many to the knowledge of the truth, yea, to the knowledge of their Redeemer.
>
> And how blessed are they! For they did publish peace; they did publish good tidings of good; and they did declare unto the people that the Lord reigneth.[1]

Having returned from their radical departure from the path of their royal fathers, the sons of Mosiah now pressed forward on that same path following the example of their fathers. Thus they "did publish peace" and "good tidings" and "did declare unto the people that the Lord reigneth," even as their grandfather, King Benjamin, had done when he "established peace"[2] and "declare[d] . . . glad tidings"[3] about "the Lord Omnipotent who reigneth."[4] And thus the sons of Mosiah became "instruments in the hands of God"[5] in blessing the people of their father's kingdom, even as their father, grandfather, and great-grandfather were all instruments in blessing this same people.

MISSIONARIES INSTEAD OF MONARCHS – THE END OF THE NEPHITE MONARCHY

Such could have been a happy and perfect ending – except that this story does not end here, for its surprises are not over. As radically as the sons of Mosiah had once parted with precedent to rebel against

---

1. Mosiah 27:35–37.
2. Mosiah 2:4.
3. Mosiah 3:3.
4. Mosiah 3:5.
5. Mosiah 27:36.

God's kingdom, so they again wished to radically part with precedent to further that kingdom—they now wished to go and preach to the very people whose murderous aggression had ever vexed the Nephites, namely, the Lamanites. Mosiah's sons proposed to

> preach the things which they had heard, and that they might impart the word of God to their brethren, the Lamanites—
> That perhaps they might bring them to the knowledge of the Lord their God, and . . . cure them of their hatred towards the Nephites, . . . that there should be no more contentions. . . .
> Now they were desirous that salvation should be declared to every creature, for they could not bear that any human soul should perish. . . .
> And thus did the Spirit of the Lord work upon them.[1]

The idea of preaching to the Lamanites was not entirely new. Nephi's brother Jacob and Jacob's son Enos both reported on efforts made to "restore the Lamanites to the knowledge of the truth" and "the true faith in God." But "it was all vain" because of the Lamanites "eternal" and "fixed" hatred,[2] so that in the days of the sons of Mosiah the idea had long been abandoned.

The sons of Mosiah may possibly have conceived the notion in response to the now-extant report of Zeniff who had seen "that which was good" among the Lamanites.[3] But the upshot of Zeniff's trusting the Lamanites had proved disastrous,[4] confirming the long-held conviction that the Lamanites were intractably hardened. (Ironically, however, Zeniff's zealous mission did finally result—years after his death—in the language of Nephi being taught among many of the Lamanites,[5] thus preparing the way for the mission of the sons of Mosiah.) Wherever, then, the sons of Mosiah got the idea, it appeared understandably preposterous to most who heard it, as would be re-

1. Mosiah 28:1–4.
2. Jacob 7:24; Enos 1:20.
3. Mosiah 9:1.
4. See Mosiah 9–10; 23:37.
5. See Mosiah 24:1–6.

called years later when Ammon reminded his brothers that their friends had "laughed [them] to scorn."

> For they said unto us: Do ye suppose that ye can bring the Lamanites to the knowledge of the truth? Do ye suppose that ye can convince the Lamanites of the incorrectness of the traditions of their fathers, as stiffnecked a people as they are; whose hearts delight in the shedding of blood; whose days have been spent in the grossest iniquity; whose ways have been the ways of a transgressor from the beginning? Now my brethren, ye remember that this was their language.
>
> And moreover they did say: Let us take up arms against them, that we destroy them and their iniquity out of the land, lest they overrun us and destroy us.[1]

Even the righteous King Mosiah was reluctant to let his sons attempt such a mission, as seen by the fact that they had to "plead with their father many days."[2] His reluctance is immediately understandable. After all, had not his own father, the righteous King Benjamin, been forced to wield the sword of Laban in defending his people against the Lamanites?[3] And had not Mosiah himself recently seen the effects of Lamanite cruelty as he had welcomed under his protection both the people of Limhi and the people of Alma, all fleeing from Lamanite bondage?[4] As noble as the motive of Mosiah's sons was, they would clearly be placing their lives in jeopardy if they even attempted such an unprecedented and dangerous mission.

And not to be overlooked was the matter of succession to the throne. If all of Mosiah's sons were allowed to leave as requested, who would succeed Mosiah as king? He naturally "was desirous to confer" the kingdom upon one of his sons,[5] but, "there was not any of his sons who would accept of the kingdom"[6] or who were "willing to take upon them the kingdom."[7] No wonder such a major difference

---

1. Alma 26:23–25.
2. Mosiah 28:5.
3. See Words of Mormon 1:13.
4. See Mosiah 22:11–16; 24:16–25.
5. Alma 17:6.
6. Mosiah 28:10.
7. Mosiah 29:3.

of opinion took "many days" to discuss![1] It was incredible enough, obviously, for the heir apparent to refuse what so many throughout history have coveted and fought to obtain. But that refusal in turn opened the door to kingship for the next son, who probably had never expected to become king. Again a refusal, and so on until each of Mosiah's sons had refused the opportunity of a lifetime. In a word, they preferred to be missionaries rather than monarchs.

But their safety was still very much at issue. King Mosiah finally took the matter to the Lord, who instructed Mosiah to let his sons go, "for many shall believe on their words, and . . . have eternal life; and I will deliver thy sons out of the hands of the Lamanites."[2] The king in turn granted his sons' request, and they departed.

This left Mosiah with the problem of a successor. He first translated for his people the twenty-four gold plates, which told the Jaredite history with its often corrupt kings—a history that caused Mosiah's people joy for the added knowledge it gave them but also sorrow for the tragedy it related.[3]

Then King Mosiah took all the sacred records that for centuries had been handed down in the Nephite monarchy and transferred them to Alma the younger, charging him to keep the records and hand them down. He then took a poll among his people about their preference for a royal successor; Mosiah's son Aaron was their choice. However, he was not only absent but had already refused to be king. Then, with one lengthy and memorable royal proclamation, King Mosiah terminated the age-old Nephite monarchy even as he paid tribute to his father and to the power of his father's example. Monarchy would be desirable, Mosiah stated, if it were always "possible that you could have just men to be your kings," men "who would do even as my father Benjamin did for this people. . . . And even I myself have labored with all the power and faculties which I have possessed, to teach you the commandments of God, and to establish peace."[4]

---

1. Mosiah 28:5.
2. Mosiah 28:7.
3. See Mosiah 28:11–19. However, a part of this history was for the time not publicly disclosed. (See Ether 4:1.)
4. Mosiah 29:13–14.

However, "because all men are not just it is not expedient that ye should have a king," for "how much iniquity doth one wicked king cause to be committed, yea, and what great destruction!"[1]

Mosiah knew whereof he spoke, for the brass plates in his possession would have spoken of the same wicked kings in ancient Israel of whom we can read today in the Old Testament. And as an added witness of these things, Mosiah and his people now had the Jaredites' history, which told that after the Jaredites arrival to their promised land and when they wanted to establish a monarchy, the brother of Jared had responded, "Surely this thing leadeth into captivity."[2] But King Mosiah then proceeded to adduce a much more recent example of an evil king well known to his people[3] — the king from whom Alma's group had fled. Indeed, Mosiah may have been quite influenced by the record of Alma's people, who, after escaping from King Noah's tyranny, desired to make Alma their king. He had refused, renouncing the monarchical system in which he had held so high a place and insisting that monarchy was incongruous with the Lord's commandment that they should "not esteem one flesh above another."[4]

What Mosiah now proposed was a government by "the voice of this people" in the form of a system of judges, for "it is not common that the voice of the people desireth anything contrary to that which is right."[5] This self-rule will, Mosiah maintained, provide the Nephites "a land of liberty," reminiscent of what Nephi had prophesied concerning this same land with respect to its latter-day Gentile occupants — that it "shall be a land of liberty unto the Gentiles, and there shall be no kings upon the land."[6] (Mosiah had possession of Nephi's record containing this prophecy. Had it influenced him with respect to his own course of action?) Mosiah noted that under this system "every man may enjoy his rights and privileges alike" and thus be responsible for his own sins, whereas under monarchies "the sins of

1. Mosiah 29:16–17.
2. Ether 6:23.
3. See Mosiah 25:6.
4. Mosiah 23:7.
5. Mosiah 29:25–26.
6. 2 Nephi 10:11.

many people have been caused by the iniquities of their kings," transferring the guilt to the kings.[1] Thus Mosiah unfolded to his people "all the trials and troubles of a righteous king, yea, all the travails of soul for their people, and also all the murmurings of the people to their king; and he explained it all unto them," saying that "the se things ought not to be; but that the burden should come upon all tl e people, that every man might bear his part."[2] This may possibly indicate once again that King Mosiah was influenced by Alma's record, which spoke of the people in the fold of God "bear[ing] one another's burdens."[3] The one trait of the good King Mosiah that seems to come more and more into focus is his openmindedness—a trait taken even further by his sons.

And such talk by Mosiah of burden, trials, and responsibility borne by monarchs speaks yet more about the man. His was a wise and eternal perspective, and quite beyond the limited view of so many of the world's monarchs who have lived in luxury at the expense of their subjects. Furthermore, the whole tenor of his proclamation bespeaks a monarch who to the very last governed not with "compulsion upon the souls of the children of men"[4] (as "almost all men" tend to do "as soon as they get a little authority, as they suppose"[5]) but rather by "persuasion, by longsuffering, by gentleness, . . . and pure knowledge"[6]—as seen by his lengthy explanation of the potential evils of monarchy ("he explained it all unto them"[7]) and by his appeal to reason ("let us be wise . . . "[8]). Here was no tyrant telling his people what to do, but a patient leader appealing to wise use of agency.

How persuasive he was is evident in the reaction of his people, who had for so long lived under a monarchy. Upon hearing Mosiah's proclamation, they "were convinced of the truth of his words" and

1. Mosiah 29:30–32.
2. Mosiah 29:33–34.
3. Mosiah 18:8.
4. D&C 121:37.
5. D&C 121:39.
6. D&C 121:41–42.
7. Mosiah 29:33.
8. Mosiah 29:10.

"relinquished their desires for a king"[1] — a long desire indeed, one that had lasted for nearly five centuries since the day when Nephi's own people wanted him to be their king, while he "was desirous that they should have no king."[2] Thus Nephi's desire finally won out, as Mosiah's people "became exceedingly anxious that every man should have an equal chance," and "every man expressed a willingness to answer for his own sins."[3] Furthermore they

> were exceedingly rejoiced because of the liberty which had been granted unto them.
>
> And they did wax strong in love towards Mosiah; yea, they did esteem him more than any other man; for they did not look upon him as a tyrant who was seeking for gain, yea, for that lucre which doth corrupt the soul; for he had not exacted riches of them, neither had he delighted in the shedding of blood; but he had established peace in the land, and he had granted unto his people that they should be delivered from all manner of bondage; therefore they did esteem him, yea, exceedingly, beyond measure.[4]

Such was the remarkable event that ended the Nephite monarchy and began the period of judges — precisely the opposite transformation that had occurred earlier in ancient Israel despite the prophet Samuel's warning (similar in many respects to that given by Mosiah) of the dangers of monarchy.[5] And if King Mosiah here departs from the kingly path of his father, grandfather, and so on, he does so with striking echoes of the pattern set by his own father. As Mosiah persuaded his people to make a dramatic change, and "they were convinced of the truth of his words,"[6] so Benjamin had persuaded his people to make a dramatic change, and they did "believe all the words which [he had] spoken."[7] As Mosiah's people now "exceedingly re-

1. Mosiah 29:37–38.
2. 2 Nephi 5:18.
3. Mosiah 29:38.
4. Mosiah 29:39–40.
5. See 1 Samuel 8–9.
6. Mosiah 29:37.
7. Mosiah 5:2.

joiced because of the liberty which had been granted unto them"[1] by their king, so Benjamin's people had also "rejoice[d] with . . . exceedingly great joy" when they were spiritually "made free" through their faith in Benjamin's words.[2] As Mosiah "had established peace in the land,"[3] so Benjamin also "had established peace in the land."[4] As Mosiah had "not exacted riches,"[5] so Benjamin had "not sought . . . riches" of his people.[6] As Mosiah had "labored with all the power and faculties which [he] . . . possessed"[7] for the benefit of his people, so Benjamin had served his people with all his "might, mind and strength."[8] And as Mosiah did "teach [his people] the commandments of God,"[9] so Benjamin had taught his people to "keep . . . the commandments of God."[10] Such remarkable repetition demonstrates the power of Mosiah's parental example.

Indeed, it is even possible to view Mosiah's termination of the monarchy as advancing and bringing to fruition the work begun by his father: Benjamin had succeeded in having the people enter into a covenant to keep God's commandments,[11] while Mosiah now succeeded in having the people enter into a political arrangement where they would always be answerable for their own sins.[12] Benjamin had helped make the people spiritually free;[13] his son Mosiah ensured that they would be able to retain that spiritual freedom by granting them their political freedom from potentially oppressive and corrupting kings.[14] The situation calls to mind the phrase that appears twice in the book of Judges: "In those days there was no king in Israel, but

---

1. Mosiah 29:39.
2. Mosiah 5:4, 8.
3. Mosiah 29:40.
4. Mosiah 2:4.
5. Mosiah 29:40.
6. Mosiah 2:12.
7. Mosiah 29:14.
8. Mosiah 2:11.
9. Mosiah 29:14.
10. Mosiah 2:31.
11. See Mosiah 5:5.
12. See Mosiah 29:30, 38.
13. See Mosiah 5:8.
14. See Mosiah 29:17, 30–32.

every man did that which was right in his own eyes."[1] These passages would have been contained on the brass plates and would have probably been familiar to King Mosiah, which indicates that he was seeking to restore a condition that had once existed among his Israelite forefathers.

THE MISSION OF THE SONS OF MOSIAH

And what of Mosiah's sons? Did their refusal of the Nephite kingship and their mission to the Lamanites constitute a departure from the path of their fathers? So it would appear; except that the more one looks at the story, the more continuity it seems to have with prior events. Their departure from home on a merciful mission of rescue to a people they did not even know, and all because "they could not bear that any human soul should perish,"[2] is at once reminiscent of the compassion and missionary zeal of Abraham, revered by both Nephites and their kinsmen Jews as "our father Abraham."[3] Tradition tells that Abraham was not content with providing hospitality to those who happened by his house but that he would often go in search of wayfarers who might need assistance.[4] And when grateful recipients of his liberal hospitality would thank him, he would teach them how to thank God, the real provider[5]—behavior later echoed, as Hugh Nibley has pointed out,[6] by one of Abraham's descendants, King Benjamin ("an ardent student of early Jewish traditions") when he tells his grateful subjects: "If I, whom ye call your king, who has spent his days in your service, . . . do merit any thanks from you, O how you ought to thank your heavenly King!"[7] Abraham's missionary zeal was so great[8] that the rabbis reported that "the nations of the world slept, and did not come under the wings of the

---

1. Judges 17:6; 21:25.
2. Mosiah 28:3.
3. See TDNT V:976; Arieti 1981:171; John 8:53.
4. See Montefiore and Loewe 1974:415.
5. See Ibid. 115; LJ I:270–271.
6. See Nibley, *Improvement Era*, November 1969:120–21.
7. Mosiah 2:19.
8. See, e.g., Abraham 2:15; LJ I:219.

Shechinah [Divine Presence or Spirit]. Who woke them up so that they might come? Abraham. . . . And not only so, but Abraham woke up Charity, which slept."[1] Hence Abraham was said to have extended God's rule on earth,[2] and all because of the Patriarch's great love for God and his fellow beings. "A man filled with the love of God," insisted Joseph Smith, "is not content with blessing his family alone, but ranges through the whole world, anxious to bless the whole human race."[3] So it was with Abraham, whose object, says Hugh Nibley, was "not to conquer or impress, but to bless all."[4] Indeed, tradition tells that Abraham himself, when returning from his battle with the marauding kings, had been hailed as a mighty king but had refused the honor, saying that "the Universe has its King, and it has its God."[5] Thus, according to Hugh Nibley, Abraham "was 'the Friend of God' because he was the friend of man."[6]

If King Benjamin had emulated Abraham in teaching the grateful recipients of his service how to thank the true provider, Benjamin's grandsons went further in following the example of Abraham. Declining the impressive honors and wealth of earthly kingship, they preferred to leave their homes and go abroad to find those who were lost, cause them to be "awakened out of a deep sleep,"[7] and bring them "to rejoice in the Lord their God, that they might become friendly to one another."[8] And by following the path of their father Abraham, the sons of Mosiah were helping to fulfil the Abrahamic covenant, whose scope of blessing was universal.[9]

That very covenant had been alluded to by King Benjamin when he reported that the angel had promised that "the time shall come when the knowledge of a Savior shall spread throughout every nation,

---

1. Montefiore and Loewe 1974:563–564.
2. See Nibley, *Improvement Era*, January 1970:59.
3. TPJS 174.
4. Nibley 1981:249.
5. LJ I:232.
6. Nibley, *Improvement Era*, November 1969:122.
7. Alma 5:7 (words of Alma the younger about the conversion process).
8. Mosiah 28:2.
9. See Genesis 22:18.

kindred, tongue, and people."[1] Other possible foreshadowings of their mission may also be discerned in the accounts of Benjamin and his son Mosiah. For example, Benjamin had taught Mosiah that the Nephites were fortunately unlike their "brethren, the Lamanites," who "have dwindled in unbelief, and . . . know nothing concerning these things [the scriptures]."[2] Years later when Mosiah had gathered his people and read to them the accounts of the peoples of Alma and Limhi, Mosiah's people "thought upon the Lamanites, who were their brethren, of their sinful and polluted state, [and] . . . were filled with pain and anguish for the welfare of their souls."[3] Such passages may well portend the mission of Mosiah's sons, for whom talking about the unfortunate Lamanites and even feeling pity for them was simply not enough. The sons of Mosiah translated their compassion into action (echoing father Abraham) in order to rectify the situation.

There was good reason, of course, why others had not undertaken such a mission, for the Lamanites' hatred of the Nephites seemed intractable. A family feud is the worst kind, especially when it drags out over generations, and the original flame of anger kindled by Laman and Lemuel for Nephi had, over the centuries, been fanned into a raging fire by the Lamanites, so that they had become "a wild and a hardened and a ferocious people . . . who delighted in murdering the Nephites, and robbing and plundering them."[4] No wonder that King Mosiah had to deliberate "many days"[5] when his sons first proposed the mission. But when he finally inquired of the Lord about the matter, he obtained a promise that the Lord would "deliver [his] sons out of the hands of the Lamanites"[6] and that it would "be unto" his sons according to his faith.[7]

As the account of their mission is related by Mormon, the clear implication is that but for this divine protection obtained through

1. Mosiah 3:20.
2. Mosiah 1:5.
3. Mosiah 25:11.
4. Alma 17:14.
5. Mosiah 28:5.
6. Mosiah 28:7; see also Alma 17:35.
7. Alma 19:23. This passage speaks specifically of Ammon.

Mosiah's faith, his sons in fact would have been killed.[1] Thus if their mission was made possible by their break with the kingly tradition of their fathers, the mission was also possible only through the faith of their father, Mosiah—illustrating the principle expressed by Joseph Smith that "the greatest temporal and spiritual blessings which always come from faithfulness and concerted effort, never attended individual exertion or enterprise."[2]

The influence of Mosiah was essential to his sons' mission in another sense also, for their experience in growing up in the royal Nephite household provided invaluable expertise in matters of royal practice and protocol, all of which would have greatly facilitated their dealing with Lamanite kings and their courts—as Ammon with both King Lamoni[3] and his father,[4] and as Aaron with King Lamoni's father.[5] The conversion of these rulers proved critical in opening the door to spread the word among their peoples.

But it was the pattern of righteousness set by Mosiah and his father and grandfather that most facilitated the mission of Mosiah's sons, who "waxed strong in the knowledge of the truth" and became "men of a sound understanding," having "searched the scriptures diligently" to "know the word of God" and having "given themselves to much prayer, and fasting." Consequently, "they had the spirit of prophecy, and the spirit of revelation, and when they taught, they taught with power and authority of God."[6] The description recalls their grandfather King Benjamin teaching his sons so that "they might become men of understanding" and "know concerning the prophecies";[7] and to this end Benjamin had spoken of the scriptures and told his sons to "search them diligently" and to "keep the com-

---

1. See Alma 17:35; 19:23.
2. TPJS 183.
3. See Alma 17–19.
4. See Alma 20.
5. See Alma 22.
6. Alma 17:2–3.
7. Mosiah 1:2.

mandments of God."[1] Further, when Benjamin taught his people, it was with great power and authority from God.[2]

The influence of their fathers is likewise evident in what the sons of Mosiah preached. To King Lamoni and his court, Ammon "expounded unto them the plan of redemption, which was prepared from the foundation of the world; and . . . made known unto them concerning the coming of Christ."[3] Precisely the same message was preached to King Lamoni's father and his court, as "Aaron did expound . . . the plan of redemption, which was prepared from the foundation of the world, through Christ."[4] Ammon and Aaron were thus preaching the same message that their grandfather Benjamin had preached when he quoted the words of the angel that "salvation was, and is, and is to come, in and through the atoning blood of Christ, the Lord Omnipotent."[5] It was also the same message that Benjamin's son Mosiah had caused to be preached to his people when they were taught "repentance and faith on the Lord."[6]

The effect of the message preached by Mosiah's sons was profound. A number of their listeners—including King Lamoni,[7] his queen and court,[8] and King Lamoni's father[9]—fell to the earth as if dead, for "the fear of the Lord had come upon them"[10] and they were "overpowered by the Spirit"[11] and "under the power of God" while "the dark veil of unbelief was being cast away from [their] mind[s]" and "the light of the glory of God . . . infused . . . joy into [their] soul[s]."[12] When they again received strength, they witnessed to a profound transformation by exclaiming such things as: "Blessed be

1. Mosiah 1:7.
2. See Mosiah 3:2–3; 4:3.
3. Alma 18:39.
4. Alma 22:13.
5. Mosiah 3:18.
6. Mosiah 25:15.
7. See Alma 18:42.
8. See Alma 19:13, 16.
9. See Alma 22:18.
10. Alma 19:15.
11. Alma 19:13, referring to Lamoni's queen.
12. Alma 19:6, referring to Lamoni.

the name of God," for "I have seen my Redeemer,"[1] and "O blessed Jesus, who has saved me from an awful hell! O blessed God, have mercy on this people!"[2] They further declared that "their hearts had been changed; that they had no more desire to do evil," and they spoke also of "things of God, and of his righteousness,"[3] and began to "minister" unto others and convert them.[4] Thus "thousands were brought to the knowledge of the Lord,"[5] being "convinced of [their] sins" and granted forgiveness through their repentance and the mercy of God.[6] "They became a righteous people," and "the Lord did begin to pour out his Spirit upon them."[7]

The sons of Mosiah also helped organize churches among them,[8] "consecrating priests and teachers throughout the land among the Lamanites, to preach and to teach the word of God."[9] They also became a "free people," enjoying "the liberty of worshiping the Lord their God according to their desires,"[10] so that "the word of God might have no obstruction, but that it might go forth throughout all the land."[11] And with all this they became peace-loving and "did lay down the weapons of their rebellion, that they did not fight against God any more, neither against any of their brethren,"[12] and even when threatened by war they would not "take up arms" nor "make any preparations for war."[13]

Such events in the mission of Mosiah's sons distinctly echo the experiences of their fathers, such as when King Benjamin preached to his people, and the entire multitude "had fallen to the earth, for

1. Alma 19:12–13.
2. Alma 19:29.
3. Alma 19:33–34.
4. Alma 22:23.
5. Alma 23:5.
6. Alma 24:9–15.
7. Alma 19:35–36.
8. See Alma 19:35.
9. Alma 23:4.
10. Alma 21:21–22.
11. Alma 23:3.
12. Alma 23:7.
13. Alma 24:6.

the fear of the Lord had come upon them," having "viewed themselves in their own carnal state." After begging for "mercy" through "the atoning blood of Christ . . . the Spirit of the Lord came upon them, and they were filled with joy, having received a remission of their sins, and having peace of conscience."[1] Their hearts were changed so that they had "no more disposition to do evil, but to do good continually."[2] They also were "made free" through Christ, first at the time of King Benjamin[3] and later under King Benjamin's son Mosiah, so that the people "exceedingly rejoiced because of the liberty which had been granted them."[4] Both kings organized churches and appointed priests to facilitate the teaching of the word of God,[5] and both "established peace in the land."[6] And as King Benjamin had told his repentant people, "ye will not have a mind to injure one another, but to live peaceably."[7] The pattern established by these fathers was thus followed closely by their posterity, the sons of Mosiah, in achieving such astonishing success among the Lamanites.

Even before the Lamanite mission of Mosiah's sons, through their missionary work in the Nephite kingdom they had become "instruments in the hands of God in bringing many to the knowledge of the truth."[8] But with the astonishing success of their Lamanite mission, that same designation as "instruments in the hands of God" is applied to them repeatedly.[9] The phrase had first occurred in the Book of Mormon when father Lehi gratefully stated that his son Nephi had been "an instrument in the hands of God, in bringing us forth into the land of promise; for were it not for him, we must have perished with hunger in the wilderness."[10] By similarly becoming instruments in God's hands in saving the Lamanites, the sons of Mosiah were

1. Mosiah 4:1–3.
2. Mosiah 5:2.
3. Mosiah 5:8.
4. Mosiah 29:39.
5. See Mosiah 6:3; 25:19.
6. See Mosiah 2:4; 29:40.
7. Mosiah 4:13.
8. Mosiah 27:36.
9. Alma 17:9, 11; 26:3, 15; 35:14.
10. 2 Nephi 1:24.

following the path of their ancestor Nephi. Coincidentally, he had become such an instrument even before his reluctant reign as the first Nephite king, while the sons of Mosiah served as such instruments after the termination of that same Nephite monarchy.

As instruments in the hands of God, the sons of Mosiah were also following the example of their more immediate fathers, like their father Mosiah, whose use of the interpreters to translate the Jaredite record allowed him "through faith" to be "a great benefit to his fellow beings";[1] and like their grandfather Benjamin, in whose powerful words his people had the faith that brought them such "great knowledge" and "exceedingly great joy";[2] and like their great-grandfather Mosiah, who had been an instrument in delivering his people out of danger, in translating Jaredite engravings, and in being a messenger to bring salvation to the lost people of Zarahemla[3] when "the Lord had sent the people of Mosiah with the plates of brass."[4] In that last role particularly, Mosiah foreshadowed his great-grandsons, who were likewise messengers of salvation to a lost people, as so gratefully expressed by one of the Lamanite kings: "I thank my God, my beloved people, that our great God has in goodness sent these our brethren, the Nephites, unto us to preach unto us."[5] So profound, in fact, was the gratitude of the Lamanites for the sons of Mosiah that they were "dearly beloved" and "were treated as though they were angels sent from God to save them from everlasting destruction."[6] That kind of love and esteem is rare, but it seems more than coincidence that Mosiah himself (father of the missionaries) had earned that same gratitude from his people, who "did wax strong in love towards Mosiah" and "did esteem him more than any other man; . . . yea, exceedingly, beyond measure."[7] And here again the pattern was an

1. Mosiah 8:18; see also 28:11–18.
2. Mosiah 5:4.
3. See Omni 1:12–22.
4. Omni 1:14.
5. Alma 24:7.
6. Alma 27:4.
7. Mosiah 29:40.

ancient ancestral one, for Nephi's people had also "loved Nephi exceedingly" for his tireless and selfless service to them.[1]

It was adherence to the path of their fathers, then, that brought the sons of Mosiah such remarkable success on their Lamanite mission, even if that mission was made possible only by their break with the monarchical tradition of their fathers extending back to Nephi. But even in making that break, the sons of Mosiah had responded to "the Spirit of the Lord," which did "work upon them"[2] in prompting them to undertake the mission to the Lamanites. And by thus being receptive, they had also responded to their grandfather Benjamin's counsel to his people to "[yield] to the enticings of the Holy Spirit."[3] Benjamin had also counseled his people "not [to] have a mind to injure one another, but to live peaceably"[4] and to freely "succor those that stand in need of your succor" without judging them.[5] In the end, no one took that counsel so seriously and so far as Benjamin's grandsons, who chose to spiritually succor the Lamanites rather than judge them or injure them. The break with the past made by Mosiah's sons thus in one sense turns out to have as much continuity as disparity with the path of their fathers.

Even so, it took just such a break to make possible the mission that persuaded the Lamanites to break with the false traditions of *their* fathers extending back to Laman and Lemuel, as one Lamanite king thanked God that he had sent the sons of Mosiah "to convince us of the traditions of our wicked fathers."[6] But the kingly tradition that the sons of Mosiah broke with was, after all, one that Nephi had begun with only the greatest reluctance, finally acquiescing in his people's desire for a king.[7] The refusal of Mosiah's sons to accept the throne thus returned things to the condition that their ancestor Nephi had hoped for in the first place. And by their refusal and the aston-

1. Jacob 1:10.
2. Mosiah 28:4.
3. Mosiah 3:19.
4. Mosiah 4:13.
5. Mosiah 4:16, 22.
6. Alma 24:7.
7. See 2 Nephi 5:18; Jacob 1:9–11.

ishing mission that it made possible, the sons of Mosiah were able, by following the pattern of powerful preaching and service set by their immediate fathers, to advance the work of their fathers further than ever before in converting rather than fighting the Lamanites. Mosiah, Benjamin, and Mosiah were all great and righteous monarchs who established peace and righteousness throughout their realm; if the sons of Mosiah refused the monarchy, it was to extend that same peace and righteousness to further realms—following the example of Abraham and helping to fulfil his covenant to bless all nations, as alluded to by King Benjamin when he said (quoting an angel) that "the knowledge of a Savior shall spread throughout every nation, kindred, tongue, and people."[1] And that Savior is, said King Benjamin, none other than "Jesus Christ,"[2] "the Lord Omnipotent who reigneth."[3] His reign was extended by the sons of Mosiah, who left their earthly kingdom to build the kingdom of God.

A PATTERN OF ANOTHER MONARCH TURNED MISSIONARY

Leaving behind a kingdom in order to minister was something the Lord himself would do, according to King Benjamin's quotation of the angelic message:

> The time cometh, and is not far distant, that with power, the Lord Omnipotent who reigneth, who was, and is from all eternity to all eternity, shall come down from heaven among the children of men, and shall dwell in a tabernacle of clay, and shall go forth amongst men, working mighty miracles.[4]

The description bears striking similarities to the Lamanite mission of Benjamin's grandsons, who likewise would leave their kingdom to go forth among men, working mighty miracles. But is it going too far to see in their mission a type of Christ? In that same speech by King Benjamin, he mentions "many signs, and wonders, and types, and shadows" that God has shown unto his people "concerning

1. Mosiah 3:20.
2. Mosiah 3:8, 17.
3. Mosiah 3:5.
4. Ibid.

[Christ's] coming."[1] While his immediate reference appears to be to the law of Moses, there seems to be no reason why the concept cannot be broader. Indeed, Benjamin himself, as discussed earlier, echoed the pattern of the ancient Melchizedek, himself a type of Christ. Furthermore, the Book of Mormon speaks repeatedly of types of Christ both within and without the law of Moses,[2] with the great prophet Nephi insisting that "all things which have been given of God from the beginning of the world, unto man, are the typifying of him."[3] And since such "things" include, according to Nephi's brother Jacob, historical events such as Abraham's offering of Isaac,[4] there is no reason that the mission of Mosiah's sons could not also typify Christ.

In fact, more parallels appear as the two stories are compared. King Benjamin (still quoting the angel) predicted that Christ "shall suffer temptations, and pain of body, hunger, thirst, and fatigue."[5] Using similar language, Mormon reports that during their mission among the Lamanites, the sons of Mosiah "had many afflictions; they did suffer much, both in body and in mind, such as hunger, thirst and fatigue, and also much labor in the spirit."[6] Furthermore, "they journeyed many days in the wilderness, and they fasted much and prayed much that the Lord would grant unto them a portion of his Spirit"[7]—foreshadowing the time when, as Matthew reports, Jesus would be "led up of the Spirit into the wilderness" and would there fast "forty days and forty nights."[8] The sons of Mosiah "had undertaken to preach the word of God to a . . . hardened and a ferocious people; a people who delighted in murdering";[9] so also Christ would go to preach to "the more wicked part of the world"[10] who would

---

1. Mosiah 3:15.
2. See Mosiah 13:31; Alma 13:16; 25:15; 33:19.
3. 2 Nephi 11:4.
4. See Jacob 4:5.
5. Mosiah 3:7.
6. Alma 17:5.
7. Alma 17:9.
8. Matthew 4:1–2.
9. Alma 17:14.
10. 2 Nephi 10:3.

"harden their hearts"[1] against him because they followed the devil, "a murderer from the beginning."[2] Despite the danger posed by the Lamanites, the sons of Mosiah fearlessly "entered into their houses and taught them, and . . . taught them in their streets; yea, and . . . taught them upon their hills; and . . . entered into their temples and their synagogues and taught them."[3] Christ also would teach his people in their houses and streets, on their hills and in their temple and synagogues.[4] The sons of Mosiah "suffered all manner of afflictions" as they were "cast out, and mocked, and spit upon, and smote upon [their] checks; and . . . stoned, and taken and bound with strong cords, and cast into prison,"[5] and scourged.[6] Christ would suffer similar things—the Book of Mormon prophets foretold that his people would "scourge him, and . . . smite him, and . . . spit upon him,"[7] and that he would be "mocked, and . . . cast out, and disowned";[8] these and similar afflictions that he suffered are recounted by the Gospel writers.[9] The sons of Mosiah were willing to suffer such hardships to bring the Lamanites "to the knowledge of the Lord their God," for "they could not bear that any human soul should perish";[10] so also Christ, in the words of King Benjamin, would come "unto his own, that salvation might come unto the children of men"[11] and would perform his atoning mission out of his great love for humanity.[12] The sons of Mosiah and their converts were filled with great and sometimes overpowering joy,[13] even as Christ spoke of his joy filling those who

1. 1 Nephi 22:5.
2. John 8:44.
3. Alma 26:29.
4. See, e.g., Matthew 4:23; 5:1–2; 8:5–15; 9:10, 35; 11:1; 13:1–2; 21:12–23.
5. Alma 26:29–30.
6. See Alma 23:2 (implying that they had been scourged).
7. 1 Nephi 19:9.
8. Mosiah 15:5.
9. See Luke 4:16–32; Matthew 13:54–58; John 8:59; Matthew 26:47–75; 27; Mark 14:43–72; 15; Luke 22:47–71; 23; John 18– 19.
10. Mosiah 28:2–3; Alma 17:9, 16.
11. Mosiah 3:9.
12. See Ether 12:33; also John 15:13.
13. See Alma 17:2, 29; 19:6, 13–14, 30; 21:21; 22:15; 25:17; 26:4, 10–11, 13, 16, 30, 35–37.

followed him.[1] Also, the sons of Mosiah achieved success because
they followed the pattern set by their forefathers and because they
were sustained by the faith of their father, whom the Lord had told
that "it shall be unto [them] according to thy faith";[2] so also Christ
would say that "My Father worketh hitherto, and I work,"[3] and "I
do nothing of myself; but as my Father hath taught me, I speak these
things. And he that sent me is with me; the Father hath not left me
alone."[4]

STANDING ON THE SHOULDERS OF GIANTS

Accordingly, the sons of Mosiah appear to typify not only the
mission of Christ, but also his relationship with the Father—an at-
tainment resulting not only from following the path of their fathers,
but also from building on the foundation laid by their fathers. And
even here they were following the example of their forefathers, each
father reaching further than the previous one. The first Mosiah was
the Lord's messenger to the people of Zarahemla; his son Benjamin
effected the profound cleansing and change of heart for every soul
of the combined peoples of Nephi and Zarahemla, thereby making
them free; his son Mosiah assured that they would be able to retain
that spiritual freedom when he terminated the monarchy and gave
them political freedom; and his sons the missionaries refused the
honor of an earthly kingdom to spread the kingdom of God among
the very people whose hatred and aggression had always threatened
their father's kingdom. The unprecedented accomplishments of Mosiah's sons were not theirs alone, but also their father's. One is reminded of what the incomparable Isaac Newton humbly remarked
about his unprecedented accomplishments: "If I have seen further it
is by standing on the shoulders of Giants."[5] Such should be our goal
as children, says Brigham Young:

---

1. See John 15:11; 17:13.
2. Alma 19:23 (here it is said of Ammon).
3. John 5:17.
4. John 8:28–29.
5. Fauvel et al. 1988:38 (reading "the" for "ye").

You may say to yourselves, "If I can do as well as my parents, I think I shall do well, and be as good as I want to be; and I should not strive to excel them." But if you do your duty you will far excel them in everything that is good— . . . for this is your privilege, and it becomes your duty.[1]

And such should be our goal for our children, as one modern expert on childhood education states: "*Our* goal in life" should be "for our children to stand on *our* shoulders and to start where *we* leave off."[2]

---

1. JD 2:18.
2. Doman 1984:101.

Chapter 4

KINGS OF
A NEPHITE
SPLINTER GROUP
• •
ZENIFF, NOAH, AND LIMHI

ZEALOUS KING ZENIFF

The brief depiction of three generations of kings ruling a Nephite splinter group stands out among the Book of Mormon's father-son portraits for two reasons. First, in its presentation of Zeniff and his son Noah, it breaks the general rule that good fathers tend to have good sons, or at least sons that finally turn out good. Second, it presents the only instance among the book's major father-son portraits of a good son, Limhi, coming from a bad father, Noah.

The story begins with the main body of the Nephites not long after arriving in the land of Zarahemla under the rule of the first King Mosiah. A certain Zeniff, who apparently had grown up[1] in the land of Nephi before the Nephites' departure,[2] was a soldier in the Nephite army sent to battle the Lamanites. In his own words, "[I was sent] that I might spy out their forces, that our army might come upon them and destroy them—but when I saw that which was good among them I was desirous that they should not be destroyed."[3]

---

1. See Mosiah 9:1.
2. See Omni 1:12.
3. Mosiah 9:1.

When Zeniff returned to camp and insisted that the Nephites make a treaty instead of war with the Lamanites, the Nephite general, "he being an austere and a blood-thirsty man," ordered the death of Zeniff. Fighting broke out, and Zeniff was "rescued by the shedding of much blood"[1] as the greater part of the Nephite army was killed in this internal strife. The survivors returned to Zarahemla.

"And yet," continues Zeniff,

> I being over-zealous to inherit the land of our fathers, collected as many as were desirous to go up to possess the land, and started again on our journey into the wilderness to go up to the land; but we were smitten with famine and sore afflictions; for we were slow to remember the Lord our God.[2]

If Zeniff is including himself, as he seems to be, among those who were slow to remember God, his very admission of the fact tends to indicate a later repentance. Perhaps, however, he speaks about the group as "we" because of his feeling of responsibility for them as their leader. As such he reports that when they finally arrived at the site of the prior conflict, Zeniff and "four of *my men*" entered a nearby Lamanite city to learn "the disposition of the king, and that I might know if I might go in with *my people* and possess the land in peace."[3]

Remarkably, the Lamanite king, whose name was Laman, offered not only to let them stay, but even to move some of his people out of the land of Nephi to make room for these Nephite newcomers; he even sealed the offer with a covenant. Only in retrospect did Zeniff discover that he had been deceived by the "cunning, and lying craftiness, and . . . fair promises"[4] of King Laman, who "yielded up the land that we might possess it," in order to "bring my people into bondage."[5] But one cannot judge the zealous Zeniff too harshly for his misjudgment; his overly optimistic assessment of Laman's response seems to have been occasioned by his zeal not only to possess

---

1. Mosiah 9:2.
2. Mosiah 9:3.
3. Mosiah 9:5, emphasis added.
4. Mosiah 10:18.
5. Mosiah 9:10.

the land, but also to see the best in the Lamanites, as when serving as a spy he had seen "that which was good among them"[1] and had insisted, even at the peril of his own life, that they not be destroyed.

Presumably after Zeniff's people moved on to their ancestral land now vacated by the Lamanites, Zeniff "was made a king by the voice of the people,"[2] and thus began his "reign in the land of Nephi."[3] King Zeniff and his people industriously restored Nephite civilization as they repaired the walls of the old cities, erected new buildings, reestablished agriculture, and all in all began to "multiply and prosper in the land."[4] In time their prosperity began to worry King Laman, "lest by any means [Zeniff's] people should wax [so] strong in the land" that the Lamanites "could not overpower them and bring them into bondage."[5] Finally showing his true colors, King Laman suddenly and without warning sent his people to battle the Nephites. The ensuing events presuppose that King Zeniff was a righteous man leading his people in the path of righteousness, for after arming themselves, King Zeniff and his people went to battle

> in the strength of the Lord . . . ; for I and my people did cry mightily to the Lord that he would deliver us out of the hands of our enemies, for we were awakened to a remembrance of the deliverance of our fathers.
>
> And God did hear our cries and did answer our prayers; and we did go forth in his might; yea, we did go forth against the Lamanites . . . until we had driven them out of our land.[6]

Significantly, King Zeniff and his people obtained divine deliverance by remembering "the deliverance of [their] fathers," a lesson repeated over and over throughout the Book of Mormon.

The number of Lamanites killed exceeded by more than one tenth the number of fallen Nephites, but the loss of even these occasioned

1. Mosiah 9:1.
2. Mosiah 7:9.
3. Mosiah 9:14.
4. Mosiah 9:9.
5. Mosiah 9:11.
6. Mosiah 9:17–18.

"great sorrow and lamentation"[1] on the part of King Zeniff and the rest of his people. Here was no hardened despot but a righteous ruler filled with compassion for his people.

Their victory was decisive enough that King Laman never again made war against them, allowing Zeniff's people to enjoy years of peace and prosperity even though they defensively stockpiled weapons, guarded their borders, and monitored Lamanite activities by a system of spies.[2] Only after King Laman's death did war again arise under his son and successor, who again sent the Lamanites to battle the Nephites. And once again a righteous King Zeniff led his people in righteousness. After hiding the women and children in the wilderness, Zeniff led into battle all his men capable of bearing arms. "We did go up in the strength of the Lord to battle,"[3] he recorded, and "I did stimulate them to go to battle with their might, putting their trust in the Lord."[4] Again the numerous Lamanite forces were driven out, this time with a slaughter so great that the dead were not counted. Zeniff finishes his record by telling that he "did confer the kingdom upon one of my sons; therefore, I say no more. And may the Lord bless my people. Amen."[5] King Zeniff's righteousness echoes that of *his* prior king, Mosiah,[6] and of the first Nephite king, Nephi himself, who may have been Zeniff's forefather.

WICKED KING NOAH

In expressing his final desire that his people be blessed, King Zeniff would hardly have done anything that he thought contrary to that end, such as choosing the wrong successor. Nor is it unreasonable to suppose that the son he chose would have been duly charged to follow the correct course, although we are not apprised of the matter, nor indeed are we told if or how Zeniff may have taught any of his sons. They at least had his conspicuously righteous example; and it

---

1. Mosiah 9:19.
2. See Mosiah 10:1–7.
3. Mosiah 10:10.
4. Mosiah 10:19.
5. Mosiah 10:22.
6. See Omni 1:12–23.

seems reasonable to suppose that a king who would take his people from a state of spiritual laxity (when they "were slow to remember the Lord [their] God"[1]) to righteousness (such that they could repeatedly at a moment's notice march to battle "in the strength of the Lord"[2]) would not neglect to teach his own sons the same principles of righteousness. This may also be hinted at in the name that Zeniff gave to the son who would succeed him—Noah.[3]

Following a custom found among the ancient Israelites and other peoples of the ancient Near East,[4] sons in the Book of Mormon were often given names that memorialized the circumstances of their birth, recalled their spiritual heritage, or expressed hope for the course of their lives. For example, one of Lehi's sons born in the wilderness was named Joseph,[5] recalling Lehi's recent discovery on the brass plates of his descent from the patriarch Joseph[6] and signaling that Joseph's ancient prophecies would be fulfilled through Lehi's posterity.[7] Helaman called his two sons Nephi and Lehi so they would remember and emulate their illustrious righteous ancestors who left Jerusalem.[8] And Mormon named his son Moroni,[9] after the early Nephite general whom Mormon so admired.[10]

Zeniff also had high hopes for his son, the one who would succeed him, when he named him Noah[11]—making him the only Nephite character in the Book of Mormon to bear the name of the ancient patriarch who survived the flood. The story of the ancient Noah would have been preserved on the brass plates, and his memory was very much alive in Nephite society, as seen in the preaching of Amulek

1. Mosiah 9:3.
2. Mosiah 9:17, 10:10, 19.
3. See Mosiah 11:1.
4. See AI 1:43–46.
5. See 1 Nephi 18:7.
6. See 1 Nephi 5:14–16.
7. See 2 Nephi 3.
8. See Helaman 3:21; 5:6–7.
9. See Mormon 6:6.
10. See Alma 48:11–18. That more such instances are not readily apparent to us probably reflects the fact that many Book of Mormon names are Egyptian in origin, as Hugh Nibley has shown. (See CWHN 5:25–34.)
11. See Mosiah 11:1.

whose passing and unintroduced reference to the ancient Noah shows that his story was familiar to Amulek's listeners.[1] Noah's receipt of the patriarchal priesthood, chronicled by Joseph Smith[2] and several ancient sources,[3] made Noah Adam's successor in kingship and gave him what Josephus called the "rulership,"[4] which surfaces in our traditional Genesis text after the flood when Noah receives the same dominion that Adam received.[5] In other words, Noah was made "equal [in] honor and kingship to Adam."[6] But Noah's most prominent personal characteristic was his exceeding righteousness, which the traditional Genesis text emphasizes when it describes Noah as "just" and "perfect"[7] (or, as most modern translations render it, "righteous" and "blameless"[8]), and even says that he "walked with God"[9] — a phrase which, as one scholar observes, "puts Noah on a par with Enoch, the only other named individual [in the Old Testament] to have walked with God."[10] A similar portrayal of Noah appears in apocryphal, pseudepigraphical, and early Christian sources, which depict him "as the exemplary righteous man of the past."[11] And besides being righteous himself, he also encouraged all others to follow the same path, so that the Apostle Peter described him as "a preacher of righteousness"[12] — a role described in greater detail in Joseph Smith's restored Genesis text[13] and in early Jewish and Christian tradition.[14]

When Zeniff conferred the name Noah on his son, then, he was apparently hoping that this son who would succeed him as king would

---

1. See Alma 10:22; also 3 Nephi 22:9; Ether 6:7.

2. See D&C 107:52; Abraham 1:2–4, 26.

3. See Combat of Adam III:V, in Malan 1882:148; and Cave of Treasures p. 104, in Budge 1927:104.

4. Jewish Antiquities I.iii.3, in *Josephus IV: Jewish Antiquities Books I–IV*.

5. See Genesis 9:1–2; Cassuto 1964:124–125; Westermann 1984:462.

6. Lewis 1978:54, citing Philo.

7. Genesis 6:9.

8. NJPS, NRSV, REB, NIV at Genesis 6:9.

9. Genesis 6:9.

10. Wenham 1987:170.

11. Lewis 1978:21, 101.

12. 2 Peter 2:5.

13. See Moses 8:19–20, 23–24.

14. See Lewis 1978:102; LJ I:153.

follow the pattern set by their ancient father Noah, himself a king[1] who had lived righteously and preached righteousness—even as Zeniff himself had done. Ironically, however, Zeniff's son Noah turned out to be one of the most wicked characters in Book of Mormon history.

Significantly, Mormon first points out Noah's departure from the path of his father in his description of King Noah's folly, which seems to indicate Mormon's awareness of the theme of fathers and sons:

> Zeniff conferred the kingdom upon Noah, one of his sons; therefore Noah began to reign in his stead; and he did not walk in the ways of his father.
>
> For behold, he did not keep the commandments of God, but he did walk after the desires of his own heart.[2]

King Noah's departure from the path of his father was not a simple case of forgetfulness or laxity but a deliberate and systematic effort that materially "changed the affairs of the kingdom" as he first "put down all the priests that had been consecrated by his father, and consecrated new ones in their stead, such as were lifted up in the pride of their hearts."[3] Surrounded by men of his own ilk who were dependent upon him for their position, he was free to do as he pleased, acquiring "many wives and concubines"[4] and "spen[ding] his time in riotous living" with them, as "did also his priests . . . with [their] harlots."[5] Thus "he did cause his people to commit sin, and do that which was abominable in the sight of the Lord" as "they did commit whoredoms and all manner of wickedness,"[6] including the sins of idolatry and wanton drunkenness.[7]

To finance such regal revelry, King Noah imposed a tax of twenty percent on all possessions so that he and his priests "were supported in their laziness, and in their idolatry, and in their whoredoms," and

---

1. On the nature of the patriarch Noah's kingship, see: D&C 107:40–52; Abraham 1:26–27.
2. Mosiah 11:1–2.
3. Mosiah 11:4–5.
4. Mosiah 11:2.
5. Mosiah 11:14.
6. Mosiah 11:2.
7. See Mosiah 11:7, 15; 12:35–37.

"thus did the people labor exceedingly to support iniquity."[1] Rich from the revenues extracted from his overtaxed people, Noah "placed his heart upon his riches"[2] and surrounded himself with opulence on a grand scale, erecting "many elegant and spacious buildings" exquisitely ornamented with the finest wood and most precious metals. His own residence was "a spacious palace" containing a highly decorated throne,[3] and he provided similar costly and gaudy seats for his priests, from where they could "speak lying and vain words to his people."[4] Little wonder, then, that the people "also became idolatrous, because they were deceived by the vain and flattering words of the king and priests."[5]

King Noah is not the only son in the Book of Mormon to deviate from the righteous path of his father; one thinks also of Laman and Lemuel, Alma the younger, and the sons of Mosiah. Unfortunately, Noah is one of the few who never reformed. He certainly had the opportunity when the prophet Abinadi boldly urged Noah's people to repent or suffer the wrath of God.[6] But when the report of Abinadi's preaching reached Noah, he angrily retorted:

> Who is Abinadi, that I and my people should be judged of him, or who is the Lord, that shall bring upon my people such great affliction?
>
>   I command you to bring Abinadi hither, that I may slay him.[7]

Thus, as Mormon comments, "King Noah hardened his heart against the word of the Lord, and he did not repent of his evil doings" — as was also the case with his people, who "sought from that time forward to take [Abinadi]."[8]

Abinadi could not be found, but his mission was not yet com-

---

1. Mosiah 11:6.
2. Mosiah 11:14.
3. Mosiah 11:8–9.
4. Mosiah 11:11.
5. Mosiah 11:7.
6. See Mosiah 11:20–25.
7. Mosiah 11:27–28.
8. Mosiah 11:29.

pleted. After two years he finally returned in disguise and resumed his preaching with added poignancy: Noah's people would be "brought into bondage," while "the life of king Noah [would] be valued even as a garment in a hot furnace"; and the only way to avoid such a fate was by repentance.[1] When Abinadi was brought before Noah, the king immediately sent him to prison and then counseled with his priests about what to do. If the king had had the benefit of wise councilors, the result might have been far different; but these men whom he had carefully selected for their compliance with his iniquity were to prove his undoing. They called for Abinadi and questioned him, but "he answered them boldly, and withstood all their questions, . . . and did confound them in all their words,"[2] as he told them plainly of their transgressions and need to reform.

Noah had heard enough: "Away with this fellow, and slay him; for what have we to do with him, for he is mad."[3] His reaction echoes that of the people who had heard the preaching of the ancient patriarch Enoch and accused him of being "a wild man."[4] When King Noah's priests "attempted to lay their hands" on Abinadi, they "durst not" because of the visibly luminous power that filled him[5] — again echoing what had transpired with Enoch when "no man laid hands on him; for fear came on all them that heard him."[6]

If Abinadi's experience recalled that of his antediluvian forefather Enoch, it also recalled that of his Israelite forefather Moses, as Mormon points out: Abinadi's face "shone with exceeding luster, even as Moses' did while in the mount of Sinai."[7] And this occurred, significantly, in the context of Abinadi speaking of the law of Moses and even quoting from the Decalogue, including the commandment to "honor thy father and thy mother."[8] The contrast is arresting: the

---

1. Mosiah 12:1–8.
2. Mosiah 12:19.
3. Mosiah 13:1.
4. Moses 6:38.
5. Mosiah 13:2–6.
6. Moses 6:39.
7. Mosiah 13:5.
8. Mosiah 13:20.

wicked King Noah who had departed from the path of his father was hearing the commandment to honor his father spoken by one who was honoring and even resembling their mutual Israelite forefather Moses. Then Abinadi pressed the theme of honoring one's father even further by testifying of the "Son of God," who would subject himself "to the will of the Father"[1] so that he — the Son — might become the father of those whose sins he had borne.[2] The implication for King Noah was obvious: if he persisted in dishonoring his righteous father by rejecting these truths, he would not be able to become a son of Christ.

It was too much to bear for King Noah. He summarily ordered Abinadi's death, which was temporarily diverted by the vigorous dissent of one of Noah's priests, Alma. But the king "was more wroth" and had Alma expelled, and then "sent his servants after him that they might slay him."[3]

Alma escaped to embark on a great mission of his own, but Abinadi's was now ending. He was sent to prison for three days and then summoned by King Noah, who demanded that he recant or die. Abinadi's resoluteness as he turned the tables by threatening Noah with dire consequences finally made an impression on the wicked king, who "was about to release him, for he feared his word; for he feared that the judgments of God would come upon him."[4] At this critical point, the only instance in the story when Noah shows any sign of change, his wicked priests truly proved his undoing, as they "lifted up their voices against" Abinadi, shouting, "He has reviled the king. Therefore," says the record, "the king was stirred up in anger against him," and had him executed by fire.[5]

Attempting to add to his murderous deeds, King Noah later sent his servants to destroy the group to whom Alma had been preaching in the wilderness; fortunately they all escaped.[6] But the pursuer soon

---

1. Mosiah 15:2.
2. See Mosiah 15:12.
3. Mosiah 17:3.
4. Mosiah 17:11.
5. Mosiah 17:12–13.
6. See Mosiah 18:32–35.

became the pursued as King Noah and his people fled before an advancing Lamanite army. He ordered the men to leave behind their wives and children and flee. Those that did escaped, but remorse caught up with them; and when their determination to return was countered by another commandment of Noah, "they were angry with the king, and caused that he should suffer, even unto death by fire."[1] He thus left his world in the way he had caused Abinadi to leave it, even as the dying prophet had foretold.[2]

Such an ignominious and tragic end to the son of a righteous father like Zeniff is as hard to comprehend as Laman's and Lemuel's refusal to follow Lehi's example. These isolated cases seem to be exceptions to the general rule, as illustrated over and over again in the Book of Mormon, that righteous parents who lovingly teach their children by example and word will eventually lead them to righteousness. This general rule has been more recently expressed by prophets of this dispensation. Quoting President Wilford Woodruff, President Harold B. Lee reiterated that "ninety-nine out of every hundred children who are taught by their parents the principles of honesty and integrity, truth and virtue, will observe them through life."[3] And quoting President Joseph F. Smith, President Lee similarly stated that "not one child in a hundred would go astray, if the home environment, example and training, were in harmony with the truth in the gospel of Christ."[4] If the exceptions, like King Noah, remind us of the reality of agency, the rule itself should encourage us never to give up on a child whose currently wrong course of conduct may, with continued parental guidance, prove to be temporary.

GOOD KING LIMHI

Perhaps the most surprising thing we learn about King Noah concerns *his* son, Limhi, who is introduced in the narrative in the same way Noah was — by contrasting him with his father. According

---

1. Mosiah 19:20.
2. See Mosiah 17:18.
3. Lee 1974b:82 (original in JD 15:12).
4. Lee 1974b:82 (original in Smith 1939:302).

to Mormon, Limhi had been "desirous that his father should not be destroyed; nevertheless, Limhi was not ignorant of the iniquities of his father, he himself being a just man."[1] Again, the introduction provided by Mormon reveals his own mindset; he appears to be much concerned with the theme of fathers and sons.

In the chaos that followed when the Lamanite army had descended on Noah and his people, many Nephites, Limhi among them, had been taken captive and restored to their land upon condition that they pay an annual tribute of fifty percent to the Lamanite king. Such was the context in which the people "conferred" the kingship upon the just Limhi,[2] and we are left to wonder if he was chosen merely because he had a claim—perhaps sole claim—to the throne, or if his being chosen was in some measure discretionary by a people abruptly brought back to their senses through adversity.

But the honor of kingship was a burden, not only because of the heavy annual tribute but also because of costly wars with and persecution by the Lamanites,[3] all resulting from the fact that his people had "not hearken[ed] unto the words of the Lord"[4] as delivered by Abinadi. No wonder their thoughts turned back to the land of Zarahemla. In fact, King Limhi dispatched a small group of men to search for it; they never located it but came upon a land covered with dry bones and ruins of buildings, where they discovered a record engraven in a strange language upon twenty-four plates of gold, which they brought back to Limhi.[5]

King Limhi had apparently relinquished hope of finding the people of Zarahemla when *they* found him by means of envoys from Zarahemla led by a certain Ammon. Limhi "was exceedingly glad," for he viewed these newcomers as deliverers.[6] The timing seems significant—it came after Limhi's people had "humble[d] themselves even to the dust" and, "in the depths of humility," cried "mightily

---

1. Mosiah 19:17.
2. Mosiah 19:26.
3. See Mosiah 20–21.
4. Mosiah 20:21.
5. See Mosiah 8:7–11; 21:26–27.
6. Mosiah 7:14–15.

to God . . . all the day long . . . that he would deliver them out of their afflictions."[1] The Lord had gradually lightened their burdens[2] and had now sent their brethren from Zarahemla to help deliver them and lead them back to the main body of Nephites.

King Limhi immediately called together his people, and what he told them reveals a realistic but righteous king drawing on his knowledge of the scriptures (or at least scriptural traditions) as he urges his people to exercise the same liberating faith as did their fathers of old:

> O ye, my people, lift up your heads and be comforted; for behold, the time is at hand, or is not far distant, when we shall no longer be in subjection to our enemies, notwithstanding our many strugglings, which have been in vain; yet I trust there remaineth an effectual struggle to be made.
>
> Therefore, lift up your heads, and rejoice, and put your trust in God, in that God who was the God of Abraham, and Isaac, and Jacob; and also, that God who brought the children of Israel out of the land of Egypt, and caused that they should walk through the Red Sea on dry ground, and fed them with manna that they might not perish in the wilderness; and many more things did he do for them.
>
> And again, that same God has brought our fathers out of the land of Jerusalem, and has kept and preserved his people even until now; and behold, it is because of our iniquities and abominations that he has brought us into bondage.[3]

King Limhi thus urges his people to do what they had done under his grandfather, Zeniff—to remember the divine deliverance of their fathers in order to exercise the faith necessary to obtain deliverance themselves. Limhi then proceeded to rehearse the circumstances of how Zeniff had been deceived by the crafty King Laman; how much of their own blood had "been spilt in vain"; and how even now they were suffering "grievous" and "great" affliction because of the heavy tribute to the Lamanites—"and all because of iniquity."[4]

---

1. Mosiah 21:13–14.
2. See Mosiah 21:15–16.
3. Mosiah 7:18–20.
4. Mosiah 7:23–24.

For if this people had not fallen into transgression the Lord would not have suffered that this great evil should come upon them. But behold, they would not hearken unto his words. . . .

And a prophet of the Lord have they slain; yea, a chosen man of God, who told them of their wickedness and abominations, and prophesied of many things which are to come, yea, even the coming of Christ.

And because he said unto them that Christ . . . should come down among the children of men, and take upon him flesh and blood, and go forth upon the face of the earth—

And now, because he said this, they did put him to death; and many more things did they do which brought down the wrath of God upon them.[1]

What Limhi says reveals much about the man; equally revealing, perhaps, is what he does not say. Conspicuously absent from his remarks is the single most important cause of the people's iniquity and suffering, and the one point to which both Alma (in the wilderness)[2] and King Mosiah (in Zarahemla)[3] would later call attention in summarizing the history of this Nephite splinter group: that the primary cause of this people's folly was a wicked king, Noah. We have seen before in the Book of Mormon the compassion and anguish of a father (Lehi) over lost sons (Laman and Lemuel);[4] we now sense in Limhi the grief of a righteous son for his lost father (Limhi's compassionate nature is attested by his grieving for the afflictions of his people[5]). Limhi's filial grief apparently prevents him from even mentioning his father's name, especially when he must now quote scripture and demonstrate to his people the fate of the wicked:

For behold, the Lord hath said: I will not succor my people in the day of their transgression; but I will hedge up their ways that they prosper not; and their doings shall be as a stumbling block before them.

And again, he saith: If my people shall sow filthiness they

1. Mosiah 7:25–28.
2. See Mosiah 23:12.
3. See Mosiah 29:17–20.
4. See 1 Nephi 8:4, 36–38.
5. See Mosiah 8:7.

> shall reap the chaff thereof in the whirlwind; and the effect
> thereof is poison.
>
> And again he saith: If my people shall sow filthiness they
> shall reap the east wind, which bringeth immediate destruc-
> tion.
>
> And now, behold, the promise of the Lord is fulfilled, and
> ye are smitten and afflicted.[1]

Nevertheless, Limhi holds out to his people this conditional promise of deliverance:

> But if ye will turn to the Lord with full purpose of heart,
> and put your trust in him, and serve him with all diligence of
> mind, if ye do this, he will, according to his own will and
> pleasure, deliver you out of bondage.[2]

Limhi himself led the way in righteousness by "enter[ing] into a
covenant with God . . . to serve him and keep his commandments";
and many of his people did the same.[3] Indeed, they "were desirous
to be baptized as a witness and a testimony that they were willing to
serve God with all their hearts."[4] Nevertheless, "there was none in
the land that had authority from God. . . . Therefore they did not at
that time form themselves into a church, waiting upon the Spirit of
the Lord."[5]

One of the first things King Limhi did after addressing his people
was ask if Ammon could interpret the twenty-four gold plates. Ammon could not, but Limhi was delighted to learn that the Nephite
king back in Zarahemla, Mosiah, had a gift from God allowing the
interpretation of unknown languages, whereupon Limhi exclaimed:

> Doubtless a great mystery is contained within these plates,
> and these interpreters were doubtless prepared for the purpose
> of unfolding all such mysteries to the children of men.
>
> O how marvelous are the works of the Lord, and how long

---

1. Mosiah 7:29–32.
2. Mosiah 7:33.
3. Mosiah 21:32.
4. Mosiah 21:35.
5. Mosiah 21:33–34.

doth he suffer with his people; yea, and how blind and impenetrable are the understandings of the children of men; for they will not seek wisdom, neither do they desire that she should rule over them!

Yea, they are as a wild flock which fleeth from the shepherd, and scattereth, and are driven, and are devoured by the beasts of the forest.[1]

Once again we see a righteous King Limhi, this time bemoaning the past blindness of his own people.

While "waiting upon the Spirit of the Lord,"[2] King Limhi and his people began plans to escape; and escape they finally did. Led by Ammon, they eventually arrived at Zarahemla, where they all became the subjects of King Mosiah, who "received them with joy."[3] Not long afterward, Alma — King Noah's dissident priest — also arrived in Zarahemla[4], whereupon King Mosiah called together all his subjects and had the records of Limhi and Alma read aloud.[5] Then Mosiah had Alma speak, and Alma

preach[ed] unto the people repentance and faith on the Lord.

And he did exhort the people of Limhi and his brethren, all those that had been delivered out of bondage, that they should remember that it was the Lord that did deliver them.

And it came to pass that after Alma had taught the people many things, and had made an end of speaking to them, that king Limhi was desirous that he might be baptized; and all his people were desirous that they might be baptized also.

Therefore, Alma did go forth into the water and did baptize them; . . . and as many as he did baptize did belong to the church of God; and this because of their belief on the words of Alma.[6]

So life is full of surprises. As a righteous young man seeing the

---

1. Mosiah 8:19–21.
2. Mosiah 21:34.
3. Mosiah 22:14.
4. See Mosiah 24:25.
5. See Mosiah 25.
6. Mosiah 25:15–18.

gross iniquity of his father and his father's priests, Limhi could hardly have dreamed that one of those same priests would one day baptize him! And no less surprising from our standpoint is the righteous course of Limhi himself, who had the benefit of no good example or teaching from his immediate father, having to look instead to his earlier fathers, like Zeniff. Indeed, Limhi stands out as the only son among Book of Mormon father-son portraits to do good despite a bad father. Not having the benefit of a good father, he nevertheless chose to be one himself—and thereby followed the example of his own ancient forefather Abraham, of whom Limhi had made mention to his people.[1] Abraham's father, like Limhi's, had been idolatrous, murderous, and in some accounts part of a royal entourage;[2] but Abraham, like his descendant Limhi, looked to and followed the righteous example of earlier fathers.[3] That same kind of ancestral example, particularly that of Abraham himself—whose works the Lord has commanded the Latter-day Saints to do[4]—beckons each of us today, whether or not blessed with immediate parents who are obedient. This is precisely the role that Abraham was designed to play when he was promised that all who "receive this Gospel shall be called after thy name, and shall be accounted thy seed, and shall rise up and bless thee, as their father."[5]

---

1. See Mosiah 7:19.
2. See Abraham 1:5–7, 30; 2:5; LJ I:186–203.
3. See Abraham 1:2–4.
4. See D&C 132:32.
5. Abraham 2:10.

Chapter 5

POWERFUL PREACHERS AND RIGHTEOUS RECORD KEEPERS

••••••••••••••••••••••••••••••••

ALMA, ALMA THE YOUNGER, AND HIS SONS

ALMA THE ELDER

In the entire Book of Mormon there is no more vivid illustration of the enduring effect of righteous parenting than that evidenced in the line of powerful preachers and righteous record keepers spanning approximately two centuries, beginning about 150 B.C. with Alma and including his son Alma, *his* son Helaman, *his* son Helaman, *his* son Nephi, *his* son Nephi, and *his* son Jonas. And that this amazing line of men could begin with an initially wicked character — Alma — strikingly demonstrates that nearly anyone in any circumstance can, with enough commitment, become a righteous parent and thereby righteously influence generations to come. The pattern is somewhat similar to the life of Abraham who, although never a wicked man, nevertheless broke with the idolatrous tradition of his immediate fathers to exert a profoundly righteous influence on future generations.[1]

As to the father of the first Alma we are told nothing, which may

1. See Abraham 1–2; LJ I:185–217.

107

mean either that Mormon had no such information at his disposal or, if he did, that Alma's father was not a righteous man, for in introducing illustrious figures into the narrative Mormon is prone to note those occasions when they fail to conform to the ways of a righteous father. What we do know for sure about Alma is that while yet a "young man"[1] he had risen – some would say fallen – to be one of the wicked priests of the infamous King Noah. They and their king are collectively portrayed as steeped in great wickedness, and there is not a shred of evidence that Alma was different from the others. They were idolatrous, profligate, vain, and vaunting.[2] The critical difference between Alma and his cronies was in their reaction to the words of the prophet Abinadi; and one cannot help but be impressed that it took just one audience with that prophet – one "missionary lesson" – to persuade Alma to change. Even before that session was over, Alma was pleading – albeit in vain – for Abinadi's life![3] Alma's audacity wrought a dramatic change in his fortune as he suddenly found his own life threatened by the king. Alma fled, and when he had reached safety, "he being concealed for many days did write all the words which Abinadi had spoken."[4] This passion to commit to writing words of inspiration would carry on throughout his life and the lives of his progeny.

The next thing we read of him is that he "repented of his sins and iniquities,"[5] or, as he later elaborated, he underwent "sore repentance" and "much tribulation" accompanied by fervent prayer.[6] But reforming his own life was just the beginning of his concern, for he immediately "went about privately among the people, and began to teach the words of Abinadi."[7] Here again we see the first of a fervent endeavor that would run throughout the rest of his life and the lives of his descendants – a passion to preach the word of God.

---

1. Mosiah 17:2.
2. See Mosiah 11.
3. See Mosiah 17:2.
4. Mosiah 17:4.
5. Mosiah 18:1.
6. Mosiah 23:9–10.
7. Mosiah 18:1.

These two governing themes — preaching and recordkeeping — are but the first of various facets of Alma's life that will prove to be prototypical for his posterity. Significantly, these two themes also echo the lives of many of Alma's righteous forefathers like Nephi, Abraham,[1] Enoch,[2] and Adam.[3]

The power of Alma's preaching may be judged by the fact that, despite an oppressive government that forced him and his followers into secrecy, "many did believe his words"[4] and were baptized by him, he "having authority from the Almighty God"[5] to baptize. Where in the world (or from another world!) he obtained that authority is not apparent, since there seems to have been no one else in the entire realm who had it.[6] An already corrupt king surrounding himself by supporters had newly appointed all of the king's priests, replacing the legitimate priests. King Noah went so far as to consecrate them himself.[7]

One possible explanation for Alma's priesthood authority is that Alma had received it sometime prior to his becoming King Noah's priest.[8] That seems unlikely, however, in light of Alma's young age even when Abinadi arrived, and because no one else in the realm ended up with the same authority. Moreover, even if Alma had once received the authority, his exceeding wickedness would probably have terminated it. More likely, Alma received the authority from a divine messenger (the same as other worthy mortals at times have received it in circumstances far away from any other authorized mortal[9]). That would also explain why Alma himself needed to be baptized with his people,[10] the same as Joseph Smith and Oliver Cowdery were baptized

---

1. See Abraham 1–2.
2. See Moses 6.
3. See Moses 5–6.
4. Mosiah 18:3.
5. Mosiah 18:13.
6. See Mosiah 21:33.
7. See Mosiah 11:4–6.
8. See Smith 1963:4:161–64.
9. See, e.g., D&C 84:12–13; JS–H 1:66–72.
10. See Mosiah 18:14–15. Another explanation has been offered: see Smith 1960:3:203–4.

after they had received the (Aaronic) priesthood from the hands of a divine messenger.[1] If Alma did indeed receive his authority directly from a divine messenger, it would be yet another foreshadowing of his descendants who would likewise be visited by divine messengers.

From whatever source Alma received his authority, he exercised it to ordain other priests and establish and preside over the church[2] (and was thenceforth remembered as the "founder" of the Nephite church[3]), just as his descendants would likewise preside over and continuously add to the organization of the same church. Even so, Alma considered himself merely "an instrument in [the Lord's] hands in bringing so many . . . to a knowledge of his truth."[4] He was also an instrument in leading them away into the wilderness and out of danger when the Lord warned him that King Noah's armies would come upon them[5] — following the pattern, of course, of his own fathers (Alma was a descendant of Nephi[6]): Lehi had led his family out of corrupt Jerusalem and later described his son Nephi as "an instrument in the hands of God, in bringing us forth into the land of promise";[7] and Nephi had later led his people away into the wilderness when the Lord had warned him to flee.[8]

Other variations on the father-son motif that so predominates in this story are seen in what Alma's instrumentality accomplishes: his people "became the children of God"[9] and immediately set out to follow an ancient ancestral political pattern rather than the monarchical tradition. Thus when Alma's people out of love for their leader wished to make him king, he declined by explaining the Lord's commandment that "ye shall not esteem one flesh above another"[10] — a

---

1. See JS–H 1:66–72, obviously breaking the usual pattern of baptism preceding any priesthood ordination.
2. See Mosiah 18:17–18; 23:15–18.
3. See Mosiah 23:16.
4. Mosiah 23:10.
5. See Mosiah 23:1.
6. See Mosiah 17:2.
7. 2 Nephi 1:24.
8. See 2 Nephi 5:5.
9. Mosiah 18:22.
10. Mosiah 23:7.

response demonstrating the long spiritual distance he had so quickly traveled from the power and opulence he enjoyed as one of King Noah's priests! The equality that prevailed among Alma's people arose from their spiritual condition, for they were taught that

> there should be no contention one with another, but that they should look forward with one eye, having one faith and one baptism, having their hearts knit together in unity and in love one towards another.[1]

But this equality extended to things temporal as well, as they were also commanded to "impart of their substance, every one according to that which he had,"[2] so that all received "according to their needs and their wants."[3] This echoes the order of Zion established by their ancient father Enoch, whose people likewise "were of one heart and one mind, and dwelt in righteousness; and there was no poor among them."[4] Alma's role as the administrator of Zion also foreshadowed the role his descendant Nephi would have with the other apostles in administering the Nephite Zion society on a much larger scale following the appearance of the resurrected Lord.[5]

What Alma's people didn't count on was that they would be forced to reenact yet another ancestral pattern, this time the bondage and Exodus of their ancient Israelite fathers. As the Israelites had experienced "bondage"[6] in Egypt, so Alma's people were "brought into bondage"[7] by a powerful Lamanite army. As the Egyptian overlords "set over [the Israelites] taskmasters to afflict them with their burdens,"[8] so the overlord's of Alma's people "put tasks upon them, and put task-masters over them," and "great were their afflictions" and their "burdens."[9] The Israelites had "sighed by reason of the bondage,

---

1. Mosiah 18:21.
2. Mosiah 18:27.
3. Mosiah 18:29.
4. Moses 7:18.
5. See Mosiah 18:21; 3 Nephi 28:23; 4 Nephi 1:2–19.
6. Exodus 1:14.
7. Mosiah 23:23.
8. Exodus 1:11.
9. Mosiah 24:9, 10, 14.

and . . . cried, and their cry came up unto God," who "heard their groaning, and . . . remembered his covenant with Abraham, with Isaac, and with Jacob."[1] In like manner, Alma's people in their afflictions "began to cry mightily to God," and when forced to stop yet continued to "pour out their hearts to him,"[2] for "none could deliver them but the Lord their God, yea, even the God of Abraham and Isaac and of Jacob."[3] In both cases, in other words, present deliverance derived from remembering the ancient Abrahamic covenant, as Nephi (son of Lehi) wrote of his forefather Israelites: God "covenanted with . . . Abraham, Isaac, and Jacob; and he remembered the covenants which he had made; wherefore, he did bring them out of the land of Egypt."[4] But since, as Moroni (son of Mormon) taught, the Lord "workest unto the children of men according to their faith"[5] and not "until after they [have] had faith in him,"[6] apparently in each case the Lord remembered his ancient covenant to Abraham only after Abraham's posterity remembered and emulated the faith of their father.

Yet other parallels between Alma's people and their enslaved Israelite ancestors are observable. As the Israelites were instructed to observe Passover in anticipation of their deliverance the following day,[7] so the glad word finally came to Alma's people that "on the morrow I will deliver you out of bondage."[8] As the Israelites were able to leave only by the divine intervention of plagues on the Egyptians,[9] so Alma's people were able to leave only with the divine intervention of a "deep sleep" that befell their overlords.[10] As the Israelites departed with their flocks,[11] so did Alma's people.[12] As Moses

---

1. Exodus 2:23–24.
2. Mosiah 24:10, 12.
3. Mosiah 23:23. This is Mormon's comment.
4. 1 Nephi 17:40.
5. Ether 12:29.
6. Ether 12:7.
7. See Exodus 12.
8. Mosiah 24:16.
9. See Exodus 7–13.
10. Mosiah 24:19.
11. See Exodus 12:32.
12. See Mosiah 24:18.

marched at the head of the Israelites while "God led the people about, through the way of the wilderness,"[1] so Alma was told, "Thou shalt go before this people, and I will go with thee," and thus God "led their way in the wilderness."[2] And as the Egyptians pursued the Israelites but were stopped by divine intervention,[3] so Alma was forewarned at a certain place in the wilderness to flee from their Lamanite pursuers, whom the Lord would stop.[4] Clearly Mormon's account, taken from the records of Alma, was patterned after the Old Testament Exodus account—as was Nephi's account of his family's departure out of Jerusalem.

If Alma's people had to remember the divine deliverance from bondage of their Israelite forefathers to effect their own deliverance, Alma's people and their posterity were thenceforth exhorted to particularly remember this more recent deliverance,[5] even though—or perhaps because—they were now safely rejoined to the main Nephite body at Zarahemla under King Mosiah. The king, however, promptly turned over to Alma the authority over the church in the entire realm.[6] When transgressors were brought for judgment before the king, he simply turned them over to Alma, who was troubled over the matter and "poured out his whole soul to God" for assistance.[7]

The Lord's response went beyond answering the specific request by Alma, who was told that his people were blessed because of their "exceeding faith in the words alone which thou hast spoken unto them," and that Alma himself was blessed for his ministry—blessed, indeed, with the ultimate blessing, even a covenant that "thou shalt have eternal life."[8] In the meantime, however, Alma was commanded to continue his labors and gather the Lord's sheep, who would ultimately be granted a place at God's right hand. An altogether different

---

1. Exodus 13:18.
2. Mosiah 24:17, 20.
3. See Exodus 14.
4. See Mosiah 24:23.
5. See Mosiah 25:16.
6. See Mosiah 25:19; 26:6–8.
7. Mosiah 26:14.
8. Mosiah 26:16–20.

destiny, however, awaited those who would not hearken to Alma; they would ultimately be consigned to "everlasting fire prepared for the devil and his angels."[1] As to the transgressors, Alma would judge them (yet another echo of Moses, who judged Israel[2]); they who confessed and sincerely repented would be forgiven, while they who did not would not be numbered among the Lord's people.[3] This revelation was, predictably, recorded by Alma,[4] who again manifests a passion for recording heavenly words vouchsafed to mortals. Then Alma went to work again, first to deal with the transgressors and then to teach the word with his "fellow laborers" despite much affliction and persecution by unbelievers.[5]

In all this are patterns that will be followed by Alma's posterity, who will likewise convince many of the truth despite occasionally heavy opposition, who will preside over the church assisted by fellow laborers, who will receive the guarantee of eternal life, and who will receive and record many revelations.

The one painful thing about the otherwise comforting revelation to Alma was the description of the awful fate of the transgressors who refused to repent. For among that group was, alas, his own son to whom he had given his own name. It is the first instance in the Book of Mormon of the ancient Israelite practice of naming a son after his father.[6] Ironically, Alma the younger was one of the most rebellious sons in the Book of Mormon.

THE FAITH OF A FATHER AND THE COURSE OF HIS SON

Alma's grief for his son is more than that of a righteous father over a wayward son; it includes also the pain and irony of a once-wayward but now-reformed father seeing his former self in his own son, who is described as "a very wicked and an idolatrous man,"

---

1. Mosiah 26:27.
2. See Exodus 18.
3. See Mosiah 26:29–32.
4. See Mosiah 26:33.
5. Mosiah 26:38.
6. See AI 1:45; Fitzmeyer (AB 28) 1981:380. The practice was less common than that of naming a son after a grandfather, but it is attested in several ancient sources.

gifted with words and "speak[ing] much flattery to the people."[1] The portrait is identical to that of his father as a young man, who, as one of Noah's wicked priests, had engaged in "abominable" and "idolatrous" practices and had used "lying and vain words" to speak "flattering things" to the people.[2] Such marked similarity leads us to inquire if the younger Alma was perhaps influenced by his wayward father before the father reformed. Was the son even alive at the time his father reformed? The chronology suggested in the notes of the current edition of the Book of Mormon would make Alma, who is expressly described as "a young man,"[3] about twenty-five years old at the time Abinadi appeared before King Noah.[4] It seems more probable than not that by that age Alma would have been married, although even this is open to question because he and the other priests spent much time with harlots.[5] Even assuming that Alma was married, his age at the time would make it unlikely that his first-born child would have been more than about eight years old. Nor are we even sure that Alma the younger was the first-born; all we are told is that he was "one of the sons of Alma."[6] Accordingly, even if Alma the younger was alive before his father reformed, the child would likely have been young enough to be impressed by the dramatic delivery from bondage of Alma's close-knit group of followers. Thus, Alma the younger's bad behavior was probably not modeled directly after that of his father.

But did the reformed Alma ever directly teach his son? We have no express record of such in the book of Mosiah, but later Alma the younger does disclose that he had heard his father prophesy to the people about the coming of Christ.[7] Moreover, we could hardly imag-

---

1. Mosiah 27:8.

2. See Mosiah 11:1–15.

3. Mosiah 17:2.

4. Alma died at age 82 in 91 B.C. (Mosiah 29:44–46). If the suggested chronology of 148 B.C. for Abinadi's appearance before King Noah is accurate or close, Alma must have been about 25 at the time (91 + 82 = 173; 173 – 148 = 25).

5. See Mosiah 11:14.

6. Mosiah 27:8.

7. See Alma 36:17.

ine Alma receiving the divine assurance of eternal life[1] had he failed in his parental duty. All of this makes Alma the younger's behavior even more baffling. The most plausible explanation seems to be simply that the young man was growing up in that "rising generation" in Zarahemla who "did not believe the [righteous] tradition of their fathers,"[2] and he seems to have been swept up in the tide of the times. Such a problem in fact seems to be the perennial predicament of human society. Ralph Waldo Emerson's essay on "Education" asserts that "it is very certain that the coming age and the departing age seldom understand each other."[3] And in the Russian novelist Ivan Turgenev's classic *Father and Sons,* a son tells his mother, "Of course you can't understand me. We belong to different generations." As one literary critic comments, "the conflict between generations" depicted in Turgenev's novel is "apparently an inherent problem in human nature."[4]

Regardless of how we try to explain Alma the younger's behavior, it clearly—and for his father, painfully—mirrored that of his father as a young man. However, the young Alma went one step further: he set out to destroy what his father had, since his reformation, dedicated his life to build. Thus he "led many of the people to do after the manner of his iniquities" and "became a great hinderment to the prosperity of the church of God; stealing away the hearts of the people" and "causing much dissension," thereby "giving a chance for the enemy of God to exercise his power over them." Simply put, Alma the younger "was going about to destroy the church of God."[5]

Such obstinate opposition to everything for which one's own father had worked for so long and so hard would have been enough to raise the wrath of most fathers. Not so with Alma, who despite his son's obdurate rebellion "prayed with much faith concerning" him[6] and even enlisted the prayers of other righteous people to the

---

1. See Mosiah 26:20.
2. Mosiah 26:1.
3. Emerson 1904:136.
4. Matlaw 1989:268.
5. Mosiah 27:8–10.
6. Mosiah 27:14.

same end. The profound depth of Alma's faith can best be judged by its astonishing result: As the young man and his friends (including the sons of Mosiah)

> were going about rebelling against God, behold, the angel of the Lord appeared unto them; and he descended as it were in a cloud; and he spake as it were with a voice of thunder, which caused the earth to shake upon which they stood;
>
> And so great was their astonishment, that they fell to the earth.[1]

The angel then singled out Alma the younger, commanding him by name to "arise and stand forth, for why persecutest thou the church of God?"[2] The angel made it crystal clear that this dramatic visit and invitation to reform was being afforded to Alma solely because of the faith of his father, and that to reform he must "remember the captivity of [his] fathers," and "remember how great things [God had] done for them; for they were in bondage and he . . . delivered them."[3]

The last thing Alma the younger heard the angel speak was a final warning to cease persecuting the church, "even if thou wilt of thyself be cast off."[4] So great was his "astonishment" that he lapsed into apparent unconsciousness,[5] even though his spirit remained keenly aware of things in a different realm. In his own words, "I was racked with eternal torment, for my soul was harrowed up to the greatest degree and racked with all my sins."[6] The excruciating pain is poignantly communicated by his repeated use of a verb translated into English as *rack,* whose primary meaning is "to torture on the rack; inflict pain or punishment by pulling or straining."[7] The idea graphically conveys his suffering: The mere thought of seeing God, he explained, "did rack my soul with inexpressible horror," causing

---

1. Mosiah 27:11–12.
2. Mosiah 27:13.
3. Mosiah 27:16.
4. Mosiah 27:16.
5. See Mosiah 27:19.
6. Alma 36:12.
7. WTNID 1871. This is not to suggest that the rack or its use was known among the Nephites.

a longing for extinction of both body and soul; "for three days and for three nights was I racked, even with the pains of a damned soul"; and again, he wrote, "As I was thus racked with torment."[1]

As one of the most impressive witnesses in the entire Book of Mormon to the importance of the parent-child relationship, Alma the younger found no relief from his excruciating pain until he "remembered also to have heard [his] father prophesy . . . concerning the coming of one Jesus Christ, a Son of God,"[2] to whom he immediately began to cry for mercy. Significantly, it was from his own father that Alma the Younger had learned of another Son, the Son of God — recalling Nephi's similar experience of learning of Christ from Lehi.

Alma the Younger's cry for mercy brought a miraculous transformation as his pain was replaced by a "joy as exceeding as was [his] pain!" And, he said, "Oh, what joy, and what marvelous light I did behold," so that "there can be nothing so exquisite and sweet as was my joy."[3] He even beheld the same scene that father Lehi had beheld — God sitting upon his throne, surrounded by the heavenly hosts.[4]

In the meantime, the limp body of Alma the younger had been carried before his grateful father, who "rejoiced, for he knew that it was the power of God."[5] Assembling the other priests, Alma directed that they all unitedly fast and pray; two[6] (or three[7]) days later the young man revived, stood up, and declared that he had been converted! For such a transformation his father, Alma, had prayed — the angel himself said it — "with much faith."[8] And although there is no mention of it here, one cannot help but recall a prior difficult and seemingly inexplicable experience in Alma's own life, when he and his righteous converts, having already forsaken not only their sins but also their homes for the truth, and having built a new city where

---

1. Alma 36:14–17.
2. Alma 36:17.
3. Alma 36:20–21.
4. Alma 36:22.
5. Mosiah 27:20.
6. Mosiah 27:23.
7. Alma 36:10.
8. Mosiah 27:14.

they could practice the principles of Zion,[1] were suddenly surrounded by a Lamanite army and brought into bondage. Why? Certainly not for their sins, for they had forsaken them. Mormon's passing comment on the matter offered no full explanation either as he simply noted that "the Lord seeth fit to chasten his people; yea, he trieth their patience and their faith."[2] Now, many years down the road and with the benefit of hindsight, Alma's prayers of "much faith" for his son may help to illuminate his own difficult experience of being brought into bondage: Would he ever have developed the faith necessary to pray down an angel from heaven to save his son if he had not known the faith-deepening adversity of his experience in bondage? And if it took such a difficult experience to develop the faith necessary to one day save his son, would he not have looked back and deemed it all worthwhile?

As soon as the newly reformed Alma the younger stood on his feet, he declared that he was a new man, having repented and been redeemed, even "born of the Spirit" and "born of God" — as all must do, he said, who would inherit the kingdom of God, for they can only do so if they have first become God's "sons and daughters." No fewer than four times, Alma the younger speaks of being born of God,[3] explaining that he had never had the experience before because he had "denied that which had been spoken of by [his] fathers" about the Redeemer.[4] Thus the entire experience turned on father-son relationships: his trouble in the first place came by rejecting the truth preached by his fathers, but the faith of his father called down divine intervention; he was told that to reform he must remember the captivity and deliverance of his fathers; even so, his excruciating pain continued until he remembered what his father had said about a Son, by whose grace Alma the younger himself became reborn as a new son, a son of God, and thereby was allowed to see what his ancient father Lehi had seen.

---

1. See Mosiah 18:21–22, 27; 23:15.
2. Mosiah 23:21.
3. Mosiah 27:24–25, 28.
4. Mosiah 27:30.

As the young Alma's intense pain was turned into joy, so his former zeal for evil was redirected for good. Having followed his father's path of "sore repentance,"[1] Alma the younger now continued in the path of his father by "zealously" preaching the word of God in the face of great persecution and opposition, thereby becoming precisely what his father had become: a divine instrument in "bringing many to the knowledge of the truth."[2] The similarities between father and son increase when Alma the younger becomes a record keeper by receiving the entire library of Nephite records from King Mosiah, along with a charge to "keep and preserve them, and also keep a record of the people."[3] Alma conferred the office of high priest upon Alma the younger, who was also appointed to be the first chief judge, again echoing his father's prior role as leader of the community in the wilderness. Finally, the son also succeeded his father as the presiding authority in the church. We are not told of Alma's feelings when he gave his son "charge concerning all the affairs of the church,"[4] but the occasion must have stirred the father's deepest feelings as he victoriously came to the end of his long and faithful ministry and could now be succeeded by this worthy son whose reformation he had been instrumental in effecting. Alma was respectfully referred to among the Nephites as "the founder of their church,"[5] but he should most be remembered as the founder of a righteous posterity who would significantly serve the church. Indeed, the most important convert Alma ever made was his own son — recalling George Durrant's premise that the time a father spends with his children *is* church work,[6] and recalling further President Harold B. Lee's counsel to fathers that "the most important of the Lord's work that you will ever do will be the work you do within the walls of your own home."[7]

---

1. Mosiah 23:9.
2. See Mosiah 27:32–37.
3. Mosiah 28:20.
4. Mosiah 29:42.
5. Mosiah 23:16; 29:47.
6. See Durrant 1976:27–31.
7. Lee 1973:7.

THE MINISTRY OF ALMA THE YOUNGER AFTER HIS FATHER'S DEATH

The lengthy and detailed record of Alma the younger's ministry, made by Mormon "according to the record of Alma [the younger],"[1] is itself evidence of how zealously he not only fulfilled King Mosiah's charge to keep the record[2] but also followed his father's example of recordkeeping. And what that record shows is that the theme of fathers and sons is as prominent in the ministry of Alma the younger as it was in that of his father. Like his father, Alma the younger and his fellow laborers endured much persecution in their preaching and ministry.[3] Nevertheless, also like his father, the son tried to establish in the church the principles of a Zion society wherein "they were all equal" and "did impart of their substance, every man according to that which he had."[4] Meanwhile, the unbelievers indulged in diverse kinds of wickedness which brought God's judgments and forced the younger Alma to do what his father had never had to do—take up arms and lead the Nephites in defense of their lands and liberties, and all because of the Lamanites' "incorrect traditions" handed down by their fathers.[5] A similar role of military leader would fall to Alma the younger's son Helaman.

When the heavy Nephite losses incurred during the war were duly recognized as "the judgments of God sent upon them because of their wickedness and their abominations,"[6] the people reformed and the work of the ministry progressed. But as the church members again grew proud and corrupt, Alma—like his father on a similar occasion[7]—grew "very sorrowful" over their wickedness.[8] With no regard for worldly honor, he simply relinquished the office of chief judge "that he might preach the word of God" full-time, "seeing no

---

1. Heading to book of Alma.
2. See Mosiah 28:20.
3. See Alma 1:19–25.
4. Alma 1:26–27.
5. See Alma 2–3.
6. Alma 4:3.
7. Mosiah 26:10, 13.
8. Alma 4:15.

way that he might reclaim them save it were in bearing down in pure testimony against them."[1]

The intense focus on father-son relationships in Alma the younger's ministry continues with, according to his own record,[2] the opening line of his first recorded sermon—reminiscent of the opening line of the Nephite record written by his ancient father Nephi[3]. Alma identifies himself and establishes his credibility and authority by reference to his father, Alma the elder: "I, Alma, having been consecrated by my father, Alma, to be a high priest over the church of God, he having power and authority from God . . . "[4] The sermon is structured around what happened to the father, whom the son notably and kindly never censures for his early wayward life but rather praises for his reformation:

> Did not my father Alma believe in the words which were delivered by the mouth of Abinadi? And was he not a holy prophet? Did he not speak the words of God, and my father Alma believe them?
>
> And according to his faith there was a mighty change wrought in his heart. . . .
>
> And behold, he preached the word unto your fathers, and a mighty change was also wrought in their hearts.[5]

Alma also reminded his listeners of their fathers' former bondage and divine deliverance[6]—demonstrating, by the way, his own obedience to the angel's instruction that he himself should remember what great things God did for his fathers.[7] In essence, then, he tells his listeners that *he* has remembered the captivity and deliverance of his fathers; then he asks: "Have you sufficiently retained in remembrance the captivity of your fathers? Yea, and have you sufficiently retained in remembrance [God's] mercy and long-suffering towards

---

1. Alma 4:19.
2. Alma 5:2.
3. See Mosiah 17:2; 1 Nephi 1:2.
4. Alma 5:3.
5. Alma 5:11–13.
6. See Alma 5:3–5.
7. See Mosiah 27:16.

them?" For God delivered them not only from temporal bondage, he explains, but also from the spiritual bondage of hell, thereby liberating them from the "midst of darkness" and the "chains of hell, and an everlasting destruction," so that "their souls were illuminated by the light of the everlasting word."[1] One immediately senses also a poignant autobiographical allusion to Alma's own experience in which he had been dramatically freed from the "darkest abyss" and the "pains of hell" and "destruction" so that his soul was filled with "the marvelous light of God."[2]

Remembering the mighty change wrought in their fathers was but the first step; Alma now asks: "Have *ye* spiritually been born of God? . . . Have ye experienced this mighty change in your hearts? Do ye exercise faith in the redemption of him who created you?"[3] The pattern is clearly that of the early Nephite fathers, such as Nephi hearkening to and remembering the words of Lehi about his revelations and then proceeding to exercise similar faith to receive the same revelations,[4] or as Enos remembering Jacob's words about eternal life and then engaging in lengthy and mighty prayer to communicate with God.[5]

Continuing his sermon, Alma relentlessly pursues the theme of fathers and sons as he explains the need to be "cleansed from all stain, through the blood of him of whom it has been spoken by our fathers"[6]—thus pointing to another father-son relationship, that of "the Son, the Only Begotten of the Father,"[7] through whose grace all those who repent may enter into yet another father-child relationship by being "born again."[8] But woe to each person who refuses to repent, for he or she ends up in still another father-child relationship as "a

---

1. Alma 5:4–10.
2. Mosiah 27:29; Alma 36:13–14.
3. Alma 5:14–15; emphasis added.
4. See 1 Nephi 8–14.
5. See Enos 1.
6. Alma 5:21.
7. Alma 5:48.
8. Alma 5:49.

child of the devil."[1] And Alma is telling all this not as something new but because, he says,

> I am commanded to stand and testify unto this people the things which have been spoken by our fathers. . . .
>
> And this is not all. Do ye not suppose that I know of these things myself? Behold, I testify unto you that I do know that these things . . . are true. And how do ye suppose that I know of their surety?
>
> Behold, I say unto you they are made known unto me by the Holy Spirit of God. Behold, I have fasted and prayed many days that I might know these things of myself. And now I do know of myself that they are true; for the Lord God hath made them manifest unto me by his Holy Spirit; and this is the spirit of revelation which is in me.
>
> And moreover, I say unto you that it has thus been revealed unto me, that the words which have been spoken by our fathers are true, even so according to the spirit of prophecy which is in me.[2]

Clearly Alma the younger's conversion was not complete with the dramatic transformation effected by the angel, but the process had required subsequent fasting, prayer, and reflection on the example of his father—not unlike the experiences of Nephi and Enos wherein they similarly sought divine confirmation of their fathers' teachings. In a larger sense, Alma the younger's words also perfectly illustrate the process provided for all people to acquire and increase in faith in their Creator. In Lecture 2 of the Lectures on Faith, Joseph Smith[3] explained that after Adam was created,

> he was not left without intelligence or understanding, to wander in darkness and spend an existence in ignorance and doubt (on the great and important point which effected his happiness) as to the real fact by whom he was created, or unto whom he

---

1. Alma 5:39–41.

2. Alma 5:44–47.

3. Although several of the Lectures were apparently principally authored by associates of Joseph Smith, recent studies and scholarship agree that Lecture 2 was probably authored directly by the Prophet Joseph Smith himself. (See Dahl and Tate 1990:8.)

was amenable for his conduct. God conversed with him face to face. In his presence he was permitted to stand, and from his own mouth he was permitted to receive instruction. He heard his voice, walked before him and gazed upon his glory.[1]

Nor did Adam's transgression deprive him of the memory of this glorious interaction with his Creator, who in fact continued to communicate to the fallen Adam and Eve by calling to them with his own voice and sending messengers and even the Holy Spirit.[2]

> Adam, thus being made acquainted with God, communicated the knowledge which he had unto his posterity; and it was through this means that the thought was first suggested to their minds that there was a God, which laid the foundation for the exercise of their faith, through which they could obtain a knowledge of his character and also of his glory. . . .
>
> From this we can see that the whole human family in the early age of their existence, . . . had this knowledge disseminated among them; so that the existence of God became an object of faith in the early age of the world. And the evidences which these men had of the existence of a God, was the testimony of their fathers in the first instance.[3]

For example, before Adam's righteous son Abel heard the heavenly voice accepting his offering, he had first "received the important information of his father that such a Being did exist who had created and who did uphold all things."[4] And from that day to this, insists Joseph Smith, the process has been much the same for the whole human family:

> The whole faith of the world, from that time down to the present, is in a certain degree dependent on the knowledge first communicated to them by their common progenitor; and it has been handed down to the day and generation in which we live, as [evident] from the face of the sacred records.[5]

1. LF 2:18.
2. See LF 2:19–25.
3. LF 2:31, 33.
4. LF 2:36.
5. LF 2:36.

And pursuant to that pattern explained by Joseph Smith, many of Adam's posterity have — as did Alma the younger — exercised faith sufficient to acquire a personal knowledge of the same things that father Adam knew. Hence the starting point for even such giants of faith as Enoch, Abraham, and Joseph Smith has always been the testimony of their fathers, either in person or as recorded in sacred writ. Before receiving his stunning revelations,[1] Enoch had listened to the voice of Adam and even been ordained by him.[2] Before conversing face-to-face with God, Abraham had carefully pored over "the records of the fathers, even the patriarchs."[3] Before his glorious visitation by the Father and the Son, young Joseph Smith had determined to pray only after being encouraged to do so by the Bible.[4] Each of these prophets left behind a record of their own revelations for the benefit of the world and particularly, as Abraham noted, "for the benefit of my posterity that shall come after me"[5] — thereby continually adding further testimony to sacred writ regarding God's existence, goodness, and accessibility through repentance and faith. Such experiences thus became part of that mounting evidence that provides humanity its first assurance of the existence of God and its encouragement to discover his existence for oneself and for certainty, even as Alma did.

Following his powerful preaching in Zarahemla regarding fathers and sons, Alma proceeded to follow his father's example in organizing the church and counseling "the children of God" to meet together often to worship.[6] He then traveled to other locales, as was his pattern, to "declare the word of God . . . , according to [that] . . . which had been spoken by his fathers, and according to the spirit of prophecy which was in him, according to the testimony of Jesus Christ, the Son of God."[7] And once again his preaching is structured around fathers

---

1. Beginning at or after age sixty-five. (See Moses 6:25–27.)
2. Ordination to the patriarchal priesthood at age twenty-five. (See D&C 107:48.)
3. Abraham 1:31.
4. See JS–H 1:10–14.
5. Abraham 1:31.
6. See Alma 6:1–6; see Mosiah 18:25.
7. Alma 6:8.

and sons. He continually testifies of the Son of God through whom, insists Alma, his listeners must "be born again" to join their fathers and "sit down with Abraham, Isaac, and Jacob . . . in the kingdom of heaven."[1] And when Alma obeys the Lord's instruction to warn one particular city, Ammonihah, to repent or be destroyed,[2] he significantly ascribes their entire problem to their having forgotten what great things the Lord did for their fathers:

> Behold, O ye wicked and perverse generation, how have ye forgotten the tradition of your fathers; yea, how soon ye have forgotten the commandments of God.
> Do ye not remember that our father, Lehi, was brought out of Jerusalem by the hand of God? Do ye not remember that they were all led by him through the wilderness?
> And have ye forgotten so soon how many times he delivered our fathers out of the hands of their enemies, and preserved them from being destroyed, even by the hands of their own brethren? . . .
> Behold, do ye not remember the words which he spake unto Lehi, saying that: Inasmuch as ye shall keep my commandments, ye shall prosper in the land? And again it is said that: Inasmuch as ye will not keep my commandments ye shall be out off from the presence of the Lord.[3]

Alma further points out that the Lamanites have indeed been cut off from the Lord's presence. Even so, the great value that the Lord places on following one's fathers seems to be implied by the fact that, as Alma also explains, "the Lord will be merciful unto [the Lamanites] and prolong their existence in the land" precisely because their errors arose not from willful rebellion but from following the incorrect "traditions of their fathers" — traditions that would eventually be corrected and rectified.[4] However, for the people of Ammonihah who had rejected the correct traditions of their own fathers, utter destruction awaited unless they would quickly repent and accept the Son of God.[5]

---

1. See Alma 7:7–25.
2. Alma 8:16.
3. Alma 9:8–10, 13.
4. Alma 9:16–17.
5. See Alma 9:18–30.

Alma's testimony to this hardened people was corroborated by that of his missionary companion Amulek, a resident of the place and now Alma's convert. Amulek similarly preaches of father-son themes, tracing his own lineage to Nephi and Lehi[1] and reminding the people of the great destruction by flood that came in the days of their still more ancient father Noah.[2] Like Alma, Amulek preached faith on the Son of God,[3] rejection of whom could make one a "child of hell."[4] Unfortunately and ironically, Amulek's own father, who had at first been blessed by Alma,[5] eventually rejected Amulek[6] and presumably his testimony.

That Amulek provided a second witness of the things Alma taught seemed to make an impression, whereupon Alma resumed his message, again emphasizing father-son themes: the Son of God,[7] who was spoken of and typified by "our fathers"[8] and particularly "our father Abraham,"[9] would soon come to complete the great plan of redemption set in motion when father Adam and mother Eve, "our first parents," partook of the tree of forbidden fruit.[10] But salvation was being offered now to these people, who were invited to obtain mercy through repentance.[11]

Many accepted Alma's offer; but most did not, and they bound him and Amulek with cords. After forcing them to witness a grisly scene of execution by fire of a number of righteous people, they committed Alma and Amulek to prison.[12] Finally, after verbal and physical abuse lasting for many days, the power of God rested mightily upon them, and after Alma prayed for "deliverance" according to

---

1. See Alma 10:2–3.
2. See Alma 10:22.
3. See Alma 11:38–44.
4. Alma 11:23.
5. See Alma 10:11.
6. See Alma 15:16.
7. See Alma 12:33–34; 13:1–16.
8. Alma 13:26.
9. Alma 13:15.
10. See Alma 12:22–26.
11. See Alma 12:34.
12. See Alma 14:1–17.

their "faith which is in Christ," they "broke the cords with which they were bound." Their terrified captors began to flee but were instantly crushed when "the earth shook mightily, and the walls of the prison were rent in twain, so that they fell to the earth,"[1] leaving Alma and Amulek unharmed[2] and able to walk away to continue their ministry elsewhere.[3] The miraculous experience not only echoes the deliverance from bondage of Alma the elder and, more anciently, of father Nephi who burst his bonds during the transoceanic journey, but it also foreshadows the later prison deliverance of Alma's own descendants (the brothers Lehi and Nephi) and the great earthquake that yet other descendants would live through at the great destruction, to become Christ's disciples, whom prisons would not be able to hold.

This power of God that had shaken the earth was something that Alma would later long for—not however for destruction but rather for salvation:

> O that I were an angel, and could have the wish of mine heart, that I might go forth and speak with the trump of God, with a voice to shake the earth, and cry repentance unto every people!
>
> Yea, I would declare unto every soul, as with the voice of thunder, repentance and the plan of redemption, that they should repent and come unto our God, that there might not be more sorrow upon all the face of the earth.[4]

Immediately apparent is the profound effect of the angel who had once stopped Alma and who had, in "a voice of thunder, which caused the earth to shake,"[5] cried repentance to him—and forever changed his life. What Alma adds to this wish then reflects his father's previous experience, as he acknowledges "that which the Lord hath commanded me, and I glory in it," not "of myself, but . . . that perhaps I may be an instrument in the hands of God to bring some soul to

---

1. Alma 14:26–27.
2. Alma 14:28–29.
3. See Alma 15–16.
4. Alma 29:1–2.
5. Mosiah 27:11.

repentance."[1] The words are similar to those once spoken by his father in the wilderness when he praised the Lord for making him "an instrument in his hands in bringing so many . . . to a knowledge of his truth. Nevertheless, in this I do not glory, for I am unworthy to glory of myself."[2] Indeed, his father's wilderness experience was very much on the Alma's mind, as he proceeds to explain: "Yea, and I also remember the captivity of my fathers"[3] (even as the angel had commanded him to so remember[4]). "For," continues Alma, "I surely do know that the Lord did deliver them out of bondage" — and then remembers the still more ancient fathers by adding: "Yea, the Lord God, the God of Abraham, the God of Isaac, and the God of Jacob, did deliver them out of bondage."[5]

The wicked citizens of Ammonihah who refused Alma's warning to remember their fathers soon met with destruction,[6] a phenomenon that occurs again and again in the Book of Mormon. Indeed, just several years later when the wicked Korihor came preaching against the possibility of revelation and Christ, his position was strikingly similar to that of the now-destroyed people of Ammonihah, as he accused the believing Nephites of "a frenzied mind" and "derangement" that came "because of the traditions of your fathers."[7] This is Korihor's major theme, and he repeats it relentlessly: "I do not teach the foolish traditions of your fathers. . . . Ye say that this people is a guilty and a fallen people, because of the transgression of a parent. . . . Ye lead away this people after the foolish traditions of your fathers. . . . And [thus] he did rise up in great swelling words before Alma, . . . accusing them of leading away the people after the silly traditions of their fathers."[8] The difference in how these traditions of the fathers were perceived by Korihor and Alma clearly lay in what

---

1. Alma 29:9.
2. Mosiah 23:10–11.
3. Alma 29:11.
4. Mosiah 27:16.
5. Alma 29:11.
6. Alma 16:1–11.
7. Alma 30:16.
8. Alma 30:23, 25, 27, 31.

each man had or had not been willing to do to discover their truth. Alma had paid the price of knowing the truth of his fathers' traditions by fasting and praying "many days,"[1] so that Korihor's denouncement of those same traditions becomes a stark admission that he had never paid the price of knowing their truth, "putting off the Spirit of God"[2] — based on the principle stated by President Spencer W. Kimball: "A testimony . . . may be enjoyed by every soul who will pay the price," and "to fail to attain this knowledge is to admit that one has not paid the price."[3] Korihor's ignominious end occasions one further remark from Mormon on the theme of fathers and children: "Thus we see that the devil will not support his children at the last day, but doth speedily drag them down to hell."[4]

Finally, it seems more than coincidental that the next wicked people whom Alma confronts in his ministry, the Zoramites, suffer from the identical problem that had plagued Korihor and the city of Ammonihah: a disbelief in the righteous traditions of their fathers. "We do not believe in the tradition of our brethren, which was handed down to them by the childishness of their fathers."[5] Ironically, this accusation of childishness could come only from people unwilling to be *childlike* in the sense that Alma's descendant Nephi would hear the resurrected Christ speak of: "Ye must repent, and become as a little child."[6]

Alma's mission to the Zoramites is instructive also for what it teaches about how he taught his own sons — by example and by involving them in his work. He took with him two of his sons yet "in [their] youth,"[7] Shiblon and Corianton, in the group of missionaries that also included Amulek, Zeezrom, and three of the sons of Mosiah. Prior to splitting up (apparently in pairs), the group heard Alma pray

---

1. Alma 5:46.
2. Alma 30:42.
3. Kimball 1982:56–57.
4. Alma 30:60.
5. Alma 31:16.
6. 3 Nephi 11:37–38.
7. Alma 36:3. The words "thou art in thy youth" were spoken after the Zoramite mission by Alma to Helaman, the oldest son of the three.

for each of his fellow laborers, including his "two sons." Alma then "clapped his hands" on each of them, whereupon they were filled with the Holy Spirit and went their ways to preach, being preserved and comforted by the fulfillment of Alma's prayer of faith.[1] Through their participation in this mission, the members of the group will become what Alma and his father had already become: "instruments in the hands of God of bringing many . . . to repentance."[2]

But even in his concern for his sons, Alma seems not to have forgotten his father, whose experience may be alluded to in what Alma tells the outcast Zoramite poor who had been banned from worshipping in the Zoramite synagogues. "Because ye are compelled to be humble," Alma tells them, "blessed are ye; for a man sometimes, if he is compelled to be humble, seeketh repentance."[3] The comment is likely autobiographical, as he himself had once been humbled literally to the dust by an angel whose voice shook the earth. But then Alma went one step further: "Do ye not suppose that they are more blessed who truly humble themselves because of the word?" Indeed, "blessed are they who humble themselves without being compelled to be humble."[4] Although Alma does not here expressly mention his father, he may well have been thinking of him whom, as he would soon say, he "always retained in remembrance"[5] and whose good example in believing Abinadi's words Alma had on another occasion preached about.[6] Alma then invokes other more ancient Israelite fathers—including the prophets Zenos, Zenock, and even Moses—who spoke clearly of the Son of God, of whom Alma himself also testifies.[7]

Such repeated emphasis on remembering the fathers is an authentic mark of ancient Israelite thought:

The saving deeds of Yahweh [Jehovah] to the fathers are

---

1. See Alma 31:7–38.
2. Alma 35:14. Of Corianton's failure in his mission through transgression, we will hear more when Alma devotes significant effort to encourage him to repent.
3. Alma 32:13.
4. Alma 32:14–16.
5. Alma 36:29.
6. See Alma 5:11–13.
7. See Alma 33.

treasured by the godly, and they receive courage and confidence from them. . . . The history of the fathers is a living heritage, from which one can receive courage and faith, or a warning.[1]

ALMA THE YOUNGER COUNSELS HIS SONS

Alma's ministerial labors had been extensive and his success significant, but if the relative volume of space that Mormon devotes to the various events of Alma's ministry is at all indicative of relative importance, then Alma's instructions to his sons as recorded in chapters 36 through 42 must qualify as the single most important event of his ministry, comprising as they do at least 20 percent of the entire account thereof.[2] This material is also the largest passage of fatherly counsel by any father in the Book of Mormon, and Mormon's delight in being able to include this material in his record is barely concealed in his remark of introduction: "And we have an account of his commandments, which he gave unto [his sons] according to his own record."[3]

The context is noteworthy: This fatherly counsel was given by Alma when "he caused that his sons should be gathered together, that he might give unto them every one his charge, separately, concerning the things pertaining unto righteousness."[4] In other words, he will speak to each son separately, but apparently in the hearing of them all—which makes this look much like a final farewell speech to his posterity. And although there is no mention of Alma's impending death or departure, within a year he will have disappeared, thought by the believers to have been "taken up by the Spirit."[5] If he had a premonition of this, we can understand why he could not tell his sons that he was about to die, and why he would not divulge the miraculous manner in which he would disappear. All the same, his calling his sons together to give them counsel shortly before his de-

---

1. TDOT I:12.
2. Excluding Alma 17–28, which do not treat Alma's ministry; 16 pages (current English edition of Alma 36–42) divided by 77 pages (Alma 1–16, 29–42) = 20%.
3. Alma 35:16.
4. Ibid.
5. Alma 45:19.

parture apparently follows the pattern set by father Lehi,[1] who, as we saw in chapter 1, was following a still more ancient ancestral pattern extending back to the patriarchs Joseph, Jacob, Abraham, and even Adam himself.

Also pursuant to the pattern set by Lehi, Alma tailors his instructions to each of his three sons, giving "every one his charge, separately."[2] The wisdom of such individualized instruction is borne out by modern authorities on child-rearing who insist, as nearly every parent of two or more children knows by experience, that from the moment of birth, children (even in the same family) differ significantly from each other.[3] This is hardly surprising, of course, in light of our premortal existence in which individual agency allowed for individual progress and differences, about which Alma[4] had preached.

ALMA THE YOUNGER TO HELAMAN

Alma's dependency on his ancestral Nephite fathers is also evident in what and how he teaches his sons, beginning with his oldest, Helaman. Alma's first point of instruction quotes a divine promise made earlier to both Nephi[5] and Lehi,[6] that "inasmuch as ye shall keep the commandments of God ye shall prosper in the land" of promise.[7] But Alma does more than repeat the promise; he emphasizes it and adds his own absolute assurance of its veracity by introducing it with the comment, "I swear unto you, that . . . "[8] This likewise recalls Nephi, who obtained personal revelation as to the veracity of things his father had spoken. Alma has done the same; and now he teaches the precious and critical truths that he knows with absolute certainty, again probably alluding to father Lehi and the precious fruit in his dream: "I have tasted," Alma testifies to his son, and therefore

---

1. See 2 Nephi 1:1 through 4:12.
2. Alma 35:16.
3. Dobson 1987:24–27.
4. See Alma 13:3–9.
5. See 1 Nephi 2:20.
6. See 2 Nephi 1:9.
7. Alma 36:1.
8. Ibid.

"I do know; and the knowledge which I have is of God."[1] President Ezra Taft Benson has observed that "in the Book of Mormon, faithful fathers constantly bore their testimonies to their sons."[2] There seems to be no substitute for the power of personal conviction in parental teaching.

Furthermore, Alma encourages Helaman to gain that conviction for himself: "Ye ought to know as I do know . . . "[3] And how could Helaman come to know what his father knew? By doing what his father had done, as Alma counsels: "I would that ye should do as I have done . . . "[4] Once again, example reigns supreme as the most effective teacher, even as Lehi had invited his family to eat the precious fruit after he himself had partaken. And what exactly had Alma done that he wanted Helaman to imitate?

> I would that ye should do as I have done, in remembering the captivity of our fathers; for they were in bondage, and none could deliver them except it was the God of Abraham, and the God of Isaac, and the God of Jacob; and he surely did deliver them in their afflictions.[5]

Remember our fathers! The same advice that Alma had heard from an angel and had in turn constantly emphasized in his own preaching, he now recommends to his son—and then repeats it over and over again in various ways. Remember, says Alma, that the same God who covenanted with our father Abraham also delivered our fathers—Alma and his people—out of bondage, so that God has,

> by his everlasting power, delivered them out of bondage and captivity, from time to time even down to the present day; and I have always retained in remembrance their captivity; yea, and ye also ought to retain in remembrance, as I have done, their captivity.[6]

---

1. Alma 36:26.
2. W&W 69.
3. Alma 36:30.
4. Alma 36:2.
5. Alma 36:2.
6. Alma 36:29.

Why the repetition? "Repetition is a key to learning," explains President Ezra Taft Benson. And as "devoted Book of Mormon fathers constantly reminded their sons of saving truths," so "our children need to hear the truth repeated, especially because there is so much falsehood abroad."[1]

One of the things Alma repeats is the need for his sons to do "as I have done." Again, the power of example. For it is one thing to say, "Go yonder," and quite another to say, "Follow me." The latter invitation not only shows the path is passable, but also conveys a sense of comfort and community and of traveling the path together.

But it can also be the better part of wisdom for a parent to say, "Avoid that—for I have been there, and know." And did Alma as he told his son of his earlier folly and the wrenching experience that had finally resulted in his conversion and his being granted a vision of heaven, "even as our father Lehi saw."[2] Hence Lehi also is one of the fathers to remember, as Alma soon notes again: "Yea, and [God] has also brought our fathers out of the land of Jerusalem."[3] And even before that, as Alma also reminds his son, God

> brought our fathers out of Egypt, and . . . swallowed up the Egyptians in the Red Sea; and he led them by his power into the promised land.[4]

All of the ancient fathers, says Alma, should be remembered.

And why? Alma answers from his own experience: when he had been "racked with torment" for three days, he was able to obtain forgiveness only after he "remembered . . . to have heard my father prophesy . . . of one Jesus Christ, a Son of God."[5] In other words, remember the fathers in order to learn of the Son of God. The effect of this teaching by Alma, notes President Benson, was to perpetuate one of the "great family legacies . . . in the Book of Mormon."[6]

---

1. W&W 69.
2. Alma 36:22.
3. Alma 36:29.
4. Alma 36:28.
5. Alma 36:17.
6. W&W 69.

Helaman was also singled out for a special charge, the keeping and transmission of the sacred records, tying Helaman even more closely to his fathers who had kept them before him. For example, Alma reminds Helaman that the brass plates contain "the genealogy of our forefathers,"[1] and together with the other Nephite records they must be carefully preserved and transmitted for the benefit of "future generations" (three times Alma mentions this[2]), making Helaman a critical link in the chain that would facilitate God's fulfilling "his promises which he has made unto our fathers."[3]

Among the sacred records and artifacts conferred on Helaman was the Liahona, or compass, miraculously given, Alma notes, to "our fathers,"[4] "to show unto our fathers the course which they should travel in the wilderness."[5] Alma uses this marvelous artifact to emphasize to Helaman one last time the necessity of remembering the fathers in order to get one's bearings on life. For as the Liahona worked only when Lehi's party exercised faith, so

> these things are not without a shadow; for as our fathers were slothful to give heed to this compass (now these things were temporal) they did not prosper; even so it is with things which are spiritual.
>
> For behold, it is as easy to give heed to the word of Christ, which will point to you a straight course to eternal bliss, as it was for our fathers to give heed to this compass, which would point unto them a straight course to the promised land.
>
> And now I say, is there not a type in this thing? For just as surely as this director did bring our fathers, by following its course, to the promised land, shall the words of Christ, if we follow their course, carry us beyond this vale of sorrow into a far better land of promise.
>
> O my son, do not let us be slothful because of the easiness of the way; for so was it with our fathers; for so was it prepared

---

1. Alma 37:3.
2. Alma 37:14, 18–19.
3. Alma 37:17–18.
4. Alma 37:38.
5. Alma 37:39.

for them, that if they would look they might live; even so it is with us.[1]

This is by no means the first time that Alma has used metaphor in his teaching, as for example when he had told his listeners that the good shepherd was calling them,[2] and that the word of God is like a seed to be planted and nourished in one's heart.[3] But Alma's metaphor here as he counsels his son to remember their forefathers strikingly demonstrates that in his very method of teaching, Alma is likewise following his forefathers, who also taught by metaphor: Lehi counseled Laman to direct his life to God as a river flowing into the Red Sea, and he counseled Lemuel to be firm as a valley in keeping God's commandments.[4] Lehi also compared the house of Israel to an olive tree,[5] while his son Nephi—drawing on prior prophetic imagery—compared the latter-day gathering of the righteous to calves being led to a stall, or to sheep being gathered by a shepherd.[6] Nephi's brother Jacob compared the atonement to Abraham's offering of Isaac[7] and went to the trouble of inscribing on the plates Zenos' lengthy allegory comparing Israel to an olive tree.[8]

In using the metaphor of the Liahona, Alma is not only reiterating the principle that remembering one's righteous fathers leads one to the Son of God, but he is also expressing more clearly that which had been merely implied before: That in remembering one's fathers, even the great ones, it is possible to learn from—and thereby avoid repeating—their mistakes. The idea was inherent, of course, in remembering the *bondage* of one's fathers. The same approach to teaching about the fathers was used in ancient Israel, as evidenced by the Old Testament's "many warnings . . . against following the bad example of the fathers." But the righteous fathers were models to emulate;[9]

---

1. Alma 37:43–46.
2. See Alma 5:38–60.
3. See Alma 32:28–43.
4. See 1 Nephi 2:9–10.
5. See 1 Nephi 10:12; 15:12.
6. See 1 Nephi 22:24–25.
7. See Jacob 4:5.
8. See Jacob 5.
9. See TDOT 1:13.

and Alma similarly points to the faith of Lehi as evidenced by the fact that he and his family did make it to the promised land. Alma concludes the metaphor by pointing to the ultimate source of life: "My son, . . . look to God and live."[1]

In drawing such lessons from the lives of his Nephite forebears, Alma was, of course, doing what they themselves had done—as when Nephi remembered the Exodus of "our fathers" from Egypt,[2] or when Lehi remembered the prophecies of his ancestor Joseph.[3] The authentically Israelite nature of this approach is seen by the similar approach used by the ancient Jewish rabbis in constructing their great commentary, or Midrash (Hebrew for "exposition" or "inquiry"),[4] on the book of Genesis. The commentary was constructed, says an eminent modern Jewish scholar, around two governing principles:

> One is that what the patriarchs and matriarchs of the book of Genesis did in their day gives the signal to the generations to come of what Israel is to do. The other is that the lives of the patriarchs and matriarchs foretell the sacred history of Israel. So the deeds of the founders teach lessons on how the children should live.[5]

Following this same approach, Alma's counsel to his son Helaman turns out to be a model of parental teaching and a powerful witness to the importance of remembering one's fathers.

ALMA THE YOUNGER TO SHIBLON AND CORIANTON

Alma turned next to counsel the two sons who had accompanied him on the Zoramite mission, Shiblon and Corianton. Alma's praise of Shiblon for his "steadiness and . . . faithfulness unto God" and for his "diligence, . . . patience and . . . long-suffering among the people of the Zoramites"[6] is but one example, as President Ezra Taft

---

1. Alma 37:47.
2. See 1 Nephi 4:2.
3. See 2 Nephi 3.
4. See Wigoder 1989:487.
5. Neusner 1985:79.
6. Alma 38:2–3.

Benson has pointed out, of how "loving fathers [in the Book of Mormon] commended their sons when they deserved it."[1] Alma also expressed his great joy over Shiblon's conduct: "I have had great joy in thee already," and "I trust that I shall have great joy in you."[2] To his already impressive array of parental teaching techniques, Alma adds yet another, communication of trust—the potential power of which is illustrated by what President David O. McKay recalled about the influence of his mother during his young manhood: "The realization of her love and her confidence gave me power more than once during fiery youth to keep my name untarnished."[3] The effect of Alma's parental love and confidence seems to have been the same on the fiery youthfulness of this son whom he counseled to "bridle all your passions, that ye may be filled with love"[4]—for even in his advanced age, Shiblon was a just man who kept the commandments.[5] To this admonition Alma adds others,[6] individualized for Shiblon, it would seem, since they are not given to the other sons. And all of this is combined with additional observations which, being of more general application, also appear in the counsel to the other sons.[7]

This was great fatherly counsel. And what if it is significantly shorter than that given to Helaman, for was Helaman not charged with the added responsibility of the records? But when we finally read Alma's much longer counsel to his last son, Corianton, and discover it to be as long as the combined counsel to both Helaman and Shiblon, we may begin to feel that Shiblon was shortchanged, especially when we discover that during the Zoramite mission Corianton had disappointed and shamed his father by actually forsaking the ministry and visiting a prostitute![8] Should such a son merit such significantly more time and attention from his father than a son so

---

1. W&W 70.
2. Alma 38:2–3.
3. Middlemiss 1976:196.
4. Alma 38:12.
5. See Alma 63:2.
6. See Alma 38:10–14.
7. See Alma 38:1–2, 6–8.
8. See Alma 39:3.

steady and faithful as the great Shiblon? Would not a stern and simple rebuke have sufficed for the weak and wayward Corianton? Evidently not. Instead, we are confronted by the remarkable phenomenon that this, the longest single passage of counsel by a Book of Mormon father to his son, is directed to a wicked man!

But Alma's approach would prove identical to that used by him of whom Alma so frequently prophesied, Jesus Christ—who during his mortal ministry told of the shepherd leaving the ninety and nine in order to find the one that had strayed,[1] and who responded to the query about why he spent so much time with sinners by explaining, "They that be whole need not a physician, but they that are sick. . . . I am not come to call the righteous, but sinners to repentance."[2] Alma had in fact used the same approach in his ministry, constantly going where the people most needed his preaching. That he should now do the same with his own children is therefore not surprising.

But we see added pain and poignancy as Alma, once a wayward son himself, now confronts his own wayward son. And if Corianton was not nearly as hardened and rebellious as the young Alma had been in his all-out campaign of destruction against the church, still Corianton's transgression was so grievous that Alma was compelled to confront him with the fact of that transgression and its awful consequences if Corianton did not repent. Alma, who was once confronted by a heavenly messenger, now finds himself ironically in the role of the messenger confronting his own wayward son and once again experiencing the pain inherent in such confrontation—but this time from the other side, and this time as a parent. Sensitive to the pain his son was feeling, which would have been somewhat the same as he himself had felt when his "soul was harrowed up"[3] through guilt, Alma explained to Corianton that "I would not dwell upon your crimes, to harrow up your soul, if it were not for your good."[4] Following the ancestral pattern of Lehi, who had pointed to Nephi as a

---

1. See Matthew 18:11–13; Luke 15:3–7.
2. Matthew 9:12–13.
3. Alma 36:12.
4. Alma 39:7.

worthy example for his other sons, Alma counsels the young Corianton to "counsel with your elder brothers in your undertakings," for "ye stand in need to be nourished by your brothers. And give heed to their counsel."[1]

Then, with seemingly infinite compassion and patience, this tender father proceeds systematically and at great length to answer Corianton's specific questions and concerns regarding important doctrinal points covering the entire sweep of the plan of salvation, including the fall of Adam, the atonement of Christ making possible rebirth for the repentant and resurrection for all, the final judgment, and the final state of eternal life for the obedient. Commenting on this teaching by Alma to Corianton, President Ezra Taft Benson has noted, "If their sons strayed, stalwart Book of Mormon fathers still continued to teach them."[2] Furthermore, says President Benson,

> the Book of Mormon, which is the most correct book on earth, demonstrates that the major responsibility for teaching our sons the great plan of the Eternal Father—the Fall, rebirth, Atonement, Resurrection, Judgment, eternal life—rests with fathers. It should be done individually as well as in the family. . . . It should be done from their youth up—and often.[3]

But more than discharging that important fatherly duty to teach those things, Alma puts together one of the most masterful doctrinal syntheses found anywhere in sacred writ on the facets of the great plan of salvation. Corianton could, of course, with enough study of scripture eventually have answered all of his own questions and attained a similar understanding. Moreover, it would have been far easier for Alma, after rebuking his son, simply to send him off to search these things out for himself. One suspects, however, that this son who had such gaps of understanding of the plan of salvation may not have been naturally inclined to pore over the scriptures, especially in his as-yet-unrepentant state.[4] The occasion clearly called for teach-

---

1. Alma 39:10; and see v. 1.
2. W&W 70.
3. W&W 71–72.
4. See Alma 39:9.

ing, for answering Corianton's questions and rounding out his knowledge as he was called upon to repent—and as a further stimulus to do so. And with consummate didactic skill, Alma rose to the occasion, drawing on experience and expertise acquired from so many years of preaching to so many people in so many circumstances. Indeed, as important as all that preaching had been *per se,* one could perhaps consider it all practice for this one sermon upon whose power and persuasiveness hinged the fate of his own precious son. With the utmost skill, Alma weaves the various strands of the plan of salvation into a breathtaking tapestry whose message is unmistakable: Corianton must repent.

But if Corianton could not mistake the message, neither could he have failed to be touched by his father's sheer patience and effort in delivering it, as well as by his father's manner. These were no pompous pronouncements issued in harshness and condescension but rather heartfelt insights and observations lovingly shared by a man who, despite his immense spiritual knowledge, freely and frequently admitted to the limits of that knowledge, even as he shared precious divine mysteries that he had learned through much prayer.[1] Moreover, all this was done in a context of carefully addressing Corianton's own concerns! It is a perfect illustration of the principles revealed through the Prophet Joseph Smith that allow the exercise of priesthood power "only by persuasion, by long-suffering, by gentleness and meekness, and by love unfeigned; by kindness, and pure knowledge," and following up any reproof prompted by the Holy Ghost with "an increase of love."[2] And such an approach, notes Joseph Smith, is the most powerful of all in leading people to repent:

> Nothing is so much calculated to lead people to forsake sin as to take them by the hand, and watch over them with tenderness. When persons manifest the least kindness and love to me, O what power it has over my mind, while the opposite course has a tendency to harrow up all the harsh feelings and depress the human mind.[3]

---

1. See Alma 39:3–8.
2. D&C 121:41–43.
3. TPJS 240.

All of this indicates that charity is not only the only thing that counts in the long run (as another father-son pair, Mormon and Moroni, would write[1]), but also the only thing that works in the short run. Alma's charity in teaching his wayward son is an enduring lesson for all parents.

Finally, to his already powerfully persuasive teaching Alma adds another dimension of persuasion, one that is easily overlooked in a casual reading of his counsel to Corianton. That dimension is discernment. Over and over again Alma discerns his son's thoughts: "You marvel why these things should be known so long beforehand."[2] "I perceive that thy mind is worried concerning the resurrection of the dead."[3] "I perceive that thy mind has been worried also concerning [the plan of restoration]."[4] "I perceive there is somewhat more which doth worry your mind, which ye cannot understand—which is concerning the justice of God in the punishment of the sinner."[5]

How did Alma discern his son's thoughts? Considered out of context, these passages could be thought mere abridgments of a dialogue in which Corianton had simply voiced his concerns and his father had answered them. In context, however, such an interpretation would be manifestly incongruent with the rest of Alma's own record, which has shown a marked propensity to describe not only what was preached but also the listeners' objections and questions.[6] What that record also discloses is that Alma (like several of his missionary companions[7]) possessed the gift of discernment, allowing him to know the thoughts of his listeners.[8] And the effect of demonstrating this gift was always profoundly convincing, as when Alma told Zeezrom that "thou seest that thy thoughts are made known unto us

1. See Mormon in Moroni 7:46–47; and Moroni in Moroni 10:20–21.
2. Alma 39:17.
3. Alma 40:1.
4. Alma 41:1.
5. Alma 42:1.
6. See, e.g., Alma 8:11–12, 18–19; 9:1–7, 31–32; 10:12–17, 24–32 (concerning Amulek); 11:20–46 (concerning Amulek); 12:7–9, 19–22; 14:6–7, 10–17, 24–26; 15:5–11; 30:21–55 (Korihor before first Giddonah and then Alma); 32:4–6; 33:1–2.
7. See Amulek in Alma 10:17; Ammon in Alma 18:16–35; 31:6.
8. See Alma 12:1–7.

by his Spirit," causing Zeezrom to be "convinced more and more of the power of God."[1] The effect could have been no less profound upon Corianton, who also needed convincing of God's power to bring him to repentance; the proof came indisputably when he heard his own thoughts repeatedly revealed by his righteous father! Here again Alma ironically assumes the role of the angel who had once ominously stood before him for the express "purpose . . . to convince thee of the power and authority of God. . . . And now behold, can ye dispute the power of God? For behold, doth not my voice shake the earth?"[2] Sensing that his own son now needed a demonstration of that same power, Alma lovingly but convincingly provided it—and by doing for his son what an angel had once done for him, in a sense fulfilled his own wish to become an angel and cry repentance.[3]

All in all, Alma's counsel to Corianton is perhaps the most remarkably effective fatherly instruction in the entire Book of Mormon, and it seems to have required the same sort of profound faith and patience that Alma's own father had needed to bring about his son's conversion—which means that by following his father's example, Alma saved his son. But did he save him? Alma's last word to Corianton was a renewal of the call to preach;[4] that Corianton honorably fulfilled his duty is evidenced in the very next verse, as Mormon resumes the narrative: "The sons of Alma" (there is no exclusion of Corianton) "did go forth among the people, to declare the word," as did "Alma, also," and "they preached the word, and the truth, according to the spirit of prophecy and revelation; and they preached after the holy order of God by which they were called."[5] We hear no more of Corianton until some twenty years later when he joined an immigration northward. But his departure is mentioned in connection with the transmission of the sacred records, which had fallen to Shiblon after Helaman's death[6]—at which point Mormon pauses long

---

1. Alma 12:3, 7.
2. Mosiah 27:14–15.
3. See Alma 29:1.
4. See Alma 42:31.
5. Alma 43:1–2.
6. See Alma 63:1.

enough to observe that Shiblon "was a just man" who "did walk uprightly before God" and "did observe to do good continually, to keep the commandments of the Lord his God; and also did his brother."[1] The "brother" is almost surely Helaman, whom Mormon had just mentioned in the previous verse. And what of Corianton? When Shiblon in turn finally sensed that his end was near, he apparently would have entrusted the records to Corianton—which would have been inconceivable had Corianton not also been a "just man" like his brothers. But Corianton had departed northward, Mormon observes. *"Therefore* it became expedient for Shiblon to confer those sacred things, before his death, upon the son of Helaman."[2] The clear implication is that the records would have gone to Corianton had he not departed. As the once-wayward Alma had been saved by his father's instrumentality, so Alma proved an instrument in saving his own wayward son. And for all the remarkable amount of good that Alma accomplished, we may well surmise that this one convert— his own son—was his most precious, and that if all of Alma's extensive efforts to preach would have done nothing more than to allow him to acquire the teaching expertise and spiritual power needed to save his son, it would have all been worth it. One thinks of the words of a latter-day revelation by the Son of God: "If it so be that you should labor all your days in crying repentance unto this people, and bring, save it be one soul unto me, how great shall be your joy with him in the kingdom of my Father!"[3] How much more for a father, then, when that one soul is his own son, so that together they can share eternally in the joy of dwelling with the Father and Son!

THE DISAPPEARANCE OF ALMA THE YOUNGER

Within a year after his momentous counsel to his three sons, Alma approached Helaman and prophesied to him of the eventual extinction of the Nephites, laying him under strict charge not to reveal the prophecy. Then Alma blessed him and his other sons; he also left a

1. Alma 63:2.
2. Alma 63:11; emphasis added.
3. D&C 18:15.

blessing on "the earth for the righteous' sake," and on the church.[1] Having done so, he

> departed out of the land of Zarahemla, as if to go into the land of Melek. And it came to pass that he was never heard of more; as to his death or burial we know not of.[2]

But if there was no hard evidence as to what had happened, there was at least a rumor among the righteous, which Mormon reports and then draws his own conclusion:

> Behold, this we know, that he was a righteous man; and the saying went abroad in the church that he was taken up by the Spirit, or buried by the hand of the Lord, even as Moses. But behold, the scriptures saith the Lord took Moses unto himself; and we suppose that he has also received Alma in the spirit, unto himself; therefore, for this cause we know nothing concerning his death and burial.[3]

Mormon's mention of the translation of Moses—of whom Alma had preached[4]—may at first surprise those familiar with the Bible, for of the Deuteronomic account as it has come down to us relates that Moses "died" and was "buried."[5] Nevertheless, the Nephite scriptural account of Moses' departure is congruent with an ancient Jewish tradition, reported in a number of rabbinic sources and alluded to by Josephus, telling that Moses was last seen being taken up in a cloud, and that he did not die but "continue[d] to minister above."[6] He also continued to minister on earth, as is apparent from his appearance to Christ on the Mount of Transfiguration.[7] The other Old Testament figure appearing on that Mount was the prophet Elijah,[8] who had

---

1. Alma 45:15; see vv. 2–17.
2. Alma 45:18.
3. Alma 45:19.
4. See Alma 33:19.
5. Deuteronomy 34:5–6.
6. LJ VI:161, and see pp. 162–64.
7. See Matthew 17:1–8.
8. Ibid. in NRSV, REB, NIV, etc.

also been taken up to heaven[1] and who, according to widespread Jewish tradition, has continued to minister to mortals.[2] Ministering is precisely the primary role played by translated beings, says Joseph Smith, who calls them "ministering angels unto many planets."[3] Thus the three Nephite disciples were also translated so that, as Jesus told them, "ye might bring the souls of men unto me, while the world shall stand."[4]

Accordingly, in the end Alma apparently got his wish to be like the messenger who had confronted him as a wayward youth—to be "an angel . . . and speak with the trump of God, with a voice to shake the earth, and cry repentance unto every people!"[5] Even when he had expressed that desire, he thought (as the three Nephite disciples later did[6]) that he sinned in his wish;[7] but (like them) he was granted it—pursuant to the principle that he himself had expressed when he had longed to be an angel: that God "granteth unto men according to their desire."[8]

In retrospect, Alma's translation also makes more meaningful his own prior mention of the righteous Melchizedek, of whom Alma had said that "none were greater";[9] for Melchizedek also had been translated.[10] Alma thus followed the path of certain of the ancient fathers—Melchizedek, Moses, and Elijah. And in his similarity to Moses, Alma also continues and completes the pattern of his own immediate father, whose similarity to Moses in leading God's people out of bondage is so marked in the Book of Mormon.

---

1. See 2 Kings 2:11.
2. See EJ 6:635–40.
3. TPJS 170.
4. 3 Nephi 28:9.
5. Alma 29:1.
6. See 3 Nephi 28:3
7. See Alma 29:3.
8. Alma 29:4.
9. Alma 13:19.
10. See JST Genesis 14:26–36; also Horton 1976.

Chapter 6

MEN OF WAR, MEN OF GOD

· ·

MORONI AND MORONIHAH

WAR FROM THE BEGINNING

According to historians, "war is one of the constants of history,"[1] and even from earliest antiquity

> the image which emerges from monuments, inscriptions, and the writings of contemporaries is that of a dangerous world where attack could come from any quarter and only the militarily strong survived. In such an environment the successful society was, by definition, the society successful at waging war.[2]

Little wonder, then, that war has occupied such a predominant place in works of history from the beginning:

> It is instructive to consider that the three greatest Greek historians, the three greatest of antiquity, for that matter—Herodotus, Thucydides, and Polybius—all chose major wars as the centerpieces of their works. Nor were they alone. Practically

---

1. Will and Ariel Durant 1968:81.
2. O'Connell 1989:33.

every history preserved from this period, and later the Middle Ages, concerns itself with war and conquest.[1]

Nephite history was no exception, as noted by its founder and first historian, Nephi, whose "full account of the history of [his] people" (written on the large plates) focused on "the reign of the kings, and the wars and contentions of [his] people."[2] But it should evoke our utmost gratitude that the Lord commanded Nephi to make also a separate and smaller account devoted primarily to spiritual and theological matters, for it is that account that constitutes the first portion of our Book of Mormon, including Nephi's first-person account.

The small account ended, however, at the time of King Benjamin[3] during the second century B.C., so that much of the subsequent Nephite record as we have it in the Book of Mormon is Mormon's abridgment of what Nephi had described as "the wars and contentions of [his] people." That such history should tell of a father-son pair of powerful Nephite generals is hardly surprising, since throughout world history "there have been martial families in which a son was always expected to follow his father's footsteps and become a soldier."[4] Such conditions have produced some exceedingly influential father-son pairs of military commanders. One need only recall, for example, Phillip II of Macedon and his son Alexander the Great who hellenized the ancient world; or the Roman commander (later Emperor) Vespasian and his son Titus (also later emperor) who destroyed Jerusalem in A.D. 70; or more recently, that American military "dynasty" of Arthur and Douglas MacArthur, the latter of whom played such a critical role in the Pacific Theater in the largest war in history, World War II. No less dominant in their own sphere were the two righteous Nephite generals Moroni and his son Moronihah.

But is the term *righteous general* a contradiction in terms? Can a

---

1. Ibid.

2. 1 Nephi 9:2, 4.

3. See Omni 1:25; Words of Mormon 1:1–11.

4. Sulzberger 1987:xix; see also 58, 1–75. For the proposition that there was a hereditary military caste in Nephite society, see John A. Tvedtnes, "Book of Mormon Tribal Affiliation and Military Castes," in Ricks and Hamblin 1990: 296–326.

man of war really be a man of God? The answers become apparent when we consider the Old Testament portrait of God himself, who is frequently depicted as a God of war,[1] beginning with the primordial conflict occasioned by a rebellion in heaven prior to the creation of the earth.[2] In the book of Moses that Joseph Smith restored, God described that primordial rebellion:

> Because that Satan rebelled against me, and sought to destroy the agency of man, which I, the Lord God, had given him, and also, that I should give unto him mine own power; by the power of mine Only Begotten, I caused that he should be cast down.[3]

Another revelation to Joseph Smith describes the one who rebelled as

> Satan, that old serpent, even the devil, who rebelled against God, and sought to take the kingdom of our God and his Christ—
> Wherefore, he maketh war with the saints of God, and encompasseth them round about.[4]

In other words, Satan's war that began in heaven is now continuing on earth, as the book of Moses depicts in describing the first wars as a result of Satan's "great dominion among men."[5] Hence, according to Elder George Q. Cannon, "the spirit that Lucifer exhibited in heaven has been manifested on earth."[6] And Satan's war against God and his people is not limited to individual temptation and adversity but has always included contention between people, for as the resurrected Lord told the Nephites, "The devil . . . is the father

---

1. See Lind 1980; Eichrodt 1961:I:228–232.

2. "Myths about a cosmic battle at the beginning of time appear in the Bible in fragmentary form." (Sarna 1989:3.) "The Bible offers no connected narrative of primordial divine combat, only poetic snippets." (Levenson 1988:7–13; see also Cassuto 1978: I:8–9.)

3. Moses 4:3.

4. D&C 76:28–29.

5. Moses 6:15.

6. Newquist 1974:1:5.

of contention, and he stirreth up the hearts of men to contend with anger, one with another."[1] Brigham Young observed that "the Devil delights in the work of destruction" and in "introducing war with its long train of dreadful consequences."[2] Under Satan's influence, as Joseph Smith lamented, "nations have been convulsed, kingdoms overthrown, provinces laid waste, and blood, carnage and desolation" have ensued.[3]

With God's people ever living under such threat of war, it is not surprising that from the beginning he has directed them as to how they should proceed when threatened. As disclosed in latter-day revelation:

> This is the law that I gave unto mine ancients, that they should not go out unto battle against any nation, kindred, tongue, or people, save I, the Lord, commanded them.
>
> And if any nation, tongue, or people should proclaim war against them, they should first lift a standard of peace unto that people, nation, or tongue;
>
> And if that people did not accept the offering of peace, neither the second nor the third time, they should bring these testimonies before the Lord;
>
> Then I, the Lord, would give unto them a commandment, and justify them in going out to battle against that nation, tongue, or people.[4]

The "ancients" who received this law included, the Lord explains, "all mine ancient prophets and apostles."[5] Under this law, then, the righteous seer "Enoch . . . led the people of God, and their enemies came to battle against them."[6] And under this law the righteous seer Nephi "wielded the sword of Laban in . . . defence" of his people.[7] Indeed, the Lord expressly states in the above-mentioned revelation

---

1. 3 Nephi 11:29.
2. JD 11:240.
3. TPJS 205.
4. D&C 98:33–36.
5. D&C 98:32.
6. Moses 7:13.
7. Jacob 1:10.

that "this is the law I gave unto my servant Nephi."[1] Thus the greatest generals in history, those who have marched with the power of God, have been righteous men—men of God by choice, and men of war by necessity.

So it was with Moroni and his son Moronihah, two righteous Nephite generals of the first century B.C. when there were "wars, and bloodsheds, and famine, and affliction, for the space of many years,"[2] broken only with short interludes of peace.[3] The problem for the Nephites was the same as it had always been—the Lamanites, whose "intention [was] to destroy their brethren [the Nephites], or to subject them and bring them into bondage that they might establish a kingdom unto themselves over all the land."[4]

It was "the tradition of their fathers that . . . caused their hatred"[5] toward the Nephites, whom they considered to be descendants of "a liar" (Nephi) who "robbed our fathers"[6] (Laman and Lemuel) of the right of government.[7] Hence the Lamanites "taught their children that they should hate [the Nephites], and that they should murder them, and that they should rob and plunder them, and do all they could to destroy them; therefore they ha[d] an eternal hatred towards the children of Nephi."[8] Accordingly, the Lamanites now demanded of the Nephites that they "subject [them]selves to be governed by those to whom the government doth rightly belong."[9] And to that end they had waged war, in order "to avenge their wrongs."[10]

For their part, the Nephites

were sorry to take up arms against the Lamanites, because they did not delight in the shedding of blood; yea, and this

1. D&C 98:32.
2. Alma 62:39; see also Alma 48:22.
3. See, e.g., Alma 46:37; 49:30.
4. Alma 43:29.
5. Alma 60:32.
6. Alma 20:10, 13; and see 54:17.
7. See 1 Nephi 16:37–38; 18:10; 2 Nephi 5:3, 19; Mosiah 10:12–13.
8. Mosiah 10:17.
9. Alma 54:18.
10. Alma 54:24. Although these words were spoken "fraudulently" by the Nephite traitor Ammoron, they nevertheless accurately reflect the mindset of the Lamanites.

was not all—they were sorry to be the means of sending so
many of their brethren out of this world into an eternal world,
unprepared to meet their God.

Nevertheless, they could not suffer to lay down their lives,
that their wives and their children should be massacred.[1]

Furthermore, the Lord had expressly given "unto them, and also
unto their fathers"[2] the law of war previously discussed. If the ag-
gressor army refused the repeated offer of peace, the Lord's instructions to the Nephites were, "Ye shall not suffer yourselves to be slain
by the hands of your enemies," but "ye shall defend your families
even unto bloodshed."[3] Under the monarchy, the Nephite king appears to have been the military commander.[4] Under the democratic
society ushered in by Mosiah, the chief military commander was at
first the chief judge and governor (as when Alma the younger was
head of the government led the Nephites into battle)[5] but later came
to be a separate post as "appointed by the chief judges and the voice
of the people."[6]

MORONI AND HIS ADMIRING BIOGRAPHER

In this scenario, Mormon introduces one of the most colorful,
charismatic, and competent characters in the entire parade of Book
of Mormon personalities—the Nephite commander-in-chief Moroni.
Moroni would prove to be the man of the hour as he appeared on
the scene just when his rare and remarkable array of talents was most
needed by an embattled Nephite society. Was his timely appearance
coincidental, or might we reasonably suppose that he had been fore-
ordained to his mission?[7]

We will see Moroni in his role of father only through his example,
for the narrative will never disclose so much as a word of what Moroni

---

1. Alma 48:23–24.
2. Alma 43:46.
3. Alma 43:46–47.
4. See Jacob 1:10; Words of Mormon 1:13–14.
5. See Alma 2:16.
6. Alma 46:34.
7. For Joseph Smith's comment on foreordination, see TPJS 365.

ever actually said to his son. But what the narrative does, fortunately, is provide a richly detailed picture of Moroni's example, allowing us to see much of what Moronihah learned from his outstanding father.

Mormon's detailed treatment of Moroni also tells us something about Mormon: he was enthralled with Moroni, with the man personally and with his military prowess. And understandably so, for Mormon—who shared many of Moroni's personal characteristics—was Moroni's eventual successor some four centuries later as Nephite commander-in-chief. Both men received their appointments at a young age: Moroni was twenty-five,[1] while Mormon was only fifteen.[2] Such commonality provided Mormon a unique understanding of Moroni's military exploits and achievements, and it assured an unusually detailed treatment of Moroni's career by the historian Mormon—similar in many respects to the historical treatment of Alexander the Great by the military commander Arrian (Greek by birth but a Roman citizen), who was similarly separated from his subject by about four centuries. Like Mormon's writing about Moroni, Arrian's treatment of Alexander is highly sympathetic with an experienced eye for detail in matters of military strategy and leadership.[3] Unlike Mormon, however, Arrian was not fortunate enough to have a godly man as his subject.

Mormon's admiration for Moroni was nearly unbounded:

> And Moroni was a strong and a mighty man; he was a man of a perfect understanding; yea, a man that did not delight in bloodshed; a man whose soul did joy in the liberty and the freedom of his country, and his brethren from bondage and slavery;
> Yea, a man whose heart did swell with thanksgiving to his God, for the many privileges and blessings which he bestowed upon his people; a man who did labor exceedingly for the welfare and safety of his people.
> Yea, and he was a man who was firm in the faith of Christ,

1. See Alma 43:17.
2. See Mormon 2:1–2.
3. See *Arrian: The Campaigns of Alexander* 1, 971.

and he had sworn with an oath to defend his people, his rights, and his country, and his religion, even to the loss of his blood.

Now the Nephites were taught to defend themselves against their enemies, even to the shedding of blood if it were necessary; yea, and they were also taught never to give an offense, yea, and never to raise the sword except it were against an enemy, except it were to preserve their lives.

And this was their faith, that by so doing God would prosper them in the land, or in other words, if they were faithful in keeping the commandments of God that he would prosper them in the land; yea, warn them to flee, or to prepare for war, according to their danger;

And also, that God would make it known unto them whither they should go to defend themselves against their enemies, and by so doing, the Lord would deliver them; and this was the faith of Moroni, and his heart did glory in it; not in the shedding of blood but in doing good, in preserving his people, yea, in keeping the commandments of God, yea, and resisting iniquity.

Yea, verily, verily I say unto you, if all men had been, and were, and ever would be, like unto Moroni, behold, the very powers of hell would have been shaken forever; yea, the devil would never have power over the hearts of the children of men.[1]

MORONI'S MILITARY LEADERSHIP

Knowing that the Nephites' public victories on the battlefield depended ultimately on their cumulative private victories in keeping God's commandments, Moroni was constantly "preparing the minds of the people to be faithful unto the Lord their God."[2] Here, as on the battlefield, he led the way with his characteristic conviction and charisma, as when on one occasion

he rent his coat; and he took a piece thereof, and wrote upon it—In memory of our God, our religion, and freedom, and our peace, our wives, and our children—and he fastened it upon the end of a pole.

---

1. Alma 48:11–17.
2. Alma 48:7.

> And he fastened on his headplate, and his breastplate, and his shields, and girded on his armor about his loins; and he took the pole, which had on the end thereof his rent coat, (and he called it the title of liberty) and he bowed himself to the earth, and he prayed mightily unto his God for the blessings of liberty to rest upon his brethren, so long as there should a band of Christians remain to possess the land. . . .
>
> And . . . when he had poured out his soul to God,. . . . he said: Surely God shall not suffer that we, who are despised because we take upon us the name of Christ, shall be trodden down and destroyed, until we bring it upon us by our own transgressions.[1]

Moroni then "went forth among the people," waving the title of liberty and inviting "whosoever [would] maintain this title upon the land" to "come forth in the strength of the Lord, and enter into a covenant [to] maintain their rights, and their religion." Moroni's fervent prayer, followed immediately by just as fervent action, provides a pattern of enduring relevance—a pattern also taught by a modern-day godly man to his son. According to President N. Eldon Tanner,

> When we pray, it is important that we set about to do all in our power to make it possible for the Lord to answer our prayers. As my father said to me when I was just a boy, "My son, if you want your prayers to be answered, you must get on your feet and do your part."[2]

The response to Moroni's action was stirring: "The people came running together with their armor girded about their loins, rending their garments in token, or as a covenant, that they would not forsake the Lord their God." Throwing their torn garments at Moroni's feet, they agreed that "God . . . may cast us at the feet of our enemies, even as we have cast our garments at thy feet to be trodden underfoot, if we shall fall into transgression."[3] Moroni then reminded them of their place in an important parent-child relationship. They were all

---

1. Alma 46:12–13, 17–18.
2. Kimball 1977:128.
3. Alma 46:22.

descendants of the patriarch Joseph, a piece of whose coat had prompted an important prophecy by Jacob on his deathbed. The story is absent in the traditional version of Genesis but is, as Hugh Nibley has pointed out, preserved in Arabic tradition.[1] As recounted by Moroni, when Jacob was about to die, he saw that a piece of Joseph's coat had not deteriorated, and he said:

> Even as this remnant of garment of my son hath been pre-
> served, so shall a remnant of the seed of my son be preserved
> by the hand of God, and be taken unto himself, while the
> remainder of the seed of Joseph shall perish, even as the rem-
> nant of his garment.[2]

Invoking that prophetic symbolism by their illustrious forefather, Moroni suggested that the part of Joseph's seed who would perish may be "those who have dissented from us. . . . Yea, and even it shall be ourselves if we do not stand fast in the faith of Christ."[3] Moroni's evocation of their righteous forefather Joseph is part of a larger pattern in which Book of Mormon prophets constantly call on the people to remember their righteous fathers. In addition, according to Hugh Nibley, when Moroni raised the Title of Liberty, he was apparently following an ancient practice of his Hebrew forefathers.[4] Moroni's astounding success, like that of so many other illustrious Book of Mormon characters, resulted directly from his remembering and emulating his righteous fathers.

Moroni's profoundly moving appeal to his people is also an ex-ample of what the eminent military historian John Keegan, in his recent study of generals and generalship, calls the "imperative of prescription," an aspect of successful command that, although almost entirely overlooked in modern military literature, was nevertheless "a well-known literary form in antiquity." This imperative requires a commander to inspire his men before the battle by communicating,

---

1. See CWHN 6:219–20.
2. Alma 46:24.
3. Alma 46:27.
4. See CWHN 6:209–21.

for example, "the justice of one's cause" or "by appealing to patriotism" in defense of "their property, religion, liberty and lives."[1]

Capitalizing fully on the stirring power of the Title of Liberty, Moroni proceeded to "raise the standard of liberty in whatsoever place he did enter," and "thousands did flock unto his standard, and did take up their swords in the defence of their freedom."[2] But Moroni's brilliant preparations did not stop with encouraging his people; he was also forever making military "preparations" (variations of this word recur constantly in the account). Thus he "prepared his people with breastplates and with arm-shields, yea, and also shields to defend their heads, and also they were dressed with thick clothing," giving Moroni's army a decided advantage over opposing forces, who were "not prepared with any such thing"[3] and accordingly suffered disproportionately heavy losses in battle.[4] Later when the Lamanites returned with identical preparations, they were "exceedingly astonished" at a yet new "manner of preparation"[5] by Moroni, who seemed always one step ahead of them: he had innovatively "built forts of security"[6] in "a manner which never had been known among the children of Lehi."[7] Moroni was always careful to leave part of his army to guard territory that stood at risk of Lamanite invasion.[8] We further read that "Moroni did not stop making preparations for war, or to defend his people."[9] He always seemed to be "preparing" and "making preparations,"[10] and thus "kept the commandments of God in preparing for the safety of his people."[11] The consequence of all these preparations was not merely greater protection but also deterrence so as to postpone and minimize bloodshed—as when Moroni's

---

1. Keegan 1987:320.
2. Alma 62:4-5.
3. Alma 43:19-20.
4. See Alma 43:37-38.
5. Alma 49:9.
6. Alma 49:13.
7. Alma 49:8.
8. See Alma 43:25; 49:2; 50:10.
9. Alma 50:1.
10. See Alma 53:7; 55:16, 25, 33; 59:5; 62:26.
11. Alma 49:27.

fortifications caused a surprised Lamanite army to continue marching in search of an easier target.[1]

But because full deterrence was impossible against this much larger force, Moroni also had to meet the opposing armies on the battlefield — which he did with extraordinary brilliance. "Knowing that it was the only desire of the Nephites to preserve their lands, and their liberty, and their church, therefore he thought it no sin that he should defend them by stratagem."[2] When possible he relied on the most effective intelligence gathering process of all, direct revelation from God through a prophet (Alma) as to movements of the opposing armies.[3] But Moroni also maximized his own resources in gathering intelligence in more traditional ways, such as by sending spies[4] or by engaging in reconnaissance himself, as when late one night he "went forth in the darkness . . . and came upon the top of the wall to spy out in what part of the city the Lamanites did camp with their army."[5] On another occasion he sent one of his men, a Lamanite by birth, incognito among Lamanites guarding Nephite prisoners of war in order to get the guards drunk.[6] Moroni is repeatedly said to have "resolved upon a plan"[7] or to have begun "again to lay a plan,"[8] as he repeatedly out-thinks, out-maneuvers, decoys, and isolates the opposing forces.[9] Such behavior exemplifies another command imperative identified by military historian Keegan — that of action.[10] And Moroni's brilliant strategy not only expedited his military success but also repeatedly resulted in minimizing the shedding of blood. For example, under Moroni's plan to free the Nephite prisoners by getting their Lamanite guards drunk, the purpose was accomplished without

---

1. See Alma 49:5–20.
2. Alma 43:30.
3. See Alma 43:23.
4. Ibid.
5. Alma 62:20.
6. See Alma 55:4–16.
7. Alma 52:21.
8. Alma 59:4.
9. See Alma 46:30–33; 50:7–12, 32–36; 52:19–37.
10. See Keegan 1987:325–29.

any loss of life on either side,[1] for "he did not delight in murder or bloodshed."[2]

The brilliance of Moroni's mind was matched by the courage of his heart, as seen for example in his candid correspondence with the opposing general[3] and with his own (apparently traitorous) head of government, to whom he wrote, "I do not fear your power nor your authority, but it is my God whom I fear."[4] Opposition or great odds never discouraged him; they only raised his determination.[5] On the one occasion in our English text when the word *fear* is used in connection with Moroni, he had just learned of the strategic loss of one Nephite stronghold, and he "was exceedingly sorrowful, and began to doubt, because of the wickedness of the people, whether they should not fall into the hands of their brethren [the Lamanites],"[6] whereupon he immediately wrote to the head of the Nephite government: "I fear exceedingly that the judgments of God will come upon this people."[7] But this use of the word *fear* may be merely idiomatic, for the emotion of fear seems to have been foreign to Moroni. Even for his own safety under the most intense conditions of battle, Moroni was fearless, heroically leading his men and fighting at the front alongside them — as is evident from his always apparently clear view of and earshot distance from the opposing forces, allowing him a battlefield position from which he could at any time call a halt to the fighting and immediately begin negotiations with the opposing army.[8] Moroni's behavior perfectly illustrates what historian Keegan calls "the first and greatest imperative of command," that of example, which means the commander must "be present in person. Those who impose risk must be seen to share it," for "it is the spectacle of heroism, or its immediate report, that fires the blood."[9]

---

1. See Alma 55:1–24.
2. Alma 55:19.
3. See Alma 54:5–14.
4. Alma 60:28.
5. See Alma 44:17; 46:11; 51:14; 54:13; 55:1; 59:13.
6. Alma 59:11.
7. Alma 60:14.
8. See Alma 43:54; 44:19; 52:36–38.
9. Keegan 1987:329.

The natural contagion of Moroni's personal courage was combined with an ability to inspire his soldiers even in the face of heaviest opposition, as during one intense battle

> when the men of Moroni saw the fierceness and the anger of the Lamanites, [and] were about to shrink and flee from them. And Moroni, perceiving their intent, sent forth and inspired their hearts with these thoughts—yea, the thoughts of their lands, their liberty, yea, their freedom from bondage.
>
> And it came to pass that they turned upon the Lamanites, and they cried with one voice unto the Lord their God, for their liberty and their freedom from bondage.
>
> And they began to stand against the Lamanites with power; and in that selfsame hour . . . the Lamanites began to flee before them. . . .
>
> Now, the Lamanites were more numerous, yea, by more than double the number of Nephites; nevertheless, they were driven.[1]

Moroni's role as commander-in-chief did not prevent him from counseling with some of his men on critical decisions, as when "Moroni . . . and many of the chief captains held a council of war—what they should do to cause the Lamanites to come out against them to battle."[2] The rapport that Moroni enjoyed with his men, and their esteem for him, is evident in a letter from one of his commanders, Helaman (son of Alma the younger), which begins: "My dearly beloved brother, Moroni, as well in the Lord as in the tribulations of our warfare; behold, my beloved brother, I have somewhat to tell you . . . "[3] The letter recounted the success and general safety of the men under Helaman's command; upon reading this letter Moroni "was exceedingly rejoiced because of the welfare, yea, the exceeding success which Helaman had had."[4] We are similarly told of another of Moroni's commanders, Lehi,

> who had been with Moroni in the more part of all his battles;

---

1. Alma 43:48–51.
2. Alma 52:19.
3. Alma 56:2.
4. Alma 59:1.

and he was a man like unto Moroni, and they rejoiced in each other's safety; yea, they were beloved by each other, and also beloved by all the people of Nephi.[1]

When the report reached Moroni of the death of Teancum, another of his commanders, Moroni was "exceedingly sorrowful."[2] Most telling of all, though, is the correspondence between Moroni and the Nephite governor, Paharon, whom Moroni scathingly criticizes even as he addresses Paharon and his colleagues as "my beloved brethren — for ye ought to be beloved."[3] Moroni's criticism of Paharon turns out to be inaccurate, but so sure is Paharon of Moroni's fair-mindedness and friendship that he can respond: "In your epistle you have censured me, but it mattereth not; I am not angry, but do rejoice in the greatness of your heart."[4] Paharon finally ends by closing his own "epistle to my beloved brother, Moroni."[5] Moroni's rapport with his men fulfills another imperative of command identified by Keegan, the "imperative of kinship," meaning a strong and trusted bond between the commander and his soldiers.[6]

But those who opposed Moroni, even among his own people, found him severe. Realizing the justness of his cause and what was riding upon the outcome — "their families, and their lands, their country, and their rights, and their religion"[7]—Moroni could allow no traitors and no dissenters anxious to defect or—as some dissenters even wished to do—to overthrow the government and establish again a monarchy.[8] Against such people Moroni had to use raw force, first defeating or capturing them, and then enforcing the law against those who had broken it,[9] while allowing others to choose between "a covenant to support the cause of freedom" or death.[10] Moroni's action

---

1. Alma 53:2.
2. Alma 62:37.
3. Alma 60:10.
4. Alma 61:9.
5. Alma 61:21.
6. See Keegan 1987:315–18.
7. Alma 43:47.
8. See Alma 51:1–9; 60:16.
9. See Alma 62:9–10.
10. Alma 46:35.

reflects Keegan's final imperative of command, that of "sanction," meaning the proper exercise of force among a commander's own troops.[1] That Moroni admirably fulfills every imperative of command that successful generals followed throughout history not only helps explain his amazing military achievements, but also may indicate that Moroni's entire leadership style followed an ancient pattern inherited from (who else?) his forefathers.

SEEKING PEACE IN WARTIME

Moroni's greatness as a man of war was fully matched by his greatness as a man of God, qualifying him for that exclusive group of history's successful *and* righteous generals. The sacred oath he had taken to defend the Nephite nation[2] had, of course, drawn a clear battle line, in defense of which he had to employ all his wits and strength. But with equal clarity he comprehended that God would preserve the Nephites—even as their ancestor Joseph's piece of coat had been preserved—only so long as they chose to "stand fast in the faith of Christ,"[3] in which case they could march into battle "in the strength of the Lord."[4] Indeed, Moroni himself set the example by being "firm in the faith of Christ"[5] and by "pour[ing] out his soul to God"[6] in mighty prayer on behalf of his people. Moroni knew that if and to the extent that the Nephites failed to keep God's command-ments—which at times happened[7]—they faced "the judgments of God,"[8] even though at times "the Lord suffereth the righteous to be slain that his justice and judgment may come upon the wicked."[9] Moroni also understood, however, that the "wicked" were not nec-essarily the warring Lamanites, for "it is the tradition of their fathers

1. See Keegan 1987:321–24.
2. See Alma 48:13.
3. Alma 46:27.
4. Alma 46:20; 60:16.
5. Alma 48:13.
6. Alma 46:17.
7. See Alma 51:2–14.
8. Alma 60:14.
9. Alma 60:13.

that has caused their hatred,"[1] and Moroni even felt "sorry to be the means of sending so many [Lamanites] out of this world into an eternal world, unprepared to meet their God."[2] Moroni's mercy toward those whose errors arose from following the tradition of their fathers indicates the great weight he placed on the principle of following one's fathers. Furthermore, this "man of a perfect understanding"[3] fully grasped the truth expressed by Hugh Nibley, that

> war [deceptively] settles everything by a neat polarization: everything evil on one side and everything good on the other. No problem remains for anybody on either side but to kill people on the other side. . . . The most significant thing about this polarization, of course, is that it puts an end once and for all to any thought of repentance, in which lies the only hope for survival and peace.[4]

It was precisely this polarization that Moroni constantly tried to counteract as he used every available opportunity to preach righteousness and repentance, not only to his own people[5] but even to the opposing armies. It was no mere rhetoric when Moroni informed a terrified Lamanite army:

> The Lord is with us [the Nephites]; and ye behold that he has delivered you into our hands. . . . because of our religion and our faith in Christ. . . .
>
> Now ye see that this is the true faith of God; yea, ye see that God will support, and keep, and preserve us, so long as we are faithful unto him, and unto our faith, and our religion; and never will the Lord suffer that we shall be destroyed except we should fall into transgression and deny our faith.[6]

Nor was it hyperbole when Moroni wrote to the Nephite traitor who became a Lamanite general, Ammoron:

---

1. Alma 60:32.
2. Alma 48:23.
3. Alma 48:11.
4. CWHN 8:526.
5. See Alma 46:12–27.
6. Alma 44:3–4.

> Behold, I would tell you somewhat concerning the justice of
> God, and the sword of his almighty wrath, which doth hang
> over you except ye repent and withdraw your armies. . . .
>   Yea, I would tell you concerning that awful hell that awaits
> to receive such murderers as thou and thy brother have been,
> except ye repent and withdraw your murderous purposes.[1]

It is impressive to see how Moroni, one of the most powerful and effective military commanders of all time, used every available forum during the war to call the attention of everyone, friend and foe alike, to life's real battle as fought within each human soul. Moroni thus knew what his great admirer Mormon had expressed, that

> we have a labor to perform whilst in this tabernacle of clay,
> that we may conquer the enemy of all righteousness, and rest
> our souls in the kingdom of God.[2]

This battle, Moroni well understood, was the most important of all. As President David O. McKay would later express: "The greatest battle of life is fought within the silent chambers of your own soul."[3] Winning that inner battle brings the inner peace that is, as latter-day revelation expresses, the reward of righteousness[4] — and this despite outward conditions. Thus Jesus could tell his Jewish apostles that even in the midst of this world's tribulation they would enjoy peace,[5] the peace that he gave them.[6] Or, as one of Jesus' latter-day apostles, Elder Joseph B. Wirthlin, has explained, "Despite dismal conditions in the world and the personal challenges that come into every life, peace within can be a reality. We can be calm and serene regardless of the swirling turmoil all about us."[7]

To allow the people to achieve that inner peace by focusing on life's real battle, Moroni attempted at every turn to bring a peaceful

1. Alma 54:6–7.
2. Moroni 9:6.
3. *Improvement Era* 70:6 (June 1967), p. 80.
4. See D&C 59:23.
5. See John 16:33.
6. See John 14:27.
7. *Ensign* 21:5 (May 1991), p.37.

resolution to the war with its deceptive polarization. Summing up several passages describing Moroni's actions, Hugh Nibley observes:

> We are often reminded that Moroni "did not delight in the shedding of blood" and would do anything to avoid it, repeatedly urging his people to make covenants of peace and to preserve them by faith and prayer. He refused to talk about "the enemy."[1] For him they were always "our brethren," misled by the traditions of their fathers. He fought them only with heavy reluctance, and he never invaded their lands, even when they threatened invasion of his own. . . .
>
> At the slightest sign of weakening by an enemy in battle, Moroni would instantly propose a discussion to put an end to the fighting. The idea of total victory was alien to him — no revenge, no reprisals, no reparations, even for an aggressor who had ravaged his country. He would send the beaten enemy home after the battle, accepting their word for good behavior . . . , even when he knew it was taking a risk.[2]

In wartime, then, Moroni sought peace — for society and for individual souls; and he did so by seeking to turn the hearts of the children to their fathers. He thereby put into practice precisely what the Lord has commanded his people of our day in the same revelation describing the ancient law of war given to the Nephites and others. The commandment is, "Renounce war and proclaim peace, and seek diligently to turn the hearts of the children to their fathers."[3]

VICTORY AND HUMILITY

With military victory finally in sight after years of war, Moroni magnanimously, in Nibley's words, "shared with Paharon the glory of the final victory — one thing that ambitious generals jealously reserve for themselves."[4] Such conspicuous lack of personal ambition characterized Moroni's entire career, as is well capsulized by his own statement: "I seek not for power. . . . I seek not for honor of the

---

1. On most occasions; for an exception see Alma 60:16.
2. Nibley 1984:45.
3. D&C 98:16.
4. Nibley 1984:45.

world, but for the glory of my God, and the freedom and welfare of my country."[1] His words were consistent with his deeds, as even during wartime he was careful to use his power only within the framework of the law,[2] when in fact he stood at the pinnacle of power in Nephite society and could easily—like so many other successful generals in history—have grasped the reigns of government. That he did not is proof that his opposition to those wishing to reestablish a Nephite monarchy had been no empty charade or devious power-play. Furthermore, Moroni could probably have gone about conquering to subdue foreign lands, like such skilled but insatiable generals as Alexander the Great, Attila the Hun, or Genghis Khan. Or, once Moroni had achieved victory and had become "the national hero," as Nibley observes, he at least "could have had any office or honor" within Nephite society.[3] Indeed, he had long been the one to whom people had directly appealed when wronged or oppressed,[4] and he was "beloved by all the people of Nephi."[5]

But Moroni claimed no credit or reward for the victory that he had long fought for. To the contrary, from the start he had insisted that their only strength was "the strength of the Lord,"[6] so that when victory was achieved, the Lord was the one who had preserved them[7] and delivered them[8] from their enemies. In fact, thanks mostly to Moroni's teachings, "the people of Nephi did thank the Lord their God"—rather than their General Moroni!—for "delivering them from the hands of their enemies."[9] In short, Moroni was one of those rare exceptions to the general rule that "almost all men, as soon as they get a little authority, as they suppose, . . . will immediately begin to exercise unrighteous dominion."[10]

---

1. Alma 60:36.
2. See Alma 51:15–16; 62:8–10.
3. Nibley 1984:45.
4. See Alma 50:27–31.
5. Alma 53:2.
6. Alma 46:20; 60:16.
7. See Alma 46:24.
8. See Alma 60:11.
9. Alma 49:28.
10. D&C 121:39.

Once the war was over "and there was once more peace established," Moroni simply "yielded up the command of his armies . . . and retired to his own house that he might spend the remainder of his days in peace."[1] Moroni's behavior bears striking resemblance to a later American general, George Washington, who led the American forces that had been foreseen by Moroni's forefather Nephi.[2] Similar to Moroni, Washington was fighting in defense of "inalienable rights" endowed by the Creator, rights which included "Life, Liberty and the pursuit of Happiness" (in the words of the Declaration of Independence). Washington's victory, like Moroni's, was achieved only after a long and arduous war. As with Moroni, Washington's military leadership and victory made him easily the most powerful and revered figure in his society, as one biographer notes: "He had no rivals. . . . No individual had national stature comparable with Washington's."[3] But also like Moroni, Washington credited his military success to "the gracious interposition of Heaven; and to that interposition let us gratefully ascribe the praise of victory."[4] Having clearly perceived what Nephi had foreseen, that the Americans "were delivered by the power of God,"[5] Washington told his troops, "It having pleased the Almighty Ruler of the Universe propitiously to defend the cause of the United American States . . . , it becomes us to set apart a day for gratefully acknowledging the divine Goodness."[6] And, like Moroni, the successful General Washington simply retired to his home, intending (although in his case it would not be so) to remain there for the rest of his life, as he wrote to a friend:

> At length . . . I am become a private citizen . . . under the shadow of my own vine and my own fig tree. Free from the bustle of a camp and the busy scenes of public life, I am solacing

1. Alma 62:42–43.
2. See 1 Nephi 13:17–19.
3. Flexner 1984:183.
4. To the Executive of New Hampshire, November 3, 1789, quoted in Benson 1979:17.
5. 1 Nephi 13:19.
6. Petersen 1975:54.

> myself with the tranquil enjoyments [of] which the soldier who
> is ever in pursuit of fame . . . can have very little conception.[1]

Such marked resemblance between these two generals each leading
his forces on the American continent seems appropriate, for while
Moroni drew upon divine power to secure liberty upon the promised
land for the Nephites who would produce the Book of Mormon,
Washington drew upon that same divine power to secure liberty upon
that same promised land in order to allow the Book of Mormon to
come forth — as the resurrected Savior had prophesied to the Nephites:

> It is wisdom in the Father that they [the Gentiles] should be
> established in this land, and be set up as a free people by the
> power of the Father, that these things might come forth from
> them unto a remnant of your seed.[2]

MORONIHAH – MAN OF WAR, MAN OF GOD

Such is the record of Moroni's illustrious life and career. Of his
son, however, we hear nothing (indeed, we are not so much as told
that he has a son) until the very moment Moroni relinquishes command of the Nephites' armies "into the hands of his son, whose name
was Moronihah."[3] Nor afterwards are we ever apprised of how or
what Moroni had taught his son about the art of war or the art of
righteousness. What is obvious, however, is that such a critical position now conferred upon Moronihah would have been entrusted
only to someone who was well trained and highly trusted; and that
as highly visible as Moroni's career was in general, it must have been
even more so to his son, who was being groomed for the same post.
Certainly years of living in military camps would have sharply cur-
tailed Moroni's opportunities to engage in otherwise normal teaching
activities for the benefit of his son. But such lack of opportunity seems
to have been compensated for by the sheer power of Moroni's example
and leadership, for the record paints Moronihah with much the same
tones as Moroni.

---

1. Flexner 1984:183–84.
2. 3 Nephi 21:4.
3. Alma 62:43.

To be sure, there is not the detail in the portrait of Moronihah that there is in that of Moroni. But this is no negative reflection on Moronihah, for as Mormon recounts the events of Moronihah's day he expressly states that "a hundredth part of the proceedings of this people . . . cannot be contained in this work."[1] The sparse information that Mormon does reveal about Moronihah, however, suggests a man much like Moroni. For example, in Moronihah's first battle as commander of the Nephite armies, they faced "a numerous army" of Lamanites who "came down . . . to war against the people of Moronihah, or against the army of Moronihah, in the which they [the Lamanites] were beaten and driven back again to their own lands, suffering great loss."[2] Moronihah displayed the same skill possessed by Moroni in defeating armies with significantly superior numbers.

It is true that Moronihah later made a grave miscalculation resulting in a heavy Lamanite incursion into the Nephite heartland, which may show that he didn't possess all of his father's foresight and brilliance. Or, such Lamanite success may be explained by God's withdrawing his protection from the Nephites. Whatever the explanation, Moronihah's response upon discovering his mistake shows the same decisiveness and determination as that of his father, and some of the same kind of effective strategy as well: Moronihah immediately sent one of his armies to head off the advancing Lamanites. When the battle had begun, he led another army behind the Lamanites and succeeded in surrounding them. Then he gave them such battle that, after much killing, the remaining Lamanites surrendered.[3] Finally, Moronihah "caused that the Lamanites who had been taken prisoners should depart out of the land in peace."[4] No revenge, no reprisals—just like Moroni.

Through his leadership, Moronihah succeeded in "establish[ing] again peace between the Nephites and the Lamanites"[5]—again an

---

1. Helaman 3:14.
2. Alma 63:15.
3. Helaman 1:25–32.
4. Helaman 1:33.
5. Helaman 2:1; and see 3:23.

echo of what his father had accomplished.[1] The events transpiring during Moronihah's peace likewise echo the pattern of events during peacetime in Moroni's day: in both cases church leaders successfully preached the word of God and significantly strengthened the church;[2] in both cases the Nephites were blessed with "exceedingly great prosperity";[3] in both cases there was "peace and rejoicing"[4] or "peace and exceedingly great joy";[5] and in both cases there was an eventual return to wickedness, whereupon the Lamanites achieved greater success in their war against the Nephites.[6]

In the case of Moronihah, the Lamanite success was so significant that they had captured "almost all" of the Nephite lands.[7] Such dire circumstances called for immediate action by the Nephite commander-in-chief; and respond he did, but not with military might that we would expect. Instead, "Moronihah did preach many things unto the people because of their iniquity," coordinating his efforts with church leaders who also preached and prophesied to the people "what should come unto them if they did not repent of their sins."[8] Such a surprising response by Moronihah at the very moment of the most ominous military threat to Nephite society can only be explained if he understood what the historian Mormon wrote: that "this great loss of the Nephites, and the great slaughter which was among them, would not have happened had it not been for their wickedness and their abomination," and that "it was because of the pride of their hearts" and "their great wickedness, and their boastings in their own strength, [that] they were left in their own strength; therefore they . . . were afflicted and smitten, and driven before the Lamanites."[9]

Moronihah clearly shared the perspective of his father, who had

---

1. See, e.g., Alma 46:37; 50:23; 62:11, 42.
2. See Alma 48:19–20; 49:30; Helaman 3:24–26.
3. Alma 49:30; Helaman 3:24.
4. Alma 46:38.
5. Helaman 3:32.
6. See Alma 59:11–12; 62:40–41; Helaman 3:34; 4:1–6, 11–14.
7. Helaman 4:13.
8. Helaman 4:14.
9. Helaman 4:11–13.

also prepared for battle by first raising the Title of Liberty and reminding his people that they would perish "if [they did] not stand
fast in the faith of Christ."¹ And later, when Moroni's people had
wavered in their righteousness, Moroni had been "exceedingly sorrowful . . . because of the wickedness of the people, whether they
should not fall into the hands of [the Lamanites],"² whereupon he
wrote, "If we had gone forth against them in the strength of the Lord,
we should have dispersed our enemies,"³ and he reminded his people
what would befall them "except [they] repent."⁴ It was just one of a
number of times when Moroni had "prepar[ed] the minds of the
people to be faithful unto the Lord their God"⁵ while coordinating
his efforts with church leaders who likewise preached the word of
God⁶ — a pattern that Moronihah would follow.

In the case of Moronihah, when he "saw that they did repent he
did venture to lead them forth from place to place . . . until they had
regained the one-half of their property and . . . lands."⁷ Once again
the pattern is that of Moroni, who had marched forth and reclaimed
Nephite lands (lost while he had been quelling an internal Nephite
rebellion⁸) only after his people had rallied to his standard of repentance and righteousness.⁹ And as Moroni had carefully stationed his
armies to guard Nephite territory,¹⁰ so we read that Moronihah "did
employ all his armies in maintaining those parts which he had taken."¹¹

That is the last word we hear of Moronihah, as Mormon shifts
the focus of his abridged narrative from the military to the ministry
and tells that many of the Lamanites repented and "did yield up unto
the Nephites the lands of their possession,"¹² ushering in an era of

---

1. Alma 46:27.
2. Alma 59:11.
3. Alma 60:16.
4. Alma 60:24.
5. Alma 48:7.
6. See Alma 48:19; 49:30.
7. Helaman 4:16.
8. See Alma 51:22–27.
9. See Alma 62:4–7.
10. See Alma 43:25; 49:2; 50:10.
11. Helaman 4:19.
12. Helaman 5:52.

"peace in all the land" among both Nephites and Lamanites.[1] Mormon has not disclosed as much about Moronihah as we might have wished. In what is disclosed, however, we see a son whose life and labors closely reflect the pattern established by his father. Each was a mighty man of war as well as a mighty man of God. And echoing statements by latter-day prophets about the supreme and surpassing importance of parenthood,[2] we might say that Moroni's success as a father was even more important than his colossal success as the Nephite commander-in-chief.

The exemplary value of Moroni's life was to extend far beyond his own son. Moroni's admirer Mormon—who, according to one scholar, may well have been Moroni's descendant[3]—would likewise follow the illustrious pattern of Moroni, whose name he would confer on his own son.[4] And the fact that one of Mormon's commanders bore the name of Moronihah[5] may manifest a reverential perpetuation in Nephite society of the memory of that first Moronihah, son of Moroni.

---

1. Helaman 6:7.
2. See Introduction.
3. See John A. Tvedtnes, in Ricks and Hamblin 1990:319.
4. See Mormon 6:6.
5. See Mormon 6:14.

Chapter 7

POWERFUL DISCIPLES AGAINST WICKEDNESS
••••••••••••••••••••••••••••••••

THE TWO HELAMANS, THE TWO NEPHIS, AND JONAS

HELAMAN IN WAR AND PEACE

The illustrious line of Alma continued to figure prominently in Book of Mormon history, and Mormon shifts the focus to Helaman, Alma's son, in an account of another father-son pair of two Nephite generals. In Mormon's account of the prolonged war, Helaman, the oldest son of Alma the younger, is first portrayed as a father, but not in the traditional sense. He is called "father" by the two thousand young Lamanite soldiers whom he led into battle and whom, out of his great love for them, he called "my sons."[1] Such usage is unique in the Book of Mormon but echoes similar usage in ancient Israel reflected in various Old Testament passages, wherein, as one eminent scholar notes, the term *father*

> is applied to a man who is considered worthy of special honor, e.g., an older man (1 S. 24:12[11]), a teacher or prophetic master (2 K. 2:12; 6:21; 13:14), a priest (Jgs. 17:10; 18:19; cf *beni*, "my

---

1. Alma 56:45–46.

son," as a word used by a wisdom teacher to address his students). [The term "father" also] sometimes means a protector, who to some extent takes the place of a father [Ps. 68:6[5]; Job 29:16; Isa. 22:21].[1]

These same roles of teacher, master, and protector are conspicuously played by Helaman, who as a prophet and teacher had counseled his young soldiers' parents not to break their covenant against taking up arms, "lest by so doing they should lose their souls."[2] Their sons, however, had made no such covenant, and they now heroically entered into a different covenant—to defend the liberty of the Nephites, who up to then had magnanimously provided military protection for these Lamanites converted by the sons of Mosiah.

Having voluntarily come forward to join the Nephite cause, these two thousand young Lamanites—"all young men, and . . . exceedingly valiant for courage, and . . . men who were true at all times in whatsoever thing they were entrusted"[3]—requested that Helaman be their leader. He consented, though there is no indication that he had ever been in battle. Thus it was that Helaman, like his father, Alma the younger,[4] took up arms in defending the liberty of his people.

Our account of Helaman and his two thousand "sons" in battle comes from what Helaman wrote to Commander-in-Chief Moroni in a lengthy letter,[5] the inclusion of which in Mormon's record demonstrates the value he placed on this material. Arguably the predominant theme is that of parents and children, beginning in a larger context with Helaman himself, whose tone and expression clearly demonstrate his obedience to the repeated counsel he had received years before from his own father to keep the commandments of God.[6]

Addressing his "dearly beloved brother, Moroni, as well in the

---

1. TDOT I:8; brackets in original except "[the term 'father' also]"; see also TDNT V:977. A somewhat similar range of meaning is likewise found in our English word *father*, which can designate one who is "a revered guide or most notable influence in another's . . . development." (WTNID 828.)

2. Alma 53:15.

3. Alma 53:20.

4. See Alma 2–3.

5. See Alma 56–58.

6. See Alma 36:1, 30; 37:13, 20.

Lord as in the tribulations of our warfare,"[1] Helaman describes his two thousand young warriors in relation to their fathers: "Ye have known that these were descendants of Laman, who was the eldest son of our father Lehi."[2] And as to their immediate fathers: "Ye also know concerning the covenant which their fathers made, that they would not take up their weapons of war against their brethren to shed blood."[3] The sons who stepped forward at the risk of their young lives became for Helaman "my little sons,"[4] whom even as they marched to war he tried to protect from the ravages of battle. Only when their support became potentially critical did he offer them the choice: "What say ye, my sons, will ye go against them to battle?" Their response stirred Helaman—"Never had I seen so great courage"—as they exclaimed: "Father, behold our God is with us, and he will not suffer that we should fall; then let us go forth."[5] Helaman's subsequent comment about his young warriors is one of the most instructive about parent-child relationships in the Book of Mormon, as he observes:

> Now they never had fought, yet they did not fear death; and they did think more upon the liberty of their fathers than they did upon their lives; yea, they had been taught by their mothers, that if they did not doubt, God would deliver them.
> And they rehearsed unto me the words of their mothers, saying: We do not doubt our mothers knew it.[6]

The battle that they engaged in was fierce, with intense fighting and tremendous loss of life. Yet these "sons" of Helaman did, in his own words,

> obey and observe to perform every word of command with exactness; yea, and even according to their faith it was done

1. Alma 56:2.
2. Alma 56:3.
3. Alma 56:6.
4. Alma 56:30, 39.
5. Alma 56:44–46.
6. Alma 56:47–48.

unto them; and I did remember the words which they said
unto me that their mothers had taught them.[1]

Their valor proved decisive, and the Nephite army carried the
day, albeit with heavy casualties. Of Helaman's two thousand "sons,"
not one had escaped receiving "many wounds"; but astonishingly,
not a single one had been killed:

> And we do justly ascribe it to the miraculous power of God,
> because of their exceeding faith in that which they had been
> taught to believe — that there was a just God, and whosoever
> did not doubt, that they should be preserved by his marvelous
> power.[2]

Helaman's conclusion about the preservation of his youthful warriors is not only a tribute to their great mothers (whose role was
discussed earlier[3]) but also an echo and confirmation of what his own
father had emphatically taught him — that "whosoever shall put their
trust in God shall be supported in their trials, and their troubles, and
their afflictions,"[4] and shall be delivered as were the fathers, for God
surely "delivered them" out of their afflictions, bondage, and captivity.[5]

Echoes of what his father taught him continue in Helaman's letter,
as when he reports hearing a fellow military officer bless the name
of God who "delivered [us] out of the hands of our enemies"; upon
hearing this, says Helaman, "I was filled with exceeding joy because
of the goodness of God in preserving us, that we might not all perish."[6]
The words are reminiscent of those he had heard from his father,
who had told of being filled with "joy" that was "exceeding"[7] upon
being liberated from his awful and painful "chains of death,"[8] follow-

---

1. Alma 57:21.
2. Alma 57:26.
3. See Introduction.
4. Alma 36:3.
5. See Alma 36:2, 28, 29.
6. Alma 57:35–36.
7. Alma 36:20.
8. Alma 36:18.

ing which he had always been "supported" and "delivered" by God.[1]

Later when Helaman reports a surprising and serious lack of provisions for his and other Nephite armies, he recounts that he (with others) was "grieved and also filled with fear, lest by any means the judgments of God should come upon [their] land, to [their] overthrow and utter destruction."[2] The situation recalls when Helaman's father had, because of the wickedness of the people, experienced "much affliction"[3] and "began to be very sorrowful"[4] shortly after his people had perceived their wartime losses to be "the judgments of God sent upon them because of their wickedness and their abominations."[5]

Distressed at the possibility that the judgments of God might be overtaking the Nephites, Helaman and others "did pour out our souls in prayer to God, that he would strengthen us and deliver us out of the hands of our enemies."[6] Here Helaman follows the example of his grandfather Alma and his people who, when oppressed by the Lamanites, "did pour out their hearts to [God]."[7] Obviously, Helaman lived up to the admonition of his father who, referring to their fathers, urged Helaman "to retain in remembrance, as I have done, their captivity."[8]

And the blessings of retaining that remembrance were the same blessings originally granted to the fathers, for, following the prayer of Helaman and his brethren, he recounts that "the Lord our God did visit us with assurances that he would deliver us" and "did speak peace to our souls."[9] So also had the Lord done for Helaman's grandfather Alma and his people, to whom the voice of the Lord had said,

---

1. Alma 36:27.
2. Alma 58:9.
3. Alma 4:7.
4. Alma 4:15.
5. Alma 4:3.
6. Alma 58:10.
7. Mosiah 24:12.
8. Alma 36:29.
9. Alma 58:11.

"Be of good comfort, for on the morrow I will deliver you out of bondage."[1]

At the time Helaman wrote his letter, full deliverance had not been forthcoming; but still following his father's counsel,[2] he remained hopeful: "We trust God will deliver us, notwithstanding the weakness of our armies."[3] And then, as the final tribute to and identification with his great father, Helaman signed off: "I am Helaman, the son of Alma."[4]

When the war finally ended and peace was established, Helaman could not rest. Like his father and grandfather before him, he "did take upon him again to preach unto the people the word of God" and worked with others. The result of his preaching was also similar to that of his father and grandfather, for he and his fellow laborers "did declare the word of God with much power unto the convincing of many people," causing them "to repent of their sins and to be baptized." And thus "they did establish again the church of God."[5]

Mormon's final word about Helaman again attests to how well he had followed his father's course and counsel: Helaman had been "a just man" who "did walk uprightly before God" and did "keep the commandments" and "did observe to do good continually."[6] By so doing, he had followed his father and grandfather and would also influence generations to come—beginning with his own son, Helaman the younger.

HELAMAN THE YOUNGER AS CHIEF JUDGE AND FATHER

The sacred records had passed from Helaman to his brother Shiblon, and finally to Helaman the Younger[7]—good evidence that this son of Helaman was, like his father, worthy to be entrusted with the sacred records passed down in the line of Alma. In fact, we are later expressly told that Helaman

---

1. Mosiah 24:16.
2. See Alma 36:3.
3. Alma 58:37.
4. Alma 58:41.
5. Alma 62:44–46.
6. Alma 63:2 (said of both Shiblon and Helaman).
7. See Alma 63:1–13.

did observe to keep the statutes, and the judgments, and the commandments of God; and he did do that which was right in the sight of God continually; and he did walk after the ways of his father.[1]

But it is his grandfather, Alma the younger, whom Helaman the younger most resembles in being elected to the highest political office in the land, that of chief judge,[2] an office he filled "with justice and equity"[3]; that same office had been first filled by Alma the younger through similar election.[4] Likewise it is Alma the younger who comes to mind when we read of the preservation of Helaman's life in the face of an assassination attempt by the band of Gadianton[5]; Alma the younger's life had also been preserved when threatened by the murderous citizens of Ammonihah.[6] The most significant resemblance, however, comes when Helaman did what his grandfather had done in teaching his sons not only the path of righteousness, but also how best to travel the path—by remembering their righteous forefathers, particularly Lehi and Nephi. That Helaman himself remembered those same fathers is suggested by his doing what father Lehi had done— naming his sons after righteous ancestral fathers. Lehi had named two of his sons Jacob and Joseph; Helaman now names his two sons (beginning with the oldest) Nephi and Lehi. Then comes Mormon's suggestive comment: "And they began to grow up unto the Lord."[7] How so? We find out two chapters later when Mormon describes what Helaman taught his sons:

> Behold, my sons, I desire that ye should remember to keep the commandments of God; and I would that ye should declare unto the people these words. Behold, I have given unto you the names of our first parents who came out of the land of Jerusalem; and this I have done that when you remember your

---

1. Helaman 3:20.
2. See Helaman 2:2.
3. Helaman 3:20.
4. See Mosiah 29:39–42.
5. See Helaman 2:3–12.
6. See Alma 14.
7. Helaman 3:21.

names ye may remember them; and when ye remember them ye may remember their works; and when ye remember their works ye may know how that it is said, and also written, that they were good.

Therefore, my sons, I would that ye should do that which is good, that it may be said of you, and also written, even as it has been said and written of them.[1]

This theme of the fathers continues as Helaman counsels his sons to do these things not to be able to boast but to acquire "that precious gift of eternal life, which we have reason to suppose hath been given to our fathers." That gift, says Helaman, is like "a treasure in heaven, yea, which is eternal, and which fadeth not away."[2]

The pattern of Alma counseling his sons continues as Helaman similarly urges his sons to remember the scriptures and their preeminent message concerning another Father and his Son, even Jesus Christ, who "hath power given unto him from the Father" to redeem all who repent.[3] It is this unique and uniquely powerful Son that Helaman recommends as the foundation upon which his own sons should build their lives:

And now, my sons, remember, remember that it is upon the rock of our Redeemer, who is Christ, the Son of God, that ye must build your foundation; that when the devil shall send forth his mighty winds, yea, his shafts in the whirlwind, yea, when all his hail and his mighty storm shall beat upon you, it shall have no power over you to drag you down to the gulf of misery and endless wo, because of the rock upon which ye are built, which is a sure foundation, a foundation whereon if men build they cannot fall.[4]

The inclusion of Helaman's fatherly counsel in the record of Mormon—especially when he has just told us that he is able to include less than a hundredth part of the recorded history available to him[5]—

1. Helaman 5:6–7.
2. Helaman 5:8.
3. Helaman 5:11.
4. Helaman 5:12.
5. See Helaman 3:14–16.

demonstrates again how highly Mormon prized the record of counsel given by righteous fathers to sons. Moreover, Mormon assures us that these "words which Helaman taught to his sons" were but a portion of the "many things" which he taught them.[1] And where is Mormon getting this material? He expressly discloses his source in the heading to the book of Helaman, abridged by Mormon from "the records of Helaman, who was the son of Helaman, and also according to the records of his sons." Helaman thus continued the long legacy of righteousness not only by teaching his sons, but also by adding to and transmitting the sacred record.

NEPHI, MAN OF POWER

Upon the death of Helaman, his son Nephi succeeded him as chief judge. Nephi's performance is appraised by Mormon in language similar to that which Mormon had used earlier when he said that

> Helaman did fill the judgment-seat with justice and equity; yea, he did observe to keep . . . the commandments of God; . . . and he did walk after the ways of his father.[2]

So now Mormon reports that

> Nephi . . . did fill the judgment-seat with justice and equity; yea, he did keep the commandments of God, and did walk in the ways of his father.[3]

Such parallel expression suggests that, for Mormon, these two men constituted similar and indispensable links in this long chain of righteous fathers and sons whose influence on Nephite civilization was so profound.

But Nephi's day was a time of great turbulence occasioned by the increasing wickedness of his people who lost the Lord's protection and were driven off nearly all their lands by the Lamanites.[4] Only

---

1. Helaman 5:13.
2. Helaman 3:20.
3. Helaman 3:37.
4. See Helaman 4:1–13.

after Nephi and Lehi, along with General Moronihah, preached and prophesied many warnings did the people repent sufficiently so that the Lord blessed them with military strength enough to recover half of their lands.[1] Even so, such was their general state of transgression that Nephi "yielded up the judgment-seat, and took it upon him to preach the word of God all the remainder of his days."[2] If Nephi thus gave up the office that was once occupied by his father and that could have been occupied by his future descendants for generations to come, he did so precisely because he remembered his father's words urging him and his brother to preach. As Mormon comments: "They did remember his words; and *therefore* they went forth, keeping the commandments of God, to teach the word of God."[3] Mormon's comment could well provide a simple but valuable guide for any parent: What will my children do when they remember my words?

In relinquishing the highest political office to preach full-time, Nephi was following the pattern of his great-grandfather Alma the younger.[4] In neither case was there any question of competency in performing the duties of the highest political office; the issue was priority, for the temporal and eternal salvation of their society depended on repentance. This voluntary relinquishment of high political office, so contrary to worldly wisdom, recalls the words of the Prophet Joseph Smith: "After all that has been said, the greatest and most important duty is to preach the Gospel."[5] For these descendants of the zealous preacher Alma the elder, this most important of all duties could not take a back seat to anything, even the office constituting the pinnacle of Nephite political power.

Nephi and his brother Lehi are said to have preached with "great power and authority . . . unto the great astonishment"[6] of their hearers, persuading many to repentance and baptism, and thereby continuing the tradition of powerful preaching passed down in the line

1. See Helaman 4:14–16.
2. Helaman 5:4.
3. Helaman 5:14; emphasis added.
4. See Alma 4:15–20.
5. TPJS 113
6. Helaman 5:17, 19.

of Alma. As another measure of the power of Nephi's and Lehi's preaching, they even converted thousands of Lamanites, who became "convinced of the wickedness of the traditions of their fathers."[1]

As Nephi's ministry unfolds, it continuously reflects that of his great-grandfather, Alma the younger. As Nephi and Lehi were preaching among the Lamanites, the two brothers were cast into prison (as Alma and Amulek had once been[2]) and deprived of food for many days. But at last they were delivered by the power of God, which shook the earth.[3] But Nephi's prison experience also foreshadows even greater events to be experienced by his son who some six decades later would witness the great destruction (at the time of Christ's crucifixion) and, shortly thereafter, the personal appearance and ministry of the resurrected Christ to the Nephites:

While Nephi and Lehi were in prison "the earth shook exceedingly,"[4] foreshadowing the future upheaval caused by "the exceedingly great quaking of the whole earth."[5] Those in the prison with Nephi and Lehi "were overshadowed with a cloud of darkness, and an awful solemn fear came upon them,"[6] foreshadowing the future "thick darkness" described as a "vapor" or "mist" of darkness that would settle in after the cataclysm and remain for three days, during which there would be "great mourning and howling and weeping among all the people."[7] Those who were in the prison with Nephi and Lehi, enveloped in the cloud of darkness, heard a voice saying, "Repent ye, repent ye, and seek no more to destroy my servants,"[8] foreshadowing the voice to be heard by the survivors of the great destruction sent because the people had killed the prophets:[9] "Will ye not now return unto me, and repent of your sins, and be con-

1. Helaman 5:19.
2. See Alma 14.
3. See Helaman 5:21–49.
4. Helaman 5:27, 31.
5. 3 Nephi 8:12, and see verses 6–19.
6. Helaman 5:28.
7. 3 Nephi 8:19–25.
8. Helaman 5:29.
9. See 3 Nephi 9:5, 7–11.

verted . . . ?"[1] The heavenly voice that came to those in the prison
was "a still voice of perfect mildness, as if it had been a whisper, and
it did pierce even to the very soul,"[2] foreshadowing the time when,
some time after the terrible destruction, a multitude around the temple
would hear a heavenly voice that was neither harsh nor loud but "did
pierce them that did hear to the center . . . [and] to the very soul."[3]
To those in the prison the heavenly voice came three times,[4] just as
the heavenly voice to be heard by the multitude at the temple would
come three times.[5] When the voice came to those in the prison for
the third time, it "did speak unto them marvelous words which cannot
be uttered by man,"[6] even as the multitude gathered around the
temple would hear the resurrected Lord utter in prayer "great and
marvelous things" which "no tongue can speak, neither can [they]
be written by any man,"[7] "neither can they be uttered by man."[8]
Those in the prison saw through the cloud of darkness that the faces
of Nephi and Lehi "did shine exceedingly, even as the faces of angels,"
while they seemed to be "talking or lifting their voices to some being
whom they beheld"[9] — foreshadowing the time when Christ's twelve
Nephite disciples, including two of Nephi's sons and one of his grandsons,[10] would pray to Christ as he stood before them while "the light
of his countenance" would "shine upon them," making them "as
white as the countenance . . . of Jesus."[11] After the cloud of darkness
dispersed in the prison, all present "were encircled about . . . by a
pillar of fire," even "as if in the midst of a flaming fire, . . . and they
were filled with that joy which is unspeakable and full of glory,"[12]

---

1. 3 Nephi 9:13.
2. Helaman 5:30.
3. 3 Nephi 11:3.
4. See Helaman 5:29–33.
5. See 3 Nephi 11:3–5.
6. Helaman 5:33.
7. 3 Nephi 17:16–17.
8. 3 Nephi 19:34.
9. Helaman 5:36.
10. See 3 Nephi 19:4.
11. 3 Nephi 19:25.
12. Helaman 5:43–44.

foreshadowing the time when the Nephites to whom Christ ministered would be filled with a joy of which "no one can conceive,"[1]
while some of the little children and the twelve disciples would be
"in the midst of fire" and "encircled about with fire."[2] To those in
the prison "the Holy Spirit of God did come down from heaven, and
did enter into their hearts, and they were filled as if with fire,"[3]
foreshadowing the time when the twelve disciples would similarly be
"filled with the Holy Ghost and with fire."[4] Those in the prison found
that "they could speak forth marvelous words,"[5] foreshadowing the
time when the children of those to whom Christ ministered would
also "speak . . . great and marvelous things."[6] To those in the prison
"angels came down out of heaven and ministered unto them,"[7] foreshadowing the time when the Nephite children and the twelve disciples would also have "angels . . . come down out of heaven
and . . . minister unto them."[8] Finally, following the marvelous experience of those in the prison, "they did go forth, and did minister
unto the people, declaring throughout all the regions round about all
the things which they had heard and seen,"[9] foreshadowing the time
when Christ's twelve disciples would go forth to teach and minister
to all who would listen.[10]

Surely such a harrowing prison experience as Nephi and Lehi had
passed through would warrant some sort of substantial rest, but their
passion for preaching seems to have equaled that of their great-grandfather Alma the younger, who "could not rest."[11] Similarly Nephi and
Lehi were soon off to yet other parts to preach the word.[12] Meanwhile,

---

1. 3 Nephi 17:17.
2. 3 Nephi 17:24; see also 19:14.
3. Helaman 5:45.
4. 3 Nephi 19:13.
5. Helaman 5:45.
6. 3 Nephi 26:14, 16.
7. Helaman 5:48.
8. 3 Nephi 19:14; 17:24.
9. Helaman 5:50.
10. See 3 Nephi 26:17–19.
11. Alma 43:1.
12. See Helaman 6:6.

the octopus-like Gadianton band was gaining an ever-greater hold over an increasingly wicked society.[1] When Nephi finally returned home and saw the wicked condition of his people, "his heart was swollen with sorrow within his breast," and he experienced "agony of . . . soul"[2] — reminiscent again of Alma, who had likewise "grieved for the iniquity of his people" and whose "heart was exceedingly sorrowful."[3] So Nephi did what Alma had done — he set about again to preach. As Alma cried repentance,[4] so now does his great-grandson Nephi.[5] As Alma scolded his listeners because "the good shepherd doth call you" but "ye will not hearken unto his voice,"[6] so Nephi scolds his listeners because "ye will not hearken unto the voice of the good shepherd."[7] And as Alma urged his listeners to remember "our fathers"[8] — including specifically Lehi,[9] Moses,[10] and Abraham[11] — in order to believe on the Son of God,[12] so Nephi urges his listeners to remember "our fathers" — including specifically Lehi, Moses, and Abraham — in order to believe on the Son of God.[13] And even as Alma exercised the convincing gift of discerning the thoughts of others,[14] so Nephi exercises the same gift and thereby convinces some of his prophetic power.[15] Furthermore, as Alma's ministry had been characterized by the word *power*,[16] so also is the ministry of Nephi;[17] indeed, as we shall see, the power granted to Nephi will exceed that of anyone in the line of Alma down to Nephi's day.

---

1. See Helaman 6.
2. Helaman 7:6.
3. Alma 35:15; see also 31:1-2; 4.15.
4. See, e.g., Alma 5:31-33.
5. See Helaman 7:17-28.
6. Alma 5:37-38.
7. Helaman 7:18.
8. See, e.g., Alma 5:21.
9. See Alma 9:9, 13.
10. See Alma 33:18-19.
11. See Alma 5:24; 7:25; 13:15.
12. See Alma 5:21.
13. See Helaman 8:11-23.
14. See Alma 12:3-7.
15. See Helaman 9:25-41.
16. See Alma 8:31-32; 14:25; 15:15; 31:35, 38.
17. See Helaman 5:17-18; 8:12.

In the many reflections of his forefathers seen in the life of Nephi, his great-great-grandfather Alma the elder figures prominently: as he had received the guarantee of eternal life with a commandment to continue his ministry,[1] so Nephi receives the same. God first commends Nephi for his "unwearyingness"—the word is used twice—in preaching the word and keeping God's commandments; therefore God promises to bless Nephi forever and commands him to continue his ministry. Then God gives him an additional blessing surpassing even the great power possessed by his previous illustrious ancestors in the line of Alma: God promises to make Nephi "mighty in word and in deed, in faith and in works; yea, even that all things shall be done unto thee according to thy word."[2] Whatever Nephi orders—whether it be a famine, the leveling of a mountain, or anything else—will be done.[3] Nephi's ministry from that time forward reflects this unprecedented power, as he does bring a famine to induce the people to repent,[4] and as he is physically conveyed by the Spirit from multitude to multitude in his preaching.[5]

For all of their marked similarities, then, the amazing men in the line of Alma all have their own strengths, and Nephi surpasses them all to that point in the amazing power granted him in his ministry. But would his accomplishments have been made without his father's superb teaching, or without the illustrious examples of his earlier fathers like the two Almas? It seems fair to say that (as was the case with the sons of Mosiah) if Nephi achieved more than his great fathers, it was because he stood on their shoulders. Furthermore, his astonishing ministry as he was transported from multitude to multitude is somewhat reminiscent of what Alma the younger had wished for himself—to be an angel and cry repentance.[6] Nephi's tremendous power is also reminiscent of his namesake forefather Nephi, whose righteous power had literally jolted Laman and Lemuel[7] and calmed

---

1. See Mosiah 26:20.
2. Helaman 10:5.
3. See Helaman 10:7–11.
4. See Helaman 11:1–17.
5. See Helaman 10:16–17.
6. See Alma 29:1.
7. See 1 Nephi 17:52–55.

the raging ocean storm[1]. And when Helaman the younger's son Nephi exercises his great power to bring on a famine, we are reminded of the Old Testament account of how Elijah similarly exercised his power to seal the heavens from sending down rain.[2]

When Nephi asked the Lord to send a famine, it was because the people's wickedness was about to bring on their destruction by the sword; Nephi prayed that they not be so destroyed but that there might be a famine to induce them to remember their God and repent. When the famine had the desired effect, Nephi prayed that the famine cease and the people be granted another chance to repent and serve God so that he could bless them.[3] Nephi's role as an intercessor for his people echoes the same role played by his ancient forefathers, the Old Testament prophets of Israel going back to Moses and even Abraham. The record of their lives, as one modern scholar observes, demonstrates that "intercession . . . is an integral component of the true prophet's mission. To be a prophet means to speak for the people to God, represent their case, and take up their cause."[4]

The repentance of Nephi's people brought prosperity, but one soon sees the same tragic pattern that so often prevails throughout the Book of Mormon: prosperity in turn brought ease, forgetfulness, and great pride, resulting in a return to wickedness.[5] And in accord with the law of witnesses, the Lord sent the people other prophets besides Nephi, including "Lehi, his brother, [who] was not a whit behind him as to things pertaining to righteousness,"[6] as well as a Lamanite prophet named Samuel who spoke to the Nephites about their forefathers,[7] including father Adam,[8] and urged them to believe in the Son of God, whose birth into mortality in but five years would be heralded by a sign from heaven: one night that would be as light

---

1. See 1 Nephi 18:13–21.
2. See 1 Kings 17–18.
3. See Helaman 11:1–16.
4. EJ 13:1171.
5. See Helaman 11.
6. Helaman 11:19.
7. See Helaman 13:25–26.
8. See Helaman 14:16.

as day.[1] Furthermore, said Samuel, Christ's death would also be marked by a sign: a terrible storm, earthquake, and massive destruction, followed by three days of darkness.[2]

The last we hear of the powerful Nephi is that he turned the sacred records over to his son Nephi and then mysteriously "departed out of the land, and whither he went, no man knoweth,"[3] for he "did not return . . . , and could nowhere be found in all the land."[4] His life, along with that of his brother, Lehi, had gloriously fulfilled their father's hope when he had named them after their two illustrious forefathers. And now, even in his departure, Nephi appears to echo the experience of other righteous fathers, for his disappearance sounds much like that of Alma the younger, who was rumored to have been translated.[5] If Nephi was indeed translated, it would be the last of many similarities to his great-grandfather and another similarity to the powerful ancient prophet Elijah,[6] one of the ancient Hebrew forefathers.[7]

NEPHI THE YOUNGER BEFORE THE GREAT DESTRUCTION

As distinctive as was the ministry of Nephi, that of his son Nephi easily qualifies as the most unusual in the Book of Mormon, although it also bears the unmistakable imprint of his father's influence and teaching (even though Mormon's highly abridged account—containing less than one percent of the records available to him for this period[8]—does not expressly describe that teaching).

It is on the occasion of Christ's birth into mortality that we get our first glimpse of the younger Nephi, who was facing a critical crisis. While there were a number of faithful believers, the majority of Nephites had become hardened, rejecting the words of the prophets

---

1. See Helaman 14:1–18.
2. See Helaman 14:20–27.
3. 3 Nephi 1:3.
4. 3 Nephi 2:9.
5. See Alma 45:18–19.
6. See 2 Kings 2:11.
7. Using the term "forefathers" in a slightly broader sense than literal ancestors, to mean "the former generations of the people." (TDOT I:7.)
8. See Helaman 3:14; 3 Nephi 5:8.

about the coming of Christ. Furthermore, they began to allege that the time had passed for the signs to be given as announced by Samuel the Lamanite. So antagonistic were the unbelievers, and so great their political power, that they had actually designated a day by which all the believers would be executed if the sign were not given.[1] Significantly, the issue that divided the believers from the unbelievers was the tradition of the fathers: the unbelievers were characterized as those who rejected the Christian "tradition, which has been handed down unto us by our fathers,"[2] while the believers were those who had "faith in the tradition of their fathers."[3]

The wickedness of the unbelievers had the same effect on Nephi as similar wickedness had had on his father, Nephi, and Alma the younger; when Nephi "saw this wickedness of his people, his heart was exceedingly sorrowful." Then, following the pattern of his father and ancient forefathers, Nephi interceded on behalf of his people as he "went out and bowed himself down upon the earth, and cried mightily to his God in behalf of his people, yea, those who were about to be destroyed because of their faith in the tradition of their fathers."[4] Nephi's mighty prayer lasted "all that day,"[5] and finally a heavenly voice was heard announcing deliverance in words much like those once spoken to his forefather Alma, who had heard the glad message: "Be of good comfort, for on the morrow I will deliver you."[6] So now Nephi heard the glad message: "Lift up your head and be of good cheer; for behold, the time is at hand, and on this night shall the sign be given, and on the morrow come I into the world."[7]

Nephi's mighty intercessory prayer had brought the announcement by the Great Intercessor himself that what father Lehi had termed the "intercession for all"[8] was about to begin. And as the divine voice

---

1. See 3 Nephi 1:5–9.
2. Helaman 16:20.
3. 3 Nephi 1:11.
4. 3 Nephi 1:10–11.
5. 3 Nephi 1:12.
6. Mosiah 24:16.
7. 3 Nephi 1:13.
8. 2 Nephi 2:10.

to Nephi continued, so did the theme of fathers and sons so prevalent in this incident:

> Behold, I come unto my own, to fulfil all things which I have made known unto the children of men from the foundation of the world, and to do the will, both of the Father and of the Son—of the Father because of me, and of the Son because of my flesh.[1]

So convincing was the great sign of Christ's birth—an entire night that remained as light as day—that most of the people believed and were converted, and Nephi, following the pattern of his forefathers, "went forth . . . baptizing unto repentance, in the which there was a great remission of sins."[2] But how soon people forget! For as Mormon had, just a few chapters back, marveled at "how quick to do iniquity, and how slow to do good are the children of men," and "how slow are they to remember the Lord their God,"[3] so now we see yet another instance of human folly as the Nephite nation began again "to be hard in their hearts, and blind in their minds, and began to disbelieve."[4] Within just two decades after the great sign came an unprecedented slaughter among the Nephites, brought on by their iniquity. Repentance followed, and in turn prosperity, and in turn pride, along with a collapse of the central government as the Gadianton band gained a stranglehold on the nation.[5]

At this point Mormon pauses briefly to sketch the sharply contrasting figure of Nephi, who had "been visited by angels and also the voice of the Lord," thus being an "eye-witness," and who "had power given unto him that he might know concerning the ministry of Christ."[6] In other words, he is clearly cut from the cloth of his forefathers—one thinks particularly of Alma the younger and Nephi the elder—and is a worthy successor to them, so that we are not

1. 3 Nephi 1:14.
2. 3 Nephi 1:23.
3. Helaman 12:4–5.
4. 3 Nephi 2:1.
5. See 3 Nephi 4–7.
6. 3 Nephi 7:15.

surprised to read that his ministry reflects so much of their ministries. Again he was "grieved" over his people's hardness and blindness, and "went forth among them . . . and began to testify, boldly, repentance and remission of sins through faith on the Lord Jesus Christ," preaching many things and ministering "with power and with great authority." Indeed, many were angry with him "because he had greater power than they, for it were not possible that they could disbelieve his words."[1] Such rare power, even among righteous missionaries, puts him squarely in the mold of his powerful father, Nephi.

So great was Nephi's faith that he heard the Lord's voice, and "angels did minister unto him daily"[2] — recalling his ancient forefather Jacob (Abraham's grandson), of whom one ancient source reports that it "was his custom every day to speak . . . with the angels."[3] One wonders if the angels who ministered to Nephi included such possibly translated beings as his father, Nephi, and forefather, Alma the younger. With great faith and power, Nephi performed many miracles, including casting out devils and even raising from the dead his brother, Timothy, who had been stoned by the people[4] (the same brother who would later serve with him as one of Christ's twelve disciples[5]). Furthermore, knowing that the time of the great destruction was not far off, Nephi continued his preaching to this hardened people, and, like his forefathers, organized the ministry and sent forth others.[6] Also like his forefathers, he kept the sacred record from which Mormon made his abridgment.[7]

Considering the power and zeal of Nephi's ministry, and considering also what was at stake for choosing whether or not to follow him, we may well be astounded that "there were but few" who chose to follow him.[8] One is reminded of the title of a relatively recent book,

---

1. 3 Nephi 7:16–18.
2. 3 Nephi 7:18.
3. Testament of Jacob 1:7, in OTP 1:914.
4. See 3 Nephi 7:16–20.
5. See 3 Nephi 19:4.
6. See 3 Nephi 7:25.
7. See 3 Nephi 8:1.
8. 3 Nephi 7:21.

The March of Folly, which chronicles famous cases throughout history of governmental blunders and begins by pointing to the "phenomenon noticeable throughout history regardless of place or period," namely "the pursuit by governments of policies contrary to their own interests."[1] Judging from Mormon's above-mentioned lament over humanity's seemingly endless propensity to choose evil over good,[2] the phenomenon of short-sighted governments is no less prevalent than that of short-sighted individuals, who, in the words of the righteous King Limhi, "will not seek wisdom" but "are as a wild flock which fleeth from the shepherd, and scattereth, and . . . are devoured by the beasts of the forest."[3]

So it was with the Nephite nation when Nephi attempted to save them from disaster. Stubbornly they would not be saved, and so great had become their wickedness on the land of promise as to trigger the long-standing curse revealed to Lehi[4] and mentioned by Alma the younger to Helaman: "There is a curse upon all this land, that destruction shall come upon all those workers of darkness, according to the power of God, when they are fully ripe."[5] Alma's descendant Nephi had done all he could to save the people from this destruction, but they refused to pause in their march of folly.

THE GREAT DESTRUCTION AND THE MINISTRY OF THE RESURRECTED CHRIST

The destruction, which was also a sign of the crucifixion and death of Jesus,[6] was swift and severe. In all of recorded Nephite history, there had never been the like of the terrible storm, tempest, thunder, lightnings, and earthquake that for three memorable hours wreaked havoc and wholesale destruction as mountains sprung up, cities were buried, and entire populations were wiped out. The horrible cataclysm was followed immediately by a mist of darkness that allowed no light

---

1. Tuchman 1984:4.
2. See Helaman 12.
3. Mosiah 8:20–21.
4. See 2 Nephi 1:7.
5. Alma 37:28.
6. See Helaman 14:20–27; 1 Nephi 19:10–12.

but was rent by the howling of terrified survivors. Suddenly the shrieks were supplanted by a voice from heaven that pronounced continued woes unless the people repented. The speaker identified himself as Jesus Christ, the Son of God, sent of the Father so that others might also become sons of God if they would but repent and come unto Christ as little children. The focus on fathers and sons continued as the voice explained that the Mosaic law and sacrifices were done away;[1] nevertheless, the connection with ancient fathers continued as these "descendants of Jacob, yea, who are of the house of Israel,"[2] were invited to repent, and if not their dwellings would become desolate "until the time of the fulfilling of the covenant to your fathers."[3]

Some time later, about twenty-five hundred people were gathered at the temple, probably, as some modern scholars have suggested, in a ritual setting as they and their Israelite forefathers had done for centuries in observance of one of the Mosaic festivals—except that now, with the Mosaic law and sacrifices fulfilled, these Nephites would have been wondering what to do next.[4] Among the multitude was Nephi, his brother Timothy, and Nephi's son Jonas. That day they and the rest of the multitude were privileged to witness an event as sublime as the destruction had been terrible. A voice from heaven suddenly interrupted their horizontal conversations, a voice that "did pierce them to the very soul, and did cause their hearts to burn."[5] They looked up and around, not understanding; again the voice, and still they continued to look up, straining to understand. And yet again the voice, and finally they understood: "Behold my Beloved Son, in whom I am well pleased, in whom I have glorified my name—hear ye him."[6] From heavenly realms a man in a white robe descended; he stretched out his hand and announced himself as Jesus Christ, who had done his Father's will in taking upon himself the sins of the

---

1. See 3 Nephi 8:1–9:19.
2. 3 Nephi 10:4.
3. 3 Nephi 10:7.
4. See Welch 1990:29–30.
5. 3 Nephi 11:3.
6. 3 Nephi 11:7.

world. He was, he said, the God of (their forefather) Israel and the God of the whole world, and he now invited each of them to come forward and feel the wounds in his side and hands and feet.[1] They did so, and the record — abridged by Mormon from the eyewitness account of Nephi — emphasizes the reality and certainty of the experience: each and every one of the large multitude

> did see with their eyes and did feel with their hands, and did
> know of a surety and did bear record, that it was he, of whom
> it was written by the prophets, that should come.[2]

They verified not only his physical existence but also his miraculous power as he healed all their sick,[3] raised a man from the dead,[4] and miraculously provided bread and wine as he instituted the sacramental meal.[5]

The wondrous and glorious things that these Nephites experienced as the resurrected Savior ministered to them surpassed even the miracles performed during his mortal ministry to the Jews, of whom he now spoke to the Nephites: "So great faith have I never seen among all the Jews; wherefore I could not show unto them so great miracles, because of their unbelief."[6] Accordingly, what he had once told his Jewish disciples about the great things they were privileged to experience seems to apply even more to these Nephites: "Many prophets and righteous men have desired to see those things which ye see, and have not seen them; and to hear those things which ye hear, and have not heard them."[7] As one of that blessed Nephite multitude, Nephi was now privileged to associate with that very Being of whom he and his forefathers had for so long prophesied and anticipated, and of whose coming to earth Nephi's forefather Alma the younger had said:

---

1. See 3 Nephi 11:8–14.
2. 3 Nephi 11:15.
3. See 3 Nephi 17:6–10.
4. See 3 Nephi 26:15.
5. See 3 Nephi 20:3–37.
6. 3 Nephi 19:35.
7. Matthew 13:17.

> There be many things to come; and behold, there is one thing which is of more importance than they all—for behold, the time is not far distant that the Redeemer liveth and cometh among his people.
>
> Behold, I do not say that he will come among us at the time of his dwelling in his mortal tabernacle. . . . Now as to this thing I do not know.[1]

What Alma the younger had longingly looked forward to without full knowledge, his descendant Nephi was now privileged to experience firsthand. But Nephi's experience resulted from exercising the same kind of faith that Alma the younger had exercised in his ministry. Later in the Book of Mormon when the last author, Moroni, is recalling miracles wrought by men of faith throughout Nephite history, he includes incidents involving the line of Alma:

> Behold, it was the faith of Alma and Amulek that caused the prison to tumble to the earth.
>
> Behold, it was the faith of Nephi and Lehi that wrought the change upon the Lamanites, that they were baptized with fire and with the Holy Ghost.[2]

But Moroni mentions another incident that also implies the faith of Nephi:

> It was by faith that Christ showed himself unto our fathers, after he had risen from the dead; and he showed not himself unto them until after they had faith in him; wherefore, it must needs be that some had faith in him, for he showed himself not unto the world.[3]

Judging from Mormon's record of Nephite history leading up to the appearance of Christ, the preeminent man of faith was Nephi— "so great was his faith on the Lord Jesus Christ that angels did minister unto him daily,"[4] and "he truly did many miracles in the name of

---

1. Alma 7:7–8.
2. Ether 12:13–14.
3. Ether 12:7.
4. 3 Nephi 7:18.

Jesus."[1] It would have been the faith of Nephi, then, along with others, that effected the glorious appearance of the resurrected Jesus. In other words, apparently Nephi continued the tradition of mighty faith already preeminent among his forefathers and took it to its culmination by bringing the greatest and most glorious miracle of all—the appearance and ministry of the resurrected Son of God.

NEPHI THE CHIEF DISCIPLE

Nephi's chief role in exercising the prerequisite faith for that miracle is also evident from the additional blessing granted him by the resurrected Christ—the opportunity to serve as the chief disciple among the twelve chosen by Christ as his agents and ministers. After Christ had first descended from heaven and the multitude had come forward and felt his hands and feet, Christ called to Nephi, who stepped forward and bowed himself to the ground, kissing the Lord's feet. He arose at the Lord's command and heard these words of empowerment: "I give unto you power that ye shall baptize this people when I am again ascended into heaven."[2] It was the same power, of course, that Nephi and his illustrious forefathers had previously possessed and exercised, now given anew by the newly resurrected and glorified Christ.

Nephi became the sixth successive man in the line of Alma the elder to serve as the presiding ecclesiastical authority in Nephite society. Indeed, his calling attests to the greatness of his father and forefathers who had prepared him for this privilege. One might even say that it took six generations of righteous and powerful fathers and sons to prepare a man worthy to fill such a high and holy calling. The influence of his parentage is further seen in the fact that one of the other disciples chosen was his brother, Timothy, whom Nephi had raised from the dead. But Nephi's own greatness as a father is attested by the selection of yet another disciple—Nephi's son, Jonas,[3] showing that Nephi followed the pattern of his forefathers not only

---

1. 3 Nephi 8:1.
2. 3 Nephi 11:21.
3. See 3 Nephi 19:4.

in his powerful ministry but also by being a great father himself. Of Nephi's relationship to his Jonas, of what or how he taught him, we know nothing directly; but this one vital piece of information—that Jonas was called to serve with his father as one of the Nephite twelve—speaks volumes about Nephi as a father and implies powerful and persistent patriarchal tutelage. (That such does not directly appear in the record is understandable in light of Mormon's passing comments about this same period in which Nephi would have been teaching Jonas—that "this book cannot contain even a hundredth part of what was done"[1] among the Nephites during this era.)

These twelve disciples were given special instructions and special experiences. After the Savior emphasized to them that he and the father were one, he urged that same oneness for them, commanding them to avoid contention—even on vital ordinances—lest they follow "the devil, who is the father of contention."[2] He told them to go forth and preach his word "unto the ends of the earth"[3] and told the multitude that they would be blessed if they gave heed to the words of these twelve.[4] The twelve were the first to receive the symbolic bread and wine from the Lord's own hand; they in turn offered it to the multitude.[5] The twelve were also baptized—Nephi being the first—during the Lord's three-day ministry (even though this was certainly a rebaptism, for Nephi had for decades preached and administered baptism); whereupon "they were filled with the Holy Ghost and with fire," and, in plain view of the multitude, "were encircled about as if it were by fire . . . from heaven," while "angels did come down out of heaven and did minister unto them."[6] Thus Nephi and his son Jonas together received the ministration of angels, recalling similar ministrations to their forefathers Nephi the elder and Alma the younger—all of which bespeaks the powerful faith in this line of men, for "it is by faith that angels appear and minister unto men."[7]

1. 3 Nephi 5:8.
2. 3 Nephi 11:27–29.
3. 3 Nephi 11:41.
4. See 3 Nephi 12:1.
5. See 3 Nephi 18:1–5.
6. 3 Nephi 19:11–14.
7. Moroni 7:37.

The angels who descended to the Nephite twelve were soon followed by Jesus himself, who also descended and ministered to the twelve. Shortly thereafter as the twelve prayed to Jesus and he prayed to the Father, the twelve became "as white as the countenance and also the garments of Jesus," white beyond anything earthly, as Jesus prayed that they would be purified and united in him.[1] Of the various father-son experiences recorded in the Book of Mormon, none is greater than this: a father and his son, Nephi and Jonas, unitedly praying to and in the very presence of the Son, whose "children" they had become[2] by their childlike[3] faith and acceptance of him.

Years before the Savior's ministry Nephi the younger had been described as an "eye-witness" to heavenly things.[4] Now the designation becomes all the more applicable. In fact, this Nephi is the only person in the Book of Mormon to be expressly described as an "eyewitness," an interesting phenomenon considering how the word is used in the New Testament. In the King James Version the word occurs only twice, once when the chief apostle Peter says that he and James and John were "eyewitnesses" of Jesus' majesty on the mount of transfiguration,[5] and once when the gospel writer Luke claims as his sources the original "eyewitnesses" to the things he writes about.[6] In addition, the author of the gospel of John says of one recorded event (as one modern translation has it), "He who saw this has testified so that you also may believe. His testimony is true, and he knows that he tells the truth."[7] (In a couple of modern translations the phrase "He who saw this" is rendered by the word "eyewitness."[8]) The significance of the testimony of such eyewitnesses is, as one scholar has observed, that "the belief in Jesus' . . . power and glory rests on

---

1. 3 Nephi 19:25; see 19:15–30.
2. See Mosiah 5:7.
3. See 3 Nephi 11:37–38.
4. 3 Nephi 7:15.
5. See 2 Peter 1:16–18.
6. See Luke 1:2 (the King James is a bit awkward here and potentially ambiguous; see NRSV, REB, NIV, and Fitzmeyer 1981 (AB 28):287.
7. NRSV John 19:35.
8. REB; Brown 1970 (AB 29A):932.

attested historical events."[1] Indeed, the New Testament indicates that the Jewish twelve apostles were "sent" forth[2] — the very word *apostle* derives from the Greek verb to send[3] — to bear witness to what they had observed as eyewitnesses.[4] Even so, the term *eyewitness* as applied to the Jewish apostles' experience must be understood as implying more than the strict definition of the word — one who has acquired visual evidence — for in claiming to be one of the "eyewitnesses" to Christ's majesty, Peter mentions not only the visible "glory" that enveloped Christ on the mount, but also the "voice which came from heaven" and which "we heard."[5] Peter additionally had acquired tactile experience when, with the other apostles, he had witnessed the appearance behind closed doors of the glorified Christ who had insisted that they feel for themselves the reality of his resurrected body, as Luke reports:

> He said to them, "Why are you frightened, and why do doubts arise in your hearts? Look at my hands and my feet; see that it is I myself. Touch me and see; for a ghost does not have flesh and bones as you see that I have." And when he had said this, he showed them his hands and his feet.[6]

And as one modern scholar observes, the early Christian martyr "Ignatius of Antioch supplies what all readers suppose: 'And they immediately touched him and believed.' "[7]

Nonetheless, according to one of the unswervingly faithful latter-day apostles, Brigham Young, the most important evidence that the ancient Jewish apostles had was not tangible but rather spiritual:

> What made the Twelve Apostles of Jesus Christ witnesses? What constituted them Apostles — special witnesses to the

---

1. Reicke 1985 (AB 37):157.
2. John 20:21.
3. See Brown 1970 (AB 29A):1022; TDNT I:421.
4. See Acts 1:21–22; Fitzmeyer 1981 (AB 28):294; Munck 1967 (AB 31):9–10.
5. 2 Peter 1:17–18.
6. NRSV Luke 24:38–40.
7. Fitzmeyer 1985 (AB 28A):1576 (parenthetical source — Smyrn. 3.1 — omitted in quote).

world? Was it seeing miracles? No. What was it? The visions
of their minds were opened, and it was necessary that a few
should receive light, knowledge, and intelligence, that all the
powers of earth and hell could not gainsay or compete with.
That witness was within them.[1]

Thus, Peter's greatest evidence for the divinity of Christ came in the
kind of revelation that had prompted him to declare that Jesus was
the Messiah, the Son of God, whereupon Jesus told him: "Blessed
are you, Simon son of Jonah! For flesh and blood has not revealed
this to you, but my Father in heaven."[2] Each of the Jewish apostles,
then, and particularly Peter, the chief apostle, had learned through
several senses—sight, hearing, touch, and revelation—that Jesus was
the Christ. One might almost see here a nuance of the law of witnesses,
that "in the mouth of two or three witnesses shall every word be
established";[3] that is, each apostle had the evidence acquired through
various senses. And together, of course, the twelve indeed constituted
a persuasive group of witnesses all establishing the truth of Jesus'
divinity.

As it was with the Jewish twelve apostles and Peter, so it was
with the Nephite twelve disciples (designated by Joseph Smith as
"apostles"[4]), including Nephi the younger: they also were eyewitnesses, having seen the resurrected Christ and his glory and miracles
and having also heard the Father's voice from heaven, felt Christ's
hands and feet, and received revelation. Of these things, they were
sent forth to bear witness.[5] All of this has tremendous significance
for the relationship of Nephi the chief disciple with both his forefathers
and his posterity. In one sense he fits the pattern of his forefathers,
as seen with particular clarity in the life of Alma the younger, whose
remembrance of his righteous fathers had led him to receive revelation
similar to what they received concerning the reality of the Son of God.
In another sense, though, Nephi is the privileged beneficiary of gen-

1. JD 3:206.
2. NRSV Matthew 16:17.
3. 2 Corinthians 13:1; and Deuteronomy 17:6; 19:15; Matthew 18:15–16.
4. Smith, *History of the Church* 4:538; see also Moroni 2:2.
5. See 3 Nephi 28:34.

erations of righteous forefathers, on whose shoulders he now stands
as he receives the supreme opportunity of walking and talking with
the newly resurrected Son of God and even representing him as his
chief Nephite disciple (or apostle). Furthermore, as the eyewitness
Jewish apostle John made a record of what he personally experienced
"so that you also may believe,"[1] so the eyewitness Nephi—following
the lead of his forefathers—made a record of his remarkable experiences, the record from which Mormon drew.[2] And the Nephite apostolic account is in fact intended to complement and verify the Jewish
apostolic account, as Mormon insists when he finishes his record:
"This is written for the intent that ye may believe that [the Bible]; and
if ye believe that ye will believe this also."[3] The same purpose for the
Nephite record had likewise been foreseen by its first author, Nephi,[4]
namesake forefather of the chief disciple. That ancient Nephi had also
foreseen in vision and recorded that his posterity would be visited
by the resurrected Christ, who would descend out of heaven and
choose twelve disciples "to minister unto [Nephi's] seed."[5] The historical reality of that event had now been recorded by his descendant,
Nephi the chief disciple.

   Hence the apostolic eyewitness experience of Nephi, while similar
to that of his righteous forefathers, was also surpassingly significant,
as seen from Joseph Smith's statement on the critical role of apostolic
testimony:

> The fundamental principles of our religion are the testimony
> of the Apostles and Prophets, concerning Jesus Christ, that
> He died, was buried, and rose again the third day, and as-
> cended into heaven; and all other things which pertain to our
> religion are only appendages to it.[6]

Nephi's apostolic experience in actually walking and talking with the

---

1. NRSV John 19:35.
2. See 3 Nephi 5:9–10; 26:6–12.
3. Mormon 7:9.
4. See 1 Nephi 13:38–40.
5. 1 Nephi 12:6–8.
6. TPJS 121.

resurrected Son of God has significant echoes of the experience of father Adam, who likewise had walked and talked with God. And as Adam's testimony of his experience became—as Joseph Smith indicated in the Lectures on Faith—foundational evidence allowing future generations to exercise faith in God,[1] so the testimony of Nephi assumed that foundational character for future generations, encouraging his posterity and all who now read his record to believe in the Son of God and become children of Christ. Nephi's apostolic experience rises to the level of that of father Adam in its significance for future generations.

Following Christ's three-day ministry among the Nephites, and pursuant to his command to the Nephite twelve to declare his word to all,[2] they "began from that time forth to baptize and to teach as many as did come unto them."[3] Within two years the entire populace, Nephites and Lamanites alike, were converted.[4] Divisiveness and contention ended "because of the love of God which did dwell in the hearts of the people,"[5] and "every man did deal justly one with another"[6] and with himself, for there was no wickedness.[7] Furthermore, they "had all things common among them; therefore there were not rich and poor, bond and free, but they were all made free, and partakers of the heavenly gift."[8] Thus "they were in one, the children of Christ, and heirs to the kingdom of God. And how blessed were they! For the Lord did bless them in all their doings," and "surely there could not be a happier people among all the people who had been created by the hand of God."[9] Such are the highlights of Mormon's tantalizingly brief description of this Nephite Golden Age, which lasted for over a century and a half. Mormon's terse treatment

---

1. See LF 2:33–36.
2. See 3 Nephi 11:41.
3. 3 Nephi 26:17.
4. See 4 Nephi 1:2.
5. 4 Nephi 1:15.
6. 4 Nephi 1:2; 3 Nephi 26:19.
7. See 4 Nephi 1:16.
8. 4 Nephi 1:3.
9. 4 Nephi 1:16–18.

of this most glorious of all eras of Nephite history—told in but four pages—seems to suggest that a fuller knowledge of that blessed age will be available to us only as we attain a similar state of righteousness.

One thing is perfectly clear from Mormon's description: these Nephites had established Zion, which had once been administered by their ancient forefather Enoch, and the principles that had been put in operation at least partially by Alma[1] and Alma the younger[2]—forefathers of the one who now administered the great and glorious Nephite Zion. And, as the earthly leader of this theocracy, Nephi's role further echoes the role played by several of his forefathers—Alma the younger, Helaman the younger, and Nephi the elder—each of whom served as the Nephite chief judge, the highest government office in the land.

But perhaps the greatest personal blessing for each of the twelve was that which the Savior spontaneously and unilaterally granted to each of them when he appeared as they "were united in mighty prayer and fasting" over what the name of the church should be.[3] After answering their collective question, he proceeded to put a question of his own to each of them: "What is it that ye desire of me, after that I am gone to the Father?"[4] It was the opportunity of a lifetime, the granting of one's greatest wish. Nine of the twelve replied without delay:

> We desire that after we have lived unto the age of man, that our ministry, wherein thou hast called us, may have an end, that we may speedily come unto thee in thy kingdom.[5]

The Lord responded that they were blessed because of their desire, which would be fulfilled for each of the nine at the age of seventy-two. Three disciples, however, remained silent and even sorrowful, as they dared not voice their wish; to which Jesus replied that he knew their thoughts: "Ye have desired that ye might bring the souls

---

1. See Mosiah 18:17–29.
2. See Alma 1:25–31.
3. 3 Nephi 27:1–3.
4. 3 Nephi 28:1.
5. 3 Nephi 28:2.

of men unto me, while the world shall stand." Therefore more blessed were they, for they would never experience death in the traditional sense, but finally at the Lord's glorious latter-day coming they would instantaneously be changed from mortality to immortality. Meanwhile they would live throughout time but would have no pain or sorrow except for the sins of the world. Then, when Jesus took leave of the twelve, the three were caught up to heaven, where they "saw and heard unspeakable things" and were changed into a sanctified state beyond Satan's power and the powers of the earth, so that from then on (until their final change into immortality) they were and are "as the angels of God."[1] In other words, they are translated beings.[2] This amazing blessing was later mentioned by Moroni as one of the great incidents of faith in Nephite history:

> And it was by faith that the three disciples obtained a prom-
> ise that they should not taste of death; and they obtained not
> the promise until after their faith.[3]

Who were those three remarkable disciples who desired above all else to help save others? Mormon was about to write their names but was forbidden.[4] But the remarkable faith that would have been required to receive such a blessing sounds like that same sort of faith that Nephi possessed. Also, one cannot help but recollect that Nephi's forefather Alma the younger himself had wished to be an angel[5] and had apparently got his wish when he was translated (so it would appear) to continue his ministry.[6] Furthermore, Nephi's own righteous father had disappeared quite like Alma and possibly had also been translated.[7] Would it not be at least plausible to suppose that Nephi likewise possessed this same desire so prominent among his forefathers to continue their ministry? One could object to this pos-

---

1. 3 Nephi 28:3–40; see especially v. 30.
2. See McConkie 1966:806–807.
3. Ether 12:17.
4. See 3 Nephi 28:25.
5. See Alma 29:1.
6. See Alma 45:19.
7. See 3 Nephi 1:3.

sibility on the basis of Mormon's comment in 4 Nephi that "Nephi, he that kept this last record, (and he kept it upon the plates of Nephi) died, and his son Amos kept it in his stead."[1] But a look at the surrounding verses and some simple arithmetic shows that the Nephi referred to in this verse cannot (contrary to the implication in the current edition's footnote) have been our Nephi, the chief disciple. Several verses back Mormon had already noted that all of the original twelve disciples except the three had died.[2] That this comment is indeed chronological with respect to the later comment concerning the death of a record keeper named Nephi becomes apparent from the data that Mormon includes about Amos, who kept the record (says Mormon) eighty-four years and then died in A.D. 194—which means that his father, "Nephi," would have died in A.D. 110. However, the nine disciples who were eventually to die were expressly told in A.D. 34 that each would die at the age of seventy-two, making it impossible that any remained alive by A.D. 110. Clearly the Nephi who died in A.D. 110 cannot have been Nephi the chief disciple.

Would it not be, then, a reasonable guess that one of the three translated disciples was Nephi, son and twice-great-grandson of men who had been granted similar blessings according to their desires? In fact, Truman Madsen reports a tradition that Joseph Smith believed that the three translated Nephite disciples included Nephi and his brother Timothy.[3] If Nephi was indeed one of the chosen three, his translation into an angelic ministrant would be yet another remarkable reflection and repetition of the possible translation of two of his fathers. In addition, Mormon reports that Christ's three translated disciples were cast into prison, but "the prisons could not hold them, for they were rent in twain."[4] The story echoes the deliverance granted to Nephi the younger's father, Nephi,[5] and forefather, Alma the younger.[6] We have already seen how one of those prison experiences,

---

1. 4 Nephi 1:19.
2. See 4 Nephi 1:14.
3. See Madsen (n.d.):46.
4. 3 Nephi 28:19.
5. See Helaman 5.
6. See Alma 14.

that of Nephi (and Lehi), paralleled the dramatic events that Nephi the younger later witnessed during the great destruction and the glorious appearance of Christ. Also, if Nephi was one of the chosen three Nephite disciples, his ministry would contain yet another echo of his father's ministry in that "the powers of the earth [can]not hold"[1] the three disciples, who "can show themselves unto whatsoever man it seemeth them good"[2]—similar to the earthly ministry of Nephi, who had been bodily transported by the Spirit from multitude to multitude.[3] We would thus see a crescendo of power from the powerful ministry of Alma the younger to the more powerful ministry of his great-grandson Nephi to the still more powerful ministry of his son Nephi the younger.

As previously noted, this long heritage in the line of Alma of righteous and powerful service was continued by Nephi's son Jonas, who served with his father as one of the original twelve disciples. And that the heritage continued even thereafter is evident from the heading to the book of 4 Nephi, which discloses its author to be Nephi, the son of Nephi the chief disciple. And as 4 Nephi narrates, the records then passed to the son of that last Nephi, named Amos, and later to his son Amos.[4] Thus the long-standing heritage of service that had spanned generations continued into future generations beyond Nephi the chief disciple.

What we have seen in this amazing line of righteous servants of God is a clear crescendo of power in the ministries of Alma, Alma the younger, Nephi, and Nephi the younger—each standing on the shoulders of his forefathers in this escalating elevation that finally prepared Nephi the younger for his high and holy calling as the resurrected Lord's chief disciple. This is not to say, however, that any one of those four was "greater" or more righteous or faithful than any of the others. We have seen that each in turn nobly rose to the particular and often varied challenges of his own day and circum-

---

1. 3 Nephi 28:39.
2. 3 Nephi 28:30.
3. See Helaman 10:16–17.
4. 4 Nephi 1:19–21.

stances with such integrity and tenacity as to enjoy fellowship with the Spirit of God. Indeed, the very first in this venerable line, Alma, although he would be succeeded by descendants whose ministries would be blessed by progressively increased power, nevertheless heard the guarantee of what the Lord in latter-day revelation has called "the greatest of all the gifts of God,"[1] namely, eternal life: "Thou art my servant; and I covenant with thee that thou shalt have eternal life."[2] Each of these men, then, faithfully fulfilled their varied missions, the assignment of which is illuminated by Joseph Smith's statement that "every man who has a calling to minister to the inhabitants of the world was ordained to that very purpose in the Grand Council of heaven before this world was."[3] An all-seeing and all-foreseeing Heavenly Father particularly tailored the calling of each of these noble men in the line of Alma so as to maximize the development of each and the good of them all and all whom they served, and with infinite wisdom the Father structured their missions so that the sons could stand on their forefathers' shoulders in the progressive preparation that would finally produce the resurrected Lord's chief disciple.

1. D&C 14:7.
2. Mosiah 26:20.
3. TPJS 365.

Chapter 8

FATHERS AND CHILDREN IN THE BOOK OF ETHER

· ·

THE LINE OF JARED

THE JAREDITE ACCOUNT

In retrospect, it seems more than accidental that the expedition sent by King Limhi to locate the land of Zarahemla became lost in the wilderness. Their wandering took them through a land covered with ruins and human bones where they discovered twenty-four gold plates filled with strange engravings. The plates were carried back to Limhi, who was extremely anxious to have them translated; but that task had to await the eventual arrival of Limhi and his people at Zarahemla, where King Mosiah, using the interpreters powered by divine inspiration, translated the record.[1] It was found to contain the history of a people who had originally come from the great tower when God confounded the language. The group had been divinely led to this new land, had flourished into a great civilization, and had finally been utterly destroyed because of wickedness.[2] Commenting on this history, Mormon observes in his narrative (at the point when King Mosiah had translated the plates) that "this account shall be

---

1. See Mosiah 8; 28:11–17.
2. See Mosiah 28:17.

written hereafter; for behold, it is expedient that all people should know the things which are written in this account."[1]

That the account was finally incorporated into the Book of Mormon, we owe directly to the power of a father-son relationship; for Mormon died before he was able to include the account in his narrative, but his son Moroni made good on his father's promise. The account taken from these twenty-four gold plates now constitutes that portion of the Book of Mormon known as the Book of Ether, and it has much to say about fathers and children.

JARED AND HIS BROTHER

Jaredite history begins with a glimpse at the most infamous building project in history—the great tower mentioned in Genesis—grinding suddenly to a halt when, as the book of Ether tells it, "the Lord confounded the language of the people" and decided "that they should be scattered upon all the face of the earth."[2] A similar report is found in Genesis,[3] but the book of Ether adds a significant detail in telling that the Lord *"swore in his wrath* that they should be scattered."[4] The Lord's displeasure with the tower-builders is emphasized in further details added to the traditional Genesis account in the Joseph Smith translation: "and they hearkened not unto the Lord," and "the Lord was displeased with their works."[5] Similar indictments of the tower-builders are found in many ancient sources, which insist that the whole enterprise was direct "rebellion against God"[6] by a proud and idolatrous multitude led by the tyrannical Nimrod (the name also appears in the book of Ether's designation of the "valley of Nimrod"[7]) who was bent on erecting an ostentatious structure to serve as both a refuge against a new flood and a temple of idolatry.[8] However, a

---

1. Mosiah 28:19.
2. Ether 1:33.
3. See Genesis 11:7–9.
4. Ether 1:33; emphasis added.
5. JST Genesis 11:6, corresponding to Genesis 11:8–9.
6. LJ I:179.
7. Ether 2:1, 4.
8. See LJ I:179; V:201–4.

few of those participating in the project were doing so against their will, as one ancient pseudepigraphical source, Pseudo-Philo, discloses.[1] Such seems to be the case also with the first two characters upon which the Ether narrative focuses, Jared and his brother, whose righteousness stands out in sharp contrast to the prevailing iniquity that had brought down God's wrath in confounding the language. According to the book of Ether,

> The brother of Jared being a large and mighty man, and a man highly favored of the Lord, Jared, his brother, said unto him: Cry unto the Lord, that he will not confound us that we may not understand our words.
>
> And it came to pass that the brother of Jared did cry unto the Lord, and the Lord had compassion upon Jared; therefore he did not confound the language of Jared; and Jared and his brother were not confounded.[2]

To see such faith against a backdrop of faithlessness is surprising; not so surprising is that these two men of faith were brothers. Although we are never told of their father or mother, one suspects that parental influence was at work in these two sons practicing righteousness in a wicked society.

Having obtained the desired blessing through the prayer of his brother, Jared felt reassured enough to submit another request, this time asking his brother to pray that the language of their friends not be confounded. Again the brother of Jared prayed; again his request was granted. Jared's confidence was growing. He now asked his brother to ask the Lord whether he was going to cause them to leave, and if so, could he please lead them to the choicest land possible. Yet again the brother of Jared prayed; and again the Lord responded favorably, promising to lead them to the choicest land on earth, where their posterity would build the greatest nation on earth.[3] "And thus

---

1. See Pseudo-Philo 6, in OTP 2:310–12.
2. Ether 1:34–35.
3. Ether 1:36–43. In Hebrew and related Semitic languages, the term for earth (Hebrew 'erets) can refer either to the planet earth or, in a more limited sense, to a particular land. (TDOT I:388–405.) As used in Ether 1:43, the term earth—in light of its usage in the previous verse 38 and 42—must necessarily refer to the planet earth.

I will do unto thee because this long time ye have cried unto me."[1]
But the high privilege of residing on that choicest of all lands would
bring high responsibility, for the Lord

> swor[e] in his wrath unto the brother of Jared, that whoso
> should possess this land of promise, from that time henceforth
> and forever, should serve him, the true and only God, or they
> should be swept off when the fulness of his wrath should come
> upon them.[2]

As the journey to that promised land got underway, there was
no question that they were being led by the Lord, who came and
spoke to the brother of Jared from a cloud.[3] After one leg of the trip
they camped for several years, during which the brother of Jared
"remembered not to call upon the name of the Lord."[4] For this he
was chastened when the Lord again came in a cloud and spoke with
him. Repenting of his forgetfulness, the brother of Jared received
fresh instructions for the next part of the trip, an ocean crossing. He
was to build, according to the Lord's specifications, eight submarine-
like vessels that could withstand submersion in a rough sea. Jared
obeyed but ended up with a problem: the vessels needed to be furnished with both air and light.

He approached the Lord on the matter, who promptly described
how to solve the air problem. But as to the problem of light, all that
the Lord seemed willing to do was to exclude some possible alter-
natives without suggesting any, leaving the brother of Jared to come
up with something on his own: "What will ye that I should do?"
"What will ye that I should prepare for you?"[5] Without any apparent
hesitation, the brother of Jared went right to work and melted from
a rock sixteen clear glass stones. Then he asked the Lord to touch
them with his finger to make them luminescent. Most modern readers
of this remarkable story are so captivated by the idea of shining stones

---

1. Ether 1:43.
2. Ether 2:8.
3. See Ether 2:4.
4. Ether 2:14.
5. Ether 2:23, 25.

that they overlook an important detail: How did the brother of Jared come up with the idea so effortlessly? According to Hugh Nibley, "The answer is indicated in the fact that he was following the pattern of Noah's ark, for in the oldest records of the human race the ark seems to have been illuminated by just such shining stones."[1] The book of Ether itself hints that the pattern of Noah's ark was followed when it describes the vessels built by the brother of Jared as "tight like unto the ark of Noah."[2] Furthermore, even our traditional text of Genesis may refer to Noah's shining stones. In Genesis 6:16, Noah is commanded to make, as the King James Version translates it, a "window" in the ark. The Hebrew word is *tsohar*, which occurs nowhere else in the Hebrew Bible and whose meaning has long been disputed.[3] To this day the word remains a point of uncertainty among modern translators, as indicated by the prestigious *New Revised Standard Version* when it notes that the meaning of the Hebrew word is "uncertain."[4] It is translated by most moderns as "roof"[5] or "sky light"[6] or "an opening for daylight."[7] But the majority opinion in rabbinic tradition held that Noah's *tsohar* was actually a brilliant gem or precious stone (or one of several such) that Noah hung in the ark to give light.[8] As told by the Midrash Rabbah on Genesis, "During the whole twelve months that Noah was in the Ark he did not require the light of the sun by day or the light of the moon by night, but he had a polished gem which he hung up."[9]

Accordingly, when faced with the same problem that Noah had faced, the brother of Jared solved it—apparently as the Lord intended and carefully led him to do—by looking backward and remembering his ancient father Noah.

---

1. CWHN 6:352.
2. Ether 6:7.
3. See Wenham 1987:173.
4. NRSV, note on Genesis 6:16.
5. NRSV, REB, NJB, REB.
6. Speiser 1979 (AB 1):47;*The Living Bible*; Fox 1983:28.
7. NJPS.
8. See LJ I:162; Lewis 1978:137; Cassuto 1964:63; Bowker 1979:159–60.
9. Genesis Rabbah 31:11, in Freedman 1983:I:244.

Then, in asking the Lord to touch the stones, the brother of Jared also looked *forward* by faith to the Lord's answering his prayer; in Moroni's words, he "beheld with an eye of faith,"[1] which seems to be the equivalent in Alma's terminology of "looking forward with an eye of faith."[2] As a result, when

> the Lord stretched forth his hand and touched the stones one by one with his finger . . . the veil was taken from off the eyes of the brother of Jared, and he saw the finger of the Lord; and it was as the finger of a man, like unto flesh and blood; and the brother of Jared fell down before the Lord, for he was struck with fear.
>
> And the Lord saw that the brother of Jared had fallen to the earth; and the Lord said unto him: Arise, why hast thou fallen?
>
> And he saith unto the Lord: I saw the finger of the Lord, and I feared lest he should smite me; for I knew not that the Lord had flesh and blood.
>
> And the Lord said unto him: Because of thy faith thou hast seen that I shall take upon me flesh and blood; and never has man come before me with such exceeding faith as thou hast; for were it not so ye could not have seen my finger. Sawest thou more than this?
>
> And he answered: Nay; Lord, show thyself unto me.
>
> And the Lord said unto him: Believest thou the words which I shall speak?
>
> And he answered: Yea, Lord, I know that thou speakest the truth, for thou art a God of truth, and canst not lie.
>
> And when he had said these words, behold, the Lord showed himself unto him, and said: Because thou knowest these things ye are redeemed from the fall; therefore ye are brought back into my presence; therefore I show myself unto you.
>
> Behold, I am he who was prepared from the foundation of the world to redeem my people. Behold, I am Jesus Christ. I am the Father and the Son. In me shall all mankind have life, and that eternally, even they who shall believe on my name; and they shall become my sons and my daughters.[3]

---

1. Ether 12:19.
2. Alma 32:40.
3. Ether 3:6–14.

The brother of Jared had first looked back to his faithful father (Noah), then forward in faith to Christ; and by so doing he had entered into a new father-son relationship by becoming a son of Christ. These themes of looking back to one's faithful father or fathers and looking forward in faith to Christ will run throughout the rest of the book of Ether as it recounts the history of the posterity of Jared and his brother.

The brother of Jared was commanded to write the things the Lord showed him, which included a vision of all the past and future inhabitants of the earth. "And," Moroni comments, "there never were greater things made manifest than those which were made manifest unto the brother of Jared."[1] But the record of this experience was reserved to be published only "after that [Christ] should be lifted up upon the cross."[2] Accordingly, King Mosiah in the first century B.C. did not make those things known when he translated the book of Ether and informed his people about some of its contents.[3] Nor do we yet have the full account; for after Moroni had written that full account, he was commanded to seal it up to be reserved until the day when mankind "shall exercise faith in me, saith the Lord, even as the brother of Jared did, that they may become sanctified in me," qualifying them to know "all my revelations, saith Jesus Christ, the Son of God, the Father of the heavens and of the earth, and all things that in them are."[4] Therefore, the Lord expressly invites the Gentiles, "Come unto me,"[5] and he extends the same invitation to the house of Israel so that they "shall . . . know that the Father hath remembered the covenant which he made unto your fathers, O house of Israel."[6] In other words, a knowledge of the glorious truths revealed to the brother of Jared is reserved for those who do as he did: remember the faithful fathers of old and look forward in faith to Christ in order to become children of Christ.

During the long transoceanic journey, which lasted nearly a year,[7]

---

1. Ether 4:4.
2. Ether 4:1.
3. See Mosiah 28:11–18; Ether 4:1.
4. Ether 4:7.
5. Ether 4:13.
6. Ether 4:15.
7. See Ether 6:11.

the group led by Jared and his brother continually thanked and praised the Lord, and when finally

> they had set their feet upon the shores of the promised land they bowed themselves down upon the face of the land, and did humble themselves before the Lord, and did shed tears of joy before the Lord, because of the multitude of his tender mercies over them.[1]

The powerful examples of Jared and his brother were combined with express and effective teaching, so that their sons and daughters "were taught to walk humbly before the Lord; and they were also taught from on high."[2] There are few greater things that today's parents can teach their children than "to walk humbly before the Lord," for the rewards of such humility are still the same, as is apparent in latter-day revelation: "Be thou humble; and the Lord thy God shall lead thee by the hand, and give thee answer to thy prayers."[3]

THE JAREDITE KINGS

When the people requested that Jared or his brother anoint one of their sons to be a king, the brother of Jared resisted, but Jared relented. Of all their many sons, however, only one was willing to accept the responsibility, a son of Jared named Orihah. The brief comment on his long life and reign again emphasizes the critical link between righteousness and remembering one's faithful fathers:

> And it came to pass that Orihah did walk humbly before the Lord, and did remember how great things the Lord had done for his father, and also taught his people how great things the Lord had done for their fathers.
>
> And it came to pass that Orihah did execute judgment upon the land in righteousness all his days, whose days were exceedingly many.[4]

---

1. Ether 6:12.
2. Ether 6:17.
3. D&C 112:10.
4. Ether 6:30; 7:1.

Throughout his very long life, he never forgot what the Lord had done for their fathers, and he never let his people forget it; and they prospered "exceedingly."[1]

As one follows the listing of Orihah's long line of descendants (who preserve the dynasty until near the end of Jaredite history), two distinct patterns emerge. First, there is a tendency for each son to follow the path of his immediate father, either for good or ill (the sometimes notable exceptions may bespeak the corrupting allurement of royal wealth, power, and fame). Second, those who are praised for their righteousness tend to be men who honor their immediate father and remember their faithful fathers of old. For example, after one of Orihah's grandsons, Corihor, rebelled against his own father and took the kingdom by force, Corihor's brother Shule gave him battle and thereby "obtained the kingdom and restored it unto his father."[2] For this act of filial loyalty Shule himself was eventually given the kingdom, and it seems more than coincidental that this man who so honored his father would also "execute judgment in righteousness"[3] and be "mighty in judgment."[4] When prophets arose during Shule's reign and threatened destruction if the people did not repent, the people's initial reaction was one of reviling. But Shule's decree and enforcement of a law protecting the prophets allowed their message to be heard and finally followed, averting disaster and bringing peace. The final comment about this good king expressly links his righteousness to his remembering his faithful fathers of old:

> He remembered the great things that the Lord had done for his fathers in bringing them across the great deep into the promised land; *wherefore* he did execute judgment in righteousness all his days.[5]

The word *wherefore* (meaning *therefore*[6]) is Moroni's powerful com-

---

1. Ether 6:28.
2. Ether 7:10.
3. Ether 7:11.
4. Ether 7:8.
5. Ether 7:27, emphasis added.
6. WTNID 2602.

mentary on the critical connection between remembering one's righteous fathers of the past and achieving righteousness for oneself.

Moroni's brief introduction to Shule's son and successor, Omer, tells us merely his name; only later do we learn that he was a righteous man when we read that Omer's son and successor Emer "did fill the steps of his father"[1] by "execut[ing] judgment in righteousness all his days."[2] But long before Emer was born, Omer had been deposed by his rebellious son Jared, who in turn was deposed by two of Omer's other sons; they restored their father to the throne. Deprived of his short-lived royalty, Jared was "exceedingly sorrowful," not out of remorse for his wrongs but rather "because of the loss of the kingdom, for he had set his heart upon the kingdom and upon the glory of the world."[3]

It comes as no surprise, then, to read that one of Jared's children, a daughter, likewise concerned herself with worldly glory as she proposed to her despondent father a cunning and murderous plan, based on the secret oaths and combinations that began with Cain, which would kill her grandfather (Omer) and restore her father to the throne. Jared would send for one Akish, before whom Jared's daughter would dance. When Akish requested her hand in marriage, Jared would consent only if Akish would bring him Omer's head. The plan proceeded accordingly, and when Akish learned the price, he instigated — presumably at Jared's behest — a secret society in order to murder Omer. But the righteous Omer was warned by the Lord in a dream and fled to safety. Jared ascended the throne, but ironically the secret combination he had organized turned against him as he was murdered by Akish. (We suspect the daughter of Jared in the matter; if she could have her grandfather murdered, why not her father, especially if she would thereby become queen?)

The ugly intrigue continued as Akish, now king, became "jealous" of his son and starved him to death in prison. Was Akish being influenced by his new wife, Jared's daughter, who wanted to place

1. Ether 9:15.
2. Ether 9:21.
3. Ether 8:7.

on the throne a son of her own rather than Akish's son by a former wife? Akish's other sons were incensed, resulting in an intense war that eventually decimated nearly all of the population—a destruction that was perhaps predictable for this civilization that apparently became engulfed by a secret combination, for, as Moroni commented, "whatsoever nation shall uphold such secret combinations, to get power and gain, until they shall spread over the nation, behold, they shall be destroyed."[1] The whole affair stands in sharp contrast to the many loving father-son relationships depicted in the Book of Mormon, and it demonstrates the deplorable depths to which men can fall in their reach for this world's glory at any price. Sadly, this is but one of several instances in Jaredite history when the nation was jeopardized by a prince or a king not honoring his father.

Finally restored to his throne, the aged Omer confered the kingdom on his son Emer, who, as noted before, "did fill the steps of his father"[2] and "did execute judgment in righteousness all his days."[3] His reign was a time of unparalleled prosperity (which followed, notably, when the king honored and emulated his righteous father). The account of Emer's life is regrettably brief, but his exceeding righteousness recalls that of his ancestral relative, the brother of Jared, who saw the Lord. In Emer's case Moroni merely reports that he "saw peace in the land; yea, and he even saw the Son of Righteousness, and did rejoice and glory in his day; and he died in peace."[4]

We would expect the son of such a man to follow the same path, and so it was: Emer's son and successor, Coriantum, "did walk in the steps of his father, . . . and did administer that which was good unto his people in all his days."[5] Unfortunately, however, the pattern didn't always hold. Two generations later a wicked son, Heth, turned to secret combinations as he "did dethrone his father" and "slew him with his own sword"[6] to obtain the throne. In response "there came

---

1. Ether 8:22.
2. Ether 9:15.
3. Ether 9:21.
4. Ether 9:22.
5. Ether 9:23.
6. Ether 9:27.

prophets in the land again, crying repentance" and foretelling that the people "should be destroyed if they did not repent."[1] But at Heth's command the prophets were mistreated, evicted, and even killed. Destruction soon followed in the form of a severe drought and famine, as well as the appearance of a multitude of venomous snakes. Faced with death all around, the people finally repented, and the Lord again sent rain.[2]

The famine had resulted in the death of King Heth and all his family except his son[3] Shez, whose memory of his fathers led him to righteousness:

> Shez did remember the destruction of his fathers, and he did build up a righteous kingdom; for he remembered what the Lord had done in bringing Jared and his brother across the deep; and he did walk in the ways of the Lord.[4]

Shez was followed by several generations of wicked kings,[5] until a certain Levi acquired the kingdom that had much earlier been wrested from his father. As the new king, Levi "did that which was right in the sight of the Lord,"[6] establishing a pattern that endured over the next several generations: Levi's son and successor, Corom, likewise "did that which was good in the sight of the Lord all his days."[7] And Corom's grandson Lib "also did that which was good in the sight of the Lord,"[8] as his people were "blessed" and "prospered by the hand of the Lord" beyond measure.[9]

Generations passed during which the secret combinations again arose; and in the terse account of the kings of this period, three in particular—successively—are singled out as wicked: Ahah "did do all

1. Ether 9:28.
2. See Ether 9:29–35.
3. See Ether 10:1; 1:25.
4. Ether 10:2.
5. See Ether 10:3–14.
6. Ether 10:16.
7. Ether 10:17.
8. Ether 10:19.
9. Ether 10:28.

manner of iniquity in his days";[1] his son Ethem "also did do that
which was wicked in his days";[2] and Ethem's son Moron similarly
"did that which was wicked before the Lord"[3]—and was overthrown,
ending the dynasty. Parental example of evil, it would seem, can be
as powerful as parental example of good.

ETHER AND THE END OF THE JAREDITE CIVILIZATION

The wicked Moron had a grandson named Ether, the author of
the Jaredite record inscribed on the twenty-four gold plates. In contrast
to his immediate fathers, Ether was a powerful prophet, who

> truly told [the people] of all things, from the beginning of man;
> and that after the waters had receded from off the face of this
> land it became a choice land above all other lands, a chosen
> land of the Lord; wherefore the Lord would have that all men
> should serve him who dwell upon the face thereof.[4]

In rehearsing such events, Ether was calling upon the people to do
as the most righteous Jaredite kings had done and, indeed, what the
brother of Jared himself had done: look back to their faithful fathers.
By so doing the Jaredites would be reminded of the condition of
residency on this choicest of all lands, as mandated when the Lord
swore in his wrath to the brother of Jared that the inhabitants must
serve God or eventually be swept off.[5] Furthermore, by recalling the
faith of their fathers, such as the brother of Jared, Ether's people
would be encouraged to exercise faith themselves.

Thus Ether told them that "by faith all things are fulfilled,"[6] and
he "did prophesy great and marvelous things unto the people."[7] At
this point Moroni pauses to editorialize, recalling, among other examples of faith, the experience of the brother of Jared who saw the

1. Ether 11:10.
2. Ether 11:11.
3. Ether 11:14.
4. Ether 13:2.
5. See Ether 2:8.
6. Ether 12:3.
7. Ether 12:5.

Lord only after he had first "beheld with an eye of faith."[1] What Ether was urging, it seems, was that his people not only look back to their faithful fathers but also follow their example in looking forward with an eye of faith.

Among the glorious things to look forward to, Ether said, was the future of this land. As reported by Moroni, Ether prophesied that

> It was the place of the New Jerusalem, which should come down out of heaven, and the holy sanctuary of the Lord. . . .
>
> And . . . [another] New Jerusalem should be built up upon this land, unto the remnant of the seed of Joseph, for which things there has been a type.
>
> For as Joseph brought his father down into the land of Egypt, even so he died there; wherefore, the Lord brought a remnant of the seed of Joseph out of the land of Jerusalem, that he might be merciful unto the seed of Joseph that they should perish not, even as he was merciful unto the father of Joseph that he should perish not.
>
> Wherefore, the remnant of the house of Joseph shall be built upon this land; and it shall be a land of their inheritance; and they shall build up a holy city unto the Lord, like unto the Jerusalem of old.[2]

As for the old Jerusalem, after being destroyed "it should be built up again, and become a holy city of the Lord; and it should be built unto the house of Israel."[3] And

> the inhabitants thereof, blessed are they, for they have been washed in the blood of the Lamb; and they are they who were scattered and gathered in from the four quarters of the earth, and from the north countries, and are partakers of the fulfilling of the covenant which God made with their father, Abraham.[4]

Conspicuous in these prophecies of Ether is the paramount role of the ancient fathers in the latter-day events of their posterity: Jo-

---

1. Ether 12:19.
2. Ether 13:3, 6–8.
3. Ether 13:5.
4. Ether 13:11.

seph's descendants would be preserved as typified by Joseph's own life and as part of the larger salvation of the house of Israel in fulfillment of the covenants made to their father Abraham. But why should Ether mention these matters, seeing that his own people were not descended from Joseph or Israel or even Abraham? Perhaps Ether was again trying to encourage his own people to look back to *their* own fathers, Jared and his brother, and to follow their example in looking forward in faith to Christ in order to become his sons and daughters.

Unfortunately, Ether's people would not heed his advice and finally refused to listen any more. "They esteemed him as naught, and cast him out; and he hid himself in the cavity of a rock by day, and by night he went forth. . . . viewing the destructions which came upon the people"[1] — destructions that eventually annihilated this nation that had once risen to be one of the greatest "upon all the face of the earth."[2] Their destruction resulted from the same behavior that throughout their long history had jeopardized their civilization: failure to honor their fathers by looking back at the great things the Lord had done for them, and failure to follow the example of those fathers by looking forward in faith to become children of Christ. There could be no greater memorial to the importance of remembering one's faithful fathers.

1. Ether 13:13–14.
2. Ether 1:43.

Chapter 9

THE FINAL AUTHORS

· ·

MORMON AND MORONI

ANNIHILATION ON THE PROMISED LAND

That the Nephites finally met with the same sort of annihilation that had earlier befallen the Jaredites should give us pause. Why, we may ask, could not these New World civilizations have simply waned away gradually like so many of the glorious ancient empires of the Old World? Why such drastically destructive fireworks at the end of both major civilizations chronicled in the Book of Mormon? The answer is found in the divine mandate given to the ancestors of those civilizations as they were first being led to this New World, which, as they were clearly told, is the choicest spot on God's earth. This highest of opportunities to reside on this land of liberty and prosperity is fraught with the greatest of responsibilities, as Moroni tells in his abridgment of the Jaredite history:

> The Lord . . . would that they should come forth even unto the land of promise, which was choice above all other lands, which the Lord God had preserved for a righteous people.
> And he had sworn in his wrath unto the brother of Jared, that whoso should possess this land of promise, from that time henceforth and forever, should serve him, the true and only

God, or they should be swept off when the fulness of his wrath should come upon them.

And now, [comments Moroni,] we can behold the decrees of God concerning this land, that it is a land of promise; and whatsoever nation shall possess it shall serve God, or they shall be swept off when the fulness of his wrath shall come upon them. And the fulness of his wrath cometh upon them when they are ripened in iniquity.

For behold, this is a land which is choice above all other lands; wherefore he that doth possess it shall serve God or shall be swept off; for it is the everlasting decree of God. And it is not until the fulness of iniquity among the children of the land, that they are swept off.

And this cometh unto you, O ye Gentiles, that ye may know the decrees of God—that ye may repent, and not continue in your iniquities until the fulness come, that ye may not bring down the fulness of the wrath of God upon you as the inhabitants of the land have hitherto done.[1]

The recurring phrase "swept off"—appearing no less than four times in the above passage—explains the devastating destruction of the once-glorious empires of the Jaredites and Nephites; indeed, the identical phrase is used in the descriptions of both the Jaredite and Nephite destructions.[2] Hugh Nibley has observed:

There are nations that were old when Nephi left Jerusalem and whose cultures and languages, customs, manners, and traditions still survive. They have all paid a high price in human suffering as they go along from folly to folly and disaster to disaster, but they are still there. It is not so in the New World, where great civilizations vanish without even leaving us their names, and where no high civilization has survived. It is significant that with all the warning and promising, only one penalty is ever mentioned. . . . The penalty is destruction; the deliverance repentance.[3]

It is wrenching, of course, to read of such destruction, especially

---

1. Ether 2:7–11.
2. See Ether 14:27; Mormon 4:18.
3. CWHN 8:506.

after becoming acquainted, through the written word, with many of the characters in those civilizations whose lives shine through the centuries as models for our generation. And particularly arresting is the contrast between the high hopes held by the founding fathers of those civilizations and the bitter tragedy that ultimately befell their descendants.

MORMON AND HIS PREDECESSORS

From the final Nephite tragedy, however, and in stark contrast to it, emerges the Book of Mormon's closing portrait of a father and his son, Mormon and Moroni. Their relationship seems the fitting culmination of the various father-son portraits running through the Book of Mormon, for here the familiar pattern of a son following his righteous father is made all the more poignant by an unsurpassed love and tenderness amid the harshness and savagery of a society being "swept off" the land by the judgments of God. And it is thanks to the mutual efforts of that father-son team that we have the Book of Mormon today.

The rapidly decaying condition of the "exceedingly wicked"[1] Nephite society became all the more evident when in about A.D. 320 the keeper of the sacred records, a certain Ammaron, was "constrained by the Holy Ghost"[2] to hide them away in the earth. We are not expressly told but can reasonably suppose that it was also the prompting of the Holy Ghost that caused Ammaron to approach a ten-year-old boy by the name of Mormon and give him these unusual and portentous instructions:

> I perceive that thou art a sober child, and art quick to observe;
> Therefore, when ye are about twenty and four years old I would that ye should remember the things that ye have observed concerning this people; and when ye are of that age go to the land Antum, unto a hill which shall be called Shim; and there have I deposited unto the Lord all the sacred engravings concerning this people.

---

1. 4 Nephi 1:45.
2. 4 Nephi 1:48.

> And behold, ye shall take the plates of Nephi unto your-
> self, . . . and ye shall engrave on the plates of Nephi all the
> things that ye have observed concerning this people.[1]

Mormon's connection with Nephi and the continuation of his work become even more emphatic in what immediately precedes and follows the above passage, which is introduced by Mormon's comment that at the age of ten he "began to be learned somewhat after the manner of the learning of my people."[2] This comment not only alludes to the preparation necessary to transmit the sacred records, but also directly echoes Nephi's comment about his own preparation as he was "taught somewhat in all the learning of my father."[3] Then, immediately after reporting Ammaron's fateful directions to continue the record on the plates of Nephi, Mormon states:

> And I, Mormon, being a descendant of Nephi, (and my
> father's name was Mormon) I remembered the things which
> Ammaron commanded me.[4]

Mormon is thus called upon to become a critical link in the long father-son chain of sacred record keepers going back to his father Nephi, who, as we have seen, was himself a link in a chain of record keepers stretching back through Joseph, Abraham, Noah, Enoch, and Adam, he who first, notes Hugh Nibley, "labored diligently to provide holy books for his descendants."[5] It should be no wonder, then, that the Book of Mormon, like a great deal of other sacred writ, owes its very existence to dutiful fathers, sons, and grandsons, all doing their divinely ordained part in a continuing cause of preserving, updating, and transmitting the sacred records.

Mormon's resemblance to his forefather Nephi did not stop with responsibilities of record keeping. As the "exceedingly young" Nephi

---

1. Mormon 1:2–4.
2. Mormon 1:2.
3. 1 Nephi 1:1.
4. Mormon 1:5.
5. CWHN 2:145.

had avoided the corruption of Jerusalem and had reported, "the Lord . . . did visit me,"[1] so a very young Mormon reported that

> wickedness did prevail upon the face of the whole land, insomuch that the Lord did take away his beloved [translated[2]] disciples, and the work of miracles and of healing did cease because of the iniquity of the people.
>
> And there were no gifts from the Lord, and the Holy Ghost did not come upon any, because of their wickedness and unbelief.
>
> And I, being fifteen years of age and being somewhat of a sober mind, therefore I was visited of the Lord, and tasted and knew of the goodness of Jesus.[3]

There must be something significant, by the way, concerning the stage of life one goes through at the age of about fourteen. Mormon's awakening to spiritual matters at about this age foreshadows a similar awakening at a similar age by the young Joseph Smith,[4] who would translate Mormon's record. And the experiences of both these men echo that of their ancient father Abraham, who was fourteen years old (according to the ancient and venerable Book of Jubilees) when he "began understanding" how society had gone astray and consequently "began to pray to the Creator" for guidance.[5] Fifteen is the age specified in Confucian tradition to set one's heart upon learning, and thirteen is the age specified in Jewish tradition for the acceptance of moral responsibility.[6] Similarly, through modern-day prophets, the Lord has specified twelve as the age when worthy young men of his church can receive the Aaronic Priesthood. What all of this seems to suggest is a heightened spiritual sense experienced at about this age—something that conscientious parents of young teenagers would do well to keep in mind.

In Mormon's experience at age fifteen, he apparently acquired

---

1. 1 Nephi 2:16.
2. See 3 Nephi 28:4–12.
3. Mormon 1:13–15.
4. See JS–H 1.
5. Jubilees 11:16–17, in OTP 2:79.
6. See Viorst 1986:395.

not only increased knowledge of deity, but also divine authority to minister, meaning (as he would later describe the acquisition of such authority) that he had been "called . . . to [the Lord's] ministry, and to his holy work."[1] In fact, in another passage he declares that he was "a disciple of Jesus Christ," having "been called of him to declare his word."[2] This echoes the life of Nephi, who similarly had been "called of God, and ordained after the manner of his holy order"[3] to engage in the ministry.[4]

By virtue of the authority Mormon received, and out of his great concern for his fellow Nephites, in his own words,

> I did endeavor to preach unto this people, but my mouth was shut, and I was forbidden that I should preach unto them; for behold they had wilfully rebelled against their God; and the beloved disciples were taken away out of the land, because of their iniquity.
>
> But I did remain among them, but I was forbidden to preach unto them, because of the hardness of their hearts.[5]

(This ban on preaching would not be permanent.[6])

But the skills of this remarkable fifteen-year-old did not end here. In that same year, as he tells it,

> there began to be a war again between the Nephites and the Lamanites. And notwithstanding I being young, was large in stature; therefore the people of Nephi appointed me that I should be their leader, or the leader of their armies.
>
> Therefore it came to pass that in my sixteenth year I did go forth at the head of an army of the Nephites, against the Lamanites.[7]

And once again we see a parallel with Nephi, who had likewise served

---

1. Moroni 8:2 (Mormon speaking of Moroni's call to the ministry).

2. 3 Nephi 5:13.

3. 2 Nephi 6:2. These words were spoken by Jacob telling of the authority he had received apparently from Nephi.

4. See 1 Nephi 9:3–4; 10:1; 19:3.

5. Mormon 1:16–17.

6. Mormon 3:2–3; Moroni 7.

7. Mormon 2:1–2.

as a "great protector" for his people, "having wielded the sword of Laban in their defence."[1]

Mormon's youthfulness in being appointed commander-in-chief of the Nephite armies is also but the first of many echoes in his lengthy life and military career (he would die in battle at about seventy-four) of that most illustrious Nephite commander-in-chief, General Moroni, who according to one latter-day saint scholar was probably Mormon's ancestor.[2] Whether ancestor or merely military predecessor, Moroni seems to have exerted a profound influence upon Mormon, who in fact devoted significant space in his abridgment of Nephite history to the life and labors of Moroni. The parallels between the two men are striking, beginning with Mormon's brief character sketch of the ancient general who was "a strong and a mighty man" possessing "a perfect understanding" and delighting "not . . . in bloodshed" but in "the liberty and the freedom of his country"; being a man also "whose heart did swell with thanksgiving to his God" even as he "did labor exceedingly for the welfare and safety of his people"; thus Moroni "was a man who was firm in the faith of Christ" and who gloried not in military victory but in the spiritual victory of "doing good" and "keeping the commandments of God"; indeed,

> if all men had been, and were, and ever would be, like unto Moroni, behold, the very powers of hell would have been shaken forever; yea, the devil would never have power over the hearts of the children of men.[3]

Mormon might just as well have been describing himself, although modesty would have prevented any such self-praise. Ironically, and fortunately for us, Mormon's magnanimity in justly praising the ancient General Moroni has left us a portrait that also conforms in every particular to Mormon himself. If Moroni was "a strong and a mighty man," so also was Mormon, who was of such "large . . . stature" that at fifteen he could be appointed to lead the armies.[4] The "perfect

---

1. Jacob 1:10; see also 2 Nephi 6:2.
2. See John A. Tvedtnes, in Ricks and Hamblin 1990:319.
3. Alma 48:11–13, 16–17.
4. Mormon 2:1.

understanding" that Moroni possessed is matched by that of Mormon, who perfectly understood the plan of salvation and the purpose of earth-life[1] and knew, as he wrote to his son, that the real battle of life is the struggle within each soul between good and evil:

> For we have a labor to perform whilst in this tabernacle of clay, that we may conquer the enemy of all righteousness, and rest our souls in the kingdom of God.[2]

As Moroni "did not delight in bloodshed," Mormon likewise abhorred the "blood and carnage"[3] occasioned by war. He fought not for conquest but rather to defend his people's homes and families[4] against attack by a people whose hatred stemmed from the wicked traditions of their fathers.[5] As Moroni's "heart did swell with thanksgiving to his God," so Mormon's focus was the "victory" gained by Christ allowing those who are guiltless to "sing ceaseless praises with the choirs above . . . in a state of happiness which hath no end."[6] As Moroni "did labor exceedingly for the welfare and safety of his people," so Mormon labored with all his might for his people, having "loved them . . . with all my heart" and prayed "all the day long for them" and even "delivered them out of the hands of their enemies" time after time.[7] Moroni was "firm in the faith of Christ," as was Mormon, who encouraged both his brethren and his readers to "exercise faith in Christ"[8] and "believe in Jesus Christ, that he is the Son of God."[9] He explained also that angels show themselves "unto them of strong faith and a firm mind"[10] (that this description also applied to himself is evident from his son's report that they both had been

---

1. See Moroni 7–9.
2. Moroni 9:6.
3. Mormon 5:8.
4. See Mormon 2:23.
5. See 4 Nephi 1:39.
6. Mormon 7:5, 7.
7. Mormon 3:12–13.
8. Moroni 7:25.
9. Mormon 7:5.
10. Moroni 7:30.

visited by the three translated Nephite disciples[1]). As Moroni had gloried not in military victory but in "doing good" and "keeping the commandments of God," so Mormon emphasized to his people the need to "do that which is good"[2] and to "lay hold upon every good thing"[3] and to thereby "love God, and to serve him."[4] Hence Mormon's concluding statement about the character of Moroni—that were all men like Moroni "the very powers of hell would have been shaken forever"—turns out to be an accurate self-portrait of Mormon. It surely seems more than coincidental that the man—and possibly his ancestor—whom Mormon seemed to admire the most, he became most like. As the ultimate tribute to the ancient general, Mormon named his own beloved son Moroni.

The parallels between Mormon and his predecessor Moroni extend into their military leadership as well. Like Moroni, Mormon led his people to "make preparations to defend [them]selves,"[5] thus "preparing their lands and their arms against the time of battle"[6] by fortifying key cities[7] and creating strongholds.[8] Also like Moroni, Mormon attempted to prepare the minds of the people (as soon as the Lord allowed him to do so) by crying repentance to them,[9] and, as Mormon recounts it, by

> speak[ing] unto my people, and . . . urg[ing] them with great energy, that they would stand boldly before the Lamanites and fight for their wives, and their children, and their houses, and their homes.[10]

Like Moroni, Mormon courageously led his armies into battle.[11] And

1. See Mormon 8:11.
2. Moroni 7:10.
3. Moroni 7:19.
4. Moroni 7:13.
5. Mormon 2:4.
6. Mormon 3:1.
7. See Mormon 2:21; 3:5–6.
8. See Mormon 5:4.
9. See Mormon 3:2–3.
10. Mormon 2:23.
11. See Mormon 6:11.

as with Moroni, Mormon's leadership inspired the Nephites to beat the odds in defeating larger[1] — sometimes much larger[2] — armies.

MORMON LEADS A FALLEN PEOPLE AND LEAVES A SACRED RECORD

But Mormon's army was not always, and — most importantly — not finally, successful. For the one vital difference between the lives of General Moroni and General Mormon was the difference between the people they served. Moroni's people qualified for the Lord's help by repenting;[3] not so with the people of Mormon. "Notwithstanding the great destruction which hung over my people," Mormon wrote, "they did not repent of their evil doings."[4] Once when it seemed otherwise, as Mormon recorded,

> I, Mormon, saw their lamentation and their mourning and their sorrow before the Lord, [and] my heart did begin to rejoice within me, knowing the mercies and the long-suffering of the Lord, therefore supposing that he would be merciful unto them that they would again become a righteous people.
>
> But behold this my joy was vain, for their sorrowing was not unto repentance, because of the goodness of God; but it was rather the sorrowing of the damned, because the Lord would not always suffer them to take happiness in sin.
>
> And they did not come unto Jesus with broken hearts and contrite spirits, but they did curse God, and wish to die. Nevertheless they would struggle with the sword for their lives.
>
> And it came to pass that my sorrow did return unto me again, and I saw that the day of grace was passed with them, both temporally and spiritually; for I saw thousands of them hewn down in open rebellion against their God, and heaped up as dung upon the face of the land.[5]

But no amount of destruction could move this people to repentance. Even when Mormon himself was commanded to tell the people,

---

1. See Mormon 2:9.
2. See Mormon 2:25.
3. See Alma 62:40–51.
4. Mormon 2:8.
5. Mormon 2:12–15.

"Repent ye, . . . and ye shall be spared," yet "it was in vain," for "they did harden their hearts against the Lord their God."[1] Such hardness resulted from an intractable pride, for, as Mormon wrote to his son, "the pride of this nation . . . hath proven their destruction."[2] Thus every time some battle would go their way, they would immediately begin to "boast in their own strength,"[3] so that indeed they "were left to [them]selves," and "the strength of the Lord was not with [them]."[4] Hence they were "without Christ and God in the world," being "led about by Satan, even as chaff is driven before the wind, or as a vessel is tossed about upon the waves, without sail or anchor, or without anything wherewith to steer her."[5] In Mormon's brief allusions to their awful wickedness, which he mercifully declines to describe in full,[6] we learn that the Nephites were overrun with secret combinations and practiced "sorceries, and witchcrafts, and magics; and the power of the evil one was wrought upon all the face of the land."[7] Furthermore the Nephites "delighted in the shedding of blood continually"[8] and sought "for blood and revenge."[9] They engaged in the most brutal and barbaric savagery as they inflicted upon prisoners of war different types of sordid abuse and torture and afterward devoured their flesh.[10] Mormon wrote to his son that the Nephites

> have become strong in their perversion; and they are alike brutal, sparing none, neither old nor young; and they delight in everything save that which is good; and the suffering of our women and our children upon all the face of this land doth

---

1. Mormon 3:2–3.
2. Moroni 8:27.
3. Mormon 3:9; see also 4:8.
4. Mormon 2:26.
5. Mormon 5:16, 18.
6. See Mormon 4:11; 5:8–9; Moroni 9:19.
7. Mormon 1:19.
8. Mormon 4:11.
9. Moroni 9:23.
10. See Moroni 9:9–10.

exceed everything; yea, tongue cannot tell, neither can it be written.[1]

It is quite simply the worst picture of evil painted in all of the Book of Mormon. Indeed, the Lord revealed to Mormon that "there never had been so great wickedness among all the children of Lehi, nor even among all the house of Israel"[2]—a statement that can hardly be appreciated without reading the Old Testament's descriptions of the appalling degradation that had set in on the kingdom of Judah just prior to the Babylonian destruction. The only thing in history known to compare with the Nephite wickedness is the infamous generation of the flood, whose degradation, depravation, and refusal to repent were similar to that of the Nephites[3]—and brought a similar result: total annihilation. And as the generation of the flood had the righteous Noah to declare repentance and warn of impending disaster if they did not repent,[4] so the Nephites had the righteous Mormon. Had they remembered their righteous father Noah and the fate that befell his generation when they refused to hearken to him, perhaps the Nephites would have hearkened to their own prophet, Mormon.

But they did not, and Mormon mourned for them: "Wo is me because of their wickedness; for my heart has been filled with sorrow because of their wickedness, all my days."[5] On one occasion after they had come out in open rebellion against God, Mormon "did utterly refuse from this time forth to be [their] commander," even though, as he wrote, he "had loved them, according to the love of God which was in me, with all my heart; and my soul had been poured out in prayer unto my God all the day long for them."[6] Only when they "began to be swept off"[7] did Mormon agree again to be their commander, writing later about his decision, "For they looked upon me

---

1. Moroni 9:19.
2. Mormon 4:12.
3. See Genesis 6:5, 11–13; Moses 7:32–41; 8:18–30; 1 Enoch 9:9, in OTP 1:17; Jubilees 7:20–25, in OTP 2:69–70; Lewis 1978:126–30; CWHN 2:178–93.
4. See Moses 8:19–24; 2 Peter 2:5; LJ I:153; Lewis 1978:37, 135.
5. Mormon 2:19.
6. Mormon 3:11–12.
7. Mormon 4:18.

as though I could deliver them from their afflictions."[1] His resumption of command is one of the great acts of charity on record. He could not refuse his service—perilous as it was for his own life—to this people whom, despite their blindness, he loved and for whom he seemed to hold out hope till the end that they might repent. They did not, and after his sizable army of 230,000 men had been reduced to a mere 24 souls, Mormon—who had been severely wounded himself[2]—gazed out over the battlefield and left us a poignant description of the carnage he beheld and the pain he felt—not for his own severe wound but for the loss of his people:

> Their flesh, and bones, and blood lay upon the face of the earth, being left by the hands of those who slew them to molder upon the land, and to crumble and to return to their mother earth.
>
> And my soul was rent with anguish, because of the slain of my people, and I cried:
>
> O ye fair ones, how could ye have departed from the ways of the Lord! O ye fair ones, how could ye have rejected that Jesus, who stood with open arms to receive you!
>
> Behold, if ye had not done this, ye would not have fallen. But behold, ye are fallen, and I mourn your loss.
>
> O ye fair sons and daughters, ye fathers and mothers, ye husbands and wives, ye fair ones, how is it that ye could have fallen!
>
> But behold, ye are gone, and my sorrows cannot bring your return.
>
> And the day soon cometh that your mortal must put on immortality, and these bodies which are now moldering in corruption must soon become incorruptible bodies; and then ye must stand before the judgment-seat of Christ, to be judged according to your works; and if it so be that ye are righteous, then are ye blessed with your fathers who have gone before you.
>
> O that ye had repented before this great destruction had come upon you. But behold, ye are gone, and the Father, yea,

---

1. Mormon 5:1.
2. See Mormon 6:10.

the Eternal Father of heaven, knoweth your state; and he doeth
with you according to his justice and mercy.[1]

Mormon's marked emphasis on various parent-child relationships
is noteworthy as he tells these "sons and daughters" and "fathers
and mothers" that "if . . . ye are righteous, then are ye blessed with
your fathers who have gone before you. . . . But behold, ye are gone,
and the Father . . . knoweth your state." In addition, Mormon's powerful lament echoes that of one of the ancient antediluvian fathers,
Enoch, who had similarly wept over the fate of another people who
had practiced such wickedness — the generation of the flood:

> Enoch . . . looked upon their wickedness, and their misery,
> and wept and stretched forth his arms, and his heart swelled
> wide as eternity; and his bowels yearned; and all eternity
> shook.[2]

Mormon's emphasis on fathers and children continued as he hast-
ily finished the sacred record. He had already written of yet other
father-children relationships: the "human family of Adam",[3] the seed
of the Lamanites,[4] the latter-day Gentiles who derive blessings from
the house of Israel[5] (an apparent allusion to becoming adopted children of Abraham),[6] the fulfillment of the covenant made by "the
Father" to (Abraham's seed of) the house of Israel,[7] the Nephites'
identity as "a remnant of the seed of Joseph" derived from "[their]
father Jacob",[8] praise to God that "he brought our fathers out of the
land of Jerusalem,"[9] and the relationship of God the Father and "his
most Beloved" Son.[10] Now, after the decisive battle that had made his

---

1. Mormon 6:15–22.
2. Moses 7:41.
3. Mormon 3:20.
4. See Mormon 5:10.
5. Ibid.
6. See Abraham 2:10; TPJS 149–50.
7. See 3 Nephi 29:1; Mormon 5:14, 20.
8. 3 Nephi 10:17.
9. 3 Nephi 5:20.
10. Mormon 5:14.

people nearly extinct, and probably believing that in his wounded state he could not survive much longer, he engraved his final words on the sacred plates—again with a marked emphasis on fathers and children. Addressing himself to the future descendants of the Lamanites, he said that his record would come to them "that they may know of the things of their fathers"[1] and believe in the Son of the Eternal Father:

> Know ye that ye are of the house of Israel. . . .
>
> Know ye that ye must come to the knowledge of your fathers, and repent of all your sins and iniquities, and believe in Jesus Christ, that he is the Son of God, and that he was slain by the Jews, and by the power of the Father he hath risen again. . . .
>
> And he hath brought to pass the redemption of the world, whereby he that is found guiltless before him at the judgment day hath it given unto him to dwell in the presence of God . . . in a state of happiness which hath no end. . . .
>
> And if ye believe this [record] ye will know concerning your fathers, and also the marvelous works which were wrought by the power of God among them.
>
> And ye will also know that ye are a remnant of the seed of Jacob; therefore ye are numbered among the people of the first covenant; and if it so be that ye believe in Christ, and are baptized, first with water, then with fire and with the Holy Ghost, following the example of our Savior, according to that which he hath commanded us, it shall be well with you in the day of judgment. Amen.[2]

To weep over the loss of one's own people is one thing; but it must have been quite another for Mormon to expend his last literary breath in extending an invitation of "happiness which hath no end" to the future posterity of the very people against whom he had been forced to fight for nearly six decades[3] and who had now destroyed his nation and severely wounded him. We would have understood had Mormon vowed to recover and fight his enemies yet another day,

---

1. Mormon 7:1.
2. Mormon 7:2, 5, 7, 9–10.
3. See Mormon 1:15; 2:1–2; 8:6.

but his was a higher vision, and one of the most moving examples of charity in the Book of Mormon. Such rare and forgiving love recalls that of Mormon's ancient father Joseph and the difficult trial of his life, which in fact had been emphasized twice before in the Book of Mormon, once by Nephi[1] (Mormon's ancestor) and once by Moroni[2] (Mormon's predecessor and possibly his ancestor), when they spoke of Joseph's being sold by his brothers. Many years later when, as Genesis records, the tables of power were dramatically turned and Joseph, now vizier of Egypt, dined with these same brothers who hadn't a clue that this was Joseph,

> Joseph said unto his brethren, Come near to me, I pray you. And they came near. And he said, I am Joseph your brother, whom ye sold into Egypt.
>
> Now therefore be not grieved, nor angry with yourselves, that ye sold me hither: for God did send me before you to preserve life . . . and to save your lives by a great deliverance. So now it was not you that sent me hither, but God. . . .
>
> [Then] he kissed all his brethren, and wept upon them.[3]

Later, according to the pseudepigraphical Testament of Joseph, as Joseph lay dying, he spoke of love and divine design:

> My brothers and my children. Listen to Joseph, the one beloved of Israel. . . . These, my brothers, hated me but the Lord loved me. They wanted to kill me, but the God of my fathers preserved me. . . .
>
> Love one another and in patient endurance conceal one another's shortcomings. God is delighted by harmony among brothers. . . . [Even] after the death of Jacob, my father, I loved [my brothers] beyond measure, and everything he had wanted for them I did abundantly in their behalf.[4]

Fittingly, then, Mormon follows the charitable example of his own

1. See 1 Nephi 5:14.
2. See Alma 46:23–26.
3. Genesis 45:4–5, 7–8, 15.
4. Testament of Joseph 1:2, 4; 17:2–3, 5, in OTP 1:819, 823.

ancient father Joseph even as he calls upon future generations to remember their ancient fathers.

THE RELATIONSHIP AND LEGACY OF A FATHER AND HIS BELOVED SON

What kind of relationship would a man like Mormon have with his own son? The disclosure of that relationship may well have been part of the reason that the Lord designed that the record should be finished not by Mormon but rather by his son, Moroni, whose first entry in the record poignantly reveals what is perhaps the most tender and loving bond between any mortal father and his son in the Book of Mormon, set in a scene of the most heartrending pathos and loneliness. Moroni, we should note, was no "wimp." He had, as we learn in passing from Mormon's own record, led ten thousand men into the final battle as one of his father's generals.[1] One of the last survivors was Moroni, who now takes up his father's record and lays bare his feelings of acute loneliness after the loss of his civilization, friends, family, and particularly his father. Twice Moroni tells us that his father has been killed, and otherwise refers to him repeatedly in this soliloquy that may be the most moving passage in all of the Book of Mormon about the bond between a mortal father and his son:

> Behold, I, Moroni, do finish *the record of my father*, Mormon. Behold, I have but few things to write, which things *I have been commanded by my father*.
>
> And now it came to pass that after the great and tremendous battle at Cumorah, behold, the Nephites who had escaped into the country southward were hunted by the Lamanites, until they were all destroyed.
>
> And *my father also was killed* by them, and I even remain alone to write the sad tale of the destruction of my people. But behold, they are gone, and *I fulfil the commandment of my father*. And whether they will slay me, I know not.
>
> Therefore I will write and hide up the records in the earth; and whither I go it mattereth not.
>
> Behold, *my father hath made this record, and he hath written the*

---

1. See Mormon 6:12.

intent thereof. And behold, I would write it also if I had room upon the plates, but I have not; and ore I have none, for I am alone. *My father hath been slain* in battle, and all my kinsfolk, and I have not friends nor whither to go; and how long the Lord will suffer that I may live I know not.

Behold, four hundred years have passed away since the coming of our Lord and Savior.

And behold, the Lamanites have hunted my people, the Nephites, down from city to city and from place to place, even until they are no more; and great has been their fall; yea, great and marvelous is the destruction of my people, the Nephites.

And behold, it is the hand of the Lord which hath done it. And behold also, the Lamanites are at war one with another; and the whole face of this land is one continual round of murder and bloodshed; and no one knoweth the end of the war.

And now, behold, I say no more concerning them, for there are none save it be the Lamanites and robbers that do exist upon the face of the land.

And there are none that do know the true God save it be the disciples of Jesus, who did tarry in the land until the wickedness of the people was so great that the Lord would not suffer them to remain with the people; and whether they be upon the face of the land no man knoweth.

But behold, *my father and I have seen them, and they have ministered unto us.*

And whoso receiveth this record, and shall not condemn it because of the imperfections which are in it, the same shall know of greater things than these. Behold, I am Moroni; and were it possible, I would make all things known unto you.

Behold, I make an end of speaking concerning this people. I am the son of Mormon, and *my father was a descendant of Nephi.*[1]

Moroni's longing for his father obviously includes not only the natural feelings of a son deprived of a beloved father, but also a profound sense of loss for a person who was Moroni's exemplar and leader, and with whom Moroni had shared the memorable spiritual experience of being ministered to by the three translated Nephite disciples.

As Moroni proceeds to instruct the latter-day generation who will

---

1. Mormon 8:1–13; emphasis added.

read his words, he makes it clear that he is not writing alone, but that the record is a joint project he and his father have done under divine direction: "*We* have written this record according to *our* knowledge," and "the Lord knoweth the things which *we* have written"; "these things are written that we may rid *our* garments of the blood of *our* brethren,"[1] and "if there be faults they may be the faults of man. But behold, *we* know no fault";[2] therefore "condemn *me* not because of mine imperfection, *neither my father*, because of his imperfection."[3] Even as he writes, Moroni follows his father's example in emphasizing yet other father-child relationships by speaking of Adam's posterity being redeemed by "the Father and the Son" pursuant to the covenant made to yet other fathers—Abraham, Isaac, and Jacob[4]—which covenant will not be fulfilled fully without the latter-day coming forth of the Book of Mormon.[5] And Mormon alludes to the righteous fathers of old and the value of their examples when he urges all mankind to "begin as in times of old, and come unto the Lord with all your heart."[6]

The joint effort of Mormon and his son Moroni in completing the sacred record is nowhere better evidenced than with the Jaredite accound added to the record. In abridging the entire span of the Nephite history up through his own day, Mormon had promised that the Jaredite account would "be written hereafter; for behold, it is expedient that all people should know the things which are written in this account."[7] The circumstances of the war and Mormon's death prevented Mormon from following through, but his son Moroni made good on his father's promise.[8] And in doing so Moroni again refers to other father-children relationships as he speaks of the faith of "our fathers"[9] and the promise obtained by "my fathers" that this record

---

1. Mormon 9:32, 34–35; emphasis added.
2. Mormon 8:17; emphasis added.
3. Mormon 9:31; emphasis added.
4. See Mormon 9:11–12 (mentioning Abraham, Isaac, and Jacob).
5. See Mormon 9:37.
6. Mormon 9:27.
7. Mosiah 28:19.
8. See Ether 1:1.
9. Ether 12:7.

would go forth to the Lamanites.[1] Then he reports Christ's own words about "the mansions of [the] Father."[2] And all of this is set in the Jaredite account, which by itself is a powerful memorial to the importance of remembering one's fathers.[3]

Having completed the Jaredite account, Moroni had fulfilled his duty regarding the sacred record. He had not planned on writing more; and understandably so, for conditions were hardly conducive to the calmness and serenity that authors commonly require. Moroni was a solitary fugitive evading the fierce Lamanite armies who were not only fighting each other but were executing "every Nephite that will not deny the Christ."[4] Refusing ever to make such a denial, Moroni was forced to wander "for the safety of [his] own life."[5] Remarkably, however, and fortunately for us, he found the opportunity to "write a few more things, that perhaps they may be of worth unto my brethren, the Lamanites, in some future day, according to the will of the Lord."[6] That this man would voluntarily write words of counsel to the posterity of the people who had killed his beloved father and were now hunting him down is witness to the powerful influence of his deceased father, who had exercised the same charity.[7] His father's influence is likewise seen in *what* he chose to write: two-thirds of this final portion of Moroni's writings, titled the Book of Moroni, is direct quotation from his father Mormon! One lengthy chapter contains "a few of the words of my father Mormon, which he spake concerning faith, hope, and charity" that Mormon had spoken "unto the people, as he taught them in the synagogue which they had built for the place of worship."[8] Mormon's discourse is the most complete in the Book of Mormon on these vital topics of faith, hope, and charity, their relationship to good and evil, and the way they allow one to "lay

---

1. Ether 12:22.
2. Ether 12:37.
3. See chapter 8.
4. Moroni 1:1–2.
5. Moroni 1:3.
6. Moroni 1:4.
7. See Mormon 7.
8. Moroni 7:1.

hold upon every good thing."[1] Moroni had probably heard this discourse long before he set about to write the Jaredite account; so it is remarkable to find that as Moroni was making that account, Christ himself tutored Moroni on these same topics, explaining, "Faith, hope and charity bringeth unto me—the fountain of all righteousness."[2] The situation recalls Nephi's divine tutorial on the topics that he had first learned about from his father, Lehi.[3]

Mormon's sermon also speaks of the "covenants of the Father, which he hath made unto the children of men"[4]—probably a reference to the patriarchs of old. Even more emphatic, however, is Mormon's focus on becoming "child[ren] of Christ"[5] and "sons of God"[6] through faith, hope, and charity. We have read before in the Book of Mormon, in the Jaredite account (with which Mormon was familiar[7]), how Christ said that through faith "mankind . . . shall become my sons and my daughters."[8] Mormon elaborates on the process, explaining that faith is but the first step, followed by hope and charity, the full acquisition of which comes about only by appeal to the Eternal Father:

> Wherefore, my beloved brethren, pray unto the Father with all the energy of heart, that ye may be filled with this love, which he hath bestowed upon all who are true followers of his Son, Jesus Christ; that ye may become the sons of God.[9]

Perhaps implicit in Moroni's inclusion of this material by his father is the concept that by following his father, he would also become a child of Christ. Mormon's own progress on that path is indicated by his designation of his listeners as "beloved," a designation occurring no less than five times in this discourse.[10]

---

1. Moroni 7:20.
2. Ether 12:28.
3. See 1 Nephi 8–14.
4. Moroni 7:31–32.
5. Moroni 7:19.
6. Moroni 7:26.
7. Mosiah 28:19.
8. Ether 3:14.
9. Moroni 7:48.
10. See Moroni 7:2, 35, 40, 46, 48.

The same designation of "beloved" begins the next body of material quoted from Mormon, which this time is a letter that Mormon had written to his son. It was one of Moroni's treasures, keeping him in mind of the beloved father whom he so profoundly admired and whom he now so terribly missed. This letter, written shortly after Moroni's "calling to the ministry,"[1] provides a window on their relationship and on the heart of Mormon as a father. The opening passage not only reveals Mormon's love for his son, but also points to the even greater love of the Eternal Father, as manifested through his Holy Child:

> My beloved son, Moroni, I rejoice exceedingly that your Lord Jesus Christ hath been mindful of you, and hath called you to his ministry, and to his holy work.
>
> I am mindful of you always in my prayers, continually praying unto God the Father in the name of his Holy Child, Jesus, that he, through his infinite goodness and grace, will keep you through the endurance of faith on his name to the end.[2]

The powerful parental bond between Mormon and Moroni is again emphasized as Mormon once more addresses Moroni as "my beloved son."[3]

The predominant theme of the letter is infant baptism, apparently a subject of dispute among the church members to whom Moroni was ministering. Mormon calls the practice a "gross error,"[4] "solemn mockery,"[5] and "awful . . . wickedness"[6] because it sets "at naught [Christ's] atonement"[7] through which "the curse of Adam is taken from [little children]," making them "whole" and "not capable of committing sin."[8] Therefore, Mormon counsels his son,

---

1. Moroni 8:1.
2. Moroni 8:2–3.
3. Moroni 8:9; and six more times as "my son." (Moroni 8:6, 24, 27, 28, 29, 30.)
4. Moroni 8:6.
5. Moroni 8:9.
6. Moroni 8:15.
7. Moroni 8:20.
8. Moroni 8:8.

> I say unto you that this thing shall ye teach—repentance and baptism unto those who are accountable and capable of committing sin; yea, teach parents that they must repent and be baptized, and humble themselves as their little children, and they shall be saved with their little children.[1]

These words of Mormon may take on even added poignancy when viewed in the context of their presentation. Reading his father's words regarding little children, Moroni may have reflected on the fact that he had once—as a little child—served as a model for his own great father. But Moroni's inclusion of this material now into the record may have also evoked acute feelings of pain, for he now had no mortal children of his own (did he have any before?) to whom he could look for this same example of innocence and purity. Perhaps his uniquely great father was example enough.

Mormon finishes his letter by sadly mentioning the demise of Nephite civilization because of pride, and then requests, "Pray for them, my son, that repentance may come unto them."[2] Separated by the cruel exigencies of war, this father and son remain united in spirit and purpose.

Finally, Moroni includes a second letter he had received from his father, this time sadly chronicling the terrible conditions of war as Mormon, the military leader, vainly attempts to persuade his people to repent.[3] "They have lost their love, one towards another,"[4] Mormon sadly writes, even as he three times addresses Moroni as "my beloved son."[5] Nowhere else in the Book of Mormon does a mortal father directly address his son as "beloved." That this designation occurs (throughout Mormon's two letters) a total of five times directed to Moroni seems noteworthy, putting us in mind of the one other Son repeatedly described in the Book of Mormon as "beloved"[6] and once by Mormon himself as "most Beloved"[7]—Christ.

---

1. Moroni 8:10.
2. Moroni 8:28.
3. See Moroni 9:3–4.
4. Moroni 9:5.
5. Moroni 9:1, 6, 11.
6. 2 Nephi 31:11, 15; Helaman 5:47; 3 Nephi 11:7; 21:20.
7. Mormon 5:14.

After describing the awful condition of his unrepentant people, Mormon tells Moroni,

> Behold, my son, I cannot recommend them unto God lest he should smite me.
>
> But behold, my son, I recommend thee unto God, and I trust in Christ that thou wilt be saved; and I pray unto God that he will spare thy life.[1]

We know about that prayer only because it was answered, thereby allowing Moroni to include this letter in the record.

The letter concludes with fatherly counsel incorporating references not only to "our fathers," but also to the Father and the Son.

> My son, be faithful in Christ, and may not the things which I have written grieve thee, to weigh thee down unto death; but may Christ lift thee up, and may his sufferings and death, and the showing his body unto our fathers, and his mercy and long-suffering, and the hope of his glory and of eternal life, rest in your mind forever.
>
> And may the grace of God the Father, whose throne is high in the heavens, and our Lord Jesus Christ, who sitteth on the right hand of his power, until all things shall become subject unto him, be, and abide with you forever. Amen.[2]

Mormon's counsel provides a pattern relevant today, according to Elder J. Richard Clarke. "I believe that would be the loving counsel of every father or mother to a son: Be faithful in Christ."[3] Also significant is *how* Mormon counseled Moroni to be faithful to the Son of God: by remembering the righteous fathers. (The connection is more than coincidental, as seen so many other times in the Book of Mormon.) Moroni *did* remember his righteous fathers and *was* faithful in Christ, as Mormon had urged.

But Mormon's influence in Moroni's addition to the sacred record does not end here, for in Moroni's final farewell chapter he returns

---

1. Moroni 9:21–22.
2. Moroni 9:25–26.
3. *Ensign* 21:5 (May 1991), 43.

to themes already dealt with by his father, like good and evil;[1] laying hold upon every good thing through faith, hope, and charity;[2] the resurrection; and final judgment.[3] Tragically, however, circumstances did not permit Moroni to fully follow the righteous example of his fathers on that occasion, the pattern whereby righteous fathers like Lehi, Jacob, Abraham, and Adam gathered together their posterity and left them final counsel and blessings before dying. Knowing that he will soon depart this life,[4] Moroni addressed the only audience he had—his future readers.

So against the dark backdrop of the unspeakable wickedness and savagery that constitutes the final scene of the Book of Mormon, we see a powerful and loving portrait of a righteous mortal father and his son—who tragically is not survived by posterity of his own, making his work of completing and sealing the Book of Mormon all the more magnanimous. For his record was directed not to his own posterity—as were most of the scriptural records of the past—but rather to his kinsmen of the house of Israel, that they, as Moroni wrote on the title page, may know "what great things the Lord hath done for their fathers," including "the covenants" to be fulfilled in the latter days. Moroni also directed his record to all humanity, to convince them "that JESUS is the CHRIST," in order that, as Mormon had written, they may become children of Christ. Childless himself, Moroni invites all to become children of Christ.

We saw in the Book of Mormon's opening line that the book owes its existence to the power of a father's influence, a fact no less conspicuous as the book draws to its close and we see Moroni completing the work his father had begun. Together, their writings constitute nearly three-quarters of the book.[5] And even though Moroni's contribution was relatively small in terms of volume—about 10 percent of the Book of Mormon[6]—it was also powerful and essential, including

---

1. See Moroni 10:6, 30; cf. Moroni 7:5–18.
2. See Moroni 10:7–25, 30; cf. Moroni 7:19–48.
3. Moroni 10:27, 34; cf. Mormon 7:7, 10.
4. See Moroni 10:34.
5. $(531 - 142) \text{ v } 531 = 73\%$
6. $(531 - 480) \text{ v } 531 = 9.6\%$

the Jaredite account that Mormon had insisted was "expedient" to be made known to "all people."[1] Indeed, Moroni was, in Hugh Nibley's words, "the editor-in-chief of the Book of Mormon."[2] And Moroni's contribution may not have ended with his writing; according to some scholars, Moroni apparently carried the record all the way from his native land, in the area of the Yucatan peninsula,[3] far north to where he finally deposited the record in the present-day state of New York, in the hill located near the future Joseph Smith farm.[4]

All in all, Moroni's contribution was significant and substantial enough that when the Lord sent a messenger to introduce young Joseph Smith to the record, that messenger was Moroni.[5] In retrospect, as the mortal Moroni finished the sacred record, his significant contribution to and care for the record probably could have warranted calling the record by his own name. But as the final tribute to his father and final memorial to the love of a son for his father, the record was called the Book of Mormon.

---

1. Mosiah 28:19.
2. CWHN 2:131.
3. See summary of various geographers in Allen 1989:181–213.
4. See JS–H 1:51.
5. See JS–H 1:27–54, 59.

Chapter 10

GOD AND HIS BELOVED SON

• •

THE ETERNAL FATHER AND JESUS

NEPHI'S TESTIMONY OF THE FATHER AND THE SON

The primary purpose of the Book of Mormon, according to its first author, Nephi, is to convince its readers of the reality of one particular father-son relationship that urgently concerns all mankind—or, as Nephi says, quoting the words of an angel, to

> make known to all kindreds, tongues, and people, that the Lamb of God is the Son of the Eternal Father, and the Savior of the world; and that all men must come unto him, or they cannot be saved.[1]

Significantly, Nephi had first learned of that Eternal Father-Son relationship from his own father, Lehi, who had spoken about the Son of God not only from the scriptural record but also from direct revelation that Lehi had received on the subject.[2] Wanting to know the truth of these matters for himself, Nephi had exercised the faith necessary to see what his father had seen—a vision of the future that

---

1. 1 Nephi 13:40.
2. See 1 Nephi 10.

included "the Lamb of God, yea, even the Son of the Eternal Father!"[1]
The persistently recurrent designation of Christ as the "Lamb" in the
account of Nephi's vision—some fifty-six times in but four chapters,
but relatively infrequently elsewhere in the Book of Mormon[2]—is
similar to the same persistent usage in the book of Revelation (written
by John). This is undoubtedly more than coincidental; the vision reported in Revelation was also a part of Nephi's vision (the part he
was commanded not to record[3]). The other New Testament book
written by John and designating Christ as the "Lamb" is the Gospel
of John[4]—the only gospel to do so. The Gospel of John also shows
striking affinities with the Nephite record of the resurrected Christ's
ministry to the Nephites.

Commentators on the New Testament usage of *Lamb* to designate
Christ have noted the natural "docility of [sheep] in following the
voice of the ram, their chief leader, and father,"[5] and the image of
the lamb connoting not only youth,[6] but also meekness and gentleness.[7] Hence, whatever else the image of Christ as the Lamb may
connote,[8] it is a fitting symbol of a son's submissiveness to his father—
as intimated also in Nephi's vision by the fact that when the designation "Lamb" is first introduced, it is used in apposition with "Son":
"Behold the Lamb of God, yea, even the Son of the Eternal Father!"[9]

We may be unprepared, then, to find that in Nephi's vision the
"Lamb" is also designated as the "Shepherd," even the "Shepherd
over all the earth,"[10] he who, as Nephi later writes, "gathereth his
children from the four quarters of the earth" and "numbereth his
sheep," for "there shall be one fold and one shepherd; and he shall

1. 1 Nephi 11:21.
2. Some five times elsewhere in Nephi's writings, and some nine times elsewhere.
3. See 1 Nephi 14:18–28.
4. See John 1:29, 36.
5. Charbonneau-Lassay 1991:70.
6. See Ibid. 72–73.
7. See Hastings 1908:II:620; Henry n.d.:V:681.
8. See Brown 1966 (AB 29):58–63.
9. 1 Nephi 11:21.
10. 1 Nephi 13:41.

feed his sheep, and in him they shall find pasture."[1] How can the "Lamb" also be the "Shepherd"? Precisely because of his lamb-like quality of submissiveness to his Father, which serves as an example of the submissiveness required of all who would join the Shepherd's flock. The Son's submissiveness to his Father is also the perfect pattern of submissiveness by children to righteous parental guidance.

Christ's example is described in Nephi's later writings as he completes his sacred record and again speaks of the "Lamb" while explaining "the doctrine of Christ":[2]

> And now, if the Lamb of God, he being holy, should have need to be baptized by water, to fulfil all righteousness, O then, how much more need have we, being unholy, to be baptized, yea, even by water![3]

Nephi speaks of Christ's future baptism—which Nephi had seen in vision[4]—as if it had already happened, and he explains what significance this act has for the sons and daughters of men:

> And now, I would ask of you, my beloved brethren, wherein the Lamb of God did fulfil all righteousness in being baptized by water?
>
> Know ye not that he was holy? But notwithstanding he being holy, he showeth unto the children of men that, according to the flesh he humbleth himself before the Father, and witnesseth unto the Father that he would be obedient unto him in keeping his commandments.
>
> Wherefore, after he was baptized with water the Holy Ghost descended upon him in the form of a dove.
>
> And again, it showeth unto the children of men the straitness of the path, and the narrowness of the gate, by which they should enter, he having set the example before them.[5]

Clearly one cannot consider the relationship of the Father and the

---

1. 1 Nephi 22:25.
2. 2 Nephi 31:2.
3. 2 Nephi 31:5.
4. See 1 Nephi 11:27.
5. 2 Nephi 31:6–9.

Son in isolation, for the Son's obedience to the Father is intended as an example for all mankind.

Continuing his exposition, Nephi reveals that he has been the recipient of remarkable revelation from not only the Son but also the Father himself, the account of which provides a unique window into the Father-Son relationship and its significance for mankind:

> He [the Lamb of God] said unto the children of men: Follow thou me. Wherefore, my beloved brethren, can we follow Jesus save we shall be willing to keep the commandments of the Father?
>
> And the Father said: Repent ye, repent ye, and be baptized in the name of my Beloved Son.
>
> And also, the voice of the Son came unto me, saying: He that is baptized in my name, to him will the Father give the Holy Ghost, like unto me; wherefore, follow me, and do the things which ye have seen me do.
>
> Wherefore, my beloved brethren, I know that if ye shall follow the Son, with full purpose of heart, acting no hypocrisy and no deception before God, but with real intent, repenting of your sins, witnessing unto the Father that ye are willing to take upon you the name of Christ, by baptism—yea, by following your Lord and your Savior down into the water, according to his word, behold, then shall ye receive the Holy Ghost.[1]

One sees in operation here the law of witnesses as three different heavenly beings—the Father, the Son, and the Holy Ghost—independently testify to the same truths, showing their perfect unity. Moreover, in speaking of his Son, the Father designates him as "my Beloved Son," a designation soon to be repeated as Nephi reports hearing again the voice of both the Son and the Father:

> But, behold, my beloved brethren, thus came the voice of the Son unto me, saying: After ye have repented of your sins, and witnessed unto the Father that ye are willing to keep my commandments, by the baptism of water, and have received the baptism of fire and of the Holy Ghost . . . , and after this

1. 2 Nephi 31:10–13.

should deny me, it would have been better for you that ye had not known me.

And I heard a voice from the Father, saying: Yea, the words of my Beloved are true and faithful. He that endureth to the end, the same shall be saved.

And now, my beloved brethren, I know by this that unless a man shall endure to the end, in following the example of the Son of the living God, he cannot be saved.[1]

Once again the Son, as he and Nephi both explain, is the example for mankind, and those who follow him witness their obedience to the Father. And once again the Father himself witnesses to Nephi of the truth spoken by his Son—"my Beloved." The Father and the Son are independent beings (Nephi will later explain[2] and demonstrate[3] that prayer should be directed to the Father in the name of Christ), and yet they are perfectly united in purpose (Nephi has previously disclosed that "the Only Begotten of the Father" even bears the title "Father" as "the Father of heaven and of earth"[4]). In fact, their unity is attested by yet another heavenly being, the Holy Ghost, who, according to Nephi, "witnesses of the Father and the Son."[5] Such is the perfect unity between all three of those independent divine personages that Nephi can describe them as "one God."[6]

That Nephi should be favored to hear the voice of the Father is remarkable because of its rarity, for judging from extant scriptural records only a few mortals on very few occasions have ever been so privileged.[7] Why was Nephi so favored? To propose the answer that

---

1. 2 Nephi 31:14–16.
2. See 2 Nephi 32:9.
3. See 2 Nephi 33:12.
4. 2 Nephi 25:12.
5. 2 Nephi 31:18.
6. 2 Nephi 31:21.
7. Possibly those present at Jesus' baptism (see Matthew 3:13–17); Peter, James, and John on the mount of transfiguration (see Matthew 17:1–6); those present with Jesus when he asked the Father to glorify his name (see John 12:28); those present at his first appearance as resurrected Lord to the Nephites (see 3 Nephi 11:7); and Joseph Smith on the occasion of his first uttered prayer (see JS–H 1:17). Other instances in which the Father appears to be speaking—such as in Moses 1—are certainly to be explained by what the First Presidency termed "divine investiture of authority"—that is, the Son speaking as if he were his Father while delivering the Father's message. (See Clark, *Messages of the First Presidency* V:31–34.)

he needed to transmit this information to mankind ("for this cause have [these things] been shown unto me, that ye might know . . . "[1]) still leaves the question of why Nephi in particular was chosen to transmit these sacred truths about the submissiveness of the Son and his perfect unity with the Father. Was it because of Nephi's own similar submissiveness to his father and Nephi's nearly perfect unity with him even in the face of life-threatening opposition on the part of some of Lehi's other children? In retrospect one can discern in Nephi's relationship with his own father a type, or figure, of the Son of God, who likewise would submit to his Father in perfect unity despite fierce and life-threatening opposition by some of the Father's other children.

LOST AND RESTORED PROPHECIES ABOUT CHRIST

Nephi and his father Lehi are not the only father-son pair in the Book of Mormon to typify the Father and Christ. We have already seen the striking similarities between the mission of Mosiah's sons who left their throne to minister, and the mission of God's Son who left his heavenly throne to minister.[2] And we have observed the loving and powerful bond between Mormon and his beloved son Moroni, a bond that much resembles that between the Father and the Son.[3] That the Book of Mormon itself should provide types of Christ is hardly surprising since it expressly asserts that "all things which have been given of God from the beginning of the world, unto man, are the typifying of [Christ]"[4] — including the ordinances pertaining to the High Priesthood of Melchizedek, which "ordinances were given . . . that thereby the people might look forward on the Son of God."[5] And when Melchizedek's friend Abraham was "obedient unto the commands of God in offering up his son Isaac," the incident was also "a similitude of God and his Only Begotten Son."[6] Again in the

---

1. 2 Nephi 31:17.
2. See chapter 1.
3. See chapter 9.
4. 2 Nephi 11:4.
5. Alma 13:16.
6. Jacob 4:5.

time of Moses the Lord showed his people "many signs, and wonders, and types, and shadows . . . concerning his coming."[1] Indeed, the rites of the law of Moses "were types of things to come,"[2] as was the brazen serpent that Moses lifted up in the wilderness, for "as many as should look upon that serpent should live, even so as many as should look upon the Son of God with faith, having a contrite spirit, might live."[3]

But accompanying all these foreshadowings of Christ, says the Book of Mormon, were plain revelations and prophecies concerning his future coming. Indeed, "all the holy prophets which were before us . . . believed in Christ and worshiped the Father in his name";[4] and of "all the prophets who have prophesied ever since the world began,"[5] "none . . . have written, nor prophesied, save they have spoken concerning this Christ."[6] For example, "Abraham saw of his coming, and was filled with gladness and did rejoice."[7] And "even since the days of Abraham there have been many prophets that have testified these things,"[8] not the least of whom was Moses, who did "prophesy . . . concerning the coming of the Messiah, and that God should redeem his people."[9] Also Isaiah and Jeremiah foretold that "the Son of God [would] come,"[10] as did other ancient Israelite prophets like Zenos and Zenock[11] whose writings the Nephites had but we do not.

What happened to those lost writings, and indeed to all the plain prophecies concerning the coming of the Son of God? How is it that they are generally not found in the Old Testament, and those that are there seem obscure enough as to yield such differing interpreta-

---

1. Mosiah 3:15.
2. Mosiah 13:31.
3. Helaman 8:15.
4. Jacob 4:4.
5. Mosiah 13:33.
6. Jacob 7:11.
7. Helaman 8:17.
8. Helaman 8:19.
9. Mosiah 13:33.
10. Helaman 8:20.
11. See 1 Nephi 19:10; Alma 33:15; 34:7; Helaman 8:19; 15:11; 3 Nephi 10:16.

tions by Jews, Christians, and biblical scholars? The Book of Mormon provides a clue when Nephi foresaw what was in store for the "record of the Jews," which would contain much of the brass plates' record as well as the record of Christ's twelve Jewish apostles—in other words, both the Old and New Testaments. After passing through "the hand of the twelve apostles," the record would go "through the hands of [a] great and abominable church," which would take "away from the gospel of the Lamb many parts which are plain and most precious."[1] This scripture is often quoted as evidence for the deletion of passages not only from the New Testament but also from the Old, particularly passages that Joseph Smith restored that plainly foretell the birth of Christ, some of which are as old as Adam.[2] But the particular editing of which Nephi spoke must have been mostly of the New Testament, for our traditional version of the Old Testament, which is based on the Jewish Masoretic text, matches closely with independent textual witnesses (as the Septuagint[3] and the Samaritan Pentateuch), establishing that our traditional Old Testament text was very much in place well before the Christian era—the time when Nephi saw the removal of many plain and precious parts of the New Testament. But that the Old Testament had already undergone similar malicious editing is apparent from the very text of the Old Testament that Joseph Smith restored: Moses was expressly told that many of the words he would write would be deleted by editors who would "esteem [God's] words as naught."[4] (If this earlier editing is not mentioned by Nephi, it is simply because his vision does not focus on the land of Palestine until the Christian era). Whenever it was that the Old Testament was so drastically edited, the thing that is obvious from the Book of Mormon is *what* primarily was deleted: plain and precious prophecies of Christ. Hence the supreme value of the Book

---

1. 1 Nephi 13:23–29.

2. See, for example, Moses 1:6, 13, 32–33; 2:26–27; 4:1–3; 5:5–9; 6:50–68; 7:23–67; 8:23–24.

3. Even here there has been some allegation of Christian editing; nevertheless, "the evidence for strict continuity in most O[ld] T[estament] books between a single pre-Christian rendering and the LXX [Septuagint] text extant in our codices is overwhelming." (NJoBC 1092.)

4. Moses 1:41.

of Mormon in demonstrating that an express knowledge of Christ and his mission was had and taught by all the ancient prophets from the beginning of time — including the Book of Mormon prophets themselves.

The Book of Mormon is equally clear in explaining why such prophecies of Christ would be deleted, for "whatsoever thing persuadeth men to . . . believe not in Christ, and deny him . . . , then ye may know with a perfect knowledge it is of the devil."[1] It would appear, then, that Satan himself, Christ's arch-rival from the council in heaven, prompted editors of the Old Testament text to excise the plain and precious passages foretelling the birth and ministry of the Son of God.

But Joseph Smith's insistence that the Old Testament is a highly edited document was in his day nothing short of heresy to many who fervently believed (as some still do) in "the Divine origin and authenticity of every single letter" of the Old Testament,[2] "every word of which" has traditionally been "considered to be divinely inspired and therefore infallible."[3] In contrast to that traditional view, advances in biblical scholarship since Joseph Smith's day have shown beyond question that, "having been handed down by human agents for . . . millennia, the text of the [Old Testament] suffered from the shortcomings of man."[4] Such shortcomings resulted not only from various kinds of scribal errors but also from deliberate alterations,[5] as emphasized recently by the highly acclaimed work of one scholar who has demonstrated that "ancient Israelite scribes were . . . involved in theological corrections or modifications of their received texts" motivated by "a perceived theological dissonance between the wording of the received" text and the scribe's own "religious values and sensibilities."[6]

---

1. Moroni 7:17.
2. Radday and Shore 1985:1.
3. Shemaryahu Talmon, "The Old Testament Text," in Ackroyd and Evans 1970:I:160.
4. Ibid.
5. See Würthwein 1979:105–10.
6. Fishbane 1985:81.

While the Old Testament text can yield itself to such analysis of astute scholars to show layers of editing, what these scholars can obviously not discover by such analysis is what was edited out! It took more than human wisdom to restore such deletions, as Joseph Smith did (at least partially) in giving the world the Book of Mormon and other revealed texts with their plain and precious prophecies of the coming of the Son of God. As it turns out, Joseph Smith's restoration of ancient prophecies of Christ accords with what some of the earliest Christians had said, that the Old Testament text had become corrupted and deprived of many of its original Messianic passages.[1] Even more remarkable is the fact that since Joseph Smith's day there has been a spectacular emergence of ancient but long-forgotten texts, a number of which—such as the Combat of Adam,[2] the Cave of Treasures,[3] the Testaments of the Twelve Patriarchs,[4] and the Testament of Adam[5]—not only purport to contain authentic "pre-Christian" prophecies of Christ but in doing so bear remarkable resemblances to the "pre-Christian" prophecies of Christ contained in the Joseph Smith material.

OTHER BOOK OF MORMON PROPHETS TESTIFY OF THE FATHER AND THE SON

Concerning the Book of Mormon's focus on Christ, President Ezra Taft Benson has observed that "over one-half of all the verses in the Book of Mormon refer to our Lord," while "some form of Christ's name is mentioned more frequently per verse in the Book of Mormon than even in the New Testament."[6] And interspersed throughout these Book of Mormon passages on Christ are explanations of his relationship to the Father. Perhaps most telling is that the Father gave the Son power to become a "father" himself, beginning with the

1. See Clementine Homilies 3:39, 43, in *The Ante-Nicene Fathers* VIII:245–46; Dialogue with Trypho 71–73, in *The Ante-Nicene Fathers* 1:234–35.
2. See Malan 1882.
3. See Budge 1927.
4. See OTP 1:775–828.
5. See OTP 1:989–95.
6. W&W 53. One set of statistics indicates that of the Book of Mormon's 6,580 verses, 3,471 refer to Christ. (Cheesman 1988:33.)

creation of the heavens and the earth, performed by the premortal Christ under direction of the Father.[1] By virtue of his role as the Creator of heaven and earth, Christ earned the title of "the Father of heaven and earth."[2] This usage of "father" as "creator" authentically echoes similar usage in ancient Israel and Mesopotamia.[3] But Christ would also be the "Father" in another sense inasmuch as he would be "conceived by the power of God,"[4] becoming uniquely "the Only Begotten of the Father"[5] and thereby inheriting "power . . . from the Father to redeem [his people] from their sins because of repentance."[6] And all those who are redeemed, whether before or after Christ's actual coming in the flesh, would be "called the children of Christ, his sons, and his daughters," having been "spiritually begotten" and "born of him."[7] Accordingly, through the power given him from his own Father, Christ became the Father of all those who believe on him—as the premortal Christ explained to an ancient prophet:

> I am Jesus Christ. I am the Father and the Son. In me shall all mankind have life, and that eternally, even they who shall believe on my name; and they shall become my sons and my daughters.[8]

And this could only come about through his own mortal birth, on the very eve of which he announced that he was coming into the world "to do the will, both of the Father and of the Son—of the Father because of me, and of the Son because of my flesh."[9] But that flesh would be "subjected . . . to the will of the Father" throughout the Son's ministry, and ultimately so when the Son would "be led, cru-

---

1. See Moses 1:32–33.
2. See Mosiah 3:8; Alma 11:39; Helaman 14:12 (and see Mormon 6:22 and Ether 4:7, by prophets after Christ's coming).
3. See TDOT I:3, 8, 18.
4. Mosiah 15:3.
5. 2 Nephi 25:12; Jacob 4:5, 11; Alma 5:48; 9:26; 12:33–34; 13:5, 9.
6. Helaman 5:11.
7. Mosiah 5:7.
8. Ether 3:14.
9. 3 Nephi 1:14.

cified, and slain, the flesh becoming subject even unto death, the will of the Son being swallowed up in the will of the Father."[1]

So spoke and wrote the Book of Mormon prophets even before the mortal birth of Christ. And the theme was afterward carried on by prophets who testified that "Jesus Christ . . . is the Son of God, and . . . was slain . . . , and by the power of the Father he hath risen again"[2] and "hath ascended into heaven, and hath sat down on the right hand of God, to claim of the Father his rights of mercy which he hath upon the children of men."[3] Hence Jesus became "the Christ, the Son of the living God" precisely so "that the Father may bring about, through his most Beloved, his great and eternal purpose."[4] Thus Christ "has shown himself unto the world, and glorified the name of the Father, and prepared a way that thereby others might be partakers of the heavenly gift"[5] if they will but "repent and come unto the Father in the name of Jesus."[6]

THE VOICE IN THE DARKNESS

But by far the most significant Book of Mormon testimony to the reality of Jesus Christ and his relationship with his Father comes from Christ's visitation to the Nephites, beginning with his words to survivors of the great destruction that occurred as he had died on the cross. While terrible howlings rent the thick darkness enveloping the violently deformed land, a voice was heard speaking "of the slain of the fair sons and daughters of my people" who are fallen "because of their iniquity and abominations."[7] This identification of those who had been slain as "sons and daughters" may well have been deliberately intended as a prelude to his own later self-identification: he was also a son who had been slain for iniquity — though not his own — and he identified himself in terms of that sonship:

1. Mosiah 15:2, 7.
2. Mormon 7:5.
3. Moroni 7:27.
4. Mormon 5:14 (the actual context of this passage is narrower in scope, speaking of the Father's purpose in restoring the house of Israel pursuant to the ancient covenant).
5. Ether 12:8.
6. Ether 5:5.
7. 3 Nephi 9:2.

> Behold, I am Jesus Christ the Son of God. I created the heavens and the earth, and all things that in them are. I was with the Father from the beginning. I am in the Father, and the Father in me; and in me hath the Father glorified his name.
>
> I came unto my own, and my own received me not. And the scriptures concerning my coming are fulfilled.
>
> And as many as have received me, to them have I given to become the sons of God; and even so will I to as many as shall believe on my name.[1]

Earlier we saw how a portion of the writing of Nephi (son of Lehi) paralleled the New Testament book of Revelation by the Apostle John in its repeated designation of Christ as the "Lamb of God." Now we see that the account of Christ's visitation to the Nephites (written by a descendant of Nephi who bears his name) contains striking parallels to another New Testament writing by the same apostle—the Gospel of John.[2] That gospel begins by identifying Christ in much the same terms as he identified himself to the Nephites; according to John,

> In the beginning was the Word, and the Word was with God, and the Word was God.
>
> The same was in the beginning with God.
>
> All things were made by him; and without him was not any thing made that was made. . . .
>
> He came unto his own, and his own received him not.
>
> But as many as received him, to them gave he power to become the sons of God, even to them that believe on his name.[3]

Further, the Gospel of John repeatedly emphasizes—as Christ now tells the Nephites—that Jesus had come to glorify the Father's name.[4] The same theme of glory appears in the book of Moses' account of what Jesus said to the Father in the premortal council in heaven: "The glory be thine forever."[5]

---

1. 3 Nephi 9:15–17.
2. On authorship, see Brown 1966 (AB 29):LXXXVII-CIV.
3. John 1:1–3, 11–12.
4. See John 12:28; 13:31–32; 17:1–5; cf. 15:8.
5. Moses 4:2.

There is a further echo from John's Gospel in Christ's next statement to the Nephites, "Behold, I have come unto the world to bring redemption unto the world, to save the world from sin."[1] John similarly reports that Jesus had come "to save the world,"[2] for he "taketh away the sin of the world."[3] Such similarities between John's Gospel and the account of Christ's Nephite ministry are the first of many.

The theme of what Christ tells the Nephites centers around fathers and sons: Jesus had become the Son to bring others also to be the sons of God. Appropriately, however, one can become a son of God only by first becoming as a little child, as Christ further explains, "Therefore, whoso repenteth and cometh unto me as a little child, him will I receive, for of such is the kingdom of God."[4]

The theme of fathers and sons continues as Christ's voice addresses the Nephites in terms of their lineage: "O ye people . . . who are descendants of Jacob, yea, who are of the house of Israel. . . . O ye people of the house of Israel . . . O ye people of the house of Israel. . . . O ye house of Israel. . . . O house of Israel."[5] The reason for the repetition is made clear—it is because these people were heirs to "the covenant to your fathers."[6] The continuation of this bond with the ancient fathers is emphasized because the voice has already severed one tie with the fathers by announcing the fulfillment and end of the law of Moses and blood sacrifices.[7] The law of Moses was at an end, but the Abrahamic covenant was not; and what the continuation of that covenant meant to these descendants of Israel is that they were still heirs to both its obligations and blessings. Accordingly, if they would not repent, "the places of your dwellings shall become desolate" to await a later fulfillment of the covenant.[8]

---

1. 3 Nephi 9:21.
2. John 12:47.
3. John 1:29.
4. 3 Nephi 9:22.
5. 3 Nephi 10:4–7.
6. 3 Nephi 10:7.
7. See 3 Nephi 9:17–19.
8. 3 Nephi 10:7.

THE APPEARANCE OF THE SON REPRESENTING THE FATHER

Some time later a group of about twenty-five hundred people was gathered at the temple, apparently in a ritual setting, as they and their Israelite forefathers had done for years in observance of one of the Mosaic festivals — except that due to the previous command they would not have been actually celebrating the festival but would rather have been wondering what to do next.[1] This adherence to the path of their righteous fathers was combined with an exercise of faith that soon the Son of God would appear[2] — a combination that was dramatically and directly rewarded by both the Father and the Son. A voice was heard from heaven, the most momentous voice in Nephite history, the voice of a father introducing and expressing love for his son: "Behold my Beloved Son, in whom I am well pleased, in whom I have glorified my name — hear ye him."[3] On the only other occasion in Nephite history when the Father's voice had been heard, it had likewise announced his "Beloved" Son[4] — the same pattern evident on other occasions when the Father's voice has been heard by mortals.

It is no wonder, then, that the Book of Mormon prophet Jacob selected from all the Old Testament types of Christ that of Abraham's offering of his son Isaac, an event similarly initiated by a heavenly voice speaking of the love of a father (Abraham) for his son (Isaac).[5] The Old Testament passage telling that God commanded Abraham to offer his beloved Isaac is the first appearance of any form of the word *love* in the Old Testament — while in the New Testament the word appears first in Matthew's account of Jesus' baptism when the Eternal Father proclaims his love for his Son. Abraham's deep love for Isaac is also emphasized in extra-biblical sources, as when Josephus (as paraphrased by one scholar) "stresses . . . Abraham's love for his son [Isaac] and the son's worthiness to be loved,"[6] or when Philo observes that Abraham "cherished for [Isaac] a great tenderness" and

---

1. See Welch 1990:29–30.
2. See Ether 12:7; 3 Nephi 11:2.
3. 3 Nephi 11:7.
4. See 2 Nephi 31:11, 15.
5. See Genesis 22:2.
6. Swetnam 1981:56 (referring to Jewish Antiquities I.xiii.1).

was "devoted to his son with a fondness which no words can express."[1] All of this mirrors all the more strikingly the Father's love for Jesus, and such a comparison between human paternal love and divine paternal love is deeply rooted in ancient Israelite theology, in which "the compassionate love of a human father for his son remains the classic symbol for the compassionate paternal love of God."[2]

The one paramount characteristic of God the Father's relationship with his Son Jesus Christ is love—a fact of no small importance in light of President Benson's insistence that our Heavenly Father is our pattern for parenthood.[3] The prophet Mormon's teaching that "all things must fail" except charity[4] applies at least as much to parenthood as to anything else; without love nothing else could work in parenting.

After hearing the Father announce his Son, the assembled Nephite multitude saw a white-robed man descend out of heaven until he stood among them. He extended his hand and identified himself:

> Behold, I am Jesus Christ, whom the prophets testified shall come into the world.
> And behold, I am the light and the life of the world.[5]

This identification immediately recalls the one made in the opening lines of the Gospel of John, which says of Christ that "in him was life; and the life was the light of men," so that Christ is "the true Light" that gives light to everyone.[6]

Another echo of John's introduction to his Gospel soon appears as Christ continues his words to the Nephites:

> I have drunk out of that bitter cup which the Father hath given me, and have glorified the Father in taking upon me the sins of the world, in the which I have suffered the will of the Father in all things from the beginning.[7]

---

1. In Abraham XXXII (in *Philo* VI:85–87).
2. TDOT II:155.
3. See TETB 503.
4. Moroni 7:46–47.
5. 3 Nephi 11:10–11.
6. John 1:4, 9.
7. 3 Nephi 11:11.

"The beginning" is also where John's Gospel starts, declaring that Christ was with God "in the beginning," meaning (as John later records) "before the world was."[1] What Christ emphasizes to the Nephites is that even "in the beginning" he was submitting to his Father's will—as the book of Moses so graphically discloses in reporting Jesus' response to the Father's plan presented in the premortal heavenly council: "Father, thy will be done, and the glory be thine forever."[2] These memorable words—"Thy will be done"—would form the theme of Jesus' mortal ministry all the way through to his last agonizing hours when he prayed, "O my Father, if it be possible, let this cup pass from me: nevertheless not as I will, but as thou wilt."[3] He then declared, "the cup which my Father hath given me, shall I not drink it?"[4]

This "cup," explains one New Testament commentator, "is not only the cup of divine wrath and judgment, but it was also an expression common in the ancient world as a symbol for destiny or fate [or] as a symbol of suffering."[5] The extensive Old Testament usage of "cup" in this metaphorical sense includes the image of cup in or from the hand of God,[6] similar to Jesus' own statements about receiving the cup from the Father. Jesus' willingness to drink the cup constituted his culminating act of submissiveness, as evident in what he told the Nephites. His perfect submissiveness to his Father is the ultimate lesson for children in submitting to righteous parental guidance.

And viewing the situation from the Father's side, his insistence that his Son—emphatically his "*Beloved* Son"—must submit to the necessary suffering is equally a lesson in perfect parental love, which is not blind to the realities of life and learning but knows that eternal joy is purchased at the price of temporary denial and discomfort. But in the Father's case there was an added dimension—his love for his other children, as expressed in the Gospel of John:

---

1. John 1:1–2; John 17:5.
2. Moses 4:2.
3. Matthew 26:39 (=Mark 14:36; Luke 22:42).
4. John 18:11.
5. Mann 1986 (AB 27):590.
6. See TDNT VI:149–50.

> God so loved the world, that he gave his only begotten Son,
> that whosoever believeth in him should not perish, but have
> everlasting life.[1]

That is, out of his love for all who might become his sons—"the sons of God"—did God give his unique Son. And why was the Son willing to go through with it? Not only out of submissiveness to his Father but also, as the Gospel of John says, out of love for his friends,[2] or, as Moroni said to Christ, "thou hast loved the world, even unto the laying down of thy life for the world."[3] This means that Christ became the spiritual Father[4] of believers by following the example of his Father's love for the world. It is the ultimate lesson for parents on the power of love: by exercising the same love as his Father had exercised, the Son became a Father himself. Furthermore, the Son became one with the Father—that is, perfectly united in mind and harmony with him, as the Son also explained to the Nephites:

> Verily I say unto you, that the Father, and the Son, and the
> Holy Ghost are one; and I am in the Father, and the Father in
> me, and the Father and I are one.[5]

That such perfect unity is intended as a pattern for us is apparent from how Christ presented it—as a prelude to his condemnation of contention, whose divisive spirit transforms those who follow it into the children of yet another father, for "he that hath the spirit of contention is not of me, but is of the devil, who is the father of contention."[6] The same principle is taught in the New Testament writings of the Apostle John, beginning with his Gospel when Jesus responds to the unbelieving Jews who claimed to be children of Abraham. Christ acknowledged their biological claim but insisted that in a higher and more important sense they were not Abraham's children because they did not do the works of Abraham. Rather, he explained,

---

1. John 3:16.
2. See John 15:13.
3. Ether 12:33.
4. See Mosiah 5:7.
5. 3 Nephi 11:27.
6. 3 Nephi 11:29.

"ye do the deeds of your father," for "ye are of your father the devil."[1]
Similarly in the first letter of the Apostle John,[2] a sharp distinction is
drawn between "the children of God . . . and the children of the
devil"[3] — the same distinction drawn by Christ as he told the Nephites
of his perfect unity with the Father. That unity is intended as a pattern
for all mankind, that they too should do "the will of my Father who
is in heaven,"[4] who "commandeth all men, everywhere, to repent
and believe in me. . . . And again I say unto you, ye must repent,
and become as a little child, and be baptized in my name. . . . And
again I say unto you, ye must repent, and be baptized in my name,
and become as a little child."[5] These instructions are, Christ insisted,
"the law and the commandments of my Father,"[6] to whom the
Nephites were commanded to pray in the name of Jesus.[7] Furthermore, those who had been baptized were commanded to periodically
"witness unto the Father" their continued obedience by partaking of
the bread and wine in remembrance of the body and the blood of
Jesus.[8]

THE SON OF GOD AND OF ABRAHAM MINISTERS TO THE CHILDREN OF ABRAHAM

Christ had told the multitude, "I am the God of Israel, and the
God of the whole earth."[9] His placement of "Israel" before the "whole
earth" was not arbitrary, as is apparent from what he had previously
said during his mortal ministry, referring to his personal presence: "I
am not sent but unto the lost sheep of the house of Israel."[10] But his
Israelite sheepfold stretched far beyond the borders of Palestine, as
he had told the Jews: "Other sheep I have, which are not of this fold:

---

1. John 8:41–44.
2. On authorship, see Myers 1987:591.
3. 1 John 3:10.
4. 3 Nephi 14:21.
5. 3 Nephi 11:32, 37–38.
6. 3 Nephi 12:19.
7. See 3 Nephi 13:6; 16:4; 19:6–8; 27:2.
8. 3 Nephi 18:6–10.
9. 3 Nephi 11:14.
10. Matthew 15:24.

them also I must bring, and they shall hear my voice; and there shall be one fold, and one shepherd."[1] Now, during his three-day[2] ministry to the Nephites, the resurrected Savior—the Lamb who had become the Shepherd—declares, "Ye are they of whom I said: Other sheep I have . . . ," for "ye have both heard my voice, and seen me; and ye are my sheep, and ye are numbered among those whom the Father hath given me."[3] Thus the Savior's entire ministry to the Nephites was predicated on father-children relationships:

> Ye are the children of the prophets; and ye are of the house of Israel; and ye are of the covenant which the Father made with your fathers, saying unto Abraham: And in thy seed shall all the kindreds of the earth be blessed.
>
> The Father having raised me up unto you first, and sent me to bless you in turning away every one of you from his iniquities; and this because ye are the children of the covenant.[4]

Clearly the interaction of the Divine Father with his Beloved Son encompasses another father-children relationship—that of Abraham and his descendants, who are beneficiaries of the covenant made on Mount Moriah after Abraham demonstrated his willingness to offer up his own beloved son. Abraham's entire life, according to Jewish tradition, had "prefigured the future history of Israel,"[5] but the "binding of Isaac as a sacrifice to God" became in Judaism the paramount "paradigmatic event in Abraham's life."[6] Thus, its selection by Nephi's brother Jacob as a similitude of the Father and Jesus is all the more significant.

The promises made to Abraham on that occasion had actually been made several times before,[7] but now they were accompanied by a divine oath unprecedented in biblical history as the Lord prefaced

---

1. John 10:16.
2. See 3 Nephi 26:13.
3. 3 Nephi 15:21, 24.
4. 3 Nephi 20:25–26.
5. Nuesner 1985:136.
6. Ibid., 97.
7. See Genesis 12:2–3; 13:14–17; 15:5; 17:1–8.

the promises with this remarkable assurance: "By myself have I sworn[1] [or 'I swear'[2]]." Commenting on this passage, the New Testament observes that "because he could swear by no greater, [God] sware by himself."[3] Or, as Martin Luther interpreted it, God was saying that "I am not only making a promise but am offering Myself as a pledge. . . . If I do not keep my promises, I shall no longer be He who I am."[4] The culminating promise sworn to Abraham was that "in thy seed shall all the nations of the earth be blessed[5] [or 'bless themselves'[6]]," and once again the New Testament offers an explanation as the Apostle Paul comments: "The promises were spoken to Abraham and his seed. The scripture does not say 'and to seeds,' meaning many people, but 'and to your seed,' meaning one person, who is Christ."[7] Paul, writing in Greek, alludes to the fact that in the Old Testament Abrahamic account the original word seed—both in the Hebrew original, zera, and in the Greek translation of the Septuagint, sperma—is a collective plural but is singular in form and can in fact (both in Hebrew and Greek) be used to indicate a single descendant.[8] Furthermore, while the plural form of the Greek sperma can designate human descendants, the plural form of the Hebrew zera cannot.[9] Accordingly, Paul, using a method of exegesis used by the Jewish rabbis,[10] insists that the term Abraham's "seed" points preeminently to Christ.[11] Christ's Abrahamic descent seems also to be emphasized by the Gospel writer Matthew, who in tracing Jesus' ancestry to Abraham[12] demonstrates, in the words of an eminent scholar, "who

---

1. Genesis 22:16:KJV, NRSV.
2. NJPS, NIV, REB, Speiser 1979 (AB 1):162.
3. Hebrews 6:13.
4. Pelikan and Hansen 1964:4:143.
5. Genesis 22:18:KJV, NIV.
6. NJPS, NJB, Speiser 1979 (AB 1):162, and see NRSV.
7. NIV Galatians 3:16.
8. See Byrne 1979:159.
9. See NJoBC 786.
10. See Byrne 1979:159.
11. See Betz 1979:156–57.
12. See Matthew 1:1–2.

Jesus is: the Messiah" and the "son of Abraham, through whom God had promised that he would bless all the families of the earth."[1]

But such blessing would begin with Abraham's other Israelite descendants, to whom Christ's personal ministry was restricted, as he himself had indicated to the Jews by stating that he was sent only to the sheep of Israel. Hence he had come to the Nephites, who were also sheep of the Israelite flock. The Son of God and of Abraham was sent personally to the other children of Abraham.

Christ reminded these Israelite children of Abraham of what their forefathers, the prophets, had spoken, explaining that he was the one of whom Moses and all the other prophets had testified.[2] He had come to urge these children of Israel to follow him and thereby become true "children of your Father who is in heaven"[3] — which would, of course, also necessarily render them "children of Christ"[4] as well as true children of Abraham (who was promised that "as many as receive this Gospel shall be . . . accounted thy seed"[5]) and heirs to his covenant.

The blessing of (Abraham's preeminent descendant) Christ upon non-Israelite mankind would then come, as Christ further told the Nephites, through the Holy Ghost:

> After that ye [are] blessed then fulfilleth the Father the covenant which he made with Abraham, saying: In thy seed shall all the kindreds of the earth be blessed — unto the pouring out of the Holy Ghost through me upon the Gentiles.[6]

In addition, there would in the latter days be further fulfillment to the descendants of Israel, the "people with whom the Father hath covenanted" through their forefathers. Regarding the descendants of father Lehi in the Americas, the Savior promised: "This people will

---

1. Albright and Mann 1971 (AB 26):5–6 (even though the genealogy given is that of Joseph, not Mary).
2. See 3 Nephi 20:23–24.
3. 3 Nephi 12:45.
4. Mosiah 5:7.
5. Abraham 2:10; see also Galatians 3:8 and TPJS 149–50.
6. 3 Nephi 20:27; see also 15:23.

I establish in this land, unto the fulfilling of the covenant which I made with your father Jacob."[1] And regarding the Jews, Christ explained: "I have covenanted with them that I would gather them together in mine own due time, that I would give unto them again the land of their fathers . . . , which is the land of Jerusalem, which is the promised land unto them forever, saith the Father."[2] All this would be in fulfillment of the ancient prophecies, particularly those of Isaiah—from which the Savior liberally quotes even as he attributes them to the words of the Father[3]—foretelling the destiny of the latter-day "daughter of Zion"[4] and "children" of Israel.[5] Indeed, the relationships of children to their forefathers would receive special emphasis in the latter days, as the Savior disclosed to the Nephites by giving them "the words which the Father had given unto Malachi"[6] regarding the latter-day coming of Elijah to "turn the heart of the fathers to the children, and the heart of the children to their fathers."[7]

PARALLELS BETWEEN THE NEPHITE RECORD AND THE WRITINGS OF JOHN

Conspicuous throughout these teachings of Christ is his repeated mention of the Father, whose agent he is. Christ clearly proclaims himself the "God of Israel,"[8] even "he that gave the law" and "he who covenanted with my people Israel."[9] And yet he also asserts that it was the Father who had covenanted with Abraham and his Israelite posterity,[10] and that it was the Father who had given his prophetic words to the Israelite prophets.[11] How so? Obviously in the same way the Father's words were now being spoken to the Nephites—by the

---

1. 3 Nephi 20:22.
2. 3 Nephi 20:29.
3. See 3 Nephi 21:29.
4. 3 Nephi 20:37 (= Isaiah 52:2).
5. 3 Nephi 22:1 (= Isaiah 54:1).
6. 3 Nephi 24:1. Malachi was a Jewish prophet who lived after Lehi left Jerusalem.
7. 3 Nephi 25:6 (= Malachi 4:6).
8. 3 Nephi 11:14.
9. 3 Nephi 15:5.
10. See 3 Nephi 20:12, 25.
11. See 3 Nephi 21:29.

Son, who is here expressly to deliver the Father's words: "Thus commandeth the Father that I should say unto you."[1] "Ye cannot understand all my words which I am commanded of the Father to speak unto you at this time."[2] And repeatedly in delivering his message, Christ reminds his listener's of its author: "thus saith the Father."[3]

Such repeated mention of and emphasis on the Father is reminiscent of the Gospel of John, in which Jesus' use of the name *Father* as a description of God is more than twice as frequent as in all the other gospels combined.[4] Indeed, "more than any other N[ew] T[estament] writing," the Gospel of John "works out the close relation of Jesus as son to God as Father."[5] As one eminent scholar points out, "the theme . . . that the Father has handed over all things to the Son . . . is a favorite one in John."[6] And "the core of Johannine proclamation" is that "the whole event of salvation is anchored in the most intimate union between Father and Son," a union in which "the main accent falls on the simple basic statement: 'The Father loves the Son.' . . . This unity finds expression in the fact that the Father determines what the Son does and says," and "the Father gives the Son a work to complete." Furthermore, "the word is taught and commanded by the Father, indeed, it is first spoken by Him to the Son." Ultimately "the unity of Father and Son finds perfect expression in the sacrifice of life on the part of the Son," to whom "the Father gives . . . the cup of suffering to drink," with "the glorifying of the Father as the final goal."[7] This scholarly summary of the Father-Son relationship as portrayed in the Gospel of John fits perfectly the account of Christ's ministry related in 3 Nephi.

Still further affinities between John's Gospel and 3 Nephi are evident in Christ's prayer uttered in the presence of his twelve Nephite disciples (apostles[8]) as compared with his great intercessory prayer

---

1. 3 Nephi 16:10.
2. 3 Nephi 17:2.
3. See, for example, 3 Nephi 16:7, 8, 10, 13, 14; 20:20, 28, 29; 21:14, 20, 29.
4. See Brown 1986:1:619.
5. Gentz 1986:355.
6. Brown 1966 (AB 29):162.
7. TDNT V:999–1001.
8. See Smith, *History of the Church* 4:538.

uttered in the presence of his Jewish apostles. To be sure, the first thing to grasp our attention in comparing the two prayers is the difference in context, for in the Nephite prayer it is the resurrected and glorified Christ speaking—a point emphasized by the fact that while Christ prays, his Nephite disciples themselves are praying—directly to him.[1] Earlier that day, before he had made his promised appearance on this the second day of his three-day[2] ministry, his disciples had—pursuant to his instructions from the previous day[3]—prayed unto the Father in the name of Jesus.[4] But now, in the personal presence of the glorified Son who had proclaimed himself one with the Father, the Nephite disciples prayed directly to Jesus, "calling him their Lord and their God."[5] He did not stop them but in his own prayer to the Father meekly observed that "they pray unto me because I am with them."[6] (The event calls to mind the observation of the eleventh-century Christian writer Anselm, who said that Christ was human before the resurrection but afterward a God.[7])

Despite that difference in context, however, Jesus' prayer with his Nephite disciples is remarkably similar to that with his Jewish disciples. In the Johannine prayer Christ had prayed that the Father would "sanctify them [the apostles] through thy truth."[8] Similarly in the Nephite prayer he thanked the Father, "Thou hast given the Holy Ghost unto these whom I have chosen"[9] and "hast purified" them.[10] In the Nephite prayer Christ states, "It is because of their belief in me that I have chosen them out of the world,"[11] as in the Johannine prayer he had said that his apostles had received "the words which thou gavest me" and "believed that thou didst send me"[12] and "are

---

1. See 3 Nephi 19:18.
2. See 3 Nephi 26:13.
3. See 3 Nephi 16:4; 17:3.
4. See 3 Nephi 19:7.
5. 3 Nephi 19:18.
6. 3 Nephi 19:22.
7. See CWHN 4:21, citing *Homilies* 7.
8. John 17:17.
9. 3 Nephi 19:20.
10. 3 Nephi 19:28.
11. 3 Nephi 19:20.
12. John 17:8.

not of the world."[1] In the Nephite prayer Christ asks the Father to "give the Holy Ghost unto all them that shall believe in their words,"[2] that "they may be purified in me, through faith on their words";[3] likewise in the Johannine prayer, after asking that his apostles be sanctified, Christ broadened his petition: "Neither pray I for these alone, but for them also which shall believe on me through their word."[4] In the Nephite prayer Christ says, "I pray not for the world, but for those whom thou hast given me out of the world,"[5] as in the Johannine prayer he said, "I pray not for the world, but for them which thou hast given me; for they are thine."[6] And in the Nephite prayer Christ prays for his Nephite disciples and their converts "that I may be in them as thou, Father, art in me, that we may be one,"[7] and "that I may be glorified in them";[8] similarly in the Johannine prayer Christ prayed that his Jewish apostles and their converts "all may be one; as thou, Father, art in me, and I in thee, that they also may be one in us," and "the glory which thou gavest me I have given them; that they may be one, even as we are one."[9] If the two prayers contained further parallels, they are currently hidden from us because part of the Nephite prayer was not written, for "so great and marvelous were the words which he prayed that they cannot be written, neither can they be uttered by man."[10] But if those words paralleled the rest of the Johannine prayer, they also went beyond it, as evidenced by what Christ told the Nephites after finishing his prayer: "So great faith have I never seen among all the Jews; wherefore . . . there are none of them that have seen so great things as ye have seen; neither have they heard so great things as ye have heard."[11]

---

1. John 17:14, 16.
2. 3 Nephi 19:21.
3. 3 Nephi 19:28.
4. John 17:20.
5. 3 Nephi 19:29.
6. John 17:9.
7. 3 Nephi 19:23.
8. 3 Nephi 19:29.
9. John 17:21–22.
10. 3 Nephi 19:34.
11. 3 Nephi 19:35–36.

278 FATHERS AND SONS IN THE BOOK OF MORMON

The repeated similarities between the Nephite writings (including Nephi's vision of the Lamb of God and the account written by Nephi's descendant Nephi describing Christ's ministry to the Nephites) and the writings of the Jewish Apostle John are all the more remarkable in view of the fact that John is the only Jewish apostle or New Testament writer to be named in the Book of Mormon.[1] How do we account for such similarities? Perhaps by the fact that John, as he emphasizes in his writings, was an eyewitness (both to Christ's glorious ministry[2] as well as to the apocalyptic vision[3]), even as the Book of Mormon writers Nephi and his descendant Nephi the chief disciple were eyewitnesses—Nephi to the vision that John saw, and Nephi the younger to the resurrected Christ's ministry among the Nephites.

THE ULTIMATE DEMONSTRATION OF CHRIST'S UNITY WITH THE FATHER

Nephi the younger was privileged (because of his people's collective faith) to witness greater things in Christ's presence than John and his people had witnessed. Unfortunately for us, however, we are excluded from the greatest of those things, not only because some of them were not written but also because others that were written were excluded from Mormon's abridgment by the express command of God. In fact, Mormon was about to reproduce the record of Christ's teachings in its entirety when the Lord forbade him, explaining that if the readers of Mormon's record accepted the little that had been written of Christ's visit they would be granted the fuller and greater record also, which is more than a hundred times larger, Mormon notes.[4] Furthermore, even what little we do have may well have been written (in certain aspects, at least) in a cryptic form so as not to openly disclose sacred mysteries that Christ taught—which is the point of John Welch's study concluding that much of our current record of what Christ taught is a richly allusive temple text.[5]

---

1. See 1 Nephi 14:27.
2. See John 1:14; 13:23–25; 19:35.
3. See Revelation 1.
4. See 3 Nephi 26:6–12.
5. See Welch 1990.

Even so, there is enough in our current record to enrapture and enthrall us with the glories revealed by the resurrected Son of God, and particularly those that provide us with the clearest window in all of scripture on the relationship between the Father and his Son. One such window is provided, in fact, in Christ's prayer with his twelve Nephite disciples, who, as noted earlier, were praying while Christ was uttering his powerful prayer, whose similarities to the Johannine prayer we have seen. But in Christ's Nephite prayer he breaks off twice to return to his nearby disciples, and what transpires during these two interludes demonstrates not only an immediate answer to Christ's prayer but also poignantly illustrates the relationship between the Father and the Son—and the sons of Christ. After commanding his disciples to kneel and pray, Jesus—the resurrected and glorified Lord—went "a little way off" and demonstrated his continuing humility before his Father by "bow[ing] himself to the earth" in prayer as he addressed the Father directly and prayed for his disciples (and their converts), requesting that he, Christ, would "be in them as thou, Father, art in me, that we may be one."[1]

> And it came to pass that when Jesus had thus prayed unto the Father, he came unto his disciples, and behold, they did still continue, without ceasing, to pray unto him; and they did not multiply many words, for it was given unto them what they should pray, and they were filled with desire.
>
> And it came to pass that Jesus blessed them as they did pray unto him; and his countenance did smile upon them, and the light of his countenance did shine upon them, and behold they were as white as the countenance and also the garments of Jesus; and behold the whiteness thereof did exceed all the whiteness, yea, even there could be nothing upon earth so white as the whiteness thereof.
>
> And Jesus said unto them: Pray on; nevertheless they did not cease to pray.[2]

Jesus turned and again went "a little way off" and again "bowed himself to the earth" in direct prayer to the Father, of whom he asked

1. See 3 Nephi 19:16–23.
2. 3 Nephi 19:24–26.

that his disciples (and their converts) would be "purified in me, that I may be in them as thou, Father, art in me, that we may be one, that I may be glorified in them."[1]

> And when Jesus had spoken these words he came again unto his disciples; and behold they did pray steadfastly, without ceasing, unto him; and he did smile upon them again; and behold they were white, even as Jesus.[2]

When Jesus returned again to pray, he spoke glorious things that cannot be written. But what is written about his two interludes with his Nephite disciples demonstrates, in the words of Truman Madsen, "the precious promised transmission of the Divine nature, from the Father to the Son to the sons" of men, thus establishing a "perfect bond between the Father and the Son and the sons of men."[3] The precious record of Christ's experience with his twelve Nephite disciples is one of our greatest windows into the relationship between the Father and his Son and the sons of men who have become sons of Christ by coming to the Father by means of the Son. The incomparably bright celestial light that once shone from the persons of Christ and the Nephite disciples shines still with a brightness that dispels the fog of centuries-old speculation by the Christian world about the nature and relationship of the Father and the Son,[4] a brightness that supremely illustrates the two principles for which Christ was praying: purity ("that they may be purified in me") and unity ("that we may be one").[5] These principles happen to be the two foundational principles of Zion, which in fact existed for over a century and a half among the Nephites after Christ's visit. By definition Zion is "the pure in heart,"[6] and its inhabitants are "of one heart and one mind."[7] And although such purity and unity must prevail among all the in-

---

1. 3 Nephi 19:27–29.
2. 3 Nephi 19:30.
3. Madsen n.d.:45.
4. See Douglas 1978:418–20, 501–2, 985–86.
5. 3 Nephi 19:23, 28–29.
6. D&C 97:21.
7. Moses 7:18.

habitants of Zion, those principles obviously begin and are centered in the primary structural unit of Zion, whether here or in eternity—the family.[1] It is no coincidence, then, that the supreme example of the purity and unity that should prevail among all members of each Zion family is found in the relationship between God the Father and his Beloved Son, as is so dramatically mirrored in the light that shone from the Nephite disciples who became purified in and one with Jesus even as he was one with his Father.

THE ULTIMATE LESSON IN CHRIST'S SUBMISSIVENESS TO THE FATHER

But perhaps the greatest recorded event in all of Christ's Nephite ministry—and indeed in all of scripture—concerned his interaction with the little children. To be sure, he had already demonstrated his affinity with children in his mortal ministry when on one occasion he became "much displeased" as his disciples attempted to deter little children from taking his time; he instructed that the children freely be allowed to approach him, "for of such is the kingdom of God." And "whosoever shall not receive the kingdom of God as a little child, he shall not enter therein." Then taking the children "up in his arms, he put his hands upon them, and blessed them."[2] On another occasion, as his disciples speculated about who would be the greatest in the kingdom of God, Jesus had called a little child to himself and explained that "whosoever therefore shall humble himself as this little child, the same is greatest in the kingdom of heaven."[3]

Jesus' own humility before his Father was also evident in his mortal ministry in how he addressed the Father in prayer—by the Aramaic word *abba*, "the warm, familiar term [for *father*] used in the everyday life of the family."[4] But it was "an unprecedented address for God"[5] that was "unthinkable for the pious Jew," for it was a

---

1. See McConkie 1966:273–74, 559.
2. Mark 10:13–16 (=Matthew 19:13–15).
3. Matthew 18:4.
4. NIDNTT 1:615.
5. Gentz 1986:355.

"childish and familiar term"[1] and "was little child's talk, addressing God as a real, intimate father, as a trusting child would."[2] Indeed, Jesus' use of *abba* indicated "both a deepened intimacy and a total obedience,"[3] showing that "God is not a distant Ruler . . . but One who is intimately close."[4] Furthermore, when "Jesus gave his disciples the Lord's Prayer, he gave them authority to follow him in addressing God as *abba*."[5]

Now, among these faithful Nephites, Jesus would again demonstrate his love and esteem for little children, but with unprecedented power and tenderness. After healing all of the multitude's sick and disabled (which probably included some of the children), he turned his attention to the children as he had all of them brought and set on the ground surrounding him. While the children remained seated he commanded the multitude to kneel, and then did so himself to pray. Hugh Nibley has alluded to the possible connection between this incident and the early Christian prayer circles reported in New Testament apocryphal sources, one of which reports of Jesus, "We made a circle and surrounded him and he said, 'I am in your midst in the manner of these little children.' "[6] Commenting on Christ's interaction with the Nephite children, Nibley observes that "the prayer circle is the nearest approach to the Lord that men make on earth—and they can approach him only 'as little children,' " as Christ had already told the Nephites three times.[7] And since the early Christian prayer circles were all derived from the temple,[8] the likelihood that Christ's prayer in the midst of the Nephite children was also a kind of temple prayer circle would increase if, as John Welch suggests, Christ's teachings

---

1. NIDNTT 1:615.
2. CWHN 4:55.
3. Gentz 1986:355.
4. TDNT V:985.
5. NIDNTT 1:615. Jesus' childlike submissiveness to his Father seems also to have been the point of his appearing in the form of a child to some of his Jewish disciples after his resurrection, as reported by apocryphal sources. (See CWHN 4:55, citing the Apocryphon of John and the Acts of John 88, translations in 1:322 and 2:225 respectively of Hennecke 1963 and 1965.)
6. CWHN 4:55, citing the Kasr al-Wazz fragment.
7. Ibid. 56; see also 3 Nephi 9:22; 11:37–38.
8. See CWHN 4:82.

up to that point had indeed revolved around sacred temple ordinances.[1]

Regardless, however, of its possible connection with a temple prayer circle, what transpired on that occasion with Jesus and the Nephite children provides perhaps our greatest window into the relationship between the Father and his Son and the sons of men. Surrounded by the seated children and the kneeling multitude, and before kneeling himself, "Jesus groaned within himself, and said: Father, I am troubled because of the wickedness of the people of the house of Israel." (The one sorrow that neither saints nor gods can ever get past is sorrow for the sins of the world.) Then Jesus "himself also knelt upon the earth; and behold he prayed unto the Father, and the things which he prayed cannot be written," being "so great and marvelous" as to defy description; those present recalled later that "no one can conceive of the joy which filled our souls at the time we heard him pray for us unto the Father."[2] It is the ultimate demonstration of Jesus' submissiveness to his Father as he kneels surrounded by little children and in the humility of a child prays to his Father words beyond human utterance which bring joy beyond comprehension — recalling Jesus' words to his Jewish disciples as reported in an apocryphal source: "I am in your midst in the manner of these little children."[3]

Still surrounded by the Nephite children, Jesus arose and instructed the multitude to arise, saying that they were blessed because of their faith. "And now," he continued, "my joy is full."[4]

> And when he had said these words, he wept, and the multitude bare record of it, and he took their little children, one by one, and blessed them, and prayed unto the Father for them.

---

1. See Welch 1990. Welch himself does not discuss the possibility of or connection with a prayer circle here; the temple connection he infers is one of sealing of these children to their parents (ibid. 79–80) — obviously not a mutually exclusive idea from that of the prayer circle.
2. 3 Nephi 17:14–17.
3. CWHN 4:55, citing the Kasr al-Wazz fragment.
4. 3 Nephi 17:18–20.

> And when he had done this he wept again;
> And he spake unto the multitude, and said unto them: Behold your little ones.
> And as they looked to behold they cast their eyes towards heaven, and they saw the heavens open, and they saw angels descending out of heaven as it were in the midst of fire; and they came down and encircled those little ones about, and they were encircled about with fire; and the angels did minister unto them.[1]

The timing of this event seems significant: it occurred on the day before the similar angelic ministrations to the Nephite twelve disciples following their baptism—demonstrating, says John Tvedtnes, that "what the adults obtained through faith, repentance and baptism was given to the children with prior conditions."[2]

Following the angelic ministrations to the children, and in dramatic illustration of what he had taught the Jews—that greatness in the kingdom of heaven is measured by the degree to which one is childlike—Jesus

> did teach and minister unto the children of the multitude . . . , and he did loose their tongues, and they did speak unto their fathers great and marvelous things, even greater than he had revealed unto the people; and he loosed their tongues that they could utter.[3]

That the Savior reserved the greatest of his teachings to be spoken by the mouths of little children was the ultimate lesson to their parents in how they themselves must approach Jesus—as little children. The most childlike of all adults, and the example for us all, is the Son of God, he who, as Nephi had said, "showeth unto the children of men that, according to the flesh he humbleth himself before the Father."[4] But we have more than the sacred record to remind us of the Son's submissiveness, for the record itself teaches that his submissiveness

---

1. 3 Nephi 17:21–24.

2. In John A. Tvedtnes, "Becoming as Little Children" (forthcoming article).

3. 3 Nephi 26:14. Also, it appears that the same phenomenon was repeated the following day. (See 3 Nephi 26:15–16.)

4. 2 Nephi 31:7.

is best exemplified by little children—a point recalling the Israelite tradition that "children are to be loved because they are in the image of God."[1] Thus the editor of the Nephite record, Mormon, instructed his own son to "teach parents that they must repent and be baptized, and humble themselves as their little children, and they shall all be saved with their little children."[2] And thus one of the Lord's modern-day apostles, Elder Boyd K. Packer, could say, "All that I have ever learned that has been most worthwhile, I have learned from my children."[3] What Elder Packer was willing to learn from his children prepared him to serve as a special witness of that Son who invites us all to follow his example of perfect child-like submissiveness to the Father and thereby become "children of Christ, his sons, and his daughters."[4]

---

1. James H. Charlesworth, in Lundquist and Ricks 1990:47.
2. Moroni 8:10.
3. Packer 1975:ix.
4. Mosiah 5:7.

Chapter 11

PATTERNS
AND REFLECTIONS
• •
FATHERS AND SONS IN
THE BOOK OF MORMON

WHY THE BOOK OF MORMON FOCUSES ON
FATHERS AND SONS

The theme of fathers and sons appears to be the predominant theme of the Book of Mormon, in which the relationship of the Eternal Father and his Beloved Son is central, and where it is taught that the son is the father of those who believe in him. The theme runs from Nephi's opening line of praise for his father all the way through Moroni's inclusion of his father's writings, and involves nearly every major event and character in the book, which from its inception owes its existence to the power of parental influence and is based on family records kept through generations — much as the Bible began as "the book of the generations of Adam."[1] It is important to recognize, however, that most of the Book of Mormon is an abridgment by one man, Mormon, of the voluminous records available to him, which would tend to indicate that he had some latitude in how he structured the

---

1. Genesis 5:1; Moses 6:8.

story. That the story is so conspicuously structured around fathers and sons may, therefore, have been at least partially discretionary by Mormon. Indeed, he not only ushers onto center stage a consecutive train of father-son pairs, but also ushers several of those characters out with a comment that this or that son did (or, rarely, did not) follow the path of his father. Mormon reports, for example, that (the second) King Mosiah set out to "do according to that which his father had done in all things,"[1] or that King Noah "did not walk in the ways of his father,"[2] or that Helaman the younger's son Nephi "did walk after the ways of his father,"[3] or that Helaman the younger likewise "did walk in the ways of his father."[4] Such remarks recall similar ones made by the authors of the Old Testament books of Kings and Chronicles as they report whether or not this or that son walked in the ways of his father (or forefather)[5]—indicating that Mormon's attention to father-son matters in making his own narrative is based on an ancient historiographic tradition handed down by his predecessor ancestral historians in ancient Israel (which means that Mormon himself was walking in the ways of his fathers).

By following that ancient pattern in abridging what was already a family record, Mormon presents us with a series of connected biographies that immediately engage our attention. "There is properly no History; only Biography,"[6] wrote Emerson, and presenting Nephite history through the experience of individuals is highly effective, especially when those individuals are connected in family relationships as fathers, sons, grandsons, and so on. Such family history tends to captivate our interest in the same sort of immediate and compelling way as do the family histories contained in the Old Testament, which,

---

1. Mosiah 6:7.
2. Mosiah 11:1.
3. Helaman 3:20.
4. Helaman 3:37.
5. See, e.g., 1 Kings 11:4, 6, 33; 15:3, 11, 26; 22:43, 52; 2 Kings 3:2; 14:3; 16:2; 18:3; 21:21; 2 Chronicles 17:3; 20:32; 28:1; 29:2; 34:2, 3. The books of Kings would probably have been included on the brass plates. (See 1 Nephi 5:10–13).
6. *The Essays of Ralph Waldo Emerson* 1987:6. In context, Emerson seems to be saying that due to its highly subjective nature, history is in a sense biography—the biography of the historian. However, Emerson's statement has popularly been interpreted as saying that the most valuable and readable form of history is biography.

as Erich Auerbach observed, are imbued with "domestic realism"; there "the sublime, tragic, and problematic take shape precisely in the domestic and commonplace."[1] It is much the same with the Book of Mormon history; its focus on the domestic bonds of fathers and sons infuses it with an inherent appeal by providing a setting to which we, as parents and children, can immediately relate.

And what magnificent fathers and sons! Beginning with father Lehi and his son Nephi, all the way down to Mormon and his son Moroni, we are treated to such a parade of outstanding father-son relationships that we may begin to wonder if Nephite society was somehow immune from what writers and philosophers have pointed to as an "inherent problem in human nature," namely, "the conflict between generations."[2] To be sure, every now and then uncommitted or even rebellious sons surface in the Book of Mormon—sons like Laman and Lemuel, Enos, King Noah, Alma the younger, Corianton, or the sons of Mosiah; but even most of these eventually turn around and carry on the righteous tradition of their fathers. Were the Nephites largely immune from the problem of generational conflict that has haunted mankind since Cain? Hardly. In fact, scrutiny of Book of Mormon history shows that, with the exception of the brief Nephite "golden age" following Christ's visit, the problem was as pervasive in Nephite society as in any other place or time. Book of Mormon prophets were forever pleading—mostly unsuccessfully—with the people to remember their righteous fathers.

This makes Mormon's presentation of so many exemplary father-son relationships all the more intriguing, for they were apparently not representative of much of Nephite society. This is dramatically highlighted in how Moroni finishes Mormon's record—by the luminous portrait of their own father-son relationship set against the dark backdrop of a decadent, decaying civilization undergoing wholesale destruction because they would not remember their righteous fathers. And as with Mormon and Moroni, so with the other remarkable father-son portraits in the Book of Mormon: they were the highlights—one

1. Auerbach 1968:22.
2. Ralph E. Matlaw, in Matlaw 1989:268.

might say lighthouses—of Nephite society. Mormon's presentation of those unique portraits may thus have been governed not only by his subject matter, but also by his audience—we to whom he was expressly and knowingly writing. President Harold B. Lee warned that when a theme is repeated over and over in the scriptures, it should merit our special attention as an urgent message from the Lord.[1] This is especially true when that theme is so conspicuously and emphatically repeated in the scriptural record that happens to be the most correct of any book on earth and was written prophetically for our day! Hence President Ezra Taft Benson has counseled,

> If [the Book of Mormon authors] saw our day, and chose those things which would be of greatest worth to us, is not that how we should study the Book of Mormon? We should constantly ask ourselves, "Why did the Lord inspire Mormon . . . to include that in his record? What lesson can I learn from that to help me live in this day and age?"[2]

What, then, does the theme of fathers and sons have to do with us today? At least as much as it has had to do with every other generation of mankind, for the central and paramount significance of the family is a timeless verity. Stable civilization has ever depended on stable families; President Benson has declared that "the home is the rock foundation, the cornerstone of civilization," so that "no nation will rise above its homes, and no nation will long endure when the family unit is weakened or destroyed."[3] President Benson has also reminded us that "the sacred title of 'father' is shared with the Almighty,"[4] which points to the fact that the central significance of the family on earth is a reflection of the family's significance in heaven, where the celestial order has ever been one of family government. Accordingly, the family is apparently the only organization created in time that endures for eternity,[5] and it is, says President Benson,

---

1. Unpublished talk to missionaries given in Salt Lake City, June 1971.
2. W&W 20.
3. TETB 522.
4. TETB 503.
5. See D&C 132:13–19.

"the most important organization in time and all eternity."[1] No wonder that modern-day prophets have spoken in superlatives about parenthood as the highest opportunity and duty that God has entrusted to mortals.[2] So it has ever been, and so it is today—which means that the Book of Mormon's teaching on fathers and sons is truly timeless.

Such teaching may be timeless in another sense as well, for Mormon's predominant focus on fathers (as opposed to mothers) in his depiction of parent-child relationships may well be more than a product of the patriarchally transmitted records from which he drew or the patriarchally structured society in which he lived. Mormon may have felt that fathers need more encouragement than mothers in fulfilling their divinely ordained parental role, and Mormon has provided that encouragement by pointing to an impressive array of the most powerful fathers who appeared in the records available to him.

The Book of Mormon's teaching on fathers and sons is also timely, for as President Ezra Taft Benson has warned, "The family is under attack today as never before."[3] Ironically, such fierce opposition to the family has arisen after the Lord has placed uniquely increased emphasis on families and family ties for our day. Already the Lord has begun to fulfil to Abraham's and Israel's descendants the covenant he made to their fathers (the beginning of the fulfillment of which, Christ told the Nephites, would be the coming forth of the Book of Mormon[4]). Already Elijah has come to turn the hearts of the fathers and the children to each other[5] (as the Nephites were told would happen[6]). And already the Lord has commanded his people to prepare for his glorious second coming (also forseen by Nephite prophets[7]) by building Zion[8]—whose central unit is always the family. In other

---

1. TETB 489.
2. See introduction to this book.
3. TETB 493.
4. See 3 Nephi 21:7.
5. See D&C 110:13–16.
6. See 3 Nephi 25:5–6.
7. See, for example, 1 Nephi 22:24.
8. Mentioned in numerous passages of the Doctrine and Covenants.

words, never has the Lord placed so much emphasis on and expected so much of the family—and never has the family been so besieged.

But as Nephi said, "the Lord giveth no commandments unto the children of men, save he shall prepare a way for them that they may accomplish the thing which he commandeth them."[1] To help parents of our day accomplish their most urgent and greatest of all tasks, the Lord has prepared the greatest of all books, the Book of Mormon; and it is more than coincidence that "the most correct of any book on earth"[2] focuses so conspicuously on fathers and sons. What the Book of Mormon teaches about fathers and sons, says President Benson, applies to all parents and children—fathers and mothers, sons and daughters.[3]

ANCIENT PATTERNS FOR MODERN TIMES

To discover that teaching, we have traced the theme of fathers and sons throughout the Book of Mormon and are now in a position to summarize and reflect upon patterns that have become perceptible. This search for patterns in the theme of fathers and sons is particularly fitting in light of the etymology of the word *pattern*, which is ultimately derived from the Latin *pater*, meaning "father."[4] The Book of Mormon fathers are indeed "patterns" whose relevance remains and is even heightened today because of the unique circumstances of our age. And in searching for those patterns, we engage in the same process that the Book of Mormon's first author, Nephi, applied, when he "did liken all scriptures unto us, that it might be for our profit and learning."[5]

But it is also important to recognize that in setting those patterns of parental instruction, the righteous Book of Mormon fathers beginning with Lehi were themselves following ancestral patterns of righteous parenting, even though the Book of Mormon never expressly says so. The closest it comes is when King Benjamin, described by

---

1. 1 Nephi 3:7.
2. TPJS 194.
3. See W&W 67.
4. WTNID 1,656–57 (entries for "pattern" and "patron").
5. 1 Nephi 19:23.

Hugh Nibley as "an ardent student of early Jewish traditions,"[1] declares that in order for parents to retain a remission of sins, they must teach their children to keep "the laws of God" and to "walk in the ways of truth and soberness."[2] We also saw that Jacob's teaching Enos "in the nurture and admonition of the Lord"[3] may well echo the Mosaic law's expectation of parents and how the ancient patriarch Jacob taught his sons. And if the Book of Mormon does not mention that Lehi's teaching Nephi was pursuant to a well-established parental duty in ancient Israel, it may be because we are apprised of that parental instruction from the perspective not of the parent but of the son. Regardless, it is clear that Lehi was fulfilling his sacred duty as a father in ancient Israel to educate his children and train them in the way they should go.[4] And how old was that duty? At least as old as Moses,[5] but beyond that the Old Testament does not indicate. However, according to Joseph Smith's restored Genesis text (which may well have been available to Lehi on the brass plates), father Adam himself had been expressly commanded by God to teach the gospel to his children.[6] In other words, the pattern of righteous parenting by the great Book of Mormon fathers throughout their widely divergent circumstances and across a millennium of history did not originate with them. By being good fathers in following the parental pattern handed down from their forefathers as far back as Adam, they were in fact being good sons. That the same pattern is as relevant for parents today demonstrates the ever-enduring paramount significance of the family.

Obedient and dutiful Book of Mormon sons were likewise fulfilling their long-established duty as children in ancient Israel to "hearken to their father"[7] and to keep the commandment in the Decalogue to "honour thy father and thy mother"[8] — a commandment of which

---

1. Nibley, *Improvement Era*, November 1969, p. 121.
2. Mosiah 4:14–15.
3. Enos 1:1.
4. See AI 1:49; TDOT I:10.
5. See Deuteronomy 6:7.
6. See Moses 6:57–58.
7. TDOT I:10, citing Proverbs 23:22.
8. Exodus 20:12.

Nephi is very much aware as evidenced by his recitation of it to Laman and Lemuel.[1] The effect of that commandment continues to be tacitly but forcefully felt throughout the generations of righteous Book of Mormon sons, much like the phenomenon pointed out by a modern biblical scholar: "In the law and the ethos of the O[ld] T[estament], regardless of the march of time, there is everywhere tacitly presupposed a basic norm which the Decalogue sets forth in the commandment: 'Honour thy father and thy mother.' "[2] Accordingly, the pattern of obedient Book of Mormon sons, like the pattern of good fathers, was an ancient one, and it has never lost its relevance.

SETTING AN EXAMPLE

How did Book of Mormon fathers teach their sons? First and foremost by example, as seen when Nephi desired to know the things that his father had seen and was granted that same vision[3] in which Lehi first ate the fruit and then beckoned his family;[4] or when Enos began his own spiritual odyssey by recognizing that his father, Jacob, was a "just man";[5] or when (the second) King Mosiah acted righteously by "do[ing] according to that which his father had done in all things";[6] or when General Moroni set a sterling example for Moronihah;[7] or when Helaman the younger kept God's commandments by "walk[ing] after the ways of his father";[8] or when Jonas was selected to be one of the resurrected Lord's twelve disciples alongside his exemplary father, Nephi.[9] Such righteous examples by Book of Mormon fathers recall the fact that in ancient Israel, "the first requirement of a father [was] to fear God; then he will be a refuge to his children."[10] And so it is in modern Israel. President David O. McKay told parents

---

1. See 1 Nephi 17:55.
2. TDNT V:964.
3. See 1 Nephi 11:3–6.
4. 1 Nephi 8:11–15.
5. Enos 1:1.
6. Mosiah 6:7.
7. See chapter 6.
8. Helaman 3:20.
9. See 3 Nephi 19:4.
10. TDOT I:10, citing Proverbs 14:26.

that "your example will teach [gospel] principles more effectively than what you say,"[1] and that "it is what the teacher is at heart that will influence the child."[2] President Harold B. Lee counseled, "You cannot lift another soul until you are standing on higher ground than he is."[3] And commenting on the great examples set by the Book of Mormon fathers, President Benson has observed, "A good model is the best teacher. Therefore, a father's first responsibility is to set the proper example."[4]

TEACHING PLAINLY THE PLAN OF SALVATION CENTERED IN CHRIST

Having first set a righteous example for their sons, Book of Mormon fathers proceeded to plainly teach the foundational gospel truths. For example, Lehi taught his sons about the fall of Adam, the redemption made by the Messiah, free agency, eternal laws with their punishments and rewards, and God's final judgment.[5] Lehi's son Nephi recorded: "We talk of Christ, we rejoice in Christ, we preach of Christ, we prophesy of Christ . . . that our children may know to what source they may look for a remission of their sins."[6] Nephi's brother Jacob taught his own son "concerning eternal life, and the joy of the saints."[7] Alma the younger emphasized to his sons the necessity of repenting and being "born of God"[8] through the mercy of Jesus, and of enduring to the end[9] so that through the justice of God they would in the resurrection be restored to happiness instead of misery, for "wickedness never was happiness."[10] Helaman the younger explained to his sons that salvation comes "only through the atoning blood of Jesus Christ," who would "come to redeem his

---

1. Burton 1970:86.
2. McKay 1957:307.
3. *Ensign* 3:7 (July 1973), p. 123.
4. W&W 67.
5. See 2 Nephi 2.
6. 2 Nephi 25:26.
7. Enos 1:3.
8. Alma 36:24–26; 38:6.
9. See Alma 38:2.
10. Alma 41:10.

people."[1] And Mormon taught his son Moroni about the exemplary innocence of little children, which all adults who would be saved must emulate by repentance, baptism, and receiving the Holy Ghost in order to obtain "hope and perfect love, which love endureth by diligence unto prayer."[2] In short, as President Benson observed, although the Book of Mormon fathers taught their sons "many things, . . . the overarching message was 'the great plan of the Eternal God' — the Fall, rebirth, Atonement, Resurrection, Judgment, eternal life." For "all truths are not of the same value. The saving truths of salvation are of greatest worth. These truths the [Book of Mormon] fathers taught plainly. . . . Are we doing likewise?"[3]

That all of these truths are centered in Christ is no accident, for as the Prophet Joseph Smith explained, our entire religion is centered in Christ.[4] According to President Spencer W. Kimball, Christ should be no less the center of parental instruction, pursuant to the pattern of Nephi, who focused on Christ so that his children would "know to what source they may look"[5] is a model for all parents.

> What inner strength would be in every person if he knew that the Master and His teachings were indeed his great source of guidance, his great source of correct example, his great source of help! That is our prime goal in all our teaching in the home.[6]

And although applicable to all parents, the examples of the Book of Mormon fathers teaching these things to their sons also demonstrates that "the major responsibility for teaching our sons the great plan of the Eternal Father . . . rests with the fathers. It should be done individually as well as in the family."[7]

---

1. Helaman 5:9–10.
2. Moroni 8:26; see vv. 4–26.
3. W&W 68–69.
4. See TPJS 121.
5. 2 Nephi 25:26.
6. Kimball 1982:333.
7. W&W 71.

TEACHING FROM AND ABOUT THE SCRIPTURES

The teachings of the great Book of Mormon fathers were centered in and focused on the scriptures, beginning with the brass plates that Lehi so ardently searched,[1] and from which he taught his sons the plan of salvation "according to the things which [he had] read."[2] King Benjamin told his sons that "were it not for these [brass] plates, which contain these records and these commandments, we must have suffered in ignorance, even at this present time, not knowing the mysteries of God."[3] Alma emphasized to his son Helaman that the sacred Nephite records "have enlarged the memory of this people, yea, and convinced many of the error of their ways, and brought them to the knowledge of their God unto the salvation of their souls."[4] Helaman the younger urged his sons to remember specific passages from the sacred Nephite scriptures.[5] And Mormon wrote to Moroni that the same destruction that once had befallen the Jaredites (as known through their records) was now threatening Nephite civilization.[6] President Benson has observed that just as the Nephite records "blessed Lehi and his descendants, so our scriptures should bless us."[7]

TEACHING BY USE OF METAPHORS

Sometimes wise Book of Mormon fathers taught important but intangible gospel principles by metaphorically likening them to things tangible. When Lehi's first campsite after leaving Jerusalem was in a valley by a river that flowed into the Red Sea, he drew unforgettable lessons from the topography to teach his two oldest sons about being directed towards righteousness—like a river "running into the fountain of all righteousness"—and about being resolute in righteousness—"like unto this valley, firm and steadfast, and immovable in

---

1. See 1 Nephi 5:10.
2. 2 Nephi 2:17.
3. Mosiah 1:3.
4. Alma 37:8.
5. See Helaman 5:9–11.
6. See Moroni 9:23.
7. W&W 71.

keeping the commandments of the Lord."[1] Later when Lehi taught his sons about the destiny of the house of Israel, he said "that they should be compared like unto an olive-tree, whose branches should be broken off and should be scattered upon all the face of the earth."[2] And in recounting his dream of the tree of life, Lehi described to his sons the various symbols he had seen, such as the iron rod, the river of water, the mists of darkness, the great and spacious building, and the precious fruit.[3] Lehi's son Jacob, writing expressly for the benefit of his posterity, compared God's giving of his Only Begotten Son to Abraham's offering of Isaac.[4] King Benjamin, quoting the words of an angel, told his people—including his sons—that the Lord had showed "many signs, and wonders, and types, and shadows . . . concerning his coming."[5] Alma the youger, who had taught the Zoramites that the word of God was like a seed to be planted in one's heart,[6] used a similar teaching technique to teach his son Helaman—to whom he had just delivered the Liahona—that "it is as easy to give heed to the word of Christ, which will point to you a straight course to eternal bliss, as it was for our fathers to give heed to this compass," whose spindles had pointed the right way in the wilderness for Lehi's party when they exercised faith.[7] And Helaman the younger explained to his sons Nephi and Lehi that eternal life is like a "treasure" that "fadeth not away,"[8] the acquisition of which depends upon building one's life "upon the rock of our Redeemer, who is Christ," a "sure foundation, . . . whereon if men build they cannot fall," despite the devil's mighty storms.[9] This method of likening intangible gospel truths to tangible and familiar objects is, according to Elder Boyd K. Packer, one of the most foundational of all

1. 1 Nephi 2:9–10.
2. 1 Nephi 10:12.
3. See 1 Nephi 8.
4. See Jacob 4:1–5.
5. Mosiah 3:15.
6. See Alma 32.
7. Alma 37:44.
8. Helaman 5:8.
9. Helaman 5:12.

teaching principles, as evidenced by the fact that it is the one teaching principle that Jesus himself used more than any other.[1]

While it is true that one of the purposes of Jesus' teaching by parables was to cloak precious truths from the unworthy,[2] such a purpose does not necessarily exclude using those same parables as vehicles to communicate those same truths to the worthy. Furthermore, Jesus' use of metaphor was not limited to the parables, as seen, for example, when he used a word-play to compare Peter to rock,[3] or when he compared God's clothing of the faithful to the beauty of the lilies.[4] Even in latter-day revelation, the Savior has continued to use parable and metaphor in teaching his Saints ("Unto what shall I liken these kingdoms, that ye may understand?"[5] and "Unto what shall I liken the children of Zion? I will liken them unto the parable of the woman and the unjust judge."[6]).

TEACHING BY PERSONAL EXPERIENCE AND TESTIMONY

To emphasize and verify the truth of what they were teaching, righteous Book of Mormon fathers — as President Benson has pointed out — "constantly bore their testimonies to their sons."[7] Through such testimonies these fathers shared their own personal and experiential knowledge and acted as instruments through which the Holy Ghost testified. For example, Lehi spoke to his sons "with power, being filled with the Spirit,"[8] and he "prophesied many things" to his family;[9] he also shared with them his dream of the tree of life.[10] King Benjamin testified to his sons that "these sayings are true, and also . . . these records are true"[11] and later shared with his people

---

1. See Packer 1975:20, and forward.
2. See Matthew 13:10–15.
3. See Matthew 16:18.
4. See Matthew 6:28–31; 3 Nephi 13:28–31.
5. D&C 88:46.
6. D&C 101:81.
7. W&W 79.
8. 1 Nephi 2:14.
9. 1 Nephi 5:19.
10. See 1 Nephi 8.
11. Mosiah 1:6.

(with his sons present[1]) the words of an angel that had appeared to him the previous night.[2] Alma the younger graphically described for his sons his own traumatic conversion experience when he had been abruptly halted by an angel and for three days been "tormented with the pains of hell"[3] until he cried to Jesus for mercy, whereupon his exquisite pain was replaced by an equally exquisite joy. Since that time, Alma continued, "I have labored without ceasing, that I might bring souls unto repentance," and "the Lord doth give me exceedingly great joy in the fruit of my labors."[4] And, he assured his sons, his knowledge about God was acquired from God, for "the Spirit of God which is in me . . . maketh these things known unto me."[5] And Mormon related to his son Moroni a revelation that he had just received from Christ regarding the heinous practice of infant baptism.[6] Such sharing of personal knowledge and testimony by the power of the Spirit is, as latter-day prophets have emphasized, critical to the conversion of those being taught. Brigham Young discovered early in his ministry that "nothing short of a testimony by the power of the Holy Ghost would bring light and knowledge to [the people]—bring them in their hearts to repentance. Nothing short of that would ever do."[7] Hence, according to Elder Boyd K. Packer, "If there is one essential ingredient for the teaching of moral and spiritual values, for the teaching of the gospel, it is to have the Spirit of the Lord with us as we teach."[8]

LEADING IN WORSHIP, ORDINANCES, AND BLESSINGS

Great Book of Mormon fathers also participated with and led their sons in worship, ordinances, and blessings. Under Lehi's direction, for example, his family "did offer sacrifice and burnt offerings unto

1. At least Mosiah, and presumably the others.
2. See Mosiah 3.
3. Alma 36:13.
4. Alma 36:24–25.
5. Alma 38:6.
6. See Moroni 8.
7. JD 5:327.
8. Packer 1975:273.

the Lord" and "gave thanks unto the God of Israel," whereupon Lehi took the brass plates "and he did search them from the beginning."[1] Lehi also blessed and prophetically counseled his several sons.[2] Alma the younger prayed with and for his missionary companions (who included two of his sons), and then imparted the Holy Spirit to them by the laying on of hands.[3] After Nephi was chosen as the chief disciple, he baptized his son Jonas and the other disciples[4] and frequently joined them in mighty prayer,[5] most memorably when the Savior himself prayed with them and their beings were filled with celestial light.[6] And Mormon and Moroni had (apparently together) been honored by the personal ministry of the three translated Nephite disciples.[7] Such shared activities of worship are similar to what President Benson has counseled fathers to do in our day:

> Give father's blessings to your children. Baptize and confirm your children. Ordain your sons to the priesthood. These will become spiritual highlights in the lives of your children.
>
> Personally direct family prayers, daily scripture reading, and weekly family home evenings. Your personal involvement will show your children how important these activities really are.
>
> Whenever possible, attend Church meetings together as a family. Family worship under your leadership is vital to your children's spiritual welfare.[8]

PRAYING FOR THEIR SONS

Book of Mormon fathers prayed not only with their sons but also for them. It was King Mosiah's prayer of faith that brought divine protection for his missionary sons among the hostile Lamanites.[9] Al-

1. 1 Nephi 5:9–10.
2. See 2 Nephi 1 through 4:11.
3. See Alma 31:26–36.
4. See 3 Nephi 19:12.
5. See 3 Nephi 19:6–9; 27:1.
6. See 3 Nephi 19:16–36.
7. See Mormon 8:11.
8. TETB 511.
9. See Mosiah 28:6–7; Alma 17:35; 19:23.

ma's prayers of faith brought down an angel to reform his rebellious son.[1] And Mormon told Moroni, "I am mindful of you always in my prayers, continually praying unto God the Father in the name of his Holy Child, Jesus, that he, through his infinite goodness and grace, will keep you through the endurance of faith on his name to the end."[2] Such frequent prayers for family welfare were recommended by Amulek when he counseled his listeners to pray "over all your household, both morning, mid-day, and evening."[3] And the resurrected Lord himself commanded the Nephites, "Pray in your families unto the Father, always in my name, that your wives and your children may be blessed."[4]

TEACHING SONS FROM THEIR YOUTH

The wise fathers in the Book of Mormon began their parental instruction while their sons were young. Lehi instructed Nephi who was "exceedingly young"[5] and Jacob who was in his "childhood" and "youth."[6] Alma the younger taught his sons and even took two of them with him on a mission while they were yet "in [their] youth."[7] Although the record does not expressly disclose when Helaman began teaching his sons Nephi and Lehi, the implication is that the process began when they were very young, for "they began to grow up unto the Lord."[8] And the ultimate demonstration in Nephite history of teaching children from their youth was given by the resurrected Lord himself when he appeared to the Nephites and, instead of excluding the little children from the meeting, showed them first priority as he gathered them around him, individually blessed them, and prayed in their midst.[9] All of this serves as a pattern for today's parents, who,

---

1. See Mosiah 27:14.
2. Moroni 8:3.
3. Alma 34:21.
4. 3 Nephi 18:21.
5. 1 Nephi 2:16.
6. 2 Nephi 2:1, 4.
7. Alma 31:7; 36:3.
8. Helaman 3:21.
9. See 3 Nephi 17:11–25.

as President Benson has counseled, should teach children "from their youth up."[1]

TEACHING BY REPETITION

Book of Mormon fathers taught their sons repeatedly, as when Lehi frequently exhorted his sons to righteousness and taught them from the scriptures,[2] or when Jacob spoke "often" to Enos about eternal life,[3] or when Mormon, separated from Moroni by the exigencies of war, taught him through letters.[4] "Repetition is a key to learning," observed President Benson. "Devoted Book of Mormon fathers constantly reminded their sons of saving truths." Likewise, "our children need to hear the truth repeated, especially because there is so much falsehood abroad."[5]

TEACHING WITH TENDERNESS

Despite the repetition, great Book of Mormon fathers tempered their teaching with tenderness borne of profound love for their sons. Thus Lehi spoke to the hardened Laman and Lemuel "with all the feeling of a tender parent."[6] Jacob taught Enos in the "nurture and admonition" of the Lord.[7] Alma the younger tempered his reproof of Corianton by explaining that it was only for Corianton's good.[8] And Mormon manifested his feeling for Moroni by repeatedly addressing him as "my beloved son."[9] This principle of influence through love exercised by righteous Book of Mormon fathers is the same as that revealed in modern times through the book's translator, the Prophet Joseph Smith, who recorded that priesthood power or influence can be exercised "only by persuasion, by long-suffering, by gentleness

---

1. W&W 72.
2. See 1 Nephi 2:9–14; 5; 8; 2 Nephi 1 through 4:11.
3. See Enos 1:3.
4. See Moroni 8–9.
5. W&W 69.
6. 1 Nephi 8:37.
7. Enos 1:1.
8. See Alma 39:7.
9. Moroni 8:2; 9:1, 6, 11.

and meekness, and by love unfeigned; by kindness, and pure knowledge."[1] He later remarked that kindness had the greatest power to
lead people to forsake sin.[2] Accordingly, President Benson has counseled parents to "treat your children with respect and kindness."[3]

TEACHING OBEDIENCE TO THE COMMANDMENTS

But such kindness did not prevent the great Book of Mormon
fathers from clearly communicating to their sons the objective of all
their teaching—to urge their sons to righteous action. Lehi exhorted
his sons to "hearken to his words" and "keep the commandments of
the Lord."[4] His dying counsel to his sons was that they "look to the
great Mediator, and hearken unto his great commandments; and be
faithful unto his words, and choose eternal life."[5] King Benjamin
counseled his sons about the scriptures, to "remember to search them
diligently, that ye may profit thereby; and I would that ye should
keep the commandments of God."[6] Alma the younger told Helaman
that "I would that ye should do as I have done, in remembering the
captivity of our fathers";[7] and "I command you, my son Helaman,
that ye be diligent in fulfilling all my words, and that ye be diligent
in keeping the commandments of God";[8] furthermore, "look to God
and live."[9] Alma the younger's counsel to Shiblon seems to combine
general instructions with more specific, personalized admonitions, as
he warns him not to be "lifted up unto pride" or to "boast in your
own wisdom, nor of your much strength"; furthermore, he is to
"bridle all your passions" and "refrain from idleness."[10] Alma the
younger likewise tailors his instructions to the errant Corianton, instructing him to "repent and forsake your sins, and go no more after

---

1. D&C 121:41–42.
2. See TPJS 240.
3. TETB 499.
4. 1 Nephi 8:37–38.
5. 2 Nephi 2:28.
6. Mosiah 1:7.
7. Alma 36:2.
8. Alma 37:20.
9. Alma 37:47.
10. Alma 38:11–12.

the lusts of your eyes," and also to "counsel with your elder brothers in your undertakings."[1] Helaman the younger admonished his sons to "build your foundation" upon "the rock of our Redeemer."[2] And Mormon told Moroni, "My son, be faithful in Christ."[3] All of these fatherly teachings have what President Harold B. Lee insisted is necessary for all effective leaders—"a certain, sure trumpet sound to their instructions."[4] And according to President Benson, these invitations to righteousness by Book of Mormon fathers who were themselves righteous constitute "a divine pattern" of powerfully effective parental teaching.[5]

TEACHING ABOUT ETERNAL REWARDS

Accompanying the admonitions to righteousness were descriptions of the rewards it would bring. Lehi, for example, described the symbolic fruit that "was desirable to make one happy" and the "most sweet, above all that I ever before tasted"[6] and then spoke of the "liberty and eternal life" conditionally available to his sons.[7] Lehi's son Jacob similarly spoke to his son Enos about "eternal life, and the joy of the saints."[8] King Mosiah urged obedience for his sons "that ye may prosper in the land."[9] That same promise was repeated by Alma the younger to his sons,[10] as he also told them that if "ye . . . put your trust in God . . . ye shall be delivered out of your trials, and your troubles, and your afflictions, and ye shall be lifted up at the last day"[11] to enjoy what Alma had had a foretaste of—"there can be nothing so exquisite and sweet as was my joy."[12] Helaman the younger

---

1. Alma 39:9–10.
2. Helaman 5:12.
3. Moroni 9:25.
4. Lee 1974a:105.
5. W&W 68.
6. 1 Nephi 8:10–11.
7. 2 Nephi 2:27.
8. Enos 1:3.
9. Mosiah 1:7.
10. See Alma 36:1; 38:1.
11. Alma 38:5.
12. Alma 36:21.

similarly spoke to his sons about "that precious gift of eternal life."[1] And Mormon wrote to Moroni about the "perfect love"[2] that fills the righteous, expressing his wish that "may Christ lift thee up, and may his . . . mercy and long-suffering, and the hope of his glory and of eternal life, rest in your mind forever. And may the grace of God . . . be, and abide with you forever."[3] To forever keep in focus "the hope of his glory and of eternal life" seems essential to their achievement.

OBEDIENT SONS

Such teaching usually had a profound effect, as illustrated in the lives of many exemplary Book of Mormon sons. The example *par excellence* of a son obediently taking direction from his righteous father is Nephi, as he first listened to and believed Lehi tell of his revelation, and then sought and received the same revelation.[4] Nephi uncomplainingly followed his father into the wilderness and into extreme hardship, and at every turn and even at the peril of his life sought to uphold Lehi's authority by trying to persuade others of Lehi's inspiration and insight. Nephi was the model son—a model followed by a number of his descendants who, like King Mosiah, "did according to that which his father had done,"[5] or, like Helaman the younger, "did do that which was right in the sight of God continually; and he did walk after the ways of his father,"[6] or, like Helaman's sons Nephi and Lehi, "did remember [their father's] words; and therefore they went forth, keeping the commandments of God."[7] This same pattern of filial recognition of and submission to righteous fathers was also seen among the Jaredites, as when Orihah "did walk humbly before the Lord, and did remember how great things the Lord had done for his father,"[8] or when the righteous Coriantum "did walk in the steps

---

1. Helaman 5:8.
2. Moroni 8:26; 7:48.
3. Moroni 9:25–26.
4. See 1 Nephi 10:17 through 14:30.
5. Mosiah 6:7.
6. Helaman 3:20.
7. Helaman 5:14.
8. Ether 6:30.

of his father."[1] All of this demonstrates, says President Benson, "the responsibility sons have to take direction from their fathers," to "listen and obey."[2]

JOY IN AND PRAISE FOR OBEDIENT SONS

Worthy sons such as these brought joy to their fathers and received encouraging commendation from them. Thus Lehi, upon hearing Nephi's faithful response to the instruction to return for the brass plates, "was exceedingly glad, for he knew that [Nephi] had been blessed of the Lord."[3] Later, after seeing his sons Nephi and Sam partake of the fruit in vision, Lehi declared, "I have reason to rejoice in the Lord because of Nephi and also of Sam."[4] In giving his all-important final instructions and blessings, Lehi directed his other sons' attention to Nephi, "whose views have been glorious, and who hath kept the commandments" and "been an instrument in the hands of God, in bringing us forth into the land of promise,"[5] so that "if ye will hearken unto the voice of Nephi ye shall not perish."[6] Alma told his righteous son Shiblon, "My son, I trust that I shall have great joy in you, because of your steadiness and your faithfulness unto God," and "as you have commenced in your youth to look to the Lord your God, even so I hope that you will continue in keeping his commandments," for "I have had great joy in thee already."[7] And writing to his "beloved son" Moroni, Mormon said, "I rejoice exceedingly that your Lord Jesus Christ hath been mindful of you, and hath called you to his ministry, and to his holy work,"[8] adding, "My son, I recommend thee unto God, and I trust in Christ that thou wilt be saved."[9] This pattern

---

1. Ether 9:23.
2. W&W 67.
3. 1 Nephi 3:8.
4. 1 Nephi 8:3.
5. 2 Nephi 1:24.
6. 2 Nephi 1:28.
7. Alma 38:2–3.
8. Moroni 8:2.
9. Moroni 9:22.

of pertinent praise is still relevant; President Benson has counseled parents, "Praise your children more than you correct them."[1]

WAYWARD SONS, WISE FATHERS

But the law of agency was as operable among the Nephites as anywhere else, and at times the best teaching by the best fathers met with indifference or even resistance. The record of how Book of Mormon fathers dealt with such situations is at once a tribute to them and a model for us. "If their sons strayed," observed President Benson, "stalwart Book of Mormon fathers still continued to teach them."[2] For example, Lehi exhorted the stubborn Laman and Lemuel "with all the feeling of a tender parent, that they would hearken to his words, that perhaps the Lord would be merciful to them."[3] They continued their murmuring, but Lehi never gave up, continuing to the end of his life to teach them, and leaving them a final plea— echoing a passage out of Isaiah[4] that speaks of the glorious restoration of latter-day Israel—to "arise from the dust" so that "my soul might have joy in you."[5] When Jacob's son Enos was apparently uncommitted for a time, Jacob did not shirk his own commitment as a father but continued to teach his son "often" about "eternal life, and the joy of the saints"[6]—teaching that eventually proved pivotal in Enos' conversion. The case of Corianton concerned a son who had started right—as a missionary—but had deviated from the straight path through the sin of immorality; his wise and powerful father, Alma the younger, began by speaking plainly about the terrible consequences of his son's sins, while assuring him that "I would not dwell upon your crimes, to harrow up your soul, if it were not for your good."[7] Then, devoting most of his time in speaking with his sons to this one who had erred, Alma decisively demonstrated the power of

---

1. TETB 499.
2. W&W 70.
3. 1 Nephi 8:37.
4. See Isaiah 52:1–2.
5. See 2 Nephi 1:13–23.
6. Enos 1:3.
7. Alma 39:7.

God by repeatedly discerning Corianton's thoughts[1] and then in patience addressing his concerns while discussing the great doctrines of the plan of salvation and relating them all to Corianton's need to repent.

But what about sons who refused even to listen to fatherly advice? Alma the younger himself seems to have been such a son. He was, in fact, one of the most openly, ardently, and influentially rebellious of all Nephite sons as he campaigned to destroy all that his father had built—the Church of God. And when his father could have no more influence directly on this son to whom he had entrusted his own name, he focused his faith on the last avenue open to him— direct appeal to God, praying "with much faith concerning" his son, and having other righteous church members join in with their prayers of faith.[2] We can judge that faith by its effect: it brought dramatic divine intervention as an angel literally stopped Alma in his tracks. Even then, however, agency reigned supreme as the angel made it perfectly clear that he had been "prayed" there, and that Alma's fate rested on his own choice.[3] He chose to repent and thus ended up owing his eternal life to this father who had refused to give up and whose righteousness and faith had called on and called down the powers of heaven for his son's eternal benefit. It is the greatest of the great works recorded of Alma the elder, and perhaps the greatest demonstration of patient and profound faith by any mortal father in the Book of Mormon. It is also an enduring lesson for modern parents, whom Elder Orson F. Whitney counseled,

> You parents of the wilful and the wayward! Don't give them up. Don't cast them off. They are not utterly lost. The Shepherd will find his sheep. They were his before they were yours— long before he entrusted them to your care; and you cannot begin to love them as he loves them. . . .
>
> Though some of the sheep may wander, the eye of the Shepherd is upon them. . . . Pray for your careless and dis-

---

1. See chapter 5.
2. Mosiah 27:14.
3. See Mosiah 27:16.

obedient children; hold on to them with your faith. Hope on, trust on, till you see the salvation of God.[1]

For wayward sons who repented, wise Book of Mormon fathers forgot past mistakes and forged ahead by trustingly involving their sons in the work to be done, as when Jacob gave Enos charge of the sacred records,[2] or when King Mosiah attempted to confer the kingdom on his repentant sons,[3] or when Alma appointed his son Alma as his ecclesiastical successor,[4] or when Alma the younger charged a reproved Corianton to continue preaching.[5]

TEACHING SONS TO CARRY ON THEIR HERITAGE

Righteous Book of Mormon fathers transmitted to their sons an enduring sense of family heritage by emphasizing their forefathers. For example, Lehi "spake much"[6] about the house of Israel and pointed to (as Nephi reports) the "covenant the Lord made to our father Abraham,"[7] later rehearsing to his sons the Lord's covenants to their forefather the patriarch Joseph.[8] King Benjamin taught his sons "in all the language of his fathers" that "they might know concerning the prophecies which had been spoken by the mouths of their fathers," and he exhorted them, "Keep the commandments of God, that ye may prosper in the land according to the promises which the Lord made unto our fathers."[9] Alma the younger urged his son Helaman, "Do as I have done, in remembering the captivity of our fathers"—Alma and his people—who were delivered from Lamanite bondage by "the God of Abraham, and the God of Isaac, and the God of Jacob."[10] He then continued the theme of the forefathers by speaking

---

1. Conference Report, April 1929, p. 110.
2. See Jacob 7:27 (presumably after Enos' conversion).
3. See Mosiah 28:10.
4. See Mosiah 29:42.
5. See Alma 43:1.
6. 1 Nephi 10:12.
7. 1 Nephi 15:18.
8. See 2 Nephi 3.
9. Mosiah 1:2, 7.
10. Alma 36:2.

about the earlier deliverance from Egyptian bondage of "our fathers," and also about "our fathers" being "brought . . . out of the land of Jerusalem"[1] and given the Liahona to guide them in the wilderness. And as it "was . . . with our fathers. . . . even so it is with us,"[2] he noted, adding, "[God] will fulfil all his promises which he shall make unto you, for he has fulfilled his promises which he has made unto our fathers."[3] Helaman the younger named his sons Nephi and Lehi after their "first parents who came out of the land of Jerusalem" so that "when you remember your names ye may remember them" and "their works," that "they were good," adding, "I would that ye should do that which is good, that it may be said of you, and also written, even as it has been said and written of them."[4] And Mormon hoped for his beloved son Moroni that Christ's "showing his body unto our fathers" would "rest in [Moroni's] mind forever."[5]

Such transmission of a sense of heritage was often accompanied by a delegation of responsibility to carry on that heritage, as when the aged King Benjamin gave Mosiah "charge concerning the kingdom,"[6] or when the aged Alma conferred the office of chief judge upon his son Alma and gave him "charge concerning all the affairs of the church,"[7] or when Alma the younger solemnly charged Helaman to preserve and add to the sacred records,[8] or when Mormon asked Moroni to "labor diligently"[9] and later delivered to him the sacred records with a command to add to them.[10]

In our day President Benson has set an example of one who likewise is determined to preserve and pass on to his posterity a noble heritage:

I am dedicated to passing on, if possible, as noble a heritage

1. Alma 36:28–29.
2. Alma 37:46.
3. Alma 37:17.
4. Helaman 5:6–7.
5. Moroni 9:25.
6. Mosiah 1:15.
7. Mosiah 29:42.
8. See Alma 37.
9. Moroni 9:6.
10. See Moroni 9:24; Mormon 8:1.

as I have received, and a name as unsullied and honorable as it was when it was given to me. To do so is to bequeath to my children and my children's children a legacy most precious above all earthly possessions.[1]

A SENSE OF CONNECTEDNESS

A son so imbued with a sense of heritage and entrusted with continuing the work to which his forefathers had devoted their lives could not help but feel a stabilizing sense of connectedness, of being a part of a continuing enterprise larger than himself and to which he could commit his entire life, as a link in a chain forged by the faith of his fathers. This is the sense conveyed, for example, in Nephi's words that "we labor diligently to write, to persuade our children, and also our brethren, to believe in Christ";[2] or in the similar statement by Nephi's brother Jacob that "we labor diligently to engraven these words upon plates, hoping that our beloved brethren and our children will receive them with thankful hearts";[3] or in the statement about Alma the younger that he "began to declare the word of God . . . according to the revelation of the truth of the word which had been spoken by his fathers, and according to the spirit of prophecy which was in him";[4] or in the assertion of Helaman's son Nephi that what he was preaching about Christ had been testified of by "all the holy prophets," including particularly Abraham, Moses, "our father Lehi," Nephi, "and also almost all of our fathers, even down to this time";[5] or in the words of a lonely and anguished Moroni dutifully writing in the wake of his father's death, "I, Moroni, do finish the record of my father, Mormon. Behold, I have but few things to write, which things I have been commanded by my father."[6] "Condemn me not because of mine imperfection, neither my father, because of his im-

---

1. TETB 469–97.
2. 2 Nephi 25:23.
3. Jacob 4:3.
4. Alma 6:8.
5. Helaman 8:11–22.
6. Mormon 8:1.

perfection, neither them who have written before him. . . . We have written this record according to our knowledge."[1]

Such a lesson on linking with past generations is especially needed in our day when increased family mobility often means that children grow up away from grandparents and without much of a sense of family heritage. But ours is also the day when fulfillment of the Abrahamic covenant is being realized for all of his actual and adopted posterity, and when, to facilitate that fulfillment, Elijah has come to "turn the hearts of the fathers to the children, and the children to the fathers"[2] — or, as Joseph Smith explained, to "reveal the covenants of the fathers in relation to the children, and the covenants of the children in relation to the fathers,"[3] or, alternately, "to seal the children to the fathers, and the fathers to the children."[4] The latter-day work of writing and gathering family histories and genealogies and sealing of ancestors is surely an essential part of instilling in children today the same sort of intergenerational connectedness and mission felt by faithful Book of Mormon sons who were a part of what President Benson calls "great family legacies."[5] And concerning our day President Benson has said that "we owe [our progenitors] much more than we can ever repay," and "we have an obligation to do [their] temple work" and "to see that we are linked to our progenitors."[6]

STANDING ON THEIR FATHERS' SHOULDERS

In carrying on their fathers' work, Book of Mormon sons often reached new heights by building on the foundation laid by their fathers. Thus Nephi, so well taught and fortified by Lehi, acquired the strength to remain faithful and open to revelation in circumstances so difficult as to cause Lehi to temporarily murmur;[7] thus the sons of Mosiah refused an earthly kingdom handed down by their righteous

1. Mormon 9:31–32.
2. D&C 110:15; see also Malachi 4:6; 3 Nephi 25:6.
3. TPJS 321.
4. TPJS 337.
5. W&W 69.
6. TETB 161.
7. See 1 Nephi 16:20–26.

forefathers in order to extend the kingdom of God;[1] thus King Mosiah secured for his people the political freedom[2] necessary for them to retain, if they chose, the spiritual freedom previously granted them by King Benjamin;[3] thus the remarkable line of Alma with its recurrent stellar prophets could, over time, produce a man (Nephi) qualified to serve as the resurrected Lord's chief disciple and the chief administrator of the Nephite Zion; and thus generations of faithful record keepers preserved, added to, and finally abridged the sacred records that we now possess in the form of the Book of Mormon. To stand on the shoulders of one's parents is something for which children today should strive, according to Brigham Young, who counseled the saints to "excel [your parents] in everything that is good . . . , for this is your privilege, and it becomes your duty."[4]

WORTHY SONS WITH UNWORTHY FATHERS

But what of Book of Mormon sons not fortunate enough to have righteous fathers? The wicked King Noah's son Limhi "was desirous that his father should not be destroyed" but "was not ignorant of the iniquities of his father, he himself being a just man"[5] — echoing the pattern of his righteous grandfather, Zeniff, or his righteous forefather, Abraham. And as to sons who were deceived because of the false traditions of their fathers (notably many of Laman's and Lemuel's descendants), they were emphatically accorded increased clemency for their errors[6] — perhaps indicative of the weight the Lord places on the commandment he gave ancient Israel to "honour thy father and thy mother."[7] Even so, the conversion process for those misled by the erroneous traditions of their fathers included a recognition of those errors, as seen in the Lamanite converts of the sons of Mosiah.[8] And

---

1. See Mosiah 28:1–10.
2. See Mosiah 29.
3. See Mosiah 5:8.
4. JD 2:18.
5. Mosiah 19:17.
6. See Mosiah 1:5; Alma 9:16.
7. Exodus 20:12.
8. See Alma 24:7.

in the background stands the great example of one who singlehand-edly overcame the false traditions of his fathers by an intense personal search for God—none other than father Abraham, whose veneration in Nephite society matched that in Judaism. And just as Abraham learned of the righteousness of his earlier forefathers, so the converted Lamanites could look to their righteous ancestors Lehi and Nephi, as evidenced by the name they took upon themselves: Anti-Nephi-Lehis.[1] The lesson here is that all are blessed with righteous exemplary ancestors, even if we must go as far back as Noah; and he who is the father of the faithful and the adoptive father of all the righteous, Abraham, was not himself fortunate enough to have a righteous fa-ther.

THE SIGNIFICANCE OF THE BOOK OF MORMON'S EMPHASIS ON FOLLOWING THE FATHERS

Such reenactment by the converted Lamanites of an ancient an-cestral pattern is, as we have seen throughout the Book of Mormon father-son portraits, only one of numerous such reenactments. Time and again righteous men mirrored ancestral patterns in the very cir-cumstances of their lives. The phenomenon is hardly surprising in-asmuch as the Nephites were, as both Lehi and Nephi say from the start, a branch broken off from the house of Israel[2]—and thus heirs to the "covenant the Lord made to [their] father Abraham."[3] Thus Nephite civilization was grounded in and grew out of the covenants to the Israelite forefathers, which was precisely the case with that other famous branch of Israelites, the Jews.[4] The Jews and Nephites also shared the same Mosaic heritage and obligation to observe the Mosaic law and remember the Exodus. Indeed, it was that very remembrance that had preserved Nephi and his family from the pen-alty of destruction for forgetting and had given rise to Book of Mormon history. The theme of remembrance continues throughout the Nephite

1. See Alma 23:17.
2. See 1 Nephi 10:12; 19:24.
3. 1 Nephi 15:18.
4. See TDNT V:977.

record with marked emphasis on remembering the forefathers. Fathers constantly reminded sons about their forefathers, and prophets forever urged the people to remember the forefathers.

Such fervent emphasis in the Book of Mormon on remembering one's fathers is reminiscent of the Jewish record, the Old Testament, which has "no hesitations in commanding memory. Its injunctions to remember are unconditional, and even when not commanded, remembrance is always pivotal" for both God and Israel, "for memory is incumbent upon both."[1] "Above all, God remembers His covenant which He made with the fathers" and "remembers the patriarchs and is thus merciful to Israel. Conversely, a basic element in O[ld] T[estament] piety is that man remembers the past acts of God,"[2] and particularly "the covenant and the patriarchs,"[3] meaning preeminently Abraham, Isaac, and Jacob, who were specially venerated in Judaism[4]—all of which is perfectly mirrored in the Book of Mormon, which has been written, says Moroni on the title page, "to show unto the remnant of the House of Israel what great things the Lord hath done for their fathers." Further, the Book of Mormon text demonstrates time and time again that remembering God's mercy and covenants to the faithful forefathers generated the faith among the Nephites necessary to call down similar blessings from God, for God "work[s] unto the children of men according to their faith" and "after men have faith"[5]—again echoing the situation in ancient Israel in which "the saving deeds of Yahweh [Jehovah] to the fathers are treasured by the godly, and they receive courage and confidence from them. . . . Thus the history of the fathers is a living heritage, from which one can receive courage and faith, or a warning."[6]

Viewed from this vantage point, the Book of Mormon constitutes a stunning performance by its twenty-four-year-old backwoods producer Joseph Smith, who claimed to have served merely as the in-

---

1. Yerushalmi 1982:5.
2. TDNT IV:675, internal citations omitted.
3. TDOT IV:81.
4. See TDNT V:976–77.
5. Ether 12:29–30.
6. TDOT I:12.

spired translator of an authentic record by ancient Israelite people—
for the woof and warp of Book of Mormon fabric turn out to match
those woven into the cloth of the Old Testament, with both records
emphasizing the critical importance of remembering the forefathers.

This should attune us to what the Prophet Joseph Smith had to
say about the importance of remembering the fathers: "The whole
faith" of mankind since the time of Adam has been "in a certain
degree dependent on the knowledge first communicated to them by
their common progenitor,"[1] and so the pattern has continued; "the
evidences which . . . men have of the existence of a God" usually
begins with "the testimony of their fathers."[2] And what the Book of
Mormon amply demonstrates is that exercising faith in that evidence
allows one to attain the same direct knowledge previously attained
by the fathers. Hence, in the Book of Mormon, remembering one's
fathers has the same object as it did throughout Old Testament history,
where "again and again memory keeps its attention riveted on the
present, even on present and future conduct."[3]

The lesson for our day is particularly timely, for according to the
Book of Mormon—which is notably our book of scripture that focuses
most on the Abrahamic covenant to Israel and its fulfillment—our day
is the day of that fulfillment. The timeless significance of remembering
the fathers accordingly becomes even more urgent for our day, for
as we remember the fathers and the covenants made to them and
thereby increase our faith, God will also remember that covenant and
increasingly fulfil it to the eternal blessing of latter-day Zion. This
mutual action by God and latter-day Israel is emphasized by Mormon[4]
and Moroni, the latter of whom bids us farewell by quoting the great
Isaiah passage (52:1–2) calling on Israel to "awake, and arise from the
dust . . . and put on thy beautiful garments"—so that, Moroni explains, "the covenants of the Eternal Father which he hath made unto
thee, O house of Israel, may be fulfilled."[5]

---

1. LF 2:36.
2. LF 2:33.
3. TDOT IV:80.
4. See Mormon 7.
5. Moroni 10:31.

And as the primary idea in Judaism of remembering the forefathers was to "remember the acts of God"[1] and the divine covenants to the forefathers, so the primary idea of remembering the Nephite fore-fathers was similarly to remember God's central act, that of giving his Son in fulfillment of the Abrahamic covenant. Among the Nephites, then, remembering the fathers brought into focus another father-son relationship, that of God and his Beloved Son, so that the faith gen-erated from remembering the fathers was faith in Christ. Conversely, it happens again and again in the Book of Mormon that those who forget or reject their righteous fathers also deny Christ.

Clearly, to forget or reject the righteous fathers is to forget or reject the Son of God, while to remember the righteous fathers is to learn of the Son of God—he who, according to the Book of Mormon, was spoken of by all the ancient prophets from the beginning of time. This necessarily means that much is missing from the text of the Old Testament. In fact, scholars now agree that it has been highly edited, and various newly discovered ancient sources show that the early Christians possessed texts purporting to contain numerous "pre-Christian" prophecies of Christ similar to those contained in the Book of Mormon.[2] Hence the value of the Book of Mormon: it not only discloses many plain and precious "pre-Christian" prophecies of Christ of the kind that were long ago edited out of the Old Testament, and not only contains a record of his glorious appearance as the newly resurrected Savior, but it also describes the all-important pattern of how to learn of the Son of God—by remembering one's righteous forefathers; whereupon one is prepared, continues the Book of Mor-mon, to enter a new parent-child relationship by coming unto the Son and becoming "children of Christ, his sons, and his daughters"[3]—as spoken of by King Benjamin, Abinadi, and the brother of Jared.

But the first step is to be childlike enough to learn of Christ from one's righteous fathers, which seems to go a long way toward putting one in the frame of mind to approach him as he commanded—"as a

---

1. TDOT IV:80.
2. See chapter 10.
3. Mosiah 5:7.

little child."[1] Hence to become children of Christ, Book of Mormon fathers remembered their fathers and also looked to their own small children in order to emulate their humility and come to Christ. Then, so that those little children would also grow up to be children of Christ, the Book of Mormon fathers taught them the gospel; and by such parental teaching the fathers would be able to retain their own status as children of Christ. The lesson is particularly relevant for our day, when Moroni's words invite us to "come unto Christ, and be perfected in him" so that "the covenants of the Eternal Father which he hath made unto thee, O house of Israel, may be fulfilled."[2]

And the ultimate example of how to come to Christ and become his children was given by Christ himself in his relationship with the Father—a relationship that is the summit of father-son portraits in the Book of Mormon and is the perfect model for all father-son relationships, not only because the Son sets the perfect example for sons, but also because, as President Benson has pointed out, "our pattern, or model, for fatherhood is our Heavenly Father," as evidenced by the fact that "the sacred title of 'father' is shared with the Almighty."[3]

THE BOOK OF MORMON FATHERS AND US

That the Nephites have bequeathed to us that poignant portrait of the Father and the Son should invoke our eternal gratitude. But our gratitude increases when we meet with the final tragedy and irony in following the theme of fathers and sons in the Book of Mormon: in the end those powerful lines of Nephite fathers and sons were left without a posterity to carry on their work! As Moroni bids his final farewell, it is not to adoring sons and grandsons hanging on his every word—as had been the pattern throughout the Book of Mormon and as far back as father Adam—but rather to us, a distant audience. For Moroni was a lonely fugitive, survivor of a once-mighty Israelite civilization whose destruction had been foreseen and foretold by their

---

1. 3 Nephi 9:22; see also 11:37–38.
2. Moroni 10:31–32.
3. TETB 503.

visionary forefather Nephi: "I beheld that the seed of my brethren did overpower the people of my seed."[1]

When Nephi saw that vision, he was but three days' journey out of Jerusalem[2] and was carrying with him his ancient Israelite heritage, whose emphasis on "seed" (Hebrew *zera*) is evident in the Hebrew Bible. As one eminent scholar explains,

> *Zera* articulates more than mere blood relationship, a shared heritage and growth; it also indicates more than the intimate solidarity of the individual with the fathers and the people. It expresses an organic cohesion within history under the same God, under his guidance in judgment and salvation, the unfolding into the future of the gifts given and promised to the fathers by Yahweh [Jehovah].[3]

The Nephite destruction, then, was more than the cutting off of beloved posterity; it was also the tragic termination of the unfolding through the Nephite line of the covenants made to their forefathers Abraham, Isaac, and Jacob. And why that termination? Precisely because the Nephites as a whole failed to remember their forefathers, even as the Jaredites had suffered annihilation for similarly failing to remember their forefathers. That should serve as a warning for us, descendants of the house of Israel through other lines. But it should also stir in us the utmost gratitude to that ancient branch of our Israelite kinsmen for living those powerful lessons on fathers and sons, and for recording those lessons in their precious family record that would have continued to pass down through their posterity. For the Book of Mormon is itself the sacred repository of the experiences of the Nephite fathers, who knew by revelation that their seed would eventually be destroyed, but who wrote the record for us!

We are in a sense, then, their honorary posterity, and all the more so because of our shared Israelite ancestry. We are the favored people entrusted with the final fulfillment of the Abrahamic covenant for which the Nephite fathers labored; and to achieve that, we have been

---

1. 1 Nephi 12:19.
2. See 1 Nephi 2:6.
3. TDOT IV:162.

given their record, which was to come forth—as the final two authors, Mormon and Moroni, repeatedly emphasize—unto the fulfilling of God's covenant with the house of Israel.[1] Indeed, the very emergence of the Book of Mormon constitutes a sign that the covenant has already begun to be fulfilled.[2] The Book of Mormon not only reminds us of that covenant given to our mutual forefathers Abraham, Isaac, and Jacob, but it also provides us with honorary Nephite forefathers as patterns to help us realize the Abrahamic covenant. As we reflect on those patterns, we would do well to remember the words of President J. Reuben Clark:

> In living our lives let us never forget that the deeds of our fathers and mothers are theirs, not ours; that their works cannot be counted to our glory; that we can claim no excellence and no place, because of what they did; that we must rise by our own labor.[3]

Rising by our own labor as we follow the patterns of the Nephite forefathers, we too shall become worthy parents and worthy children and thereby "children of Christ,"[4] for whose glorious coming we are privileged to prepare.

---

1. See Mormon 5:12; 9:31–37. Moroni 9:31.
2. See 3 Nephi 21:7; 29:1–3.
3. Clark 1947:28.
4. See Mosiah 5:7.

BIBLIOGRAPHY

· ·

Ackroyd, P. R., and C. F. Evans. *The Cambridge History of the Bible, Vol. 1: From the Beginnings to Jerome.* Cambridge: Cambridge University Press, 1970.

Albright, W. F., and C. S. Mann. *Matthew: A New Translation with Introduction and Commentary.* The Anchor Bible, vol. 26. Garden City, New York: Doubleday & Company, 1971.

Allen, Joseph L. *Exploring the Lands of the Book of Mormon.* Orem, Utah: S.A. Publishers, 1989.

The Ante-Nicene Fathers. 10 vols. Edinburgh: T&T Clark; and Grand Rapids, Michigan: Wm. B. Eerdmans Publishing Company, 1985–86. Reprint.

Arieti, Silvano. *Abraham and the Contemporary Mind.* New York: Basic Books, 1981.

Arrian: The Campaigns of Alexander. Middlesex, England: Penguin Books, 1971.

Arrington, Leonard J., and Susan Arrington Madsen. *Mothers of the Prophets.* Salt Lake City: Deseret Book Company, 1987.

Auerbach, Erich. *Mimesis: The Representation of Reality in Western Literature.* Princeton, New Jersey: Princeton University Press, 1968.

Bartlett, John. *Familiar Quotations,* 14th ed. Boston: Little, Brown, and Company, 1968.

Benson, Ezra Taft. *A Witness and a Warning: A Modern-day Prophet Testifies of the Book of Mormon.* Salt Lake City: Deseret Book Company, 1988.

———. *The Teachings of Ezra Taft Benson.* Salt Lake City: Bookcraft, 1988.

———. *This Nation Shall Endure.* Salt Lake City: Deseret Book Company, 1979.

Betz, Hans Dieter. "Galatians: A Commentary on Paul's Letter to the Churches in Galatia." In *Hermenia — A Critical and Historical Commentary on the Bible.* Philadelphia: Fortress Press, 1979.

Botterweck, G. Johannes, and Helmer Ringgren, eds. *Theological Dictionary of the Old Testament.* Grand Rapids: Wm. B. Eerdmans Publishing Co., 1974–.

Bowker, John. *The Targums and Rabbinic Literature: An Introduction to Jewish Interpretations of Scripture.* Cambridge: Cambridge University Press, 1979.

Brown, Collin, ed. *The New International Dictionary of New Testament Theology.* 4 vols. Grand Rapids: Zondervan Publishing House, 1986.

Brown, Raymond E. *The Gospel According to John I–XII: A New Translation with Introduction and Commentary,* 2d ed. The Anchor Bible, vol. 29. Garden City, New York: Doubleday & Company, 1966.

———. *The Gospel According to John XIII–XXI: A New Translation with Introduction and Commentary.* The Anchor Bible, vol. 29A. Garden City, New York: Doubleday & Company, 1970.

Brown, Raymond E., Joseph A. Fitzmeyer, and Roland E. Murphy, eds. *The New Jerome Biblical Commentary.* Englewood Cliffs, New Jersey: Prentice Hall, 1990.

Budge, E. A. Wallis. *The Book of the Cave of Treasures.* London: Religious Tract Society, 1927.

Burton, Alma P. *Doctrines from the Prophets: Choice Selections from Latter-day Leaders.* Salt Lake City: Bookcraft, 1970.

Byrne, Brendan. *"Sons of God"—"Seed of Abraham."* In Analecta Biblica 83. Rome: Biblical Institute Press, 1979.

Cassuto, U. *A Commentary on the Book of Genesis.* 2 vols. Jerusalem: Magnes Press, 1961–64.

Charbonneau-Lassay, Louis. *The Bestiary of Christ.* New York: Parabola Books, 1991.

Charlesworth, James H., ed. *The Old Testament Pseudepigrapha.* 2 vols. Garden City, New York: Doubleday & Company, 1983, 1985.

Cheesman, Paul R. *The Book of Mormon: The Keystone Scripture.* Provo, Utah: Religious Studies Center, Brigham Young University, 1988.

Clark, J. Reuben, Jr. *To Them of the Last Wagon.* Salt Lake City: Deseret News Press, 1947.

Clark, James R. *Messages of the First Presidency.* 6 vols. Salt Lake City: Bookcraft, 1965–75.

Cowley, A. E., ed. *Gesenius' Hebrew Grammar.* Oxford: Clarendon Press, 1980.

Dahl, Larry E., and Charles D. Tate, Jr. *The Lectures on Faith in Historical Perspective.* Religious Studies Center Monograph Series, vol 15. Provo, Utah: Religious Studies Center, Brigham Young University, 1990.

Danielou, Jean. *From Shadows to Reality: Studies in the Biblical Typology of the Fathers.* Westminister: The Newman Press, 1960.

Dobson, James C. *Parenting Isn't for Cowards: Dealing Confidently with the Frustrations of Child-Rearing.* Waco, Texas: Word Books, 1987.

The Doctrine and Covenants of The Church of Jesus Christ of Latter-day Saints. Salt Lake City: The Church of Jesus Christ of Latter-day Saints, 1981.

Doman, Glenn. *How to Multiply Your Baby's Intelligence.* Garden City, New York: Doubleday & Company, 1984.

Douglas, J. D., ed. *The New International Dictionary of the Christian Church,* rev. ed. Regency Reference Library. Grand Rapids: Zondervan Publishing House, 1978.

Durant, Will, and Ariel Durant. *The Lessons of History.* New York: Simon and Schuster, 1968.

Durrant, George D. *Love at Home Starring Father.* Salt Lake City: Bookcraft, 1976.

Eichrodt, Walther. *Theology of the Old Testament.* The Old Testament Library, vol. 1. Philadelphia: The Westminster Press, 1961.

Encyclopedia Judaica. Jerusalem: Keter Publishing House, 1972.

Emerson, Ralph Waldo. *The Essays of Ralph Waldo Emerson.* Cambridge, Massachusetts: Belknap Press of Harvard, 1987.

———. *Lectures and Biographical Sketches.* Boston: Houghton Mifflin Company, 1904.

Fauvel, John, Raymond Flood, Michael Shortland, and Robin Wilson, eds. *Let Newton Be!* Oxford: Oxford University Press, 1988.

Fishbane, Michael. *Biblical Interpretation in Ancient Israel.* Oxford: Clarendon Press, 1985.

Fitzmeyer, Joseph A. *The Gospel According to Luke I–IX: A New Translation with Introduction and Commentary.* The Anchor Bible, vol. 28. Garden City, New York: Doubleday & Company, 1981.

———. *The Gospel According to Luke X–XXIV: A New Translation with Introduction and Commentary.* The Anchor Bible, vol. 28A. Garden City, New York: Doubleday & Company, 1985.

Flexner, James Thomas. *Washington: The Indispensable Man.* New York: Signet, 1984.

Fox, Everett. *In the Beginning: A New English Rendition of the Book of Genesis.* New York: Shocken Books, 1983.

Fraade, Steven D. *Enoch and His Generation: Pre-Israelite Hero and History in Postbiblical Interpretation.* Society of Biblical Literature Monograph Series, No. 30. Chico, California: Scholars Press, 1984.

Freedman, H., and Maurice Simon, eds. *Midrash Rabbah.* 10 vols. London: Soncino Press, 1983.

Gentz, William H., ed. *The Dictionary of Bible and Religion.* Nashville: Abingdon, 1986.

Ginzberg, Louis. *The Legends of the Jews.* 7 vols. Philadelphia: Jewish Publication Society, 1937–66.

Hanks, Marion D. *Steps to Learning.* In Brigham Young University Speeches of the Year, 1959–60. Provo, Utah: Brigham Young University, May 4, 1960.

Hastings, James, ed. *A Dictionary of Christ and the Gospels.* 2 vols. Edinburgh: T. & T. Clark, 1906–8.

Hennecke, Edgar. *New Testament Apocrypha,* vols. 1–2. Philadelphia: Westminster Press, 1963–64.

Henry, Matthew. *Matthew Henry's Commentary on the Whole Bible,* rev. ed. McLean, Virginia: MacDonald Publishing Co., n.d. Reprint.

Hollander, H. W., and M. de Jonge. *The Testaments of the Twelve Patriarchs: A Commentary.* Leiden: E. J. Brill, 1985.

Horton, Fred L., Jr. *The Melchizedek Tradition: A Critical Examination of the Sources to the Fifth Century A.D. and in the Epistle to the Hebrews.* Society for New Testament Studies, Monograph Series, no. 30. Cambridge: Cambridge University Press, 1976.

Joseph Smith's "New Translation" of the Bible. Independence, Missouri: Herald Publishing House, 1970.

Josephus IV: Jewish Antiquities, Books I–IV. The Loeb Classical Library, no. 242. Cambridge, Massachusetts: Harvard University Press; and London: William Heinemann Ltd., 1978.

Journal of Discourses. 26 vols. Liverpool and London: Latter-day Saints Book Depot, 1855–86.

Keegan, John. *The Mask of Command.* New York: Viking, 1987.

Kimball, Spencer W. *The Teachings of Spencer W. Kimball.* Edited by Edward L. Kimball. Salt Lake City: Bookcraft, 1982.

Kimball, Spencer W., et al. *Prayer.* Salt Lake City: Deseret Book Company, 1977.

Kittel, Gerhard, and Gerhard Friedrich, eds. *Theological Dictionary of the New Testament.* 10 vols. Grand Rapids: Wm. B. Eerdmans Publishing Company, 1964–76.

Kobelski, Paul J. *Melchizedek and Melchiresa.* The Catholic Biblical Quarterly Monograph Series, no. 10. Washington, D.C.: The Catholic Biblical Association of America, 1981.

Lee, Harold B. *Stand Ye in Holy Places.* Salt Lake City: Deseret Book Company, 1974.

———. *Strengthening the Home.* Salt Lake City: The Church of Jesus Christ of Latter-day Saints, 1973.

———. *Ye Are the Light of the World.* Salt Lake City: Deseret Book Company, 1974.

Levenson, Jon D. *Creation and the Persistence of Evil: The Jewish Drama of Divine Omnipotence.* San Francisco: Harper & Row, 1988.

Lewis, Jack P. *A Study of the Interpretation of Noah and the Flood in Jewish and Christian Literature.* Leiden: E. J. Brill, 1978.

Lind, Millard, C. *Yahweh Is a Warrior: The Theology of Warfare in Ancient Israel.* Scottdale, Pennsylvania: Herald Press, 1980.

The Living Bible. Wheaton, Illinois: Tyndale House Publishers, 1971.

Lundquist, John M., and Stephen D. Ricks, eds. *By Study and Also by Faith.* Salt Lake City and Provo, Utah: Deseret Book Company and Foundation for Ancient Research and Mormon Studies, 1990.

Madsen, Truman. *Christ and the Inner Life.* Privately published, n.d.

Malan, S. C. *The Book of Adam and Eve, Also Called The Conflict of Adam and Eve with Satan.* London: Williams and Norgate, 1882.

Mann, C. S. *Mark: A New Translation with Introduction and Commentary.* The Anchor Bible, vol. 27. Garden City, New York: Doubleday & Company, 1986.

Master Study Bible: New American Standard. Nashville: Holman Bible Publishers, 1981.

Matlaw, Ralph E., ed. *Fathers and Sons,* 2d ed. A Norton Critical Edition. New York: W. W. Norton & Company, 1989.

McConkie, Bruce R. *Mormon Doctrine,* 2d ed. Salt Lake City: Bookcraft, 1966.

McKay, David O. *Pathways to Happiness.* Salt Lake City: Bookcraft, 1957.

Meyers, Carol L., and M. O'Connor. *The Word of the Lord Shall Go Forth.* Philadelphia: American Schools of Oriental Research, 1983.

Middlemiss, Clare, ed. *Cherished Experiences from the Writings of President David O. McKay.* Salt Lake City: Deseret Book Company, 1976.

Montefiore, C. G., and H. Loewe. *A Rabbinic Anthology.* New York: Schocken Books, 1974.

Munck, Johannes. *The Acts of the Apostles: A New Translation with Introduction and Commentary.* The Anchor Bible, vol. 31. Garden City, New York: Doubleday & Company, 1967.

Myers, Allen C. *The Eerdmans Bible Dictionary.* Grand Rapids: Wm. B. Eerdmans Publishing Company, 1987.

Neusner, Jacob. *Genesis and Judaism: The Perspective of Genesis Rabbah — An Analytical Anthology.* In Brown Judaic Studies, no. 108. Atlanta: Scholars Press, 1985.

Newquist, Jerreld L., ed. *Gospel Truth: Discourses and Writings of President George Q. Cannon,* vol. 1. Salt Lake City: Deseret Book Company, 1974.

Nibley, Hugh. *Abraham in Egypt.* Salt Lake City: Deseret Book Company, 1981.

———. *An Approach to the Book of Mormon,* 3d ed. The Collected Works of Hugh Nibley, vol. 6. Salt Lake City and Provo, Utah: Deseret Book Company and Foundation for Ancient Research and Mormon Studies, 1988.

———. *Enoch the Prophet.* The Collected Works of Hugh Nibley, vol. 2. Salt Lake City and Provo, Utah: Deseret Book Company and Foundation for Ancient Research and Mormon Studies, 1986.

———. "Leadership versus Management." *BYU Today* 38, no. 1 (February 1984): 16–19, 45–47.

———. *Lehi in the Desert/The World of the Jaredites/There Were Jaredites.* The Collected Works of Hugh Nibley, vol. 5. Salt Lake City and Provo, Utah: Deseret Book Company and Foundation for Ancient Research and Mormon Studies, 1988.

———. *Mormonism and Early Christianity.* The Collected Works of Hugh Nibley, vol. 4. Salt Lake City and Provo, Utah: Deseret Book Company and Foundation for Ancient Research and Mormon Studies, 1987.

———. "Setting the Stage—The World of Abraham." In "A New Look at the Pearl of Great Price," part 9, continued, *Improvement Era* 72, no. 11 (November 1969).

———. "Setting the Stage: The World of Abraham," in "A New Look at the Pearl of Great Price," part 9, continued, *Improvement Era* 73, no. 1 (January 1970).

———. *The Prophetic Book of Mormon.* The Collected Works of Hugh Nibley, vol. 8. Salt Lake City and Provo, Utah: Deseret Book Company and Foundation for Ancient Research and Mormon Studies, 1989.

North, Christopher R. *The Second Isaiah: Introduction, Translation and Commentary to Chapters XL–LV.* Oxford: Clarendon Press, 1964.

O'Connell, Robert L. *Of Arms and Men: A History of War, Weapons, and Aggression.* New York: Oxford University Press, 1989.

Packer, Boyd K. *Teach Ye Diligently.* Salt Lake City: Deseret Book Company, 1975.

Pelikan, Jaroslav, and Walter A. Hansen, eds. *Luther's Works,* vol. 4. Saint Louis: Concordia Publishing House, 1964.

Petersen, Mark E. *The Great Prologue.* Salt Lake City: Deseret Book Company, 1975.

Philo VI. Loeb Classical Library, no. 289. London: William Heinemann Ltd.; and Cambridge, Massachusetts: Harvard University Press, 1967.

Radday, Yehuda T., and Haim Shore. *Genesis: An Authorship Study.* Analecta Biblica, no. 103. Rome: Biblical Institute Press, 1985.

Reicke, Bo. *The Epistles of James, Peter, and Jude: A New Translation with Introduction and Commentary,* 2d ed. The Anchor Bible, vol. 37. Garden City, New York: Doubleday & Company, 1985.

Ricks, Stephen D., and William J. Hamblin, eds. *Warfare in the Book of Mormon.* Salt Lake City and Provo, Utah: Deseret Book Company and Foundation for Ancient Research and Mormon Studies, 1990.

Sarna, Nahum M. *Genesis.* The JPS Torah Commentary. Philadelphia: Jewish Publication Society, 1989.

Smith, Joseph. *Teachings of the Prophet Joseph Smith.* Edited by Joseph Fielding Smith. Salt Lake City: Deseret Book Company, 1938.

Smith, Joseph F. *Gospel Doctrine*. Salt Lake City: Deseret Book Company, 1939.

Smith, Joseph Fielding. *Answers to Gospel Questions*. 5 vols. Salt Lake City: Deseret Book, 1957–75.

Sorenson, John L., and Melvin J. Thorne, eds. *Rediscovering the Book of Mormon*. Salt Lake City and Provo, Utah: Deseret Book Company and Foundation for Ancient Research and Mormon Studies, 1991.

Speiser, E. A. *Genesis: A New Translation with Introduction and Commentary*, 3d ed. The Anchor Bible, vol. 1. Garden City, New York: Doubleday & Company, 1979.

Sulzberger, C. L. *Fathers and Children*. New York: Arbor House, 1987.

Swetnam, James. *Jesus and Isaac*. Analecta Biblica, no. 94. Rome: Biblical Institute Press, 1981.

Tanakh: A New Translation of the Holy Scriptures According to the Traditional Hebrew Text. Philadelphia: Jewish Publication Society, 1985.

Tuchman, Barbara W. *The March of Folly: From Troy to Vietnam*. New York: Alfred A. Knopf, 1984.

Vaux, Roland de. *Ancient Israel*. 2 vols. New York: McGraw Hill, 1965.

Vawter, Bruce. *On Genesis: A New Reading*. Garden City, New York: Doubleday & Company, 1977.

Viorst, Judith. *Necessary Losses*. New York: Simon and Schuster, 1986.

Webster's Third New International Dictionary of the English Language, Unabridged. Springfield, Massachusetts: Merriam-Webster Inc., 1981.

Welch, John W. *The Sermon at the Temple and the Sermon on the Mount*. Salt Lake City: Deseret Book Company, 1990.

Wenham, Gordon J. *Genesis 1–15*. Word Biblical Commentary, vol. 1. Waco, Texas: Word Books, 1987.

Westermann, Claus. *Genesis 1–11: A Commentary*. Minneapolis: Augsburg Publishing House, 1984.

———. *Genesis 12–36: A Commentary*. Minneapolis: Augsburg Publishing House, 1985.

———. *Isaiah 40–66: A Commentary*. Philadelphia: The Westminister Press, 1969.

Widengren, G. "Early Hebrew Myths and Their Interpretation." In S. H. Hooke, ed., *Myth, Ritual, and Kingship: Essays on the Theory and Practice of Kingship in the Ancient Near East and in Israel*. Oxford: Clarendon Press, 1958.

Wiesel, Elie. *Messengers of God: Biblical Portraits and Legends*. New York: Pocket Books, 1977.

Wigoder, Geoffrey, ed. *The Encyclopedia of Judaism*. New York: Macmillan, 1989.

Würthwein, Ernst. *The Text of the Old Testament: An Introduction to the Bible Hebraica*. Grand Rapids: William B. Eerdmans Publishing Co., 1979.

Yerushalmi, Yosef Hayim. *Zakhor: Jewish History and Jewish Memory*. Philadelphia and Seattle: Jewish Publication Society of America and University of Washington Press, 1982.

INDEX

● ●

327

relationships, 239–40; echoes Enoch,
239; finishes sacred record, 239;
invites enemy's posterity to
happiness, 240–41; forgiveness of,
recalls ancient Joseph, 241–42; and
legacy of father and son, 242–51
Moron, 223
Moroni, General: in role of father
through example, 154; prepares
people to be faithful, 156–57; raises
Title of Liberty, 156–57, 159; reminds
people of parent-child relationship,
157–58; evokes forefather Joseph,
157–58; always preparing, 159–60;
gathered intelligence, 160; brilliant
strategist, 160–61; mind of, matched
by courage, 161; fear foreign to, 161;
counseled with men, 162; rapport
with men and administrators, 162–
63; and Pahoran, 163; used force
against traitors, 163–64; merciful
toward vanquished, 165; preached
righteousness and repentance, 165;
writes to Ammoron, 165–66; sought
to turn hearts of children to fathers,
167; exhibited lack of personal
ambition, 167; words of, consistent
with deeds, 168; claimed no credit
for victory, 168; resembles George
Washington, 169; success as father,
174
Moroni, son of Mormon: on brother of
Jared, 217; commanded to seal up
full account, 217; on examples of
faith, 223–24; praised by Mormon,
232; difference between, and General
Mormon, 235; as one of Mormon's
generals, 242; takes up father's
record, 242; instructs latter-day
generation, 243–44; writes few more
things for Lamanites, 245–49;
influenced by father's charity, 245;
quotes father's discourse, 245;
follows father to become child of
Christ, 246; addresses future readers,
250; messenger sent to Joseph Smith,
251; final tribute to father, 251
Moronihah, 170–74
Mosaic law done away, 196
Moses: attributes Enos's righteousness

to Seth, 40; writing of, a gift of God,
42; translation of, 147; Alma's
similarity to, 148
Mosiah, father of Benjamin, 49–50
Mosiah, son of Benjamin: replaces
Benjamin as king, 57–58; consecrated
as king by Benjamin, 60–61; follows
pattern of father, 62; as seer, 62;
benefits people as grandfather did,
63; joined by other peoples, 63; calls
together all his people, 63–64; life of,
echoes Benjamin's, 67; reluctance of,
to send sons to Lamanites, 70–71;
transfers records to Alma the
younger, 71; terminates Nephite
monarchy, 71–72; proposes system of
judges, 72; as patient leader, 73;
echoes pattern of father, 74–75; frees
people politically, 75; obtains
promise of Lord, 78; influence of,
essential to sons' mission, 79; earns
gratitude of people, 83; summarizes
history of Nephite splinter group,
103; gives Nephite records to Alma
the younger, 120; did not make some
things known, 217
Multitude at temple, 196

Names given sons, 32–34, 94, 114, 181
Nephi: influence of fathers in record of,
1–5; record of, guides generations, 2;
applies scriptures to own experience,
2; remembers fathers, 3; account of,
parallels Exodus account, 4; identifies
with father, 6; obeys and honors
father, 8; sees what father saw, 11–
13; learning of, from Lehi, 12; vision
of, illustrates power of parental
example, 13; and Abrahamic
covenant, 15–16; feels pain of
righteous parent, 16–17; spiritual
progress of, 17–18; loyalty of, to
Lehi, 18; reluctance of, to chasten
Lehi, 20–21; concerned about respect
for Lehi, 23–24; upholds Lehi as
patriarch, 23; recounts his
weaknesses, 27; feels loss of father,
27–28; relies on Redeemer, 28;
Mormon's parallel expressions
concerning, and Helaman, 183